ORGANIZING KNOWLEDGE

An Introduction to Managing Access to Information

Fourth Edition

Acclaim for the third edition

'This book covers a great deal of ground ... invaluable for students (and their lecturers), but it also provides clear, mostly jargon-free, discussion of a range of topics useful to practitioners ... remarkably good value.' *Information Management Report*

'... fast becoming a standard introductory reference text on the organisation and retrieval of information through physical and electronic library systems. It fully deserves such a positioning, as it is a rich and challenging summary of a wide range of library-related subjects and it certainly helped this reader ... The authors are to be congratulated. They write authoritatively and engagingly on subjects which, written by another hand, could easily be as interesting to read as watching paint dry ... I can imagine *Organizing Knowledge* proudly occupying a place on the shelves of both corporate libraries and student bedrooms for some time to come. It is quite simply a very well-researched and well-written reference work ... I would strongly advise all such [information] professionals to carry a copy of *Organizing Knowledge* as a navigational aid.' *Managing Information*

'*Organizing Knowledge* is above all easy, in spite of being English; it is extremely well constructed and clear and does not use technical language ... Its translation into French would be very welcome ... Few professional works are as complete on such a complex subject. The question of organization and structuring of knowledge is central at present and shows, if needs be, the important role that information professionals play. Thanks to pertinent examples, the authors clarify the questions and integrate both traditional and up-to-date components in their work. The reader therefore has a more global understanding of the subject and can introduce new elements into their professional practice. Surely this is the objective of any professional work?' *Bulletin des Bibliothèques de France* [French Libraries' Bulletin]

'A thorough introduction to the whole subject of managing information and knowledge. Full of useful material.' *Long Range Planning*

'This book can be recommended for any library and information science collection and might be useful as a textbook for an introductory graduate or intermediate undergraduate course.' *Canadian Library Association*

'This book is a comprehensive and accessible introduction to knowledge organization for both undergraduate and postgraduate students of information management and information systems.' *European Foundation for Management Development*

'*Organizing Knowledge* deserves to retain its place as a key introductory textbook in this subject area because Rowley has a good grasp of what lecturers like myself are able to cover in the time available to teach this subject.' *Aslib Program*

'Intended primarily as a textbook for first professional studies it succeeds admirably in this respect, providing a very broad sweep of subject content within one volume ... Rowley and Farrow write in a clear, concise style, eminently suited to the purpose. Any student of LIS should find the book helpful in their understanding of the subject and it will certainly serve the student as a useful reference source for the basics of several different operational areas. In this respect it is also to be recommended to the practising non-specialist ... The text is well supported by graphics, and ample illustrations and examples are provided in every section ... it represents extremely good value for money, and will certainly be on my reading list for next year's information retrieval course.' Vanda Broughton, Lecturer in Library and Information Studies, University College London, in *Library and Information Research News*

'This work has much to commend it to a wide audience ... This work is essential for both undergraduate and postgraduate students, and anyone who is interested in learning the basic components of information management and information systems. It is highly recommended as a required text in relevant LIS courses.' *Library Collections, Acquisitions and Technical Services* (New Zealand)

ORGANIZING KNOWLEDGE

An Introduction to Managing Access to Information

Fourth Edition

Jennifer Rowley and Richard Hartley

ASHGATE

First edition published in 1987, second edition 1992, third edition 2000, by Ashgate Publishing Limited.

This edition published by
Ashgate Publishing Limited

Ashgate Publishing Limited
Gower House
Croft Road
Aldershot
Hampshire GU11 3HR
England

Ashgate Publishing Limited
Suite 420
101 Cherry Street
Burlington, VT 05401-4405
USA

Ashgate website: http://www.ashgate.com

Jennifer Rowley and Richard Hartley have asserted their rights under the Copyright, Designs and Patents Act 1988 to be identified as the authors of this work.

British Library Cataloguing in Publication Data
Rowley, J. E.
    Organizing knowledge : an introduction to managing access
    to information. - 4th ed.
    1. Information storage and retrieval systems - Management
    I. Title   II. Hartley, Richard J.
    025.5'24

Library of Congress Cataloging-in-Publication Data
Organizing knowledge: an introduction to managing access to information
Jennifer Rowley and Richard Hartley. -- 4th ed.
        p. cm.
    Includes bibliographical references and indexes.
    ISBN: 978-0-7546-4431-6
    1. Information organization -- English-speaking countries. 2. Cataloguing -- English-speaking countries.   I. Rowley, J. E.   II. Hartley, Richard J.

    Z666.5.R69 2007
    025.5'24--dc22   2007018836
                        ISBN: 978-0-7546-4431-6

Typeset by IML Typographers, Birkenhead, Merseyside.
Printed and bound in Great Britain by MPG Books Ltd, Bodmin, Cornwall.

Contents

List of figures

Dedication

This book is dedicated to three people who have shared in and supported our professional and other lives, but who sadly are no longer with us:

John Farrow, co-author of the third edition of this book; many of John's quirky and humorous asides, coupled with his impressive scholarship, remain in evidence in this fourth edition;

Gwendoline Rowley, Jennifer's mother-in-law;

and **Edward Hartley**, Richard's father.

Introduction

There is an increasing recognition of the value of knowledge and information to individuals, organizations and communities. Individuals are expected to become ever more adept at identifying, locating, interpreting and using information. This information may come from a wide variety of different sources, in diverse formats, and be used for many different purposes. As availability of, and access to, information increases, the need to be able to locate and retrieve information becomes all the more pressing. Tools that support or assist in the process of information retrieval are becoming increasingly important and also increasingly sophisticated. In keeping with a long tradition, this book uses the phrase 'the organization of knowledge' to encompass the tools and the processes associated with providing access to knowledge and information. We are aware that some authors might have a preference for the term 'information' instead of 'knowledge'; this debate is visited in Chapter 1.

One of the other objectives of Chapter 1 is to establish the complexity of the field of the organization of knowledge. Tools such as Google are so superficially effective that it is possible to be lulled into a belief that the one-stop shop for information has arrived. But this is to overlook the wide variety of different contexts in which knowledge is organized. These include libraries, public record offices, archives, corporate databases, museums, government files, content management systems, and knowledge-based systems. Not so long ago all of these applications were relatively separate islands. The advent of Web technologies has provided exciting opportunities for networked access to a wide variety of digital content, and interoperability has become a shared agenda. This makes understanding the organization of knowledge all the more challenging, because it is no longer acceptable to work within one of these arenas and to ignore the developments in others. In addition, although there are some common principles, standards and agendas, each professional community (such as information professionals, archivists or record managers) faces challenges that are unique to its own documents, databases and communities.

This book seeks to identify and explain the principles that underlie the structuring of knowledge in a wide variety of different contexts. It seeks to strike a balance between the identification of principles, and the description of their application in specific contexts.

This fourth edition continues the tradition of earlier editions in offering a broad-based overview of approaches and tools in the organization of knowledge, written in an accessible style, and well illustrated with figures and examples. There are, however, significant changes between this and the previous edition. These changes reflect the ongoing shift towards a networked and digital information environment which has many consequences for and impacts on documents, information, knowledge, information services and users. The book has been structured into three parts and twelve chapters and has been thoroughly updated throughout. Topics that are either new to this edition or have undergone significant development include:

- ontologies and taxonomies
- information behaviour
- systems contexts, including digital libraries and content management systems
- markup, metadata, interoperability and the Semantic Web
- evaluation of information retrieval systems
- authentication and security
- project management
- managing change.

The text has also been thoroughly revised to take into account the most recent editions of key standards such as MARC, AACR (including RDA), DDC, LCC, LCSH and BS 8724-2: 2005 for thesauri. Also, the balance of treatment of topics has been adapted. Most significantly, there is no longer a separate chapter on the Internet and its applications, since these topics are now integrated throughout the book.

Part I discusses the nature, structuring and description of knowledge. Chapter 1 argues the case for the organization of knowledge, discusses basic definitions and gives an overview of the contexts and processes for the organization of knowledge. Chapter 2 examines the different ways in which knowledge is packaged and structured using databases and documents. It then goes on to discuss the relationships between documents. Finally, it introduces ways in which digital documents can be structured and labelled using markup and metadata. Chapter 3 examines some specific types of metadata that are used to describe the content of documents: citations, abstracts, bibliographic records, bibliographic description and the MARC format.

Part II, with its five chapters, lies at the core of the book, focusing as it does on access to information. Chapter 4 sets the scene by considering users and their behaviour, including different models of information behaviour and the concept of usability and its application. Chapter 5 is the first of three chapters on subject access. Chapter 5 introduces the basic challenges of the provision of subject access, such as deciding what a document is 'about', and differentiates between the two main approaches: natural and controlled indexing languages. Two major sections follow, one on thesauri and the other on searching facilities. Chapter 6 switches the focus from alphabetical indexing languages to classification and order, and the challenges associated with examining the relationships between subjects. It explores the elements of bibliographic classification schemes: schedules, notation, alphabetical indexing and revision strategies. Chapter 7 starts by exploring in more detail the concept of pre-coordination. This is used as a platform for the analysis of traditional subject access tools, such as subject headings lists, and bibliographic classification schemes. A discussion of special bibliographic classification schemes leads naturally into an exploration of taxonomies and ontologies. The final chapter in Part II shifts the focus towards access through author names and titles. It introduces and illustrates the issues associated with the choice of access points, and the selection of headings for persons, corporate bodies and uniform titles.

Part III explores the different types of knowledge organization systems, and considers some of the management issues associated with such systems. Chapter 10 reviews the range of digital systems, and illustrates how the organization of knowledge is achieved through those systems. Chapter 11 perhaps sits a little less comfortably in the systems section, but it takes an important opportunity to explore a number of issues relating to print documents and indexes, such as book indexing, document arrangement, and filing orders and sequences. Finally, Chapter 12 offers an overview of some key aspects of the management of knowledge systems, including authority control, user support, security, systems development and managing change.

Each chapter commences with an introduction which specifies the learning objectives for the chapter. Chapter coverage is revisited at the end of each chapter, in the chapter summary, and every chapter has a list of references for further reading. Throughout the text, key points are illustrated with the use of a range of different figures. Checklists are offered in places where a summary of features or factors can most effectively be summarized in such a form.

AUDIENCE

In common with the earlier editions of this book, this edition is written for undergraduate and postgraduate students of information management. It is intended to be an introductory textbook. These students need to understand the organization of knowledge for three reasons. First, they may be involved in the design of information retrieval systems. Secondly, as information intermediaries and designers of information systems they themselves need to be exemplary searchers of information. Success in searching will not be achieved solely through the identification of an appropriate source, but also depends on skills in extracting the information from that source. Finally, they are likely to act as trainers in assisting others in effective information retrieval. Information retrieval, despite the plethora of information available to us, is not simple and requires considerable skill if the best information or document for the purpose is to be extracted.

ACKNOWLEDGEMENTS

It would be impossible to list all of those to whom the authors owe some debt in the creation of this book. The ideas gathered here have been drawn from many authors, and represent a melding of the traditional contributors to the debates around cataloguing and classification, and the more recent enthusiasts who are members of the Internet generation. The authors would like to acknowledge all the publishers, authors and systems suppliers who have permitted them to make use of extracts from their works. These are individually acknowledged at the point at which they are included in this work. We have made every effort to contact the copyright holders for the relevant figures but if any have been inadvertently overlooked we will rectify this at the first opportunity. The honing of the ideas in this book has been undertaken with innumerable cohorts of students; their questions and difficulties in understanding have driven the authors to seek to think more clearly about the concepts in the area described as the Organization of Knowledge.

The authors would also like to take this opportunity to acknowledge their publisher's patience as one personal challenge after another managed to get in the way of the timely completion of this manuscript.

List of acronyms and abbreviations

Note: This is a list of the more common abbreviations and acronyms used in the text. It is not an exhaustive list.

AACR	Anglo-American Cataloguing Rules
ABN	Australian Bibliographic Network
ALA	American Library Association
ANSI	American National Standards Institute
BC	(Bliss) Bibliographic Classification
BC2	(Bliss) Bibliographic Classification, 2nd edn
BL	British Library
BNB	British National Bibliography
BT	broader term
CC	Colon Classification
CCF	Common Communications Format
CD	compact disc
CD-ROM	compact disc read-only memory
CIP	Cataloguing in Publication
DAML	DARPA Agent Markup Language
DBMS	database management system
DDC	Dewey Decimal Classification
DMOZ	Directory Mozilla
DTD	document type definition
DVD	digital versatile disc
DVI	digital video interactive
ERIC	Educational Resources Information Center

FID	Fédération Internationale d'Information et de Documentation
GUI	graphical user interface
HTML	Hypertext Markup Language
HTTP	hypertext transfer protocol
IFLA	International Federation of Library Associations
IIB	Institut International de la Bibliographie
IR	information retrieval
ISBD	International Standard Bibliographic Description
ISBN	International Standard Book Number
ISO	International Standards Organization
ISSN	International Standard Serial Number
KWIC	keyword in context (index)
LC	Library of Congress
LCC	Library of Congress Classification
LCSH	Library of Congress Subject Headings
LMS	library management system
MARC	Machine-Readable Cataloguing
MeSH	Medical Subject Headings
NT	narrower term
OCLC	Online Computer Library Center (originally Ohio College Online Computer Library Center)
OPAC	online public access catalogue
PC	personal computer
PDF	portable document format
PRECIS	Preserved Context Index System
RDA	Resources Description and Access
RLG	Research Libraries Group
RSS	Really Simple Syndication
RT	related term
SGML	Standard Generalized Markup Language
SN	scope note
TT	top term
UDC	Universal Decimal Classification
UF	use for
URL	Uniform Resource Locator
Web	World Wide Web
WWW	World Wide Web

Part I
Structuring and Describing

1 Knowledge, information and their organization

INTRODUCTION

In the knowledge-based society of the 21st century, data, information and knowledge are integral to our existence. Information and our ability to retrieve, select, evaluate, process and use it are pivotal to the survival and success of individuals, groups, organizations and communities. As quantities of information increase, means of organizing information so that it can be retrieved are becoming increasingly important. This introductory chapter sets the scene for more in-depth consideration of the tools and approaches in the organization of knowledge and information retrieval. At the end of this chapter you will:

- appreciate the need to organize knowledge
- have considered definitions of data, information and knowledge and the relationship between these
- be aware of the need for sophisticated and diverse tools for the organization of knowledge and information retrieval
- have considered some of the basic elements of the engagement of people and computers in the organization of knowledge and information retrieval
- appreciate some of the characteristics of knowledge that are important to its organization and use.

WHY ORGANIZE KNOWLEDGE?

Knowledge is becoming ever more important to individuals, groups, organizations, communities, societies and nations. Compared with, say, 20 years ago individuals, organizations and communities experience:

- more information, communicated from
- a greater range of sources, through
- a wider range of channels, many of which have
- faster response and turnaround times.

Knowledge is viewed as an important, or arguably the most important asset. Knowledge and knowing is power. That power may bring political, social or economic success. Most developed countries are concerned to develop and capitalize on their knowledge assets to generate wealthier societies and economic growth. In order to achieve this they focus on both the development of learning environments (schools, colleges, universities, workplaces, virtual learning environments) and the development of, and networked access to, knowledge resources. This central significance of knowledge means that it is important that a user has convenient and appropriate access to the best information or knowledge at the right time, and in the most appropriate format. In order to make this possible it is necessary to organize knowledge. The organization of knowledge is the other face of information retrieval. The better organized that knowledge is, the easier it is to retrieve specific items of knowledge.

The overriding objective of the organization knowledge is the retrieval of information, hence the title of this book. We visit the distinction between information and knowledge below, but here we treat the two terms as synonymous. So, in principle it is necessary to organize things (books, DVDs, database records, the products sold by a supermarket and displayed on its shelves, paper files in filing cabinets and information on a website) in order to be able to find and locate, or retrieve, that required information easily. Organization of concepts is at the core of learning. Babies start their learning by organizing things into basic categories such as 'faces' or 'things to eat'. As they grow, children develop their collection of categories and the number of items grouped into those categories. We learn by analysing and organizing data, information and knowledge.

Information and knowledge is also used for a wide range of other purposes, including:

- decision making
- problem solving
- communication and interpersonal relationships
- entertainment and leisure
- citizenship
- enhancing business and professional effectiveness, performance and success.

All of these processes benefit from access to appropriately organized information and knowledge.

This all sounds straightforward and intuitive – why, then, is the organization of knowledge so complex? Later in this chapter, we answer this question through two different routes: first, by considering the limitations of a popular information retrieval tool, the widely used search engine Google, and secondly, by considering the elements in the process of organizing and retrieving knowledge, and the contexts in which this occurs. But first we start with some definitions of information and knowledge.

DEFINING 'INFORMATION' AND 'KNOWLEDGE'

What is this entity, knowledge, that is to be organized, and how does it relate to the notion of information? There are a number of different ways to approach a discussion of the nature of information and knowledge. One of the useful starting points is to examine the DIKW hierarchy shown in Figure 1.1, which defines information in terms of data, knowledge in terms of information, and wisdom in terms of knowledge.

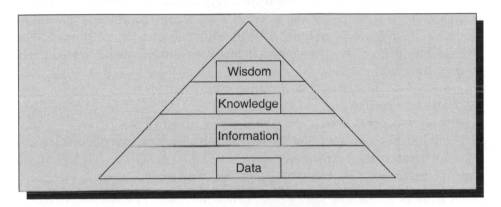

Figure 1.1   The DIKW hierarchy

In proposing this hierarchy, Ackoff (1989) offers the following definitions of data, information, knowledge and wisdom, and their associated transformation processes:

- *Data* is defined as a symbol that represents a property of an object, an event or of their environment. It is the product of *observation* but is of no use until it is in a usable (that is, relevant) form. The difference between data and information is functional, not structural.
- *Information* is contained in *descriptions*, answers to questions that begin with such words as 'who', 'what', 'when' and 'how many'. Information systems generate, store, retrieve and process data. Information is inferred from data.

- *Knowledge* is know-how, and is what makes possible the transformation of information into instruction. Knowledge can be obtained either by transmission from another who has it, by instruction, or by extracting it from experience.
- *Wisdom* is the ability to increase effectiveness. Wisdom adds value, which requires the mental function that we call judgement. The ethical and aesthetic values that this implies are inherent to the actor and are unique and personal.

More recently, Rowley (2006) summarizes definitions in a number of textbooks, and proposes the following definitions of data, information and knowledge. Embedded in these definitions are implicit statements about the relationship between data, information and knowledge.

- *Data* can be characterized as being discrete, objective facts or observations, which are unorganized and unprocessed and therefore have no meaning or value because of the lack of context and interpretation.
- *Information* is described as organized or structured data, which has been processed in such as way that the information now has relevance for a specific purpose or context, and is therefore meaningful, valuable, useful and relevant.
- *Knowledge* is generally agreed to be an elusive concept which is difficult to define. Knowledge is typically defined with reference to information. For example the processes that convert information into knowledge are variously described as:
  - synthesis of multiple sources of information over time
  - belief structuring
  - study and experience
  - organization and processing to convey understanding, experience, accumulated learning and experience
  - internalization with reference to cognitive frameworks.

Other authors discuss the 'added ingredients' necessary to convert information into knowledge and suggest variously that knowledge is:

- a mix of contextual information, values, experience and rules
- information, expert opinion, skills and experience
- information combined with understanding and capability
- perception, skills, training, common sense and experience.

These various perspectives all take as their point of departure the relationship between data, information and knowledge. This tight coupling between these concepts means that organizations, communities and nations need to integrate the management of data, information and knowledge, and that more specifically the organization of knowledge is likely to involve the organization of data and information.

The knowledge management literature (for example Nonaka and Takuchi, 1995) identifies two different types of knowledge: explicit knowledge and implicit or tacit knowledge. Tacit knowledge, or know-how, refers to personal knowledge embedded in the human mind through individual experience and involving intangible factors such as personal belief, perspective and values. Explicit knowledge, on the other hand, is knowledge that is codified and recorded in books, documents, reports, White Papers, spreadsheets, memos and other documents so that it can be shared. Tacit knowledge may be converted into explicit, objective or public knowledge through public expression such as speech, writing or the creation of images or performances. Some information scientists would argue that explicit knowledge is the same thing as information (Wilson, 2002; Taylor, 2004a). For example, Taylor (2004a, p. 2) argues that 'it seems to me that I can use my knowledge to write a book, but until you read that book, understand it, and integrate it into your knowledge it is just information'. This comment reflects the essential feature of knowledge, which is that it involves understanding. There would appear to be an ongoing debate on whether explicit knowledge can be described as knowledge or is better described as information. However this debate is resolved, this book is concerned with the organization of explicit knowledge. The debate on the relationship between knowledge and information does serve to emphasize the tight coupling between the two. Certainly the process of searching and retrieval involves cognition and knowledge of both the subject or items being sought and the search process, and it could be said that as the searcher pulls together information resources as part of a search he or she 'organizes knowledge'. In addition, if the term 'explicit knowledge' is used, the indexing and organization of packages of information or documents can be described as the organization of knowledge.

Published in 1987, the first edition of this book by the present authors was titled *The Organization of Knowledge and Information Retrieval*. Perhaps this wording might be seen as an attempt to have it all ways! In fact it followed in the tradition of earlier versions of the book which covered similar subject matter, written by another author working in the 1960s and 1970s.

WHY ISN'T GOOGLE SUFFICIENT?

People who have grown up and been educated with the rich resources available through the Internet, networked learning and information environments are inclined to the belief that if an Internet search engine, such as Google, cannot satisfy all of their information needs on the entry of a keyword or two, it can certainly take a very significant step in that direction. Google is becoming an indispensable aid to modern living and studying, to such an extent that in popular parlance it has generated the verb 'to google'. Quite apart from the fact that such a transition is a major commercial achievement for any brand, such an accessible route to a diverse collection of information resources predisposes users to believe that knowledge is organized for them, and little effort is required in the organization of knowledge or information retrieval on their part. Google is a very powerful retrieval tool, and in its universality has achieved scope and coverage only dreamt of by the founders of information retrieval, with their visions of 'universal bibliographic control'. Arguably even more significantly, Google has achieved a position as one of the leading global brands in a very short period of time. When previously has a tool that does no more and no less than offer an information search facility achieved such an elevated brand reputation and such significant global business success?

If Google were indeed the be-all and end-all for information retrieval, then this book would need to go no further than possibly explaining some of the more sophisticated search features offered by Google, and how to design optimum Google search strategies for different kinds of searches. Unfortunately, things are not that simple, and Google is only one tool in an armoury of different approaches to information retrieval. Figure 1.2 summarizes some of the advantages and

Advantages	Disadvantages
Fast	The user is not aware of the details of the search that has been undertaken, and may therefore have difficulty refining the search in a meaningful way
Simple keyword searching	Irrelevant hits or missing of relevant sources due to non-exploration of synonyms or related terms, or to the definition of relationships between words in search phrases
Underpinned by powerful search technology that delivers highly relevant top ten hits, from millions of websites and documents	It is difficult to distinguish between keywords used as author and those used as subject (such as 'Shakespeare'), without being able to indicate field or data type
Simple search interface, which is the same anywhere in the world (with language changes as necessary)	There can be a sense that Google provides too many hits, leaving it to the user to decide on their cut-off point in scanning lists of hits. Ranking of hits may not always show the best sources for the searcher's query on the first screen, and scanning several screens of hits is tedious
Automatic spellchecking Virtually always delivers something that is relevant	Relevant items may be scattered amongst many other items; the onus is on the user to evaluate and select
Searches on a range of file formats (such as PowerPoint slides, PDF files) Most hits have hyperlinks that give immediate access to the full text of documents or websites	Authority and quality of content of sources varies, and the user needs skills and judgement in selection

Figure 1.2 Evaluating Google

disadvantages of Google as an information retrieval tool. The disadvantages identified lead into the wider debate as to what an information retrieval tool should do. On the other hand, it is important to note that the pre-eminence of Google as a first port of call derives from advantages such as its speed, ubiquity and convenience, which are characteristics that should be firmly placed at the forefront of the design of other information retrieval systems.

TOOLS FOR ORGANIZING KNOWLEDGE AND INFORMATION RETRIEVAL

What happens to information? The greater part by far of information stored in the brain is discarded after immediate use. The time of day is important only for planning some subsequent action; the phase of a set of traffic lights serves only the immediate purpose of crossing the road or proceeding across a junction. We do not record this information, or retain it in our long-term memory. Some background information we do retain in long-term memory because we need to use it frequently: how to tell the time, or to proceed on green – this is part of our personal knowledge base. In between, there is information that we may possibly need to re-use at some future date or time, and this we record in personal information files. At their most basic, these files may be notes scribbled on the backs of envelopes, but most of us maintain more sophisticated databases: diaries, address books, lists of telephone numbers, filofaxes and electronic personal organizers or, in the case of researchers, personal databases of documentary sources. Everybody needs to organize their own information sources. There is no single way of doing this – each of us structures our information to suit ourselves.

Once we move outside the area of personal and domestic information and into published and organizational information, the pattern changes. The information we use in our professional lives – indeed, in all contexts outside the home – has a corporate existence. Many people may need to access it. We will be accessing information that others have created or organized. The organization of information in professional, academic and research contexts is complex and highly formalized. In this work we are concerned with the organization of knowledge and information retrieval in these specific contexts. In particular we are concerned with those techniques that are of interest to information and knowledge professionals. These will include techniques and tools found and used in libraries, as well as other approaches used in the management of information in organizations. However, one important feature to note about such systems is that some of them do not, in fact, organize or retrieve information. Some are actually concerned with the organization and retrieval of documents or references to documents. Conventionally, librarians have concentrated on documents and resources that have been generated elsewhere and bought in, whereas information managers have specialized in the records or files that an organization generates internally: letters, leaflets, personnel documents and a host of other items. Even this distinction is no longer clear-cut. What is clear, however, is that resources of all kinds, irrespective of their source, need organizing so that their contents can be retrieved when required. If we need our personal organizers and other devices to store and retrieve our personal, professional and domestic information, how much more true is this of libraries and organizations of all kinds?

The tools for the organization of knowledge have been developed, designed and used in a wide range of different contexts and amongst different professional communities. Key amongst these fields are the following:

- *Catalogues and bibliographies* are created and used by librarians to list the documents in a collection or within a specified field. Catalogues are used to list the print and electronic documents within a library collection for purpose of inventory and access. Electronic catalogues are known as online public access catalogues (OPACs). Bibliographies typically focus on a specific field (for example, ceramic art) and seek to list the documents that have been published within that field in a defined time period to capture the knowledge base of the field, and to support scholars and others in their investigations in that field.
- *Indexing and abstracting services* are used by information managers to identify the documents that are required to meet a specific subject request. Indexing and abstracting services regularly scan new publications and resources in a given subject field (for example, forestry) and add records relating to those publications to their databases. Users may search these databases for information on a given topic, or receive regular alerts of new publications.
- *Publishers and third party aggregators* offer access to electronic journals and e-books, and require mechanisms to support the searching of their databases.
- *Records management systems*, which are the responsibility of records managers and archivists, maintain an orderly collection of records or archive of the documents and transactions of the organization. Such record repositories may include paper records, but significant proportions of such archives are now electronic. Records may include licences, personnel contracts and files, manuals, details of product trials, historical documents and a wide range of other items.
- *Knowledge management systems* are designed and maintained by knowledge professionals in organizations in order to support knowledge-based processes, such as knowledge capture, knowledge creation, knowledge sharing, knowledge dissemination, and knowledge access in relation to the knowledge base of a specific organization and, sometimes, its partner organizations. Such knowledge repositories often focus on explicit information in the form of, for example, market research reports, technical research reports, manuals and

policy documents, but some also seek to embrace tacit or explicit knowledge (know-how) through embedding it in expert systems or through databases of experts.

- *E-commerce*, where services and goods are sold through websites. E-commerce sites may be launched by e-tailers (such as eBay or Amazon), by brick retailers (such as Tesco, Boots or Barnes & Noble) or by manufacturers (such as Dell or Ford). Such sites may have significant product ranges amongst which the consumer needs to be able to locate a specific item. Some also have significant information resources available to customers.

- *E-government*, in which government agencies use the Web to enhance their interactions with their citizens, to enhance service delivery and to encourage more active participation in citizenship and democracy. Such applications are diverse, including for example, websites offering online health information, tax and revenue information and transactions, local authority information and services and employment and training information.

- *Digital libraries* (DLs) are organizations that seek to offer intellectual access to, interpret, distribute, preserve the integrity of and ensure the persistence over time of collections of digital works for the benefit of specific communities. They often involve large volumes of documents or data located within multiple repositories managed by different organizations. The user is able to move from one source to another, seeking and linking information automatically to solve their information problems. The design of DLs involves considerable attention to the way in which knowledge is organized and represented in these different repositories and, increasingly, the 'interoperability' between repositories.

- *Content Management Systems* (CMSs) are widely used to manage the content of large websites and for providing access to a repository of information resources via a range of different delivery channels, such as customer call systems, digital TV, intranets and internets. CMSs support the collection, management and publication of content. This typically involves the indication of subject keywords, descriptive indicators, access rights, renewal dates and content originators. The content may be document-based or generated from a database.

Taken together, the above list of contexts in which knowledge must be organized and accessed means that numerous different types of organizations are involved in the development of approaches to support access to information, documents and knowledge. More importantly, users are increasingly accessing information in a wide range of different contexts, for different purposes, and engaging with different tools and approaches to the structuring of knowledge. Against this backdrop it is useful to restate three of the long-standing principles associated with the organization of knowledge:

1. knowledge needs to be organized for communities, which in turn means that all knowledge providers need to know their communities
2. in designing tools to support the organization of knowledge, community members' linguistic, semantic and cognitive frameworks must be the central consideration
3. standards and standardization enhances interoperability between systems, which has benefits for both systems designers and organizers and the communities that they serve.

There is, however, an inherent tension between the design of systems for specific communities and the ever-present need for standardization, as is very evident in the use and development of the tools discussed throughout this book.

APPROACHES TO INFORMATION RETRIEVAL: WHAT PEOPLE DO

In any of these environments, the objective of the organization of knowledge is successful subsequent retrieval. Different people may wish to retrieve a document or unit of information for different reasons, and may therefore approach the retrieval process in different ways. There are two fundamental approaches to seeking information, namely information searching, where the information seeker attempts to locate information which meets specified search criteria, and browsing, where the information seeker browses through an information source in the hope of spotting something useful.

A fundamental difference in searching strategy is between known-item searching and subject searching. *Known-item searching* is performed by users when they know what they are looking for and usually possess some clue or characteristic by which they can identify the item, such as its author or all or part of its title. *Subject searching* is performed by users who do not have a specific item in mind. Although it is called subject searching, in practice all manner of other considerations come into play, such as literary form, level of difficulty, the author's viewpoint, whether designed for continuous reading, among others. *Browsing* describes the situation when users have a less precise view of the information or documents that may be available or are not sure whether their requirements can be met. It is often used for the activity of scanning through a number of documents in order to refine the user's requirements. *Surfing* is its Web equivalent – though this includes browsing with no purpose other than to revel in the sheer range and diversity of available resources.

There are a number of types of subject information need. A common one is for a specific item of information: the searcher knows what information is required, but is less certain where to look for it. Another very common situation is for one or more documents to be required, but less than the total available. Less frequently a comprehensive (exhaustive) search may be required when it is important not to overlook any significant piece of information. This kind of information need is often encountered in the early stages of research to avoid duplicating research that has already taken place. What is common to all these types of subject information need is that they are *retrospective*: the searcher is looking backwards over available resources. A quite different kind of subject need is for *current awareness*: the need for professionals, academics and keen amateurs to keep abreast of developments within their areas of interest.

Irrespective of the type of information need, there are (from the point of view of the information professional) two methods of conducting a search. The first kind of search is user-conducted: the documents or resources are organized and accessed such that users can retrieve information for themselves. Information that is obtained in this way is said to be *heuristic*: users can modify their search requirements as they go along. The second kind uses an information professional as an intermediary to carry out the search on behalf of the end-user. If the user is present when the search is taking place, this kind of search may also be heuristic. If not, the search is *iterative*: if the search results do not adequately match the end-user's requirements, the search has to be started again from scratch.

APPROACHES TO INFORMATION RETRIEVAL: WHAT COMPUTERS DO

Computers make a significant contribution in the organization of knowledge and information retrieval. Typically they support information retrieval through:

- *Storing metadata and associated index files* needed to identify and locate documents or other information objects. As the scale of digital information increases so computers are increasingly being used to automatically generate the metadata which is used subsequently for retrieval.
- *Storing the full text of documents and any index files* needed to support the searching of these documents. The full text may be web pages, journal articles or reports. Where this is stored digitally all or some elements of it can be used to support the retrieval of appropriate documents. Index files may support the operation of search engines.
- *Search engines* have become the most common way to search web-based and other digital resources. They provide an interface through which the user can enter some search terms, and then seek these terms in documents or indexes in order to generate a list of items that are potentially relevant to the search. This process of matching words in a query against words in a document is by far the most widely used computer-based tool. Search engines typically also

offer advanced search facilities that conduct searches based on other parameters, such as dates and journal titles.

- *Citation indexing* makes use of the citations (references) appearing at the end of many documents, particularly research papers. Effectively, the author of a paper has established a link between the paper and those earlier documents that are cited at the end. A citation index makes a separate record for each cited document. Documents in the citation index are linked to a separate file (source index) of their source documents. Searching begins with a document known to be relevant, and it is possible to check either which later documents have cited it or which earlier documents it cites. Searches can be recycled backwards and forwards to build up a file of promising-looking citations.

- *Hypertext links* are closely identified with the World Wide Web, even though their history goes back to the 1960s and they have many other applications. A hypertext link consists of an identifier – a highlighted word or phrase in a passage of text or a button to be clicked – and a link to a related document or to another part of the same document.

- *Information filtering* is one name given to techniques for pre-sorting large volumes of data in response to a given search in order to eliminate the least relevant. A further search or data analysis is then conducted on a subset of the database. Another name for this is *data mining*.

- *Image and sound processing*. With the escalation of digital imaging, techniques for indexing images are becoming ever more important and there is considerable development occurring in this arena, but the indexing, matching and retrieval of images is much more complex than the matching of words in text.

CHARACTERISTICS OF INFORMATION AND KNOWLEDGE

Any discussions about the way in which knowledge and information can be managed, or structured, need to take into account a number of their inherent characteristics. These include objectivity, accessibility, relevance, currency, structure and systems. We discuss each of these characteristics in turn.

OBJECTIVITY

The debate associated with the objectivity of knowledge is relevant to all types of knowledge and all disciplines. All knowledge is a product of the society and cultural environment in which it is created. However, the issue of objectivity has been most hotly debated in the social sciences. Social science researchers and knowledge users have been acutely aware of the difficulties associated with creating a shared reality which could be regarded as valid and transferable objective knowledge. Science and technology, on the other hand, often investigate problems and environments where experiments can be repeated under similar conditions to give consistent results and thus what can be identified as objective knowledge. Related to the issue of objectivity are those of reliability and accuracy. *Accuracy* means that data or information is correct. *Reliability* implies that the information is a true indicator of the variable that it is intended to measure. Users often judge reliability of information on the basis of the reputation of the source from which it has been drawn.

ACCESSIBILITY

This is concerned with the availability of knowledge to potential users. The distinction between implicit or tacit knowledge and explicit knowledge is relevant here. Tacit knowledge is subjective knowledge, which is owned by the individual or team. Most explicit knowledge is stored in the printed and electronic archives of societies (libraries) and organizations, and is, in general, likely to be more accessible than tacit knowledge. However, the storage and communication media and the form and style of communication are also important. Knowledge may be stored and communicated via people, print or electronic media. A real challenge for most individuals and organizations is the integration of information that is presented in different formats. Also the form and style of communication needs to be amenable. The user's subject knowledge, environmental context, language used and preferences all influence the success with which a message is received.

RELEVANCE

Knowledge available to an individual must be appropriate to the task in hand. Knowledge available to an organization must be relevant, or pertinent, to its current direction, vision and activities. Knowledge is relevant when it meets the user's requirements and can contribute to the completion of the task in which the user is engaged, whether that task is decision making, problem solving or learning. Relevance can be assessed in relation to many of the other characteristics listed in this section, such as currency and accuracy, but may specifically be judged in terms of level of detail and completeness. *Completeness* is normally judged in relation to a specific task or decision; all of the material information that is necessary to complete a specific task must be available. In addition the level of detail, or *granularity*, of the information must match that required by the task and the user. We return to the concept of relevance and define a more specialized use of the term in Chapter 10.

CURRENCY

Currency and life span of knowledge are important for two reasons – some information may supersede other information; the most current information is required, and outdated information needs to be discarded. Each type of information has its own *life cycle*. At one end of the timescale there is a core of relatively stable knowledge for each discipline, such as the way in which the heart functions or the process for the refining of steel. Other information (for example, the weather report) loses its immediacy within hours, but may still be valuable for the detection of trends or for historical purposes. There is a real challenge in being able to recognize the positioning on a timescale of specific knowledge and to be able to manage that knowledge in accordance with its life cycle. Users need to be presented with information that is still current, and collections of knowledge need to be weeded of redundant and outdated material.

STRUCTURE AND ORGANIZATION

All knowledge has a structure. At the individual cognitive level, the brain holds associations between specific concepts. Structure is important to understanding. This cognitive structure is reflected in the way in which individuals structure information in their communications in the form of verbal utterances, text and graphical representations. Some disciplines have inherent structures; biology, for example, is organized in accordance with a structure that reflects the structure of living matter, and documents on biology can be organized in a way that is consistent with this structure. Newspapers, similarly, group information into categories such as news, politics and sport. The two important features of this structure are:

- the way in which items are grouped into categories
- the relationships between these categories.

SYSTEMS

Structure is often imposed by systems, whether those systems are conceptual frameworks, communication systems or information systems. Knowledge will be communicated through information systems and stored in information systems. Such systems embrace people as well as hardware and software. The central theme of this book is the nature of systems for the organization of knowledge. These systems need to be designed in order to achieve effective and efficient information retrieval.

SUMMARY

This chapter has explored the nature of information and knowledge and has sought to discuss the processes associated with the organization of knowledge and information retrieval. It has discussed the role of computers and people, respectively and introduced some of the tools for organizing knowledge and information retrieval. This chapter has started to demonstrate that the theory and practice of systems for the organization of knowledge and information retrieval is complex. Much of this complexity derives from the wide variety of different contexts in which knowledge has been and continues to be organized. Approaches to and systems for the organization of knowledge embrace systems designed for a number of different user groups and of knowledge and document formats; such approaches use varied technologies and have evolved considerably over the past 50 years. More specifically, the complexity of systems, the range of systems, and the different terminologies and conceptual frameworks associated with information retrieval have their origins in:

1. The evolving technological landscape, in relation to, for example, storage media, network technologies, metadata protocols and standards, and database platforms and search technologies. This means not only that continuing innovation is required in information retrieval systems, but also that many organizations responsible for organizing information (libraries, archives, business organizations, public records offices) sometimes have large quantities of data stored and indexed in legacy systems. In addition, metadata standards embed concepts (such as main entry) that derive from earlier generations of information retrieval systems.
2. The wide range of different but overlapping disciplinary and professional perspectives that have influenced the design of information retrieval systems. This leads to overlapping conceptual frameworks and systems with similar, but not identical objectives. Professional groups that make contributions to the practice and theory of the organization of knowledge include librarians, publishers, psychologists, educationalists, archivists, museum curators, knowledge managers and information systems professionals.

REVIEW QUESTIONS

1. Why do communities need to organize knowledge?
2. Using your own words and examples, illustrate the relationships between data, information, knowledge and wisdom.
3. Google is a wonderfully effective search tool, but it has its limitations. What are they?

17

4. Tools for the organization of knowledge are used in a wide variety of different fields. Briefly explain their use in four of these fields.
5. Briefly explain the relationship between knowledge and communities, and the consequences that this has for interoperability.
6. Explain the difference between known-item searching, subject searching and browsing.
7. Briefly explain some of the key contributions that computers make to the organization of knowledge and information retrieval.
8. What do you understand by each of the following in relation to information and knowledge: objectivity, accessibility, relevance and currency?

REFERENCES AND FURTHER READING

Ackoff, R.L. (1989) From data to wisdom. *Journal of Applied Systems Analysis*, **16**, 3–9.

Awad, E.M. and Ghaziri, H.M. (2004) *Knowledge Management*. Upper Saddle River NJ: Pearson Education International.

Battelle, J. (2006) *The Search: How Google and its rivals rewrote the rules of business and transformed our culture*. London: Nicholas Brealey.

Brookes, B.C. (1974) Robert Fairthorne and the scope of information science. *Journal of Documentation*, **30** (2), 139–52.

Chowdhury, G.G. (2003) *Introduction to Modern Information Retrieval*. London: Facet.

Chowdhury, G.G. and Chowdhury, S. (2006) *Organizing Information*. London: Facet.

Floridi, L. (2003) Two approaches to the philosophy of information. *Minds and Machines*, **13**, 459–69.

Floridi, L. (2004) Afterword – LIS as applied philosophy of information: a reappraisal. *Library Trends*, **52** (3), 658–65.

Herold, K. (2004) The philosophy of information – introduction. *Library Trends*, **52** (3), 373–6.

Jashapara, A. (2005) *Knowledge Management: An integrated approach*. Harlow: FT Prentice Hall.

Jeanneney, J.N. (2006) *Google and the Myth of Universal Knowledge: A view from Europe*. Chicago IL: University of Chicago Press.

Joachim, M.D. (2003) *Historical Aspects of Cataloguing and Classification*. Binghamton NY: Haworth Press.

Kakabadse, N.K., Kakabadse, A. and Kouzmin, A. (2003) Reviewing the knowledge management literature: towards a taxonomy. *Journal of Knowledge Management*, **7** (4) 75–91.

Koniger, P. and Janowitz, K. (1995) Drowning in information, but thirsty for knowledge. *International Journal of Information Management*, **15** (1), 5–16.

Nonaka, I. and Takuchi, H. (1995) *The Knowledge Creating Company*. Oxford: Oxford University Press.

Rowley, J.E. (1998) What is information? *Information Services and Use*, **18**, 243–54.

Rowley, J.E. (2000) Knowledge organization for a new millennium: principles and processes. *Journal of Knowledge Management*, **4** (3), 217–23.

Rowley, J.E. (2007) The wisdom hierarchy: representations of the DIKW hierarchy. *Journal of Information Science* **33** (2), 163–80.

Spender, J.C. (1996) Organizational knowledge, learning and memory: three concepts in search of a theory. *Journal of Organizational Change*, **9**, 63–78.

Spink, A. and Cole, C. (2004), A human information behaviour approach to a philosophy of information. *Library Trends*, **52** (3), 617–28.

Taylor, A.G. (2004a) *The Organization of Information*, 2nd edn. Westport CT: Libraries Unlimited.

Taylor, A.G. (2004b) *Wynar's Introduction to Cataloging and Classification*. Westport CT: Libraries Unlimited.

Taylor, A.G. (2006) *Introduction to Cataloguing and Classification*, 10th edn. Westport CT: Libraries Unlimited.

Vise, D.A. (2006) *The Google Story*. Pan.

Wilson, T.D. (2002) The nonsense of 'knowledge management', *Information Research*, **8** (1), 144–54.

2 Formatting and structuring knowledge

INTRODUCTION

Chapter 1 established the importance of organizing knowledge and information retrieval. This chapter introduces some of the basic tools for formatting and structuring knowledge into and within 'information packages' which act as the foundations for the organization of knowledge discussed in subsequent chapters. At the end of this chapter you will:

- appreciate the different types of databases that might be important in the organization of knowledge
- be aware of the need for database structures
- learn how text is organized into documents
- understand the formats in which documents are presented
- be aware of intellectual relationships between documents
- understand the forms and roles of markup and metadata that are applied to electronic and printed documents.

DATABASES

Library and information managers have always compiled files of information, in the form of catalogues and lists of borrowers. Early computer-based systems in many businesses held master files typically containing data relating to payroll, sales, purchase and inventory. Such applications comprise a series of related and similarly formatted records. External databases may be accessed through the online service suppliers through the Internet or acquired on CD-ROM. The information manager may download sections of these databases, with appropriate licensing arrangements, to integrate into local databases. Since databases are central to the way in which data is stored and retrieved, it is important for the information manager to be aware of the types of database that are available, any standard record formats that are likely to be encountered and approaches to database structure.

Databases may be stored on magnetic or optical media such as discs, and accessed either locally or remotely. This may include access to an organization's database covering transactions and financial records or other databases that might be accessed remotely. Some of these databases will hold publicly accessible information, such as abstracting and indexing databases, full texts of reports, encyclopaedias and directories, while others will be databases that are shared within an organization or group of organizations.

There are two main types of databases that might be available to information users in the public arena: reference databases and source databases.

REFERENCE DATABASES

These refer or point the user to another source such as a document, an organization or an individual for additional information, or for the full text of a document. They include:

1. *Bibliographic databases*, including citations or bibliographic references, and sometimes abstracts of literature. They tell the user what has been written and in which source (for example, journal title, conference proceedings) it can be located and, if they provide abstracts, will summarize the original document. Figure 2.1 shows part of a bibliographic database. Even though a number of the large bibliographic databases have been available in machine-readable form for more than 20 years, the basic elements in the database still have their roots in the printed product (often an abstracting or indexing tool with which they are associated), and this influences their structure and the options for information retrieval. The databases often also have spin-off products in addition to the options for online access, such as alerting services, links to full-text documents, and search aids.
2. *Catalogue databases*, which show the stock of a given library or library network. Typically, such databases list which monographs, journal titles and other items the library has in stock, but do not give much information on the contents of these documents. Catalogue databases are a special type of bibliographic database but, since their orientation is rather different from that of the other bibliographic databases, they are worth identifying as a separate category. Figures 2.2 to 2.5 show a search conducted on a catalogue database.
3. Referral databases offer references to information or data such as the names and addresses of organizations, and other directory-type data.

TI:	Title
	Population genetics meets behavioral ecology
AU:	Author
	Sugg, DW; Chesser, RK; Dobson, FS; Hoogland, JL
AF:	Author Affiliation
	Div. Wildl. Ecol. and Toxicol., Univ. Georgia's Savannah River Ecol. Lab., Aiken, SC 29802, USA
SO:	Source
	TRENDS ECOL. EVOL., vol. 11, no. 8, pp. 338–342, 1996
IS:	ISSN
	0169-5347
AB:	Abstract
	Populations are often composed of more than just randomly mating subpopulations – many organisms form social groups with distinct patterns of mating and dispersal. Such patterns have received much attention in behavioral ecology, yet theories of population genetics rarely take social structures into account. Consequently, population geneticists often report high levels of apparent inbreeding and concomitantly low effective sizes, even for species that avoid mating between close kin. Recently, a view of gene dynamics has been introduced that takes dispersal and social structure into account. Accounting for social structure in population genetics leads to a different perspective on how genetic variation is partitioned and the rate at which genic diversity is lost in natural populations – a view that is more consistent with observed behaviors for the minimization of inbreeding.
LA:	Language
	English
SL:	Summary Language
	English
PY:	Publication Year
	1996
PT:	Publication Type
	Journal Article; Review
DE:	Descriptors
	population genetics; social behavior; behavioral genetics; dispersal; reviews
CL:	Classification
	D 04615 Ecology studies – general; Y 25521 General; G 07280 Behavioral genetics
SF:	Subfile
	Ecology Abstracts; Animal Behavior Abstracts; Genetics Abstracts
AN:	Accession Number
	3952287

Figure 2.1   Bibliographic database (record from Animal Behaviour Abstracts database)

Source: <www.csa.com/factsheets/animal-Behaviour-set-c.php>

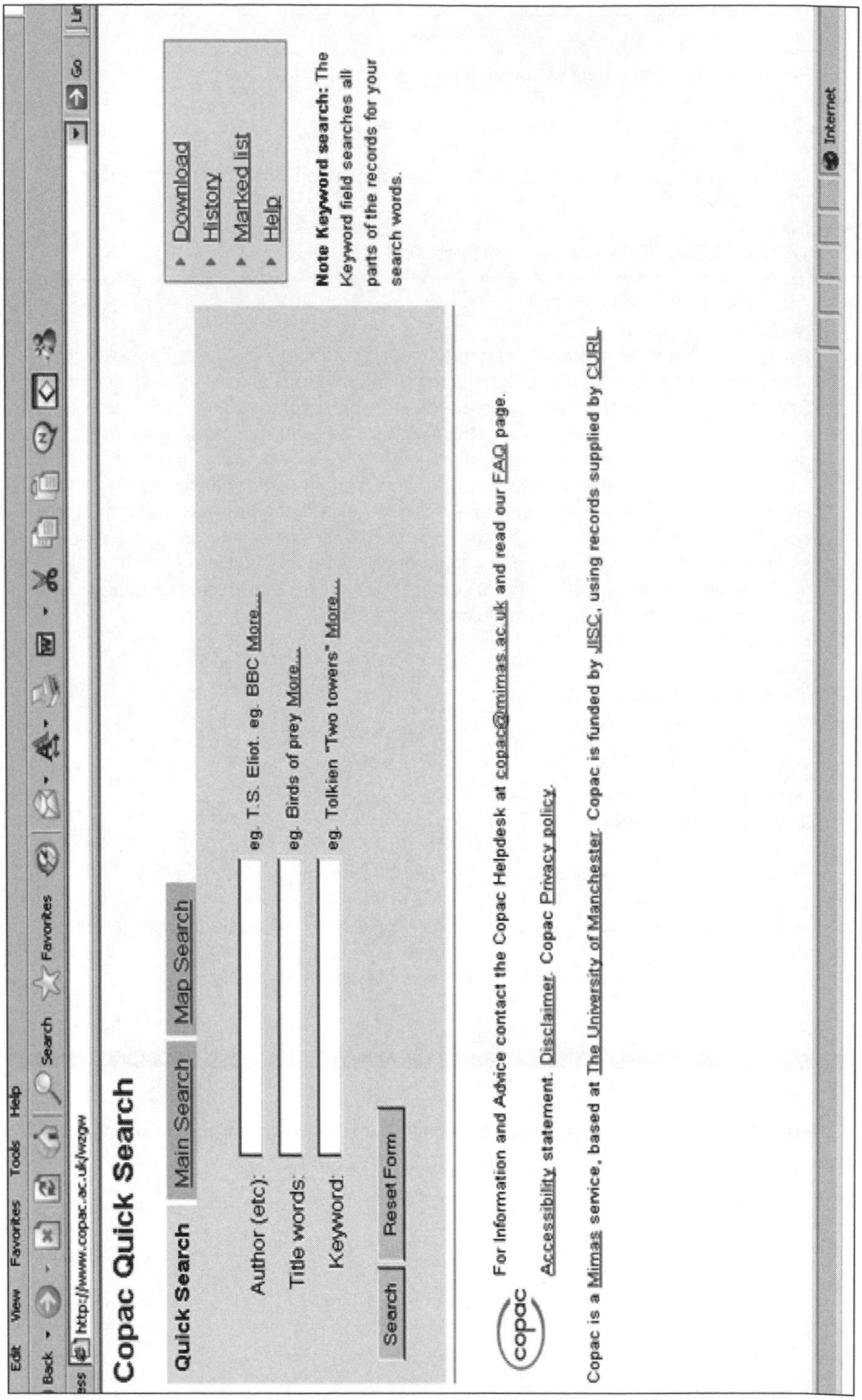

Figure 2.2 Catalogue database 1: OPAC search screen

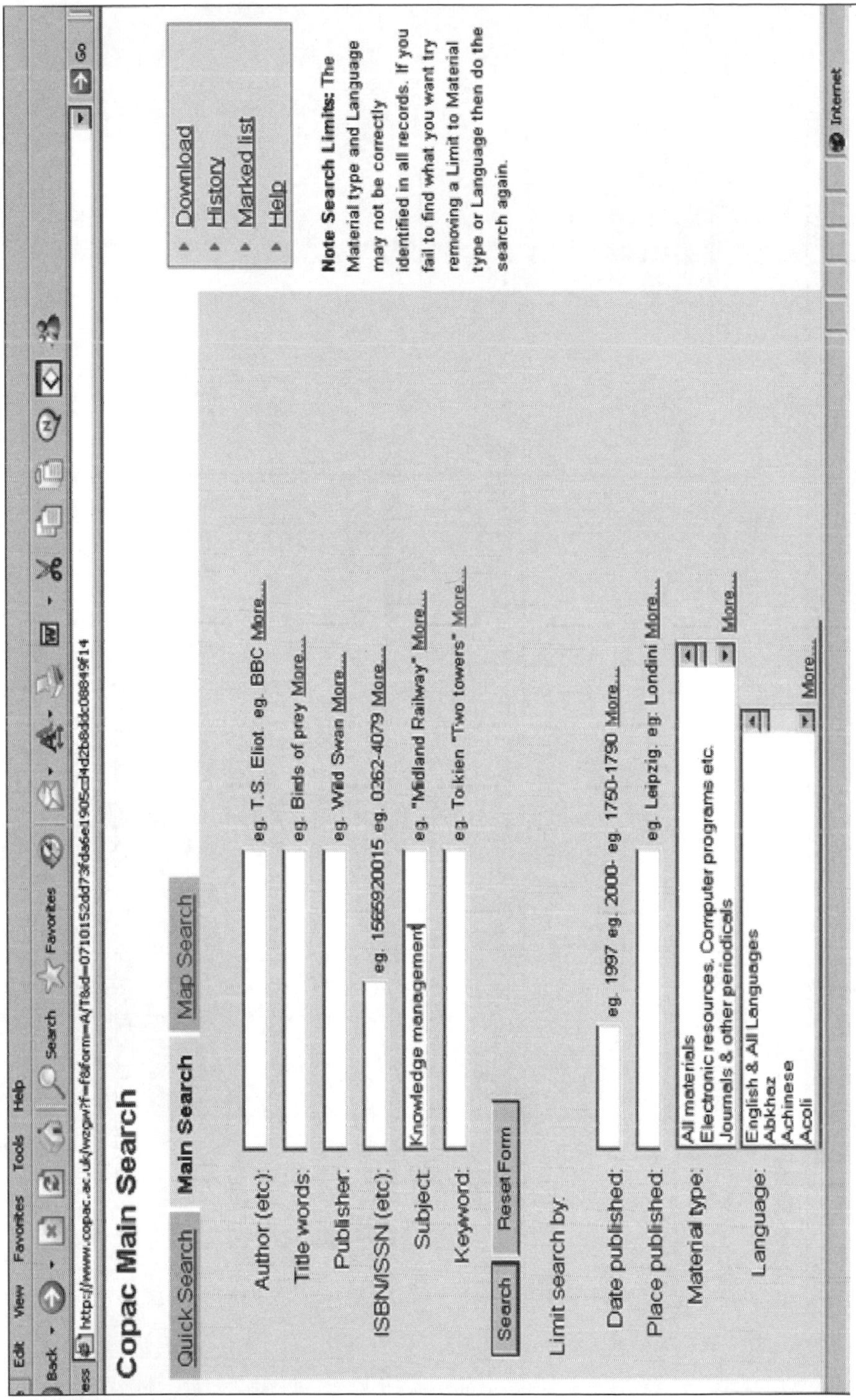

Figure 2.3 Catalogue database 2: OPAC subject search

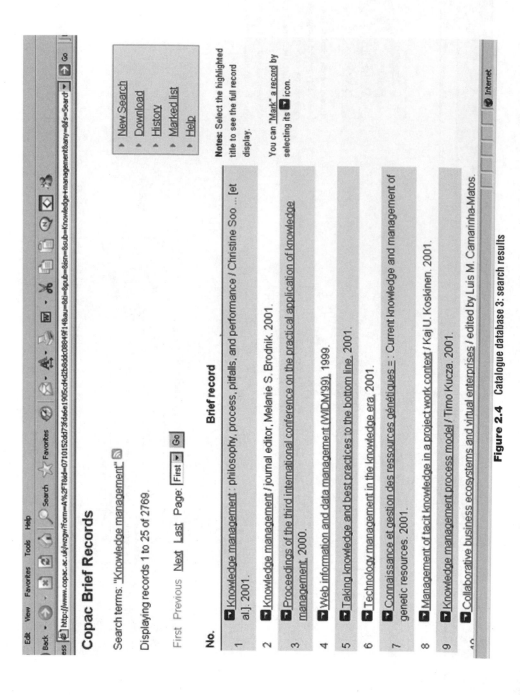

Figure 2.4 Catalogue database 3: search results

Figure 2.5 Catalogue database 4: full record details

SOURCE DATABASES

These contain the original source data, and are one type of electronic document. After successful consultation of a source database the user should have the information that is required and should not need to seek information in an original source (as is the case with reference databases). Data is available in machine-readable form instead of, or as well as, printed form. Source databases can be grouped according to their content:

- numeric databases, which contain numerical data of various kinds, including statistics and survey data
- full-text databases of journal articles, newsletters, newswires, dictionaries, directories and other source materials
- text-numeric databases, which contain a mixture of textual and numeric data (such as company annual reports) and handbook data
- multimedia databases, which include information stored in a mixture of different types of media, including, for example, sound, video, pictures, text and animation.

Many, although not all, source databases have a print equivalent. Some source databases do not contain the complete contents of the print equivalent, but only offer selected coverage. Some referral databases can also be regarded as source databases when, for instance, they contain the full text of a directory.

DATABASE STRUCTURES: THE INVERTED FILE

The crudest way to search a database is to go through it record by record looking for the appropriate data element. As this is slow, alternative methods of locating specific records have been developed. The online search services and other applications that use document management systems have always used the *inverted file* approach described below. This is useful for searching complex text-based databases, where the searcher does not know the form in which the search key may have been entered in the database, and has, essentially, to guess the most appropriate form.

Transaction-processing systems, such as library management systems, travel bookings information systems, and sales and marketing information systems, may also use this approach to locate individual records within a database, but these also need a mechanism for linking a series of distinct databases together so that information can be drawn from more than one database for display on the screen or printing at one time as discussed in subsequent sections on database structures.

The *inverted file* is similar to an index. In the inverted file approach there may be two or three separate files. The two-file approach uses two files – the text or print file and the inverse or index file. The text file contains the actual records: the index file provides access to these records. The index file contains a record for each of the indexed terms from all of the records in the database, arranged in alphabetical order. Each term is accompanied by information on its frequency of occurrence in the database, the file in which it is to be located, the record in which it is entered, and possibly further location information such as the paragraph (or field) within which it is located. When a new record is added to the database, it is necessary to update the index file. These files are used together in the search of a database. A user who is interested in performing a search on the word 'hedges', for instance, will enter the term at the keyboard, and the system will seek the term in the index file. If the term is not present in the index file, the system responds by indicating that there are no postings for that term. If the term is found, the user will be told how many postings, or occurrences, of the term there are in the database.

To display the records, the text file location is used to locate records in the text file. If three files are used, there is an intermediate file that allows search terms input at the keyboard to be checked quickly and the number of postings displayed on the screen. This is particularly useful with a complex search that may involve using the index file records for a number of search terms.

The above description is intended to offer a simple introduction to the basic concept of an inverted file. In practice, file structures may be more complicated, as the following examples indicate:

- If it is possible to search terms in proximity to other terms (for example, terms within two words of each other), the index file must contain information about word positions within a field for each term.
- Inverted files are often created for a number of fields within a record.
- However, not all fields are usually indexed, because each index takes disc storage space; indexes are created for those fields that are commonly searched. Inverted files are often created for author names, title words, subject-indexing terms and author-title acronyms.
- Long full-text records need to be split into paragraphs and those paragraphs must be assigned identifiers before indexing can commence. Alternatively, the positions of individual words in the file can be used as identifiers.

DATABASE STRUCTURES: THE RELATIONAL MODEL

In the early days of computing, business and library systems worked with a series of individual master files covering, for example, in the case of libraries, borrowers and books in stock or, in the case of many businesses, payroll, sales and inventory. It soon became apparent that programs for, say, circulation control in a library needed to access two or more different files, and it was appropriate to start to examine the relationships between these files. This led to the introduction of the concept of a database, and the software to manage such databases, known as database management systems (DBMSs). It then became necessary to examine the optimum way to structure data or to develop data models to support specific applications.

Relational databases use one type of database structure, which has been widely adopted in database systems. In relational systems, information is held in a set of relations or tables. Rows in the tables are equivalent to records, and columns in the tables are equivalent to fields. The data in the various relations are linked through a series of keys. Figure 2.6 shows a simple example of a relation known as catalogued-book. In this relation the International Standard Book Number (ISBN) is the primary key and may be used in other relations to identify a specific book. For example, if we maintain the relation order-book the ISBN acts as a link to the order-book relation. If we wish to complete an order form with details from the order file, data for each book can be extracted from the catalogue file and incorporated into the order form alongside data from the order file.

(a) Catalogued-book relation occurrences

ISBN	Title	Author	Year
0-82112-462-3	Organic chemistry	A.J. Brown	2005
0-84131-460-7	Alchemy	R.M. Major	2004
0-69213-517-8	Expert systems	S. Estelle	2006
0-93112-462-1	Computer science	S. Estelle	2006
0-71143-526-6	Bibliography	J. Johns	2001

(b) Order-book relation occurrences

Order no.	ISBN	Quantity ordered
678	0-82112-462-3	1
678	0-84131-460-7	4
678	0-69213-517-8	20
679	0-93112-462-1	2
680	0-82112-462-3	3
681	0-71143-526-6	2

Figure 2.6 Two simple relations

DATABASE STRUCTURES: THE OBJECT-ORIENTATED MODEL

The object-orientated approach is an alternative to the relational database model; it is important in the Web environment. The object-oriented approach to programming and database design constructs systems and databases as collections of reusable interacting objects. An object model for a database consists of a collection of objects. An *object* may be a person, a thing (such as a document) or a concept. An object combines data structures with any functions needed to manipulate the object or the data that it holds. Objects may be grouped in *object classes* on the basis of common attributes, relationships or methods. An *attribute* is a property of an object class. A *relationship* is some connection between object classes. A *method* establishes some behaviour expected of a class.

The object-oriented approach is attractive because:

- since objects are self-contained they are easy to change and develop, without necessarily changing any other part of the system
- new objects can be easily created from existing objects
- objects can be copied or transferred into new systems with little difficulty.

COMPLEX DATABASE STRUCTURES

Standard database design focuses on data in a limited range of data types, such as integer and text. Other data types, such as images, audio and video present special challenges for database design. Such data types need special approaches to their storage and to their indexing and retrieval. Multimedia DBMSs (MM-DBMSs) are used to manage such databases. As pictures, animation, sound, text and data tables have very different storage needs, MM-DBMSs seek to use a range of technologies, such as relational technology for tables, text databases for documents and image storage devices for graphics and animation. In networked environments, object-orientated database models are being used to develop systems to handle different data types; a digital object within such a system can be in any one of a wide range of data types. One of the advantages of the object-oriented approach is that processing information can be stored alongside data.

TEXT AND MULTIMEDIA

Historically, databases have been compiled from representations of documents, or document surrogates, rather than the documents themselves. It is only since the mid-1980s that it has become technically and economically feasible to store whole documents in an immediately accessible digital format, and the computer storage of graphics, sound and multimedia resources is more recent still. Many of the tools and techniques originally developed for organizing document representations have been adapted to whole documents. Others are new. The rapid growth of the Internet has produced a whole new generation of information specialists from a variety of backgrounds whose interest is in the retrieval of networked documents and other resources – whole documents and not representations of documents. This section therefore discusses the formats of knowledge itself – documents and resources in their various guises – before progressing to consideration of document representations in Chapter 3.

The rise of multimedia notwithstanding, text remains the basis of information. In the global society, it is worth pausing briefly to consider some of the implications of this statement. Most of the world's languages have no written codes. On the other hand, English has effectively replaced Latin as the lingua franca of international communication. The Latin alphabet used by the English language has variants and extensions when applied to other European languages. Many Asian languages, and a few European ones, use other alphabets, and transliteration standards are needed to represent one language in the script of another. Two major languages – Japanese and Chinese – have non-alphabetic writing systems: the one is syllabic, the other logographic, with each symbol representing a complete word. The study of written languages recognizes two basic components. A language has a *vocabulary* of words, and a *syntax* – a set of rules for stringing words together to make meaningful statements. Semantics is the name given to the study of meaning in language. We will meet these terms again in Chapter 5.

The word is the unit on which many retrieval systems operate, but what is a word? Is *folk-lore* one word or two? (Some retrieval systems will make three words out of it: *folk*, *lore*, *folk-lore*.) Most of us recognize that many words are inflected – that is, they have different inflections (endings) according to their grammatical function – but many languages take this far beyond the simple *dog – dogs* or *bark – barks – barked – barking* of the English language. Retrieval systems can easily reconcile different word endings, but sometimes languages are agglutinative – they attach prefixes to words, or string several words together to make portmanteau words. Important in German and some other languages, in English this is a problem that needs to be systematically addressed, mainly in chemical information retrieval systems.

It is important to be aware of the structure of text. We – not just information professionals, but any literate person – can become more effective in understanding the gist of a document by skimming it if we have some idea how text is structured, so we know where to look and where to skip. Computers can be made to mimic human processes and apply them to text analysis. Two important structural patterns are:

- *Problem–solution*: at its simplest, a problem is stated and a solution proposed. A four-part variant is often found in research papers: introduction (statement of the problem to be solved); method; results; discussion and conclusions. Another variant is: statement of problem; discussion of one or more inadequate responses; and, finally, a successful response.
- *General–particular*: a generalization is made, and provided with one or more examples. There may be hierarchies of generalizations in that a sentence may

function both as an example to a generalization and as a generalization which is itself exemplified. This hierarchical organization of text is explicit in report writing.

These structural patterns are often found in combination. Anyone used to skimming text to obtain its gist soon learns to look for cues that help to establish the subject matter. These include elements such as section headings, or stock phrases like 'In this paper we ...', 'This paper seeks to ...', and so on. Additionally, the hierarchical organization of text teaches us that the more significant parts of a text are likely to be found near the beginning of the whole document, of individual sections and of paragraphs. Not only can we learn to do these things ourselves, we can also design our search systems to act in a similar way, for example, by giving greater weight to words found near the beginning of a document.

Multimedia pose problems not encountered with text. Many non-textual collections – images, video clips, mixed media – are now held online, ranging from the large-scale digitization projects of national libraries and art galleries to personal collections. The types of verbal and structural cues that text offers are simply not available. Images do not even have titles, so viewers have to rely on their own conceptual interpretations. The same image can be studied at different generic levels and from a range of disciplinary viewpoints. A set of pictures of Hardwick Hall ('more glass than wall') in Derbyshire might be of interest to historians, architects, art historians or to someone researching the history of windows; it is an example of Elizabethan architecture, and a source of the social history of the sixteenth-century English upper classes; the National Trust (its present owner) calls it 'a magnificent statement of the wealth and authority of its builder, Bess of Hardwick'; and its setting might be studied by landscape historians, or by a film or television producer looking for a setting for a costume drama. Faced with complexity of this order, the manual indexing of non-text media is inevitably subjective and slow. Researchers into the automatic indexing and retrieval of images by their content have an uphill struggle. Some success has been reported with systems operating on simple graphic shapes within limited domains, like engineering drawings, plant-leaf types or, operationally, fingerprints.

DOCUMENTS

A document is a record of knowledge, information or data, or a creative expression. A document's creator has recorded ideas, feelings, images, numbers or concepts in order to share them with others. Until recently, this would have been a sufficient definition. Documents were normally text-based, but the definition could easily be extended to include the minority of documents which expressed themselves in some other way. Basically, stored data, in any form, constitutes a document. Documents include, for example, broadcast messages and three-dimensional objects such as models and realia. This is not a new idea: the suggestion that everyday objects could be considered to be documents goes back to the early years of this century, if not earlier: did not Shakespeare find 'tongues in trees, books in the running brooks, Sermons in stones ...'? (Incidentally, a study in the 1950s concluded that an antelope was a document if kept in a zoo as an object of study, but not when running wild.)

Documents are traditionally perceived by the unaided eye, less commonly by touch. Formats requiring optical apparatus – slides, microforms, etc. – have been with us for a long time. Electronically readable formats have a shorter history but are revolutionizing our notions of a document. Libraries have conventionally been concerned with books. Most libraries have also collected conference proceedings, reports, microforms, serials, maps, videos, slides, filmstrips and computer software; some, specializing in such media, are often described as resource centres. Libraries have always been network-conscious, with their well-established and efficient networks for interlending books. Over the last 30 years, libraries have made increasing use of computer networks, sometimes for operational tasks like acquisitions and cataloguing, but increasingly to obtain information electronically – references to documents, actual documents, factual information, images, software, interactive media. Some people are still happy to call these documents, but it is now more conventional to use the word resources for networked resources of all kinds. The term *digital library* is also used of the range of networked resources.

Schamber (1996) identified some characteristics of electronic documents. They are:

- easily manipulatable, in that they can be cut-and-pasted, rotated, etc.
- internally and externally linkable, through hyperlinks
- readily transformable, onto disc, print, etc.
- inherently searchable, by means of search software
- instantly transportable, via electronic networks
- infinitely replicable, in that copying does not degrade the quality of the original.

The growth of electronic documents has given rise to some alternative notions of a document. A document can be considered in any of the following ways:

- a homogeneous item; that is, a physical entity
- linked heterogeneous items; for example, a mixture of full text and abstracts in a database
- a contextual display of related items; for example, the results of a search on such a database

- homogeneous items created by the user, such as a Web home page with its unstable set of links.

To reconcile these different perspectives, Schamber (1996, 670) defines a document as a unit:

- consisting of dynamic, flexible, non-linear content
- represented as a set of linked information items
- stored in one or more physical media or networked sites
- created and used by one or more individuals
- in the facilitation of some process or project.

In the context of networked resources, definitive lists of resource types and formats are being prepared by the Dublin Core (see below). These include: collection, dataset, event, image, interactive resource, moving image, physical object, service, software, sound, still image and text. Definitions are to be found in the DCMI Type Vocabulary at <http://purl.org/dc/dcmitype>.

A more generic approach to items of intellectual content in the digital environment is embedded in the work on digital object identifiers (DOIs). A DOI is a unique name for an entity on digital networks. The DOI system introduces the concept of a digital object for an item of intellectual property on a digital network that has been precisely defined by means of structured metadata.

While the formats of networked resources are still being formalized, the forms of presentation and arrangement of text-based documents are well established. Figure 2.7 is based on the categories found in a major classification scheme, the Bliss Bibliographic Classification. This is not a comprehensive listing, but simply serves to illustrate some of the more common formats. Each format has its own features and problems of indexing and retrieval. The contents of encyclopaedias and dictionaries, for example, are virtually self-indexing, and information professionals need do little more than identify them and indicate where they are located. The contents of periodicals, on the other hand, require massive and complex organization. Also, specialist areas of knowledge have their own specialized information formats. Figure 2.8 shows the formats recognized by the Educational Resources Information Center (ERIC).

BIBLIOGRAPHIC RELATIONSHIPS

Documents seldom exist in isolation from one another, but draw on each other in all kinds of ways. In literary studies this is known as intertextuality, and includes a range of pursuits from the tracking down of passing allusions, to full-blown parody. Information retrieval makes use of relationships between documents in a

Comprehensive works
Introductory works
Reference works: encyclopaedias, dictionaries
Partially comprehensive works: periodicals, newspapers, yearbooks, directories
Works for a particular class of reader: by subject interest (for example, for nurses); sociological
characteristics (for example, for women); or by level of understanding (for example, for children)
Surveys, reports, reviews
Research reports
Forward-looking: proposals, recommendations, forecasts, feasibility studies
Critical studies
Notices, bulletins, announcements, manifestos, agendas, circulars
Composite works: essays, speeches, interviews, conference proceedings, anthologies, readings
Study aids: syllabuses, exercises, identification manuals, digests
Tabulated information: timetables, chronologies, almanacs, technical data, formulae
Numerical information: statistics, accounts
Imaginative literature
Personal observations
Case studies

Figure 2.7 Forms of presentation and arrangement of documents

Books
Book product reviews
Collected works
General
Dissertations/theses
ERIC products
Guides – general
Guides – classroom, learner
Guides – classroom, teacher
Guides – non-classroom
Historical materials
Information analyses
Journal articles
Legal/legislative/regulatory materials
Numerical, quantitative data
Opinion papers
Reference materials
Reports – general
Reports – descriptive
Reports – evaluative
Reports – research
Speeches, meetings, papers
Tests and questionnaires

Figure 2.8 Document types recognized by ERIC

number of ways. It is clear that if some kind of intellectual relationship exists between two documents, a user who is interested in one may well be interested in the other as well. One way is through *citation indexes*. These are reverse indexes to the lists of cited works that appear at the end of research and other documents, and enable researchers to see which later documents have cited an earlier one. Another way concerns cataloguers in particular, who are engaged in a re-examination of what used to be known as the bibliographic unit problem. The problem is one of identifying the overt relationships between two or more documents. Research has identified seven categories of relationship:

1. *Equivalence relationships* between exact copies of the same manifestation of a work. These include copies, issues, facsimiles, photocopies and microforms.
2. *Derivative relationships*, also called horizontal relationships, are between a bibliographic item and modifications based on the same item, including variations, versions, editions, revisions, translations, adaptations, and paraphrases.
3. *Descriptive relationships*: the relationship between a work and a description, criticism, evaluation or review of that work. These include annotated editions, casebooks, commentaries, critiques, etc.
4. *Whole–part relationships*, also called vertical or hierarchical relationships, are between a component part of a work and its whole; for example, a selection from an anthology, collection or series. This may even apply to the chapters of a book, as it is sometimes more convenient to regard an electronically stored book as a coordinated collection of documents rather than as a single document.
5. *Accompanying relationships*, where two works augment each other, whether equally (as with supplements) or with one subordinate to the other (as with concordances and indexes).
6. *Sequential relationships*, also called chronological relationships, where bibliographic items continue or precede one another, as with successive titles in a serial, sequels of a monograph, or parts of a series.
7. *Shared characteristic relationships*, where items not otherwise related have, coincidentally, a common author, title, subject or other characteristic used as an access point. This relationship differs from the other six in that there is no intellectual relationship between the works.

The *Functional Requirements for Bibliographic Records* (*FRBR*), issued in 1998, in discussing the unit that should be the focus of bibliographic description, identified a different set of relationships in the definition of the concepts: work, expression, manifestation and item:

- *Work*: an intellectual or artistic creation, that exists in the mind of the creator. Examples of works include Shakespeare's *Hamlet* or Lennon and McCartney's *Hey Jude*.

- *Expression*: the intellectual or artistic realization of a work through which the work can be read, seen, heard or felt. There can be more than one expression of a work, as in successive translations, performances or copies. For example, in the case of a sculpture, expressions of the original may take the form of copies, photographs or digital representation on the Web.
- *Manifestation*: the physical embodiment of a work, or the format in which one of the expressions of the work can be found. For example, a journal article might have manifestations as paper format, an HTML file or a PDF version.
- *Item*: a single exemplar of a manifestation; for example, a copy of a book. Exemplars are usually identical to each other, unless factors such as the condition or location of a copy are important.

This approach is particularly useful for digital and multimedia resource environments. Bibliographic description, as discussed in Chapter 3, is normally performed at the level of the manifestation, unless there are significant differences between copies, in which case description may be performed at the item level.

TEXT ANALYSIS

Computers are able to process very large quantities of text. With text analysis we can automate such processes as:

- extracting keywords
- preparing document representations; for example, by scanning title pages of books to generate catalogue descriptions or by processing the text to generate an abstract
- determining various characteristics of a text; for example, its level of reading difficulty, its authorship, its chronological place within the canon of its author's works, or the attitudes or beliefs of its author translating the text into another language.

There are broadly two approaches to text analysis:

1. *Statistical analysis* is based on counting the frequency of particular words in the text, together with a range of more sophisticated devices, including phrases, pairs of words or clusters of words in proximity to one another. Concept frequency is another such device, where the text is analysed to generate a thesaurus, or list of words that share some aspect of their meaning, or a semantic network of words that are to be found in association with one another.
2. *Structural analysis*, or knowledge-based analysis, scans the text for words,

phrases or sentences that are in significant positions within the text. For example, for indexing purposes one might look for section headings and figure captions; for abstracting purposes and also for indexing, one might examine the first and final paragraphs of sections, the opening sentences of paragraphs, or the positions of such cue words and phrases as 'in this paper we', 'method', 'results show' or 'in conclusion'. For abstracting, translation and other applications which generate sentences, the text is parsed – parsing is a word-by-word analysis of each sentence using an algorithm which gradually builds up an interpretation of the text.

Knowledge-based text-processing systems – expert systems – use many forms of knowledge representation. One that is commonly found is the *frame*, which is based on human mental processes. A frame is a receptacle for information about an entity or event. It contains slots to hold the attributes of the entity. As the text is parsed or the cues read, the slots are gradually filled in. A simple frame, which could be used for newspaper stories, is shown in Figure 2.9. Text analysis is easier within fairly specific domains, such as news items or papers in medicine. The new generation of search engines and data-mining tools use advanced text analysis techniques that are less domain-specific.

Slot	Look for indicator
Type of disaster	look for indicator word such as *train wreck, earthquake*
Where	look for place name
When	look for time words: *yesterday, Friday*, etc.
Number of dead	look for *killed* or *dead* and a number close by
Number of wounded	look for wounded or *injured* and a number close by
Amount of damage	look for £, $ or *dollar* adjacent to a number, especially when close to *damage* or *worth* or *destroyed*

Figure 2.9 Frame for understanding and summarizing 'Disasters'

TEXT MARKUP AND ENCODING

Electronic text at its most basic uses the ASCII character set. This includes all the characters found on a keyboard plus a few others. Extended ASCII character sets (256 characters) also include the diacriticals found in many European languages. (Chinese logograms are a problem apart. One encoding system has 65,536 possible characters, enough for everyday use but not for advanced work.) ASCII does not include any of the elements which define the layout of text into paragraphs, etc., or its actual appearance, as for example the use of bold type or different fonts. Word-processing and publishing software have used their own codes, and this has lessened the portability of documents between systems.

Also, within an organization it is often necessary to store documents for retrieval and re-use. Often only parts of a document will be re-used, and selective revision and reformatting may be applied. The application of *markup* to plain (ASCII) text enables electronic documents to be stored and re-used efficiently.

Markup is of two kinds:

- *Procedural markup* originally denoted the handwritten instructions that would tell typesetters how to lay out text for printing. Word-processing and desktop publishing software use procedural markup in the same way. Procedural markup defines the final presentation of a document and so is specific to the application as, for example, when we instruct our word processor to change the font size or insert a page break.
- *Descriptive* (or *generic*), *markup* defines the headings, content lists, paragraphs and other elements which make up the structure of a document, without reference to its appearance on the page.

Standard Generalized Markup Language (SGML) is the international standard (International Standards Organization, ISO 8879: 1986) for embedding descriptive markup within a document, and thus for describing the structure of a document. Standard Generalized Markup Language formally describes the role of each piece of text, using labels enclosed within <brackets> (see Figure 2.10 for an example). It is a descriptive, not a procedural, markup language. It separates document structure from appearance, and so allows documents to be created that are independent of any specific hardware or software, and thus these are fully portable between different systems.

```
<memo> <to>
A.C. Stanhope
</to><from>
Earl of Chesterfield
</from><date>
12 October 1765
</date><subject>
Advice
</subject><text><para>
In matters of religion and matrimony I never give any advice; because I will not have anybody's
torments in this world or the next laid to my charge.
</para></text></memo>
```

Figure 2.10 A simple SGML document

Hypertext Markup Language (HTML) is a subset of SGML – formally, it is an SGML document type definition – that has been specially developed for creating World Wide Web documents. HTML is used to define the display of Web documents, including features such as font size and type, background and text colours, the use of bold and italic, and page layout (see Figure 2.11 for an example). As with SGML, an HTML document can be created using any text editor. There are also a number of HTML editors, some within word-processing packages, which insert the markup automatically.

```
<html>
<head>
<title>This is an example of HTML</title>
</head>
<body>
<hl>Here is an example of a link</hl>
<p>The Department of Information and Communications at Manchester Metropolitan University
has its own
<a>href='http://www.mmu.ac.uk/h-ss/dic/'>Home Page</a>.</p>
<p>In it you will find links to a wide range of useful sources.</p>
</body>
</html>
```

Figure 2.11 A simple HTML document

XML (eXtensible Markup Language) is a version of SGML that can be used on the Web. As compared with HTML, XML is extensible in the sense that new markup tags can be created to facilitate searching and exchange of information. HTML tags are restricted to those useful for formatting and linking of web pages. Because XML can be used to define the elements of any type of structured data, it has a wide range of applications in information exchange and e-commerce. The tags effectively act as a standard set of database field descriptions so that data can be exchanged between companies once a standard has been agreed. An XML implementation typically consists of three parts: the XML document, a document type definition (DTD) (see below) and a style sheet (XSL).

The markup languages all share a common structure. The text of a document is divided into a number of elements and sub-elements, each of which is named and allocated a start tag and an end tag. Tag names can be single letters (such as <p>), abbreviated words (such as <li>), single words (such as <title>) or several words (such as <PublisherName>). The actual text sits between the start and end tags; for example, <title>Organizing knowledge</title>.

Non-text resources (images, sound, video, multimedia) are especially reliant on markup, as systems which can automatically analyse sounds and images for retrieval are very much in their infancy.

Document Type Definitions (DTDs) are SGML or XML applications that define the structure of a particular type of document, using markup. A DTD defines the elements or fields in a document in accordance with its document type. This combination of fields or metadata elements defines the metadata structure of a document. An *XML Schema* is a richer form of a DTD that defines not only the structure, but also the content and semantics or meaning of documents. Both DTDs and XML schemas define:

- elements that might be part of a particular document type
- element names and whether they are repeatable
- the content of elements (in general terms)
- what kinds of markup can be omitted
- tag attributes and their default values
- names of permissible entities.

A DTD or schema can be created for one document, but generally it is more appropriate to create DTDs or schemas for many documents. Examples of such schemas are:

- TEI DTD – for encoding web pages
- MTML/XHTML – for encoding web pages
- MARC DTDs and SXML schema – for encoding MARC21 records.

METADATA

WHAT IS METADATA?

The previous paragraph started to use the term 'metadata'. Here we take a step back and consider what metadata is and how it is used.

Metadata is 'data about data'. Assuming that an information package such as a website, a journal article, a digital map, an MP3 or a learning object is data, metadata is the data created to describe or represent the attributes and contents of that information package. Such metadata is structured information that aids in the identification, discovery, retrieval, manipulation, management and use of digital objects in a networked environment. Metadata may be used by people or computer programs. Apart from level 1 metadata (see below), metadata differs from markup in being distinct from, rather than integrated with, the body of the resource: in the HTML example above, the metadata is included in the <head> section. So metadata is a form of document representation, but it is not a document surrogate in the way that a catalogue entry is. Metadata is linked directly to the resource, and so allows direct access to the resource.

Metadata also differs from bibliographic or cataloguing data in that the location information is held within the record in such a way as to allow direct document delivery from appropriate applications software; in other words, the records may contain detailed access information and network addresses. In addition, biblio-graphic records are designed for users to use both in judging relevance and making decisions about whether they wish to locate the original resource, and as a unique identifier of the resource so that a user can request the resource or document in a form that makes sense to the recipient of that request. These roles remain significant. Internet search engines (see Chapter 10) use metadata in the indexing processes that they employ to index Internet resources.

The term 'metadata' is generally applied to the data used to represent Internet and digital resources, but some would argue that cataloguers have been creating metadata, in the form of catalogue records, for centuries. Catalogue records are created for the purposes of keeping a record of library resources, information retrieval and access to resources, and the management of those resources. The attributes that allow users to identify and select information packages are relatively common, including, for example, titles, creators, creation dates and subject matter. Others would argue that there is a significant difference between cataloguing and metadata. Key differences derive from the key characteristics of electronic sources:

- The challenges associated with identifying the boundary of an 'information package' in the absence of an identifiable physical item. Is the unit a single web page, or an entire website?
- Absence of physical carrier for Web resources removes the need for a physical description, covering, for example, number of pages, or size.
- The concept of edition is more elusive with electronic resources. What, for instance, constitutes or denotes the release of a new edition of a website?
- Location information for Web resources is based on URL, and there is an expectation that when users locate a metadata record they will be able to click through to a URL; on the other hand, URLs are relatively volatile, when compared with library location data.
- Electronic resources require not only descriptive metadata of the kind typically used to describe their content, but also extensive structural metadata in order for them to be displayed and function appropriately.

THE PURPOSES OF METADATA AND ITS CLASSIFICATION

According to Haynes (2004) there are five purposes of metadata:

1. *Resource description* – so that a clear list of the documents and resources held by an organization can be created. This is particularly important for public authorities and government agencies that are required to identify their

information and publications, and also for both public and corporate sector organizations that need to compile information asset registers.

2. *Information retrieval* – to support resource discovery across Web resources and electronic books and journals.

3. *Management of information resources* – to support the management of the retention and disposal of records and the publication of Web content using content management systems applications. Typical metadata that may assist in the management of record life cycles includes: authorship, ownership, date of creation and date of modification.

4. *Documenting ownership and authenticity of digital resources* – digital documents are increasingly being used in e-commerce contractual situations as evidence of contract. Metadata provides a way of declaring the ownership of the intellectual content and layout of a document, and a record of the authenticity of the document.

5. *Interoperability* – metadata acts as an enabler of information and data transfer between systems, and metadata standards are a key component in the drive towards interoperability. When a piece of data is passed from one system to another the accompanying (or embedded) metadata allows the new application to make sense of the data, and to make appropriate use of it. For example, in the book trade, where suppliers use different software, the ONIX standard allows different participants in the chain from the author to reader to exchange data without the need to integrate their systems.

Metadata systems can be classified into three levels:

1. The metadata is some unstructured data found in the information package itself; this is the approach adopted on the Web with search engines that identify metadata in the content of web pages.

2. The metadata is in a structured format, using a basic template for metadata creation. The Dublin Core (see below and Chapter 3) fits into this category.

3. The metadata is in rich format to support specific applications, such as those used by libraries, archives and museums. At this level, metadata elements are more detailed and may combine metadata elements with encoding and content standards, such as MARC, AACR2R and EAD (see Chapter 3).

METADATA SCHEMAS

A number of metadata schemas have been developed in order to standardize and control metadata. The basic components of metadata are the schema and the elements. Metadata elements are the individual categories or fields that hold the pieces of description of an information package, such as title, creation, creation date and subject identification. Metadata schemas are sets of elements designed to meet the needs of particular communities, such as the book trade or government agencies; they may focus on specific types of data such as web pages, geospatial information or graphics resources. Figure 2.12 shows some metadata schemas and their domains. A listing of schemas can be viewed on the SCHEMA website (<www.schema-forum.org>). The different communities and resources covered by metadata schemas mean that the schemas vary considerably, in terms of the data elements included, the use of mandatory and repeatable elements, encoding, and the use of controlled vocabularies. In addition, whilst most schemas contain descriptive elements to support resource identification and discovery, some schemas also include elements to support administrative and structural functions.

Schemas and modelling languages	Domain or purpose
IEEE Learning Object Metadata	Education
Australian Government Locator Service	Government
E-Government Metadata Standard	Government
Government Information Locator Service	Government
JPEG-2000	Images
Machine Readable Cataloguing (MARC)	Libraries
Moving Picture Expert Group MPEG-2 1	Multimedia
Moving Picture Expert Group MPEG-7	Multimedia
ONIX	Publishing industry
Indecs	Rights management
Extensible Rights Metadata Language (XrML)	Rights management
Open Digital Rights Language (ODRL)	Rights management
Dublin Core Metadata Element Set	Web

Figure 2.12 Some metadata schemas and their domains

There are a number of general-purpose metadata schemas, arguably the most significant of which is the Dublin Metadata Core Element Set, referred to as the Dublin Core; this was developed in the mid-1990s as a metadata standard to assist the management of electronic resources. The Dublin Core is discussed below. Others, such as ISBD and AACR2R, that define metadata content are discussed in Chapter 3.

THE DUBLIN CORE

The Dublin Metadata Core Element Set, known simply as the Dublin Core, is a list of metadata elements originally developed at a workshop in 1995 organized by OCLC (the Online Computer Library Centre) and NCSA (the National Centre for Super Computer Applications). The objective was to improve the indexing and bibliographic control of Internet documents by defining a set of data elements for metadata records of 'document-like objects' – the scope was deliberately left open. The intention was to make the data element set as simple as possible, so that the developers of authoring and network publishing tools could incorporate templates for this information in their software. Authors and publishers of Internet documents could thus create their own metadata. This approach is akin to the practices of research publishing, where contributors to primary journals commonly supply their own abstracts, subject keywords, and affiliation details when submitting papers for publication. The Dublin Core does not prescribe any record structure and originally excluded details of access methods and constraints, though these have subsequently been added. All elements are optional and repeatable, and can be extended as required. Controlled vocabularies are also being developed for certain of the data elements, as an aid to consistency.

The data elements are:

1. *Title* – the name given to the resource by the creator or publisher.
2. *Creator* – the person or organization primarily responsible for creating the intellectual content of the resource.
3. *Subject* – the topic of the content of the resource, expressed in keywords or phrases that describe its subject or content. The use of controlled vocabularies and formal classification schemas is encouraged.
4. *Description* – a textual description of the content of the resource, including abstracts in the case of document-like objects or content descriptions in the case of visual resources.
5. *Publisher* – the entity responsible for making the resource available in its present form, such as a publishing house, a university department, or a corporate entity.
6. *Contributor* – a person or organization responsible for making contributions to the content, such as an editor, transcriber, illustrator or other person or organization who has made significant intellectual contributions to the resource, but secondary to that specified in a creator element label.
7. *Date* – date associated with an event in the life cycle of the resource; this might include dates when the resource was created, made available, submitted, modified, or copyrighted or made available in its present form. The recommended format is an eight-digit number in the form YYYY-MM-DD.
8. *Type* – the nature or genre of the content of the resource, such as home page, novel, poem, working paper, technical report, essay, dictionary.

9. *Format* – the physical or digital manifestation of the resource, used to identify the software and possibly hardware that might be needed to display or operate the resource.

10. *Identifier* – a string or number used to identify the resource uniquely. Examples for networked resources include Uniform Resource Locators (URLs) and Uniform Resource Numbers (URNs, when implemented). Other globally unique identifiers, such as ISBNs or other formal names would also be candidates for this element in the case of offline resources.

11. *Source* – a string or number used to uniquely identify the work from which this resource was derived, if applicable. An example might be the ISBN for the physical book from which the portable document format (PDF) version of a novel has been derived.

12. *Language* – the language(s) of the intellectual content of the resource.

13. *Relation* – the relationship of this resource to other resources; for example, the relationship to other versions of the resource.

14. *Coverage* – the extent or scope of the content of the resources, possibly in terms of the spatial and/or temporal characteristics of the resource.

15. *Rights* – information about rights held in and over the resource, such as links to a copyright notice, to a rights-management statement, or to a service that would provide information about terms of access to the resource.

METADATA AND INTEROPERABILITY

As identified above, one of the key functions of metadata is interoperability. Metadata acts as an enabler of information and data transfer between systems. In order to allow software applications that have been designed independently to pass data between them, a common framework for describing the data being transferred is needed, so that each 'knows' how to handle the data. For example, in the book trade, the widely used ONIX metadata standard allows different participants in the supply chain (from author to reader) to exchange data without the need to integrate their systems. Another example of interoperability is the Internet, where Internet resources can be viewed using proprietary browsers which are able to interpret the marked-up HTML text. A useful working definition of interoperability is given by Shirky (2001): 'Two systems are interoperable if a user of one system can access even some resources or functions of the other system'.

In the same way that metadata may operate at three levels, so interoperability can be defined at the following three levels:

1. semantic interoperability – achieved through agreements about content description standards, such as AACR2 and Dublin Core

2. structural inoperability – achieved through a data model such as RDF, that is used to specify semantic schemas
3. syntactic interoperability – achieved through schemas like XML which provide a syntax for expressing metadata.

Interoperability at all of these levels is necessary for two metadata systems to be interoperable. In the context of digital libraries, Arms et al. (2002) propose three levels of interoperability:

1. *federation* – where bodies of metadata from different sources all conform to a particular standard, as for example in the use of Z39.50 to achieve interoperability of library catalogues
2. *harvesting* – where each participant makes metadata about its collections available in a simple exchange format (OAI is an example of this approach)
3. *gathering* – where publicly available metadata is gathered, as for example when such data is gathered by search engines on the Web.

The proliferation of metadata standards developed by different but often overlapping communities of interest is undermining the opportunities for exchange of metadata. In metadata standard development there is a tension between opting for a minimal set of data elements, as exemplified by the Dublin Core, or seeking a larger number of elements that allows improved management of the resources, as exemplified by the ONIX standard used in publishing, and the MARC21 standard used in libraries. There has been considerable work in recent years towards the identification and comparison of different metadata standards. Work has been undertaken on metadata registries (collections of metadata standards), the development of metadata exchange standards such as METS (the Metadata Encoding and Transmission Standard) and crosswalks, which map metadata elements between two or more metadata schemas.

Figure 2.13 summarizes some of the salient points covered above in considering the metadata elements of a photograph of the first public telegram in the world – URL: <http://moriarty.bobst.nyu.edu/markup/Notebook/Morse/morse6.JPG>.

TRADITIONAL FORMS OF METADATA USED BY INDEXERS

While the term metadata is applied to networked resources, we should not forget that traditional printed materials have always had what is, in effect, their own metadata, which for books is called the *preliminaries*: the parts of a book that precede (and follow) the actual text. The preliminaries are the principal source of information, both in preparing document representations and in providing the

Metadata in File Header:
```
<HTML>
<HEAD>

<META NAME = 'DC.title'
CONTENT = 'Photograph of the first public telegram in the world'>
<META NAME = 'DC.creator' TYPE = 'Name.Personal' CONTENT = 'Hering, Daniel Webster,
1850–1938'>

<META NAME = 'DC.subject'
SHEME = 'LCSH'
CONTENT = 'Telegraph-History'>

<META NAME = 'DC.subject'
SHEME = 'LCSH'
CONTENT = 'New York University-History-19th century'>

<META NAME = 'DC.subject'
SHEME = 'AAT'
CONTENT = 'Photoprint'>

<META NAME = 'DC.description'
CONTENT = 'Photograph of the original message sent over ten miles of wire in the City
University of New York, January 24, 1838. The message was loaned to the University for
exhibit on occasion of the Columbian Exposition of 1893. The photo accompanies a
biographical essay of Samuel Morse'>

<META NAME = 'DC.publisher'
CONTENT = 'New York University Libraries'>

<META NAME = 'DC.date'
CONTENT = '1997'>

<META NAME = 'DC.type'
CONTENT = 'photograph'>

<META NAME = 'DC.format'
CONTENT = 'JPEG image'>

<META NAME = 'DC.identifier'
CONTENT =
'http://moriarty.bobst.nyu.edu/markup/Notebook/Morse/morse6.JPG'>

<META NAME = 'DC.language'
SCHEME = 'Z39.53'
CONTENT = 'eng'>

<META NAME = 'DC.relation'
TYPE = 'Relation.IsMemberOf'
CONTENT = 'Hering, Daniel Webster, 1850-1938. Papers, 1889-1939'>

<LINK REL = SCHEMA.dc
HREF = 'http://purl.org/metadata/dublin-core-elements'>

</HEAD>
<BODY>
. . .
```

Figure 2.13 Example of Dublin Core metadata

49

index terms used to access documents. They consist of the title, contents list, preface and introduction, plus the index and the blurb on the dust jacket. Any or all of these may be of value in determining the subject.

TITLES

Printed documents of all types have *titles*, almost always given by their authors. Indexes based on titles go back at least 150 years. A title is the author's own summarization, identifier and retrieval cue. Research papers can usually be relied on to have informative titles, partly because editors of most primary journals issue guidelines to authors on the content of titles. For subject searching, titles summarize the content of a document at its most basic level. Searching is often based on keywords in titles, so it is important that titles so indexed should adequately reflect the subject content of the document. Less frequently, and mostly in the case of books, an author may feel that it is more important that the title should attract attention: *Women, Fire and Dangerous Things* (a study of the mental processes of categorization) and *How to Hold up a Bank* (a civil engineering manual) are two examples among many. Having decided on an oblique title, the author may make amends by means of an explicit subtitle (*What Categories Reveal about the Mind*). A few bibliographic search services provide title enrichment – the addition of a few extra keywords, or even a short annotation – to supplement titles that are perceived to be inadequate. This, however, requires the service of a human indexer with the knowledge to perceive and remedy the inadequacy; which in turn affects the cost and currency of the service.

It is virtually unknown for a published text not to have a title that has been assigned at or before publication. Non-textual media (such as graphic and cartographic material) may well not be furnished with titles and, similarly, unpublished text may also do the same – many untitled documents find their way on to the Web.

CONTENTS PAGES

These are usually to be found in books and journals. Their main purpose is to guide the reader through the book or journal, once it has been selected. The Institute for Scientific Information publishes a range of current Contents indexes, based on the contents pages of issues of journals for current awareness. Some have suggested ways in which the contents pages of books may be used as an extra subject approach in catalogues and indexes. By including tables of contents into the bibliographic record, chapter and section headings become available as additional keywords for searching.

OTHER FORMS OF METADATA

In addition to titles and contents pages, the preface and introduction, book indexes and publisher's blurbs may all be useful sources of the scope and purpose of a document.

GENERAL APPROACH

In practice, indexers examine sections of the document itself in addition to its preliminaries. The relevant international standard (ISO 5963: 1985E), *Methods for Examining Documents, Determining their Subjects, and Selecting Indexing Terms*, recommends that important parts of the text need to be considered carefully, and particular attention should be paid to the following:

- the title
- the abstract, if provided
- the list of contents
- the introduction, the opening phrases of chapters and paragraphs, and the conclusion
- illustrations, diagrams, tables and their captions
- a word or groups of words which are underlined or printed in an unusual typeface.

SUMMARY

This chapter has gathered together a number of important themes relating to the formatting and structuring of knowledge, embracing issues that are relevant for print and electronic documents, and for text and multimedia. In so doing, it has introduced many of the building blocks of the organization of knowledge and information retrieval that will be revisited in different guises later in this book. Two important sections explore how knowledge is formatted, respectively, into databases and into documents or information packages. Key concepts in respect of databases are the inverted file, and relational and object-oriented database structures. In the context of the nature and role of documents, we have explored the different document types, and explored the nature of a document and bibliographic relationships between documents. An introduction to the ways in which computers can be used to analyse text is followed by exploration of the nature and use of metadata. In relation to metadata, text markup and coding, the definition and purposes of metadata and metadata schemas are described. Two key themes in this section relate to the Dublin Core and metadata and interoperability. The chapter concludes with consideration of the traditional forms of metadata used by indexers.

REVIEW QUESTIONS

1. Discuss the purposes and contents of the different types of databases.
2. Explain the difference between an inverted file and a relational database.
3. What do you understand by the word 'text'? Discuss why text is important in information retrieval systems.
4. What is a document? What did Schamber say about the unique characteristics of electronic documents?
5. Make a list of the different types of bibliographic relationships, and offer a definition for each type.
6. What important concepts did the *Functional Requirements for Bibliographic Records* (FRBR) introduce in relation to the unit of bibliographic description.
7. There are two kinds of text markup: procedural and descriptive (or generic). Explain the difference between these two.
8. What is metadata? Identify some of the key differences between traditional cataloguing metadata and metadata for digital resources.
9. Haynes suggested that there were five purposes of metadata. What are they?
10. There are many metadata schemas. Why? Illustrate your answer with reference to one schema such as the Dublin Core.
11. How can metadata interoperability be achieved?
12. Titles, content pages and back-of-the-book indexes are traditional metadata. What do they each tell the indexer or reader about the book?

REFERENCES AND FURTHER READING

Arms, W.Y., Hillmann, D., Lagoze, C., Kraft, D., Marisa, R., Saylor, J., Terrizzi, C. and Van de Sompel, H. (2002) A spectrum of interoperability: the site for science prototype for the NSDL. *D-Lib Magazine*, **8** (1). See <www.dlib.org/dlib/january02/arms/01arms.html> [accessed 18 October 2006].

Berners-Lee, T. 2001) The semantic web. *Scientific American*, May, 34–43. Also available at <http://www.sciam.com/article.cfm?articleID=00048144-10D2-1C70-84A9809EC588EF21> [accessed 18 October 2006].

Beynon-Davies, P. (2004) *Database Systems*, 3rd edn. London: Palgrave.

Boman, J.H. (2003) *Essential Cataloguing*. London: Facet.

Buckland, M.K. (1997) What is a 'document'? *Journal of the American Society for Information Science and Technology*, **48** (9), 804–9.

Burke, M.A. (1999) *Organization of Multimedia Resources: Principles and Practice of Information Retrieval*. Aldershot: Gower.

Caplan, P. (2003) *Metadata Fundamentals for All Librarians*. Chicago IL: American Library Association.

CORES Registry website, see <www.cores-eu.net/registry> [accessed 18 October 2006].

Dale, P. (ed.) (1997) *Guide to Libraries and Information Sources in Medicine and Health Care*, 2nd edn. London: British Library, Science Reference and Information Services.

Dawson, A. (2004) Creating metadata that work for digital libraries and Google. *Library Review*, **53** (7), 347–50.

Day, M. (2001) Metadata in a nutshell. *Information Europe*, **6** (2), 11.

DCMI (2004) Dublin Core Metadata Initiative overview. See <DCMI http://dublin-core.org> [accessed 18 October 2006].

Dekker, M., Causton, L., de Jong, A., Duval, E., Day, M. and Napier, M. (2001) SCHEMA Project. SCHEMAS-PwC-WP2-D28-Final-20011217 Metadata Watch Report 7, London: pricewaterhouseCoopers. Available at <www.schmas.forum.org/metadata-watch/d28/mwr7.htm> [accessed 18 October 2006].

Haas, S.C., Henjum, E., O'Daniel, M.A. and Aufmuth, J. (2003) Darwin and MARC: a voyage of metadata discovery, *Library Collections, Acquisitions and Technical Services*, **27**, 291–304.

Hansen, J. and Andersen, L. (2003) AC – Administrative component. Dublin Core DCMI administrative metadata, final version. See <http://dublincroe.org/groups/admin/> [accessed 18 October 2006].

Haynes, D. (2004) *Metadata for Information Management and Retrieval*. London: Facet.

Heery, R. (1996) Review of metadata formats. *Program*, **30** (4), 345–53. Also at <http://www.ukoln.ac.uk/metadata/review> [accessed 18 October 2006].

Hillmann, D.I. and Westbrooks, E.L. (2004) *Metadata in Practice*. Chicago IL: American Library Association.

International Organization for Standardization (1985) *Documentation – Methods for Examining Documents, Determining their Subjects and Selecting Indexing Terms*. ISO 5963: 1985. Geneva: ISO.

International Organization for Standardization (1986) *Information Processing – Text and Office Systems – Standardized Generalized Markup Language (SGML)*. ISO 8879: 1986. Geneva: ISO.

Kunze, J. *Guide to Creating Dublin Core Descriptive Metadata*. Available at <http://purl.oclc.org/metadata/dublin-core/guide> [accessed 18 October 2006].

Library of Congress (2003) *METS: An overview and tutorial*, Washington DC: Library of Congress. See <www.loc.gov/standards/mets/METSOverview.v2.html> [accessed 18 October 2006].

Meadow, C.T. (1996) *Text Information Retrieval Systems*. San Diego CA: Academic Press. (See especially Chapters 1–3.)

Mostafa, J. (1994) Digital image representation and access. *Annual Review of Information Science and Technology*, **29**, 91–135.

Pearlson, K.E. and Saunders, C.S. (2006) *Managing and Using Information Systems: A strategic approach*. New York: Wiley.

Rasmussen, E.M. (1997) Indexing images. *Annual Review of Information Science and Technology*, **32**, 169–96.

Schamber, L. (1996) What is a document? Rethinking the concept in uneasy times. *Journal of the American Society for Information Science and Technology*, **47** (9), 669–71.

Shirky, C. (2001) Interoperability, not standards. The O'Reilly Network (15 March). See <www.openp2p.com/lpt/a/680> [accessed 18 October 2006].

Tillett, B.B. (1991) A taxonomy of bibliographic relationships. *Library Resources and Technical Services*, **35** (2), 150–158.

Tough, A. and Moss, M. (2003) Metadata, controlled vocabulary and directories: electronic document management and standards for records management. *Records Management Journal*, **13** (1), 24–31.

Tozer, G. (1999) *Metadata Management for Information Control and Business Success.* Boston MA: Artech House.

UK Office of the e-Envoy (2001) *E-government Metadata Framework.* London: Office of the e-Envoy.

Vellucci, S.L. (1997) Options for organizing electronic resources: the coexistence of metadata. *Bulletin of the American Society for Information Science*, **24** (1), 14–17.

Vellucci, S.L. (1998a) Metadata. In M. Williams (ed.) *Annual Review of Information Science and Technology*, vol. 33, 187–222. Medford NJ: Information Today Inc.

Vellucci, S.L. (1998b) Bibliographic relationships. In J. Weihs (ed.), *The Principles and Future of AACR: Proceedings of the International Conference on the Principles and Future Development of AACR, Toronto, Ontario, Canada, October 23–25, 1997*, 105–47. Ottawa: Canadian Library Association.

Vickery, B.C. (1997) Knowledge discovery from databases: an introductory review. *Journal of Documentation*, **53** (2), 107–22.

Weibel, S. (1997) The Dublin Core: a simple content description model for electronic resources. *Bulletin of the American Society for Information Science*, **24** (1), 9–11.

3   Describing documents

INTRODUCTION

This chapter looks at document and information resource representations and surrogates; that is at metadata that identifies and characterizes, and often serves as a key for retrieving the actual documents. This chapter focusses on the principles and problems of document representations and surrogates such that at the end of this chapter you will:

- understand the construction and use of citations
- appreciate the purposes of abstracts and related kinds of document summary
- be able to discuss record formats in abstracting and indexing services
- the nature of bibliographic records for a wide range of different document types
- how to prepare a bibliographic description according to the Anglo-American Cataloguing Rules (AACR2)
- the principles and structure of the Machine-Readable Cataloguing (MARC) format.

This chapter is concerned with document *representation*, not with document *access*, which is dealt with in Chapters 4 to 8. Various other forms of metadata, as discussed in Chapter 2, are also a form of document representation, but these are distinct from the metadata discussed in this chapter because they are invariably associated with the document or information resource.

CHARACTERISTICS AND PROBLEMS OF DOCUMENT REPRESENTATION

In many information retrieval situations, we are unable to work with documents themselves, but have to rely on representations, or document 'surrogates'. It is only in recent years that it has become technically and economically possible to directly retrieve documents. Previously, we constructed indexes consisting of brief records of documents, and retrieved those surrogates in advance of retrieving the actual documents. Library catalogues, citations, abstracts and bibliographies are typical examples. Hypertext links, class marks, keywords and abstracts are other forms of surrogate, but are usually embedded in larger records. Identification keys – ISBNs, International Standard Serial Numbers (ISSNs), Digital Object Identifiers (DOIs) and URLs – are another type of document surrogate. All these document surrogates represent individual documents in an information retrieval system.

As discussed in Chapter 1, knowledge organization occurs in a range of different contexts, including: catalogues, bibliographies, individual documents, indexing and abstracting databases, record management systems, museum inventories, content management systems and digital libraries. In all of these contexts it is necessary to create metadata that describes or represents the document or resource, although the context and nature of the resource and the identification of the item will vary.

Some common and persistent characteristics and problems of document representation in all of the above contexts are:

1. *Defining the document* – as was discussed in Chapter 2.
2. *Identification* – any representation of a document or resource must be sufficient for it to be identified uniquely, by both computer software and people.
3. *Granularity* – at what level should a document be described and indexed? Should, for example, individual contributions to a journal be indexed separately? Similar questions arise in respect of (for example): papers in a set of conference proceedings; two or more musical works on one CD; a school resource kit containing pupils' workbooks, wall charts, a teacher's book, etc.; or, pages other than the home page of a website. Some considerations influencing the granularity of description include the following:
   - Is the more detailed description available within the document? For example, many books have contents pages and back-of-book indexes, or large websites may have an internal search engine.
   - Are there other sources that perform the same task? Most libraries, for example, do not record journal articles or contributions to published conference proceedings in their catalogues, as there are specialist indexing and abstracting services that perform this function.
   - Will the use justify the extra cost? Sometimes detailed description for rapid retrieval is vital, as with a television news service's film archive, or a fire service's database of information on hazardous materials. In other cases it may be cheaper to carry out time-consuming sequential searching for seldom-required items; for example, in archives of local history materials.

– Will the extra detail merely lead to added complexity and near duplication? This can happen with some Web search engines when they record numerous hits, mostly to different parts of the same site.

4. *Selection* – the description must always uniquely identify the document it represents. Many representations go further, by indicating related documents, or by including information which characterizes the document. An important function of document representation is to act as a selection filter, enabling users to decide whether or not they wish to obtain the actual document.

5. *Search keys* – document representations for manually searched databases need search keys; that is, headings under which they are filed for manual searching. In the case of networked resources, 'semantic interoperability' requires such devices as metadata and the Z39.50 search and retrieve protocol.

6. *Location and accessibility* – a document representation loses much of its purpose if users are not given enough information to enable them to locate the document itself. In the case of books and journals, bibliographic control is well enough established for the conventional publication details to suffice for this purpose. In the case of non-print materials:

– bibliographic control is often less well organized than with printed materials
– the extent of the item may not be immediately obvious in the way that it can be judged by counting or estimating the number of pages in a book or journal article
– in many cases the material can only be used via some mechanical, optical or electronic device.

Networked resources may have specific hardware (for example, free disc space) and/or software requirements (such as Adobe Acrobat). Locations may well be remote, unlike library catalogues, which typically list only locations within the institution. A networked resource may be available to all, or access may be restricted; for example, to members of an organization or on payment of a fee.

RECORDS

For web pages and some other digital documents the descriptive metadata may be embedded in the document. For books, journals, and a wide variety of other information resources, such as sound recordings, maps and objects, a separate record is created to describe or represent the item. Such a record contains the information relating to and describing one document. Other similar documents will also be represented by records. A database is a collection of similar records.

Records are composed of a number of fields. The types of fields used, their length and the number of fields in a record must be chosen in accordance with a specific application. There are two types of field: fixed-length and variable-length. A *fixed-length field* is one that contains the same number of characters in each record. Since field lengths are predictable, it is not necessary to signal to the computer where each field begins and ends. Fixed-length fields are economical to store and records using fixed-length fields are quick and easy to code. However, fixed-length fields may not adequately accommodate variable-length data. Fixed-length fields are ideal for codes, such as ISBNs, reader codes, product codes, bank account numbers, dates and language codes, where the length of the information will be the same in each record. With variable-length data variable-length fields are necessary. A *variable-length field* will consist of different lengths in different records. Here, the computer cannot recognize when one field ends and another starts, so it becomes necessary to flag the beginning and end of fields. In addition, objects (such as pictures and video clips) may be stored as separate files linked to records that contain primarily fixed-length or variable-length fields.

Within fields, individual data elements or units of information may be designated as *subfields*. Subfields need to be flagged so that they can be identified. The discussion of the MARC format, later in this chapter, has examples of the two types of field and subfields.

CITATIONS

WHAT ARE CITATIONS AND HOW ARE THEY USED?

We start with citations, as these have an honourable and familiar place in the academic world: the mechanism by which scholars acknowledge the work of their predecessors, and students ward off accusations of plagiarism in essays. Citations are the author's way of making links between his or her contribution and that of other authors. In this digital age, when cut-and-paste is all too easy, it is all the more important to respect and acknowledge the work of others, and in turn to create a unique and different essay, article, paper or other creative expression.

Citations are a relatively uncomplicated form of document representation and one that every student, irrespective of discipline, is required to create. This section discusses the format of citations, and when to make them. Citations form the basis for structuring the records used in indexing and abstracting services. The purpose and making of abstracts are described in the following section, and the records used in indexing and abstracting services are described in 'Bibliographic record formats' later in this chapter. *Citation indexes*, a method of retrieval based on the lists of references at the end of scholarly papers, are discussed in Chapter 9. There are a number of published standards for ensuring uniformity, notably British Standard 5605: 1990 *Recommendations for Citing and Referencing Published Material*, and British Standard 1629: 1989 *Recommendations for References to Published Material*; the *Chicago Manual of Style*; and K.L. Turabian's *A Manual for Writers of Term Papers, Theses and Dissertations*. In spite of the existence of standards, publishers of primary journals continue to maintain a wide range of house styles for citations and bibliographies. This causes difficulties in any attempts to merge records from, for example, different publishers, leading to:

- Authors (including students) needing to create all citations using a standard citation practice in the document that they are creating, and ensuring that their citations are consistent with that standard. Authors may also need to convert citations for publication in different journals. Personal bibliographic software can assist authors in switching between citation formats, but in order to make use of these the author needs to take a systematic approach to the management of citations.
- Abstracting and indexing services needing to adopt a standard for entries in their own databases. The section later in this chapter under the heading 'Citing and metadata in abstracting and indexing services' discusses this topic further, and the variability of journal article citations in different sources is illustrated by Figure 3.6.

For each reference it is essential to record sufficient information to identify precisely the source cited. There are a number of published standards for ensuring this. Two separate methods of referencing documents are permitted: the *Harvard* (name and date) system, and the *Numeric* (Vancouver) system (Figures 3.1 and 3.2). The Harvard system is generally easier to apply, and is used in the majority of scholarly journals in the natural and social sciences. The Numeric system is more likely to be found in the arts and humanities.

COMPILING CITATION LISTS

Data for citations should be obtained from the following sources, in order of preference: (1) the title page, or a substitute (cover, caption, masthead, etc.); (2) any other source which is part of the item; (3) any other source which accompanies the item and was issued by the publisher (for example, a container, a printed insert).

The citation elements are:

1. *primary responsibility* (author, editor, etc.)
2. *year* (the position of this element varies according to the display style chosen: this is the position if using the Harvard style)

With this system, authors' names and dates of publication are given in parentheses within the running text or at the end of block quotations. They are keyed to a list of works cited, arranged alphabetically by author, and placed at the end of the text. Cited publications are referred to in the text by giving the author's surname and the year of publication:

In a recent study Schamber (1996) argued that ...
In a recent study (Schamber, 1996) it was argued that ...
In their first work, Westlake and Clarke (1987) ...
The more recent study by Farmer et al. (1998) ... (for more than two authors)

To acknowledge direct quotations or to refer to individual pages of a particular book or article the page number(s) are given after the date, separated from it by a comma, and within the parentheses:

(Eason, 1999, p. 49)

The list of references is a single alphabetical list, at the end of the text. Date of publication appears immediately after the author's name:

Colley, A.M. and Beech, J.R., eds. (1989) *Acquisition and performance of cognitive skills.* Chichester: Wiley.
Cathro, W. (1997) Metadata: an overview. http://www.nla.gov.au/nla/staffpaper/cathro3.html
Ericsson, K.A. and Oliver, W.L. (2004). A methodology for assessing the detailed structure of memory skills. In: Colley, A.M. and Beech, J.R., eds. (2004), pp. 46–58.
Rowley, J. (1988) *Abstracting and indexing.* 2nd ed. London: Bingley.
Schamber, L. (1996) What is a document? rethinking the concept in uneasy times. *Journal of the American Society for Information Science,* **47**(9), pp. 669–71.

Figure 3.1   Citation: the Harvard (name and date) system

With this system, cited publications are numbered in the order in which they are first referred to in the text. They are identified by a number given in square brackets (round brackets and superscript numerals are also found):

In a recent study, Schamber [5] argued that ...
As Carson [7, p. 46] has argued ...
A number of studies [2, 3, 4] have demonstrated ...

Entries are listed in numerical order in the list of references to match the sequence of references cited in the text. Sources not specifically referred to in the text must be given in a separate list of sources or bibliography.

1. Cathro, W. (1997) Metadata: an overview. 2005.
http://www.nla.gov.au/nla/staffpaper/cathro3.html
2. Colley, A.M. and Beech, J.R. Acquiring and performing cognitive skills. In: Colley A.M. and Beech, J.R., eds. *Acquisition and performance of cognitive skills.* Chichester: Wiley, 1989, pp. 1–10.
3. Schamber, L. What is a document? rethinking the concept in uneasy times. *Journal of the American Society for Information Science,* **47**(9), 1996, pp. 669–71.
4. Colley, A.M. and Beech, J.R. (ref. 2, p. 3).
5. Rowley, J. *Abstracting and indexing.* 2nd ed. London: Bingley, 1988.
6. Ericsson, K.A. and Oliver, W.L. A methodology for assessing the detailed structure of memory skills. In: Colley and Beech (ref. 2), pp. 46–58.

Figure 3.2   Citation: the Numeric (Vancouver) system

3. *title* (of a book, or in the case of a journal article, of the article)
4. *type of medium* (if needed)
5. *publication details* (place, publisher for books, journal title for journal articles)
6. *series* – normally only needed for reports, or where there might be confusion between the title proper and the series title (as with some kinds of audio and visual material)
7. *numeration* within the item (if the item is in more than one part, or if part of an item is cited, including, in the case of journal articles, volume and part number and page numbers).

For further examples of how these elements are combined into citations examine Figures 3.5 and 3.6.

NON-PRINT MEDIA

Citations for non-print media include any of the above elements that are appropriate, but will often also need to include as many of the following as are appropriate:

- the *medium* (for example, filmstrip, video, compact disc (CD), etc.)
- *how accessed* – with audio and visual materials, in many cases this information need only be given if a non-standard system is required (such as for Betamax videos)
- *duration* of films, videos, etc., if easily established
- frequency of *update*.

Most materials that comprise a single intellectual unit can be treated broadly as books.

ELECTRONIC DOCUMENTS

These include electronic monographs, databases and computer programs, electronic serials, electronic bulletin boards, Web documents and e-mail. As they exist only in electronic format, it is vital to show how the item can be accessed. In the case of Internet resources, the 'generic' location description is the URL. References are cited in the text in the usual way. If using the Harvard style, the list of references then follows the general form: Author (year, date). Title (version) [medium]. Location. Place of publication: Publisher.

- *(Year, Date)*. Adding *Date* (month, day, even time of day) to the scheme overcomes the problem of transient or dynamically updated sources.
- *Version* is the online equivalent of *edition*. The *Date* may be optional if a particular version number is identified.

- [*Medium*] will be given as [Online] in the case of sources referenced over a telecommunications link. For non-networked formats use [CD-ROM], [DVD], etc., as appropriate.
- *Page numbers* are not usually a feature of electronic documents, as page layout is dependent on the viewing method.
- *Location* refers to the URL in the case of Internet resources; otherwise a generic online location. ISO 690-2 (ISO, 2004) recommends the style: Available from *source*: *<location>*; for example, 'Available from World Wide Web: <http:// www.collectionscanada,ca/iso/tc46sc9/standard/690-2e.htm>'.
- On the Internet, anyone can be a publisher, and *Publisher* may be omitted where the author has self-published. However, electronic publishing online is becoming an industry in itself, and whilst the publisher's role is evolving many of the functions of publishers remain important.

See Figure 3.3 for examples.

Sample citation for a book that is available electronically
Kurland, Philip B., and Ralph Lerner, eds. *The Founders' Constitution*. Chicago: University of Chicago Press, 1987. Also available online at http://press-pubs.uchicago.edu/founders/ and as a CD-ROM.

Sample citation for a journal article that is available electronically
Hlatky, Mark A., Derek Boothroyd, Eric Vittinghoff, Penny Sharp, and Mary A. Whooley. 'Quality-of-Life and Depressive Symptoms in Postmenopausal Women after Receiving Hormone Therapy: Results from the Heart and Estrogen/Progestin Replacement Study (HERS) Trial.' *Journal of the American Medical Association* 287, no. 5 (February 6, 2002), http://jama.ama-assn.org/issues/v287n5/rfull/joc10108.html#aainfo.

Figure 3.3 Sample citations for electronic documents
Source: based on <www.chicagomanualofstyle.org/tools.Documentation.html>

FOLLOWING GOOD ACADEMIC PRACTICE FOR CITATIONS

The following rules of thumb are offered as a general guide to good citation practice for students:

1. Always acknowledge your sources.
2. Keep a record of the bibliographical details of those sources as you consult them.
3. If you have a significant number of sources, maintain a card or simple electronic listing of the sources you have used.
4. Record all bibliographical details as indicated in this book.
5. Be particularly attentive in recording details of electronic sources such as

home pages – these can be surprisingly difficult to locate on subsequent occasions without the URL.

6. Arrange your bibliography in alphabetical order by the author's surname or family name, irrespective of the form of document.
7. Any items you have read, but not cited, may optionally be added under a heading such as 'Other sources'.
8. Many universities and departments have their own guidelines. Follow any local guidelines that may be issued.

PERSONAL BIBLIOGRAPHIC FILE MANAGEMENT SOFTWARE

A number of bibliographic file management programs are available for managing personal file collections such as those developed by researchers and other authors. These packages are primarily intended for information users rather than information professionals, so it is especially important that they should be easy to use. Other desirable features include: predefined fields, the ability to import citations from external sources, so that online search results can be downloaded directly into the correct fields; adding extra fields for personal use, such as keywords and annotations; field or term search capability; detecting duplicates; editing globally; and predefined output formats for generating bibliographies in a variety of journal formats.

Notice that, while 'bibliographic' is properly confined to databases containing surrogate records of books, the word is also used more loosely in relation to surrogate records of all kinds of documents and associated databases.

ABSTRACTS

THE USE AND TYPES OF ABSTRACTS

Abstracts are included and used in the primary literature, such as journals, reports and conference papers, and in abstracting and indexing services and other tools designed to help users to navigate knowledge bases. Within the primary literature, an abstract normally appears at the front of the item, usually immediately preceding the text. In this way, readers are able to identify the basic content of a document quickly and accurately to determine its relevance to their interests, and thus to decide whether they need to read the document in its entirety. If the document is of fringe interest, reading the abstract may make it unnecessary to read the whole document (ISO, 1976).

Abstracts are recommended to accompany journal articles and any other material in journals that has a substantial technical or scholarly content (for example, discussions and reviews). It is normal for the writers of journal articles and similar primary material to include an abstract when submitting material for publication. Abstracts should also accompany reports (whether published or unpublished) and theses, monographs and conference proceedings (including chapter abstracts if each chapter covers different topics), and also patent applications and specifications.

The other major use of abstracts is in secondary services (such as abstracting databases). These services often use the original (author's) abstracts – either as they stand, or amended. Where these are lacking or considered unsuitable, an abstract has to be written from scratch, adding to the cost and often reducing the currency of the service.

There are many types of abstract (see Figure 3.4), according to the requirements of particular applications, as influenced by the language, length and readership of the document, the intended audience of the abstract and the resources of the abstracting agency. For texts describing experimental work and documents devoted to a single theme, an *informative abstract* is recommended. This type of abstract presents as much as possible of the quantitative and/or qualitative information contained in the document. This includes in particular a note of the results and conclusions of any experimental work. Such an abstract can be a substitute for the full document when only a superficial knowledge is required. Informative abstracts can extend to 500 words or more, though 100–250 words is the norm.

An *indicative* abstract is usually much shorter; merely an indication of the type of document, the principal subjects covered, and the way the facts are treated. This type of abstract is often applied to opinion papers and papers generally which do not report research, or where the text is discursive or lengthy, such as broad overviews, review papers and entire monographs. A *short abstract* comprises only one or two sentences supplementing the title, and may be valuable in current awareness services where speed is essential. In an *indicative-informative* abstract the primary elements of the document are written in an informative way, while the less significant aspects have indicative statements only.

A *slanted* abstract is one which concentrates on those topics within a document that are of interest to the abstracting service's user community. A development of this is the *critical* abstract – one that evaluates the abstracted item. Both types are expensive to produce, as the abstractor requires detailed knowledge of the subject and the user community as well as abstracting skills; they are uncommon, and very seldom found in published abstracting services.

A *structured* abstract is one that is divided into a number of related sections. Structured abstracts are widely used in the medical, clinical and psychology fields, and some social science and business publishers also make use of structured abstracts. Typically they are written in a number of sections with

Below are five different types of abstracts relating to the following document:
Urquhart, C. et al. Student use of electronic information services in further education. *International Journal of Information Management*, 25 (2005) 347–62.

Informative abstract

This paper presents a profile of user behaviour in relation to the use of electronic information services (EIS), information skills, and the role of training and wider learning experiences in UK further education colleges. The research was conducted under the JISC User Behaviour Monitoring and Evaluation Framework. Work was conducted in two strands, by two project teams, JUSTEIS and JUBILEE. JUSTEIS profiled the use of EIS and assessed the availability of EIS. JUBILEE objectives focused on understanding the barriers and enablers, with a view to developing success criteria. JUSTEIS used a multi-stage stratified sampling process, and collected data from 270 respondents from 17 departments in the baseline survey (2001/2002). JUBILEE conducted in-depth fieldwork in five institutions and snapshot fieldwork in ten institutions, collecting data from 528 respondents. Information skills and experience develop across work, home and study. There is a growing use of EIS in curriculum, but practice varies between institutions and disciplines. Tutors express concern about students' ability to evaluate and use the information that they find. Assignments can promote EIS use. The main categories of EIS used by students are search engines and organizational websites. Search engines are the preferred search tool, and search strategies are basic. Information skills are acquired through a variety of routes, with peer instruction, surfing and personal experience, instruction from tutors, and LIS induction and training all making an important contribution. The solutions to improving students' information skills may include use of the Virtual Training Suites, but librarians need to adopt different roles in promoting and evaluating use of such tools.

Indicative abstract

This paper presents a profile of user behaviour in relation to the use of electronic information services (EIS), information skills, and the role of training and wider learning experiences in UK further education colleges. The research was conducted in two strands; one strand profiled the use of EIS and assessed the availability of EIS; and the other strand focused on understanding the barriers and enablers. The research methodology, which involved extensive interviews and questionnaires, is outlined. Findings relating to the use of EIS in the curriculum, and the development of information skills in both everyday information seeking and in study contexts are presented. Student approaches to information searching and the options for enhancing information skills, together with tutors' and library and information professionals' roles, are discussed.

Extract

The objectives of the baseline study in further education were to:

● examine uptake and use of EIS among academic staff and students (JUSTEIS)
● provide, through an understanding of the context of use, a basis for the longitudinal tracking of users to determine success criteria for information seeking from the users' points of view (JUBILEE).

Short abstract

This paper presents a profile of user behaviour in relation to the use of electronic information services (EIS), information skills, and the role of training and wider learning experiences in UK further education colleges. This multi-method study investigates and reports on student information behaviour and skills, and the ways in which these can be enhanced, and discusses the evolving roles of library and information services staff.

Structured abstract

Purpose   This paper presents a profile of user behaviour in relation to the use of electronic information services (EIS), information skills, and the role of training and wider learning experiences in UK further education colleges.

Approach The research was conducted under the JISC User Behaviour Monitoring and Evaluation Framework. Work was conducted in two strands, by two project teams, JUSTEIS and JUBILEE. JUSTEIS profiled the use of EIS and assessed the availability of EIS. JUBILEE objectives focused on understanding the barriers and enablers, with a view to developing success criteria. JUSTEIS used a multi-stage stratified sampling process, and collected data from 270 respondents from 17 departments in the baseline survey (2001/2002). JUBILEE conducted in-depth fieldwork in five institutions and snapshot fieldwork in ten institutions, collecting data from 528 respondents.

Findings Information skills and experience develop across work, home and study. There is a growing use of EIS in curriculum, but practice varies between institutions and disciplines. Tutors express concern about students' ability to evaluate and use the information that they find. Assignments can promote EIS use. The main categories of EIS used by students are search engines and organizational websites. Search engines are the preferred search tool, and search strategies are basic. Information skills are acquired through a variety of routes, with peer instruction, surfing and personal experience, instruction from tutors, and LIS induction and training all making an important contribution. The solutions to improving students' information skills may include use of the Virtual Training Suites, but librarians need to adopt different roles in promoting and evaluating use of such tools.

Practical implications Library and information professionals and tutors need to work together to develop student information skills and the effective use of EIS. They need to recognize that students develop information skills in a variety of contexts and develop training and support modes accordingly.

Figure 3.4 Examples of different types of abstracts

headings. In Figure 3.4 the headings used are: 'purpose', 'approach', 'findings' and 'practical implications'. Another set of headings could be: 'objective', 'methods', 'results' and 'conclusions', as suggested at <http://research.mlanet.org/structured_abstract.html>. Structured abstracts are designed to support searching by both people and computers.

The structuring of abstracts is one of the steps that are taken to make abstracts more suitable for a digital environment. This reflects some concern that the structure, form and content of abstracts need to change to accommodate the networked environment in which they are now used.

The major purposes of abstracts, as shorter versions of a longer document, are to:

● support current awareness of new documents
● save reading time and support browsing
● aid in document selection
● aid in literature searching by mapping scope and key themes
● improve indexing efficiency and effectiveness
● aid in the preparation of literature reviews and bibliographies on specific topics.

ABSTRACTING SKILLS AND PROCESSES

The skills needed in an abstractor are essentially:

- a good standard of literacy, particularly the ability to write clearly and concisely
- detailed knowledge of the subject field of the material being abstracted
- an awareness of the patterns of text structures in the materials being abstracted
- an awareness of the kinds of people who will be using the abstracts, and of the environment of information access generally
- an ability to work methodically and accurately.

The tendency is for as much use as possible to be made of author abstracts. Professional abstractors often have formal qualifications in both information science and the subject field in which they are working. They are typically employed by producers of abstracts, databases and services.

When writing informative abstracts it is useful to take the following points into account:

1. Most documents describing experimental work conform to the sequence: *Purpose – Methodology – Results – Conclusions*. Readers in many disciplines are accustomed to this pattern.
2. Begin the abstract with a topic sentence that is a central statement of the document's major theme, unless this is already well stated in the document's title or can be derived from the remainder of the abstract.
3. Give only a brief statement of methodology, unless a technique is new. Results and conclusions, however, should be clearly presented.
4. If the findings are too numerous for all to be included, give the most important. Any findings or information incidental to the main purpose of the document but of value outside its main subject area may be included, so long as their relative importance is not exaggerated.
5. Abstracts must be self-contained and retain the basic information and tone of the document. They must be clear and concise, and must not include information or claims not contained in the document itself.
6. Unless the abstract is a long one, write it as a single paragraph. Write in complete sentences, and use transitional words and phrases for coherence.
7. Use verbs in the active voice and third person whenever possible. Use significant words from the text. Avoid unfamiliar terms, acronyms, abbreviations or symbols, or define them the first time they occur.
8. Include short tables, equations, structural formulas and diagrams only when necessary for brevity and clarity and when no acceptable alternative exists.

OTHER KINDS OF DOCUMENT SUMMARIES

An *annotation* usually appears as a note after the bibliographic citation of a document. It is a brief comment or explanation about a document or its contents, or even a very brief description.

An *extract* comprises one or more portions of a document selected to represent the whole – often a sentence or two indicating the results, conclusions or recommendations of a study. It is usually shorter than an abstract, and requires less effort to produce.

A *summary* is a brief restatement of a document's salient findings and conclusions. It occurs within a document, usually at the end, less frequently at the beginning. Summaries are most often found in reports, where they are mainly intended for busy people who do not have time to do more than skim through the full text; and increasingly in the chapters of textbooks as an aid to orientation.

Other forms of text reduction, such as reviews, synopses, abridgements, digests, precis and paraphrases, have applications that are outside the scope of the present work.

AUTOMATIC INDEXING AND TEXT SUMMARIZATION

Abstracting by professional abstractors is expensive and time-consuming. Author abstracting produces inconsistencies in style and quality. Accordingly, since the early work by Luhn in 1958 there has been an active research tradition which seeks to find ways in which abstracts can be computer-generated. These endeavours are related to the work on natural language processing and indexing, discussed in later chapters of this book, although the challenge of creating a coherent and representative abstract automatically are considerably greater than those associated with the use of computer processing of the text of documents or records to aid indexing of document collections. The basic approach builds on sentence extraction, in which the abstract is created by extracting key sentences from a document. Various algorithms have been created for selection of these sentences, based on the types of words and phrases included in the sentences. More recent work on text summarization uses a variety of approaches to summarize texts, based on phrases, sentences or paraphrases which are selected on the basis of linguistic and/or statistical criteria. More sophisticated systems may merge two or more sentences or generate summaries from different, but identified areas of documents. Some use discourse analysis with a thesaurus for recognition and selection of the most pertinent elements in the text. There are some grounds for believing that entirely computer-based text summarization will never be successful because words are always a poor representation of meaning. Craven (2000) suggests that hybrid abstracting systems, in which some tasks are performed by human abstractors and others by assistance software, are likely to be a more successful option.

CITATIONS AND METADATA IN ABSTRACTING AND INDEXING SERVICES

For the large public databases, there has been little pressure to accept a standard format, and each database producer has in general chosen a record format to suit the particular database. The nearest applicable standard is the *UNISIST Reference Manual* (UNESCO, 1986). Even one database may emerge in different record formats according to the online search service on which it is mounted. Figure 3.6 shows how one journal article may be represented in different databases. Note the details in the order of the elements, and the abbreviations and punctuation. The citations shown in this figure are a simplification of the situation; some databases list different document details in different listings (for example, for ordering a journal article, or when listing the article as a hit in a search output) and formatting and display style vary considerably from one listing to another. In addition to elements shown in Figure 3.6 some databases may also include the ISSN for the journal, and/or the digital object identifier (DOI) for the individual article. Each database compiler has their own standards concerning the fields to be included in a citation and the subject indexing made available. Yet another variable factor is the presence of full-text, and more recently multimedia, databases which demand a somewhat different record format from bibliographic records if the information is to be appropriately displayed.

This variability in citation format makes it difficult to merge two databases, and can cause difficulties in cross-database searching. The Common Communications Format (CCF) was thus designed and published by UNESCO in 1984 with the aim of facilitating the communication of bibliographic data among the sectors of the information community. In common with MARC, the CCF constitutes a specific implementation of ISO 2709. In other words, it adopts the general structure of bibliographic records specified by ISO 2709 and has the following elements: 'Label, Directory, Data fields, and Record separator'. The CCF, then,

- specifies a small number of mandatory data elements that are recognized to be essential in order to identify an item
- provides mandatory elements that are sufficiently flexible to accommodate varying descriptive practices
- provides a number of optional elements, which permit the originating agency to include non-standard elements which are considered useful within its system
- provides a mechanism for linking records and segments of records without imposing on the originating agency any uniform practice regarding the treatment of related groups of records or data elements.

This last provision shows one difference from MARC. The CCF has been designed from the outset to:

- link records at different bibliographic levels (for example, series – monograph – analytic), as this has always been an important feature of indexing services
- accommodate different kinds of records such as those for books, reports, periodicals, theses, cartographic materials, patents and standards, as well as profiles for projects, institutions and persons.

CCF was designed to be simple and permissive; rather than users adapting to the format, the format was designed to be adaptable to a range of practices.

Accession No: EJ699817
Author(s): Stevens, Lori
Title: Loving Those Abstracts
Source: *School Arts: The Art Education Magazine for Teachers* v103 n5 p28 Jan 2004 (2 pages)
Standard No: ISSN: 0036-6463
Language: English
Abstract: The author describes a lesson she did on abstract art with her high school art classes. She passed out a required step-by-step outline of the project process. She asked each of them to look at abstract art. They were to list five or six abstract artists they thought were interesting, narrow their list down to the one most personally intriguing, and do a bit of research, and finally complete a paper in which they included a little biography, information regarding the timely importance of their artist, and short critiques of two artworks they photocopied or printed. Their personal critiques were imperative. They structured their final painting to resemble the style of their chosen artist in their final project. A 'Web Link' list of websites related to topics discussed in the article is included.

SUBJECT(S) Descriptor: (Minor): Studio Art
Visual Arts
Artists
Art History
Art Appreciation
Art Education
High School Students
Rural Schools
Student Projects
Art Activities
Identifier: California
Document Type: Journal Article (CIJE)
Record Type: 080 Journal Articles; 141 Reports—Descriptive
Announcement: DEC2005
Availability: Level: 3
Alternate: Davis Publications, Inc., 50 Portland St., Worcester, MA 01608. Web site: http://www.davis-art.com.
Database: ERIC

Figure 3.5   Citation with abstract (from ERIC via FirstSearch)

Sage Publications (the publisher)
Do structured abstracts take more space? And does it matter?
Hartley *Journal of Information Science.* 2002; 28: 417–422

ISI Web of Knowledge (an indexing service)
Hartley, J
Do structured abstracts take more space? And does it matter?
J INFORM SCI 28 (5): 417–422 2002

ERIC (Dialog DataStar)
Do structured abstracts take more space? And does it matter?
Journal of Information Science, 2002, vol.28, no.5, p.417–422
Hartley-James

ERIC (FirstSearch)
Hartley James
Do structured abstracts take more space? And does it matter?
Journal of Information Science v28 n5 p417–422 2002

Figure 3.6   Varying citation formats for the same journal article listed in different databases

BIBLIOGRAPHIC RECORD FORMATS

THE ROLE OF BIBLIOGRAPHIC RECORD FORMATS

All records in one file have a standard format. In order to facilitate exchange of records between different computer systems, there have been attempts to develop some standard record formats. Such formats were seen to be particularly beneficial in cataloguing applications, where a standard format, which also embodies an agreement on the elements or content of a bibliographic record, has been particularly attractive in allowing the exchange of cataloguing records. This exchange has minimized the need for local cataloguing, as libraries can make use of records that others have created. Accordingly, one of the fields in which a standard record format is best established is in the creation of cataloguing records.

The exchange of machine-readable records has necessitated the standardization of bibliographic record formats. There is an International Standard Bibliographic Description (ISBD) for most categories of material. These include ISBD(M) for monographs, ISBD(S) for serials, ISBD(PM) for printed music, ISBD(CM) for cartographic materials, and ISBD(ER) for electronic resources – this is not by any means a complete list. All follow the general framework of ISBD(G), which recommends:

- what information should be given in the description, including the extent of detail required
- the order in which the information should be given
- the punctuation needed to divide and distinguish between the elements of the description.

The programme of ISBDs brought about the reconciliation of two earlier sets of standards for bibliographical description: AACR, originally published in 1967 and extensively revised in 1978 (AACR2), and MARC, first implemented in 1968.

AACR2 AND RDA

Since the publication of AACR2 in 1978, there has been a series of amendments and updates, arguably the most significant of which was the issue of AACR2R2 in 2002. Nevertheless, and not withstanding the introduction of new or revised chapters to better accommodate electronic resources, and integrating resources, the structure of AACR2 has remained relatively stable for some 40 years.

AACR2 is organized into two parts, one entitled 'Description' and the other 'Headings, uniform titles and references'. These indicate AACR2's two distinct functions of document representation and document access. However, AACR2 restricts itself to document access by names and titles, and makes no provision for subject access. As we shall see later in this section, the MARC format embraces both document representation and document access, including provision for subject access. Three subject access systems are included in the USMARC record format: the Dewey Decimal Classification (DDC), the Library of Congress Classification (LCC) and Library of Congress Subject Headings (LCSH).

AACR has its roots in card and printed catalogues and is largely owned by the library community. Part I of AACR2 concerns itself with the description of the information resources. Chapter 1 provides general rules that apply to all materials, and Chapters 2 to 12 offer more detailed rules for specific types of material such as music, serials and electronic resources. Chapter 13 covers analysis. Part II offers guidance on access points. Chapter 21 offers guidance on the choice of access points, including rules for both main and added entries. Chapters 22, 23 and 29 contain rules that determine the form that each heading will take. Chapter 25 addresses the issue of uniform titles, when titles are to be used as access points, and Chapter 26 covers references.

Despite its major contribution to standardization in digital environments, AACR is perceived to have a number of limitations, such that a significant review is under way. The proposal is that a new code, Resources Description and Access (RDA) will replace AACR2. RDA will be designed specifically to support integrated and networked systems, and its goal is to be used as a metadata content standard by a wide range of communities. RDA will be more closely aligned with FRBR and FRAR (Functional Requirements for Authority Records) models, and the link with ISBD will be lessened such that ISBD will be only one of several options. The FRBR is an entity-relationship or conceptual model of the bibliographic universe, designed to determine an overall perspective rather than provide specific rules, instructions or specifications. The RDA perspective is that of cataloguing a 'resource' rather than an 'item'. AACR's term 'Heading' will be replaced with 'Access point', 'Main entry' becomes 'Primary access point' and 'Added entry' becomes 'Secondary access point'. The RDA will be organized into three parts, as shown in Figure 3.7. However, as is evident in Figure 3.8, document representation under RDA has a lot in common with AACR2. At the time of writing the RDA project is very much ongoing. The best place to check for current developments is the Joint Steering Committee for Revision of Anglo-American Cataloguing Rules RDA website (<www.collectionscanada.ca.jsc/rda.html>).

Part I – Resources Description
- Functional objectives and principles

Part II – Relationships
- Persons, families and corporate bodies
- Citations for related works
- Instructions for particular types of works

Part III – Access Point Control
- Formulating access points
- Recording data used in access point control

Figure 3.7　Contents of the RDA standard

Title proper
Earlier/later variations in the title proper
Statement of responsibility
Edition statement
Numbering
Publisher, distributor, etc. (1st one)
Date of publication, distribution, etc.
Title proper of series
Numbering within series
Resource identifier
Form of carrier
Extent
Scale of cartographic content
Coordinates of cartographic content

Figure 3.8　The mandatory elements in RDA

73

BIBLIOGRAPHIC DESCRIPTION

FUNCTIONS AND BASIC ELEMENTS

The description of a document as part of a catalogue entry acts as a document surrogate. The word 'bibliographic' denotes the large degree of overlap between catalogues and bibliographies. The catalogues of major national libraries are often effectively major bibliographies in their own right, and the libraries themselves may be national agencies for preparing catalogue copy for distribution to subscribers.

The traditional functions of description are to:

● describe each document as a document – that is, to identify it
● distinguish it from other items
● show relationships with other items.

Again, notice that considerations of document access are excluded.

In preparing the description of a document it is necessary to make certain preliminary decisions if different cataloguers are to produce identical records from the same document. These considerations include:

1. *The source of the information for the description.* A 'chief source of information' is designated, to ensure consistency among different cataloguers (for example, in the treatment of books whose title-page title differs from that found on the cover or spine). In order of preference, information is taken from: the item itself; its container; other accompanying material; other external sources. According to the material, a source of information may be unitary (a title page) or collective (the sequence of credits on a film or video). Specific sources of information are prescribed for different parts (areas) of the description. So for books, the prescribed source of information for the title and statement of responsibility is the title page, but for the physical description the whole publication is examined.
2. *Organization of the description.* The description is organized into eight areas, based on the layout of a catalogue entry as it has evolved over a century and a half. The areas are:
   - title and statement of responsibility
   - edition
   - material-specific (or publication type-specific) details
   - publication, distribution, etc.
   - physical description
   - series
   - note
   - standard number and terms of availability.

The sequence of the areas is as shown. If an area is not applicable to an item, it is simply omitted. The areas are described in detail below. The organization of the MARC record format follows this sequence.

3. *Punctuation.* Consistent punctuation aids the recognition and rapid scanning of the various areas of the description in manually searched indexes and on-screen displays, and is particularly important for the international exchange of records. In MARC records, the prescribed punctuation for each area of the description is built into the subfield structure.

4. *Levels of detail in the description.* Different applications may demand different degrees of detail in the description. AACR2 identifies three levels of detail: compare Level 1 in Figure 3.9 with Level 2 in Figure 3.10. Level 3 is seldom used (see next section). In a small general library simple records may be adequate, whereas a large research collection may require rather more detail. National bibliographic agencies may apply different levels of description to different categories of material, with, for example, fiction and books for children being catalogued at the simplest level.

Castles and palaces map of the British Isles. – Bartholomew, [198-]. – 1 wall chart

English madrigals/The King's Singers. – HMV Classics, c1995. – 1 sound disc. + 1 leaflet. – Compact disc. – HMV 5 69009 2

Frink/Edward Lucie-Smith and Elisabeth Frink. – Bloomsbury, 1994. – 138p. – ISBN 0-7475-1572-7

Geoff Hamiltons [sic] 3D garden designer. – Computer program. – GSP, c1998. – 1 computer optical disc; 4¾ in. – System requirements: Windows 95 or higher. – GSPCD125

Mystic Meg's lucky numbers. – Warner, 1996. – 289 p. – ISBN 0-7515-1875-1

Rainfall in Birmingham, 1940–1979 / J. Kings and B.D. Giles. – 2nd ed. – Department of Geography, University of Birmingham, 1982. – 87p. – ISBN 0-7044-0575-X

Salmond and Heuston on the law of torts. – 20th ed. – Sweet & Maxwell, 1992. – 604p. – ISBN 0-421-45980-8

Site layout planning for daylight and sunlight. – Building Research Establishment, 1991. – 85p. – ISBN 0-85125-506-X

Soba/by D.A. Welsby and C.M. Daniels. – British Institute in Eastern Africa, 1991. – 363p. – 2 maps on folded leaves in pocket. – Bibliography: pp. 356–60

Total eclipse/produced by Jean-Pierre Ramsey Levi. – Video Collection International, 1998. – 1 videocartridge. – VHS. – VC3636

Figure 3.9 Descriptive cataloguing examples: Level 1

MORE DETAIL ON COMPONENTS OF THE DESCRIPTION

A bibliographic description compiled in accordance with ISBD and AACR2 is divided into a number of areas. The MARC bibliographic record format has corresponding groups of fields. These areas apply to all types of material, but some are more appropriate for some types of resources than others. First we

Castles and palaces map of the British Isles. – Edinburgh: Bartholomew, [198-]. – 1 wall chart: col.; 101 x 75 cm (fold to 26 x 16 cm)

English madrigals/The King's Singers. – [London]: HMV Classics, c1995. – 1 sound disc (73 min.): digital, stereo; 4¾ in. + 1 leaflet (6 p.: col. ill.; 13 cm.). – (HMV Classics; 145). – Compact disc. – 'The principal composers in this collection are Thomas Morley and Thomas Weelkes' – accompanying notes. – HMV 5 69009 2

Frink: a portrait/Edward Lucie-Smith and Elisabeth Frink. – London: Bloomsbury, 1994. – 138p, [16]p of plates: ill (some col.).ports; 22 x 23 cm. – Ill. on lining papers. – ISBN 0-7475-1572-7

Geoff Hamiltons [sic] 3D garden designer. – Computer program. – St Ives, Cambs: GSP, c1998. – 1 computer optical disc; 4¾ in. – System requirements: Windows 95 or higher. – Summary: Plant encyclopedia and graphic editor producing plans for gardens and parks. – GSPCD125

Mystic Meg's lucky numbers: for life, love and the lottery/illustrations by Caroline Smith. – London: Warner, 1996. – 289p: ill; 18 cm. – ISBN 0-7515-1875-1

Rainfall in Birmingham, 1940–1979: a statistical analysis by weeks / J. Kings and B.D. Giles. – 2nd ed. – [Birmingham]: Department of Geography, University of Birmingham, 1982. – 87p: ill; 30 cm. – (Occasional publication; no.14). – ISBN 0-7044-0575-X

Salmond and Heuston on the law of torts. – 20th ed. / by R.F.V. Heuston and R.A. Buckley. – London: Sweet & Maxwell, 1992. – 604p; 24cm. – ISBN 0-421-45980-8

Site layout planning for daylight and sunlight: a guide to good practice/P.J. Littlefair. – Watford: Building Research Establishment, 1991. – 85p: ill; 30 cm. – (Building Research Establishment report; 209). – ISBN 0-85125-506-X

Soba: archaeological research at a medieval capital on the Blue Nile / by D.A. Welsby and C.M. Daniels; with a preface by Sir Lawrence Kirwan; and cont[r]ibutions by L. Allison-Jones ... [et al.]. – London: British Institute in Eastern Africa, 1991. – 363p: ill, maps; 31 cm. – (Memoirs of the British Institute in Eastern Africa; no.12). – 2 maps on folded leaves in pocket. – Bibliography: pp. 356–60

Total eclipse / produced by Jean-Pierre Ramsey Levi. – London: Video Collection International, 1998. – 1 videocartridge (108 min.). – Cast: Leonardo DiCaprio (Arthur Rimbaud); David Thewlis (Paul Verlaine). – Credits: script: Agniezka Holland; music: Jan J.P. Kaczmarec; editor: Isbel Lorente. – Made in 1995. – VHS. – Summary: Chronicles the volatile relationship between the 19th century French poets Verlaine and Rimbaud. – VC3636

Figure 3.10 Descriptive cataloguing examples: Level 2

discuss the generally applicable areas, and later we explore some of the challenges associated with creating descriptions for specific document types.

Title and statement of responsibility

These form one area instead of two because one or the other may be lacking (as with anonymous works, or a book of reproductions of art works which has only the artist's name on the title page), or the two may be grammatically inseparable (for example, *Poems of William Wordsworth*). In many cases, Author + Title proper + Date adequately identify an item, fulfilling the first purpose of description. Early cataloguers, who had to physically type or write each catalogue card, soon realized that time and card space could be saved by omitting the author's name from the description where it was recognizably the same as the author heading appearing immediately above the description (that is, in the great majority of cases), and this interdependence of description and heading has been built into the MARC record format. The following elements are distinguished:

- title proper; this is transcribed exactly as found
- optionally, a general material designation: a word or short phrase from a prescribed list, indicating the type of material (for example, [text], [music])
- parallel title: where the title appears in more than one language
- other title information: usually a subtitle
- statements of responsibility.

Optionally, a *uniform title* – a cataloguer's filing title, preceding the title proper – may be assigned in cases where different editions of the same work may appear under different titles (see Chapter 8).

The statement of responsibility is given as found within the chief source of information. Its purpose is to describe; it is not intended to serve as an access point. Access points use headings derived from the statement of responsibility according to a complex set of rules. These are described in Chapter 8. A heading is often permanently associated with a description, and in such cases Level 1 description permits the omission of the statement of responsibility when it is recognizably the same as the main entry heading.

The principles of description were laid down before online access became an everyday reality. Title keywords are now a significant access mechanism in OPACs and other computerized search systems. Subtitles are not required in a Level 1 description, but in view of their usefulness in keyword access it would be sensible to include them even in the most abbreviated formats.

Edition

The principal elements are:

- the edition statement as found in the document, except that abbreviations (such as 'Rev. ed.') may be used, and a statement of first edition is by convention omitted
- statements of responsibility relating to the edition.

The concept of the edition derives from the printed book in the days when type was set by hand. A new edition implied a resetting of the type, which usually implied some revision of the content. A valid distinction could thus be made between an edition and a reprint, a new printing from a photographic or mechanical copy of the text, with no change in the content. Today, many kinds of documents are produced from a digital-held file that can be updated instantly. For books, the idea of the edition still has some validity but, in general, edition statements are less appropriate in digital environments, although there is still a pressing need for some kind of version statement and associated version control.

Material-specific (or publication type-specific) area

This is used only for specific physical formats. The most important uses are:

- cartographic materials – used for the scale and projection of maps and atlases
- serials – used for the volume and part numbers and dates of issue
- electronic resources – used for the extent and type of resource.

Publication, distribution, etc., area

The principal elements are:

- place of publication
- name of publisher, distributor, etc.
- date of publication.

If the description is to be used for current bibliography – that is, as a selection tool – this area should give enough information to identify and locate the source from which the item may be obtained. For books, the publisher and distributor are usually one and the same, and directories of publishers are readily available, making it unnecessary to give more than the publisher's name for trade publishers. In other cases the full postal address may be required. Year of publication refers to the edition, and so if an item was published in 1894 and a library's copy is of a reprint dated 1912, AACR2 still regards its date as being 1894 – a view to which an antiquarian bookseller might not subscribe.

Physical description area

This has four elements:

- extent of item
- other physical details
- dimensions, and (occasionally)
- accompanying materials.

The nature of these varies considerably depending on the physical form of the resource that is being catalogued. For books, cataloguers are advised to specify: the number of volumes and/or pagination; illustrative matter; and dimensions.

Series area

The principal elements are:

- title proper of series; in many cases this is all that is required
- statement of responsibility only if necessary to identify the series
- numbering within the series.

The series statement helps to identify an item and to characterize it by giving some idea of its status and subject. Series can be problematical, in that it is not always easy to distinguish title proper from series title when both appear on the chief source of information. So one work might be catalogued as *The Buildings of England: Suffolk* and another as *Essex – ... (The Buildings of England)*. On many search systems a title or title keyword search will also retrieve series titles.

Notes area

Notes contain information considered necessary to fulfil the purposes of description but which cannot conveniently be given in one of the earlier, more formal, areas of the description. Notes may be taken from any available source: for all previous areas any information not derived directly from the item's prescribed chief source of information must be enclosed within square brackets. These are some of the commoner categories of notes:

- notes citing other editions and works
- notes describing the nature, scope, or artistic form of the work; or a list or summary of its contents
- notes expanding on the information given in the formal description
- notes on the particular copy being described, or on a library's holdings, or restrictions in its use.

Standard number and terms of availability area

ISBN for books and ISSN for serials can be added in this area. Terms of availability is an optional addition. Normally the price is shown. A standard number provides a check on an item's identity, provided one bears in mind some of the limitations of ISBNs in that different editions of a work will normally carry the same ISBN or, conversely, the same work may bear two or more ISBNs if it comes in hardback and paperback formats or is published jointly by two or more publishers.

DESCRIPTIVE CATALOGUING CHECKLIST

The full AACR2 provides for three levels of description; the Concise AACR2 approximates to Level 2 description. In the full AACR2, Chapter 1 gives rules for describing materials generally, and these are expanded in Chapters 2–12 for specific types of material, with the rules numbered in parallel with Chapter 1. UKMARC records currently use either Level 2 or Level 1 descriptions. Only the more common patterns are shown here: this checklist does not attempt to cover every eventuality. Level 3 description is identical to Level 2 for the majority of items. Only rarely will items be found where Level 3 prescribes more detail. Examples include second and subsequent place of publication and/or publisher, and parallel series title and/or other series title information.

Sources of information for the various areas (fields) of a description are rigidly prescribed. Any information that is taken from outside a prescribed source is enclosed within square brackets.

The sources shown in Figure 3.11 apply to books. Chief sources of information are specified by AACR2 for each different types of resource. For example, for sound recordings, there is a list of different sources depending on the physical form of the recording. For videos, information is preferred from within the item itself or, secondly, from its container. For electronic resources, such as a web page, information within the resource itself, such as on the initial display of the page, is preferred. The areas (fields) follow an invariable sequence, as do the subfields within them. Fields or subfields not needed to describe a given item are simply omitted. Punctuation conforms to a rigid pattern (and, in UKMARC records, is generated by the system); for the most part it introduces the information that follows. Figure 3.11 shows the sequence of areas in a bibliographic description, including the source of the content for each area, and the punctuation.

Overall layout (1.0D; Concise 1C, 1D)
Title and statement of responsibility. – Edition. – Material (etc.) specific details. – Publication etc. – Physical description. – Series. – Notes. – Standard number

Title and statement of responsibility area (1.1)
Source: Title page.
Level 1: Title proper / first statement of responsibility only if different from main entry heading.
Level 2: Title proper: other title information / first statement of responsibility; each subsequent statement of responsibility.

Edition area (1.2)
Source: Title page, or a formal statement made by the publisher elsewhere in the item.
Level 1: . – Edition
Level 2: . – Edition / statement of responsibility for the edition

Material (or type of publication) specific area (1.3)
Used as described above. Consult AACR2 for full instructions.

Publication, distribution, etc., area (1.4)
Source: Title page, or a formal statement made by the publisher elsewhere in the item.
Level 1: . – First named publisher, year of edition
Level 2: . – City of publication: first named publisher, year of edition

Physical description area (1.5)
Source: Anywhere in the item.
Level 1: . – Extent of item
Level 2: . – Extent of item: other physical details; dimensions. For books this mostly means:
 – Last numbered page: illustrations; height in cm.
Series area (1.6)
Source: Anywhere in the item.
Level 1: Not required at Level 1.
Level 2: . – (Title proper of series / statement of responsibility only if necessary to identify the
 series; numbering within the series).

Notes area (1.7)
Source: Any available source.
Level 1/2: . – Note. – Note (Repeat as needed)

Standard number(1.8)
Source: Any suitable source.
Level 1/2: . – ISBN 0-123-45678-9

Figure 3.11   Areas in a bibliographic description

DESCRIPTION AND SPECIFIC DOCUMENT TYPES

GENERAL ISSUES

It was common in the past for libraries to maintain two catalogues, one for books and one for non-book media, or even separate sequences for each type of media. Practice today has moved towards integration, which AACR2 is designed to facilitate. Nevertheless, the traditions of cataloguing are rooted in the cataloguing of books, which means that the standard model of description needs adaptation to accommodate different document types. There are common issues that apply to many document types:

● Many media cannot be browsed like a book. Equipment may be needed to view or play the item, which can be slow and calls for special expertise in the media and its equipment. The description may need to include a summary of the contents.

● Granularity can be difficult to establish, and a fine judgement is needed in deciding the level at which to describe a composite item. Typical examples include a school teaching pack containing a range of separate items including

81

audio visual and printed material, or a music CD with works by different composers or players on different tracks. Another aspect of this problem is that some documents are distributed in a complex pattern of series and subseries.

- Responsibility for the creation, production and distribution of some documents can be complex and diffuse.
- There is far less standardization of presentation than with monographic materials. Titles may be difficult to establish, and other necessary information (for example, date) may be difficult or impossible to establish. External sources of information – for example bibliographies and distributors' lists – may have to be consulted.
- There is no standard numbering system, and consequently less likelihood of finding a centrally produced record. Local indexing or abstracting is more likely to be required.
- Descriptions can be complex, with much necessary information that may not fit easily into the formal areas of description. Extensive notes are therefore often needed.
- For some sources, notably networked electronic resources, the notion of publication is elusive. Such resources are considered by AACR2 to be published, but it may be difficult to establish publishers, place or date.
- The physical description area needs to be adapted to suit the type of material. For networked electronic resources such as websites, no physical description is given.

ISSUES FOR SPECIFIC TYPES OF DOCUMENT

The following notes briefly characterize some of the problems specific to categories of documents. The categories are those used by AACR2.

Cartographic materials

This category includes any representation of the whole or part of the earth or any celestial body, and extends to aerial photographs and three-dimensional maps and plans. These have a Mathematical data area, corresponding to the Material-specific (or publication type-specific) area, to record scale and projection. Some examples are:

- scale 1:50,000
- scale 1:23,000,000; azimuthal equal-area projection
- not drawn to scale.

The physical description merits special attention. This could be: the number of physical units of an item (for example, 'one map on four sheets'); other physical details, such as the number of maps in an atlas, the use of colour, the material from which it is made, if significant, and any mounting (for example, 'one globe: col., wood, on brass stand'). Finally, the dimensions of maps often mean height × width (for example, 'one map: col., 35 × 50 cm').

Manuscripts

AACR2 gives a chapter to these, but as a manuscript is by definition unique and often of incalculable value, handling them demands specialist training, which places them outside the scope of the present work.

Music

This covers published music only; books about music and musicians are treated like any other book. Sound recordings are treated separately, but share some of the problems of music scores. Problems are more of access than of representation, for two reasons: firstly, music publishing is highly international, and the music cataloguer is likely to be handling a disproportionate number of foreign language documents; and secondly, classical music in particular may require a uniform title – see Chapter 8 for a brief description of these.

Sound recordings

These share with printed music many problems of description and access. Physical description is a particular problem, because of the wide and changing range of formats. AACR2 has detailed instructions on such matters as: playing time; type of recording (analogue, digital, optical, magnetic, etc.); the playing speed of discs and film; whether mono, stereo or quad; and so on.

Motion pictures and video recordings

These, even more than sound recordings, are subject to rapid technological change. The physical description is along the same lines as sound recordings.

Graphic materials

AACR2 defines 20 types of graphic materials, from activity cards to wall charts, and taking in such categories as art reproductions, filmstrips, radiographs and slides. Sources of information may be incomplete, and even titles may need to be supplied from external sources, or made up by the cataloguer. As always, the rules for physical description should be studied carefully; many of them are highly medium-specific.

Three-dimensional artefacts and realia

Nine types are listed generically in the physical description area (art original, art reproduction, Braille cassette, diorama, exhibit, game, microscope slide, mock-up, model); otherwise the cataloguer has to state the specific name of the item. To this is added information on the extent of the item, its material, colour, dimensions and any accompanying material. The items are tangible enough, but chief sources of information may be lacking.

Microforms

These are often reissues of ordinary full-sized materials. This gives two possibilities: to catalogue them as material in their own right (AACR2's implied preference), or to prepare a description based on the original, with a note indicating a microform reproduction, as is the Library of Congress's practice in USMARC records.

Continuing resources

Continuing resources or serials, such as journals, newspaper and magazines, differ from other forms of publication in that publication is intended to be continued indefinitely. If the title proper of a serial changes, a new description is made using the new title. Statements of responsibility tend to involve corporate bodies rather than personal authors, and exclude editors of serials. Serials have a Material-specific (or publication type-specific) area, to record the chronological or numeric designation of the first issue. Here, as in the date and the 'extent of item' part of the physical description, an 'open' entry is normally made. A note records the frequency. The following example shows the general pattern:

> Jewellery International. – Oct./Nov. 1991- . – London:
> Jewellery Research and Publishing, 1991- . – v.: ill. -
> Six issues yearly. – ISSN 0961-4559

The ISSN International Centre in Paris has responsibility for ISSN allocation, The National Serials Data Program within the Library of Congress is the US centre of the ISSN Network, and the British Library manages the ISSN UK Centre.

DESCRIBING ELECTRONIC AND INTERNET RESOURCES

We deal with electronic and Internet resources here separately from other non-book resources since they are a growing and important category of resources. Other later chapters in this book discuss the tools and approaches for searching such resources: here the focus is on their description. Such resources are diverse, as an examination of the different types of resources of any of the major Web search engines will reveal, and as illustrated in Figure 3.12. Cataloguing codes for their description need to accommodate this diversity. Further, libraries and archives are presented with a further dilemma and that is which resources to select for cataloguing.

AACR has recently published a new chapter on electronic resources to replace the chapter on computer files, and there is also an ISBD for electronic resources (ISBD (ER)), but a more complete picture can be gathered by additional reference to OCLC's manual for cataloguing Internet resources.

Although the general framework of the ISBD and AACR2 for description is followed, there are a number of challenges associated with the cataloguing of Internet resources:

- It is necessary to distinguish between direct access resources, which have a physical carrier and must be inserted directly into a computerized device (such as CDs), and remote access resources, where access is to a resource across a network.
- The chief source of information is 'the resource itself' instead of the 'title screen'. Formally presented evidence, such as the home page, title page or encoded metadata, is preferred.
- The statement of responsibility – it can be difficult to determine who is responsible for an Internet resource, because a web page may contain several pieces of information that are created or owned by different users.
- Edition statement – the content of a web page may change frequently, and often different versions or revisions are not specifically marked.
- File characteristics – there are a wide range of different file types. The ISBD (ER) identifies the file types shown in Figure 3.12.
- Physical description – this is not normally appropriate and therefore not usually given.

THE MARC FORMAT

THE DEVELOPMENT OF MARC

The MARC format was designed in the late 1960s as a standard format for representing bibliographic information, so that libraries could store, communicate and reformat bibliographic information in machine-readable form. It was first implemented in the US by the Library of Congress in 1968 and in the UK by the British National Bibliography in 1971. The format was to be hospitable to all kinds of library materials, and is flexible enough to be used in a variety of applications, not only in libraries and bibliographic agencies but within the book industry and the information community at large. As more countries exploited MARC,

Electronic data
  Electronic font data
  Electronic image data
  Electronic numeric data
    Electronic census data
    Electronic survey data
  Electronic representational data
    Electronic map data
  Electronic text data
    Electronic bibliographic database(s)
    Electronic document(s) (e.g. letters, articles)
    Electronic journal(s)
    Electronic newsletter(s)
Electronic program(s)
  Electronic application program(s)
    Electronic CAD program(s)
    Electronic database program(s)
    Electronic desktop publishing program(s)
    Electronic game(s)
    Electronic spreadsheet program(s)
    Electronic word processor program(s)
  Electronic system program(s)
    Electronic operating system program(s)
    Electronic programming language(s)
    Electronic retrieval program(s)
  Electronic utility program(s)
    Electronic data and program(s)
    Electronic interactive multimedia
    Electronic online service(s) (e.g. bulletin boards, discussion groups and lists, World Wide Web sites)

Figure 3.12   File types for electronic resources as identified in ISBD(ER)

variations in practices spawned deviations from the original format. The UNIMARC format was developed for international exchange of MARC records. National organizations creating MARC records have used national standards within the country and reformatted records to UNIMARC for international exchange. Recently, however, a number of major suppliers of MARC records have agreed to use the MARC21 format. MARC21 was developed in 2000 as a result of the development and integration of the US and Canadian MARC formats. The British Library adopted MARC21 in 2001. As well as the format for Bibliographic Data, there are MARC21 formats for Community Information, Holdings Data, Classification Data and Authority Data. Figure 3.13 shows an example of a MARC21 record.

Leader	01041cam 2200265 a 4500
Control No.	001 ###89048230
Control No. ID	003 DLC
DTLT	005 19911106082810.9
Fixed Data	008 891101s1990 maua j 001 0 eng
LCCN	010 ## $a ###89048230
ISBN	020 ## $a 0316107514:
	$c $12.95
ISBN	020 ## $a 0316107506 (pbk.):
	$c $5.95 ($6.95 Can.)
Cat. Source	040 ## $a DLC
	$c DLC
	$d DLC
LC Call No.	050 00 $a GV943.25
	$b .B74 1990
Dewey No.	082 00 $a 796.334/2
	$2 20
ME:Pers Name	100 1# $a Brenner, Richard J.,
	$d 1941-
Title	245 10 $a Make the team.
	$p Soccer:
	$b a heads up guide to super soccer! /
	$c Richard J. Brenner.
Variant Title	246 30 $a Heads up guide to super soccer
Edition	250 ## $a 1st ed.
Publication	260 ## $a Boston:
	$b Little, Brown,
	$c c1990.
Phys Desc	300 ## $a 127 p.:
	$b ill. ;
	$c 19 cm.
Note: General	500 ## $a 'A Sports illustrated for kids book.'
Note: Summary	520 ## $a Instructions for improving soccer skills. Discusses dribbling, heading, playmaking, defense, conditioning, mental attitude, how to handle problems with coaches, parents, and other players, and the history of soccer.
Subj: Topical	650 #0 $a Soccer
	$v Juvenile literature.

Figure 3.13   Sample of a MARC21 record
Source: Furrie, 2003

THE MARC FORMAT

The MARC record format complies with ISO 2709: 1996 *Information and Documentation: Format for Information Exchange* (ISO, 1996), and with ISO 1001: 1986 *Information Processing: File Structure and Labelling of Magnetic Tapes for Information Interchange* (ISO, 1986). The components of the format are:

Sample brief record display as seen by a user

TITLE: Make the team. Soccer: a heads up guide to super soccer! / Richard J.
                Brenner.

AUTHOR: Brenner, Richard J.

PUBLISHED: Little, Brown, c1990.

MATERIAL: 127 p.
Copies Available: GV943.25 .B74 1990

Sample of a full record display as seen by a patron

TITLE: Make the team. Soccer: a heads up guide to super soccer! / Richard J.
                Brenner.

ADDED TITLE: Heads up guide to super soccer

AUTHOR: Brenner, Richard J., 1941-

PUBLISHED: 1st ed. Boston: Little, Brown, c1990.

MATERIAL: 127 p.: ill.; 19 cm

NOTE: 'A Sports illustrated for kids book.'

NOTE: Instructions for improving soccer skills. Discusses dribbling, heading,
                playmaking, defense, conditioning, mental attitude, how to handle
                problems with coaches, parents, and other players, and the history of
                soccer.

SUBJECT: Soccer—Juvenile literature.
                Soccer.

Copies Available: GV943.25 .B74 1990

Figure 3.14   Sample records derived from the MARC21 record in Figure 3.13

- *Leader* – supplied by the program and placed at the beginning of the record.
  The label contains information about the record, such as, for example, its
  length and status (new, changed, etc.), type and class.
- *Directory* – a plan that lists, for every field, the tag, the number of characters in
  the field, and the starting character position within the record. Directories are
  also supplied by the program, and are not required to be input by the
  cataloguer.
- *Control fields* – fixed-length fields that contain control numbers and other
  control and coded information, such as the date and time of processing, type of

material, physical characteristics and standard numbers. Each control field is identified by a field tag and contains either a single data element or a series of fixed-length data elements in specified positions.

- *Variable fields* – these fields contain the main bibliographic data such as the description, main and added entries, subject entries (subject headings) and classification (and location).

The following elements, called field enumerators, define the data content of each field.

Tag – a three-digit number within the range 000–945

The tags have a mnemonic structure in that they follow the order of a catalogue record, and the tags for added entries mirror those for main entry headings. The variable fields are grouped in blocks according to the first character of the tag:

0xx Control information, number, codes
1xx Main entries
2xx Titles and title paragraph (title, edition, imprint)
3xx Physical description, etc.
4xx Series statement
5xx Notes
6xx Subject access fields
7xx Added entries other than subject or series
8xx Series added entries
9xx Local data, such as holdings, and location.

Tags for specific fields are created by entering digits in the final two places; for example:

100 Personal author main entry heading
110 Corporate name main entry heading
240 Uniform title
250 Edition and statement of edition author, editor, etc.
260 Publication, distribution, etc.
300 Physical description.

A personal author's name generally has '00' in the second and third positions, so that:

100 is used for a main entry personal author heading
600 is used for a personal author subject heading
700 is used for a personal author added entry heading.

Indicators

These are the two characters (normally digits) which follow the tag, and introduce the variable-length fields that contain bibliographic data. Indicators are unique to the field to which they are assigned, and are used for such purposes as: to distinguish between different types of information entered in the same field; to provide for title added entries; and to indicate the number of characters to be dropped in filing titles.

Subfields

These indicate smaller distinct units within a field, which may require separate manipulation. Typical subfields in the imprint area are place of publication, publisher and date of publication. Subfields are preceded by a subfield code, which consists of a single non-alphanumeric symbol (such as '$') and a single letter. The imprint might be coded as: 260.00 $aLondon: $bPitman, $c1996. Subfield codes control such factors as appearance and layout. So, for example, the subfield coding just shown for the 260 field would generate the statement London: Pitman, 1996 in a Level 2 or Level 3 description, or Pitman, 1996 for a Level 1 description. Subfield codes are defined in the context of the field in which they are used, but similar codes are used in parallel situations. For example, the subfield codes for a person's name are constant, regardless of whether the name is main or additional author, or subject entry heading.

Field mark

The hash (#) represents the end of a field. This is necessary when variable-length fields are used.

THE USE OF MARC

MARC records can be used in the following kinds of application:

1. *Information retrieval*. Most of the fields and subfields can be searched on, and together provide an exceptionally wide range of access points. In practice, different applications make their own selection of search keys from those available.
2. *Displaying citations*. Records are rarely displayed in their 'raw' MARC format, except for cataloguers. For most applications, the tags are either suppressed or replaced with appropriate verbal descriptions (for example, *Imprint:* in place of 260), and unnecessary fields and subfields suppressed. Many applications allow the data to be displayed or printed in more than one format (see Figure 3.14).

3. *Cataloguing.* Cataloguers can call up MARC records using control numbers, or by the search keys available for information retrieval, or by acronym searches. For example , records may be selected online from a central database.
4. *Identifying new publications.* The major national bibliographic agencies operate Cataloguing-in-Publication (CIP) programmes. Arrangements are made with individual publishers to supply advance copies so that a skeleton MARC record can be made available in advance of publication. A full MARC record is made after publication and legal deposit, replacing the CIP record.
5. *Resource sharing.* The MARC format was designed from the start to facilitate the exchange of bibliographic data. Many library consortia have a central database in MARC format to which members can contribute records, and from which they copy records for local use.

MARC can be applied to other book and non-book (including electronic) materials, provided they have been catalogued using AACR2. Both use the same MARC format and content tags, but there are adjustments for specific kinds of materials. For example the following adjustments are made for electronic resources:

006 – specifies material type, showing m = computer file/electronic resources and d = document
007 – physical description field uses: c = electronic resource, and r = remote specific material designation
245 – shows a general material designation of 'electronic resource'
300 – physical description is not given for a resources available by remote access
500 – source of the title proper, indicates the date on which the item was viewed for description
516 – shows type of computer file
530 – gives any additional physical form note
538 – includes a mode of access note, and a systems requirements note where appropriate
856 – electronic location and access, points either to the original host server carrying the item, or to an e-mail address.

THE FUTURE FOR MARC

MARC21 is an important metadata standard, but it needs to continue to evolve and develop to position itself within the broader metadata landscape. The Library of Congress has launched a number of major initiatives relating to the continuing viability of the MARC format. These include:

- The development of an XML schema for a bibliographic element set that may be used for a variety of purposes, the Metadata Object Description Schema (MODS). MODS is intended to be able to carry selected data from existing MARC21 records as well as to enable the creation of original resource description records. It includes a subset of MARC fields and uses language-based tags rather than numeric ones, in some cases regrouping elements from the MARC21 bibliographic format.
- The development of a new XML schema for authorities called Metadata Authority Description Schema (MADS). MADS may be used to provide metadata about agents (people, organizations), events and terms (topics, geographics, genres, etc.) and serves as a companion to MODS. As such, MADS has a relationship to the MARC21 Authority format, similar to that which MODS has to MARC21 Bibliographic – both carry selected data from MARC21.
- Translation of the MARC format into the XML environment as MARCXML.
- The development of a number of crosswalks between MARC and various other metadata standards.

There is a general belief that the widespread use of the MARC format in library operations will persist, perhaps largely due to the inertia of existing massive MARC databases, and the extent to which it is embedded in systems. Nevertheless, MARC is recognized to have limitations that derive from its origins in the computer creation of printed and card catalogues, its long-standing association with AACR2 which also suffers from the limitations deriving from similar roots, and the evolutionary path that it has followed since its inception. There is a need to revisit its idiosyncratic record structures and coding, inconsistent granularity, technical obsolescence, and its lack of scalability to digital materials.

SUMMARY

This chapter has examined document representations and surrogates, introducing a range of different practices and associated standards along the way. Many of the approaches discussed in this chapter are long-established, but there is an ever-present need for adaptation to accommodate the increasing shift towards digital documents and other digital objects in their various forms. However, it is important to remember that information is and will continue to be packaged in a variety of media and that practices and standards to accommodate access to documents in a wide variety of formats are essential. This involves the use and development of content standards, such as cataloguing rules, as well as metadata standards that support interoperability at a range of levels. This chapter has introduced two key standards, AACR2 and MARC21. Both are under evolution. For AACR2 the evolution is towards the more open and adaptable RDA. RDA seeks to provide relatively simple content rules that could be adopted by various metadata communities, but which remain independent of any specific metadata standard. For MARC, key developments relate to the accommodation of an ever-changing range of digital objects and ensuring interoperability with other metadata standards and schemas.

REVIEW QUESTIONS

1. Discuss what is meant by document representation. Explain some of the persistent characteristics and problems associated with document representation.
2. What are citations and how are they used? Give examples that demonstrate that you understand the elements of a citation.
3. How might citations for electronic documents differ from those for print documents?
4. Discuss the difference between an informative and an indicative abstract. Explain what is meant by a structured abstract.
5. Write a brief checklist of points to help a new abstractor learn to produce abstracts.
6. Explain what AACR2 and RDA are. Why are they important in the context of bibliographic record formats?
7. What are the basic elements of a bibliographic description. Are they all necessary for every document type?
8. Choose two different non-book document types and discuss the special problems that they pose for bibliographic description.
9. Describe the structure of the MARC record format.
10. Justify the continuing importance of bibliographic description.

REFERENCES AND FURTHER READING

ABSTRACTS AND ABSTRACTING

Borko, H. and Bernier, C.L. (1975) *Abstracting Concepts and Methods*. New York: Academic Press.
Craven, T.C. (2000) Abstracts produced using computer assistance. *Journal of the American Society for Information Science*, **51**, 745–56.
Cremmins, E.T. (1982) *The Art of Abstracting*. Philadelphia PA: ISI Press.

Fidel, R. (1986) Writing abstracts for free-text searching. *Journal of Documentation*, **42**, 11–21.

Hartley, J. (2000) Are structured abstracts more or less accurate than traditional ones? A study in the psychological literature. *Journal of Information Science*, **26** (4), 273–7.

International Standards Organization (ISO) (1976) *Documentation: Abstracts for Publication and Documentation*. ISO 214: 1976E. Geneva: ISO.

Jizba, L. (1997) Reflections on summarizing and abstracting: implications for Internet Web documents, and standardized library databases. *Journal of Internet Cataloging*, **1** (2), 15–39.

Lancaster, F.W. (2003) *Indexing and Abstracting in Theory and Practice*, 3rd edn. London: Facet.

Luhn, H.P. (1958) The automatic creation of literature abstracts. *IBM Journal of Research and Development*, **2** (2), 159–65.

Montesi, M. and Urdiciain, B.G. (2005) Recent linguistic research into author abstracts: its value for information science. *Knowledge Organization*, **32** (2), 64–78.

Montesi, M. and Urdiciain, B.G. (2005) Abstracts: problems classified from the user perspective. *Journal of Information Science*, **31** (6), 515–526.

Pinto, M. (2003) Abstracting/abstract adaptation to digital environment: research trends. *Journal of Documentation*, **59** (5), 581–608.

Rowley, J.E. (1988) *Indexing and Abstracting*, 2nd edn. London: Library Association.

Salton, G. (1989) *Automatic Text Processing: The transformation, analysis and retrieval of information by computer*. Reading MA: Addison-Wesley.

Wheatley, A. and Armstrong, C.J. (1997) Metadata, recall, and abstracts: can abstracts ever be reliable indicators of document value? *Aslib Proceedings*, **49** (8), September, 206–13.

CITATION PRACTICES

British Standard 1629: 1989 (1989) *Recommendations for References to Published Material*. London: British Standards Institution.

British Standard 5605: 1990 (1990) *Recommendations for Citing and Referencing Published Material*. London: British Standards Institution.

The Chicago Manual of Style: For authors, editors and copywriters (2005), 15th edn. Chicago IL: University of Chicago Press.

International Standards Organization (ISO) (2004) *Information and Documentation – Bibliographic References – Part 2: Electronic Documents or Parts Thereof*. ISO 690–2. Geneva: ISO.

Turabian, K.L. (1996) *A Manual for Writers of Term Papers, Theses and Dissertations*, 6th edn. Chicago IL: University of Chicago Press.

BIBLIOGRAPHIC RECORDS AND MARC

Aliprand, J.M. (2005) The structure and content of MARC21 records in the Unicode environment. *Information Technology and Libraries*, **24** (4), 170–179.

American Library Association (2005) Update on major metadata standards. *Library Technology Reports*, **41** (6), 20–33.

Andrew, P.G. (2003) *Cataloguing Sheet Maps: The basics*. Binghamton NY: Haworth.

Anglo-American Cataloguing Rules (AACR2) (2004), 2nd edn, revd. 2002, 2004. London: Library Association.

Bluh, P. and Hepfer, C. (2006) *Managing Electronic Resources: Contemporary problems and emerging issues*. Chicago IL: American Library Association.

Bowen, J. (2005) FRBR: coming soon to your library? *Library Resources and Technical Services*, **49** (3), 175–88.

Burke, M.A. (1999) *Organization of Multimedia Resources: Principles and practice of information retrieval*. Aldershot: Gower.

Dempsey, L. and Heery, R. (1998) Metadata: a current view of practice and issues. *Journal of Documentation*, **54** (2), 145–72.

Dowski, C.A. (2005) Cataloguing at the crossroads; now that we have AACR2 revised chapter 12, where do we go from here? *Technical Services Quarterly*, **23** (1), 75–86.

Eden, B.L. (2004) MARC and metadata: METS, MODS and MARCXML: current and future implementations; theme issue. *Library Hi-Tech*, **22** (issues 1 and 2).

Fritz, D.A. (1998) *Cataloging with AACR2R and USMARC: For books, computer files, serials, sound recordings, video recordings*. Chicago IL: American Library Association.

Furrie, B. (2003) Understanding MARC. Available at <http//:www.loc.gov/mar/umb/>.

Gorman, G.E. and Dorner, D.G. (2003) *Metadata Applications and Management: International Yearbook of Library and Information Management 2003-4*. London: Facet.

Gorman, M. (2004) *The Concise AACR2*, 4th edn. London: Facet.

Hill, R.W. (1999) *Setting the Record Straight: A guide to the MARC format*, 3rd edn. London: British Library.

International Standards Organization (1986) *Information Processing – File Structure and Labelling of Magnetic Tapes for Information Exchange*. ISO 1001: 1986. Geneva: ISO.

International Standards Organization (1996) *Information and Documentation – Format for Information Exchange*. ISO 2709: 1996. Geneva: ISO.

ISBD(G) (1992) *General International Standard Bibliographic Description: Annotated text*. Rev. edn. London: IFLA.

ISBD(M) (2002) *International Standard Bibliographic Description for Monographic Publications*. Rev. edn. London: IFLA. Available at: <www.ifla.org/VII/s13/pubs/isbd m0602.pdf> [accessed 18 October 2006].

Joint Steering Committee for the Revision of AACR (2002) *Anglo-American Cataloguing Rules*. Rev. edn 2002, updated 2004. Chicago IL and London: CILIP.

Joint Steering Committee for the Revision of AACR (2005) *RDA: Resource description and access*. Available at <www.collectionscanada.ca/jsc/rdapresentations.html> [accessed 18 October 2006].

Jones, W. (2002) *Cataloguing the Web: Metadata, AACR and MARC21*. Lanham MD: Scarecrow.

Library of Congress, Network Development and MARC Standards Office (2003) *MARC 21 Concise Format for Bibliographic Data*. Library of Congress. Available at: <http:// lcweb.loc.gov/marc/bibliographic> [accessed 18 October 2006].

Medeiros, N. (2005) The future of the Anglo-American cataloguing rules. *OCLC Systems and Services: International Digital Library Perspectives*, **21** (4), 261–3.

Reser, D. and Hawkins, L. (2005) Defining and 'Access Level' catalog record using MARC21 and AACR2. *Serials Review*, **31** (3), 218–219.

Taylor, A.G. (2000) *Wyner's Introduction to Cataloguing and Classification*. 9th edn, with D.P. Miller. Englewood CO: Libraries Unlimited.

Tennat, R. (2005) MARC must die. *Library Journal*. Available at <www.libraryjournal.com.article/CA250046.html>.

UNESCO (1986) *UNISIST Reference Manual for Machine-Readable Bibliographic Descriptions*, 3rd edn. Comp. and ed. by H. Dierickx and A. Hopkinson. Paris: UNESCO.

Weitz, J. (2006) *Cataloguing Electronic Resources: OCLC-MARC coding guidelines*. Available at <www.oclc.org/support/documentation/worldcat/cataloging/electronicresources/default.html> [accessed 18 October 2006].

Part II
Access

4 Users and user behaviour

INTRODUCTION

Knowledge systems exist to enable users to find the information they require. Therefore it is incumbent upon designers of these systems to have an understanding of users and their information-seeking behaviour. In this chapter we focus on the user and consider various models of information behaviour. At the end of this chapter, you will be aware of:

- be aware of different ways of categorizing users
- understand the complementarity between indexing and searching
- be able to evaluate different models of information behaviour
- appreciate the concept of usability and its application.

USERS

Information seeking is an activity crucial to human survival; it has always been thus. Information scientists have long studied information-seeking behaviour. However, in reality what they studied was more likely to be the information sources used than the information seekers and their behaviour. Not only has there been a revolution in information storage and retrieval systems, resulting in a revolution in information access and use, but there has also been a revolution in the study and understanding of information behaviour. Early studies paid more attention to information sources rather than information users, notwithstanding the fact that they were often referred to as studies of information needs and use. Furthermore they concentrated almost exclusively on information seeking in professional, work-related contexts. So the information needs of engineers, chemists, historians or social workers were the subject of study whilst the information needs associated with everyday living or leisure activities were almost completely ignored.

Case (2002) argues that a key player in the shift from system-centred to user-centred theories and methods was Dervin. She presented ten myths about information and information seeking which are crucial to an appreciation of the changing nature of information seeking and its investigation. Those myths are that:

1. only 'objective' information is valuable
2. more information is always better
3. objective information can be treated out of context
4. information can only be acquired through formal sources
5. there is relevant information for every information need
6. every need situation has a solution
7. it is always possible to make information accessible
8. functional units of information such as books or TV programmes always fit the needs of individuals
9. time- and space-individual situations can be ignored in addressing information seeking and use
10. people make easy, conflict-free connections between external information and internal reality.

These myths are worth some brief comment. It is now widely recognized that, whether in professional life or everyday activities, people make wide use of informal information sources, as exemplified by widespread consultation with colleagues at work or reliance on traffic news on the radio (most of which is sourced from other travellers' phone calls). It is now widely understood that too much information leads to information overload – a major problem for many professionals – giving rise to the need for more effective filtering or targeting of information. Furthermore, it should be recognized that there will be situations in which the necessary information is not available, or the cost of acquiring it is too high and, thirdly, whilst in general terms it may be desirable that information be made available in accessible format, there may be situations in which this is simply not possible. Finally, it is now apparent that there is frequently not an exact match between information objects and the sought information; the latter frequently has to be acquired from numerous sources and re-packaged or recombined to resolve an information need.

A further myth which was widely propounded in the literature in the early days of electronic information resources was the notion that users could somehow be categorized as 'naïve' users or 'experienced' users. These myths expose the limitations of early research concerning users and their information-seeking behaviour. It is now recognized that information is sought for a much broader range of activities than work. Users may seek information in relation to work, learning, commercial activities, leisure activities and domestic life. Indeed the same person is likely to seek information in several different contexts at different times: the historian or the engineer will seek information in support of leisure activities, whether it be bird watching or movie watching; they will also seek information concerning domestic life, whether it be locating a source for obscure ingredients in a recipe or new shoes for the children.

Until the last decade our understanding of human information behaviour has been developed through studies of peoples' use of print products such as abstracts, indexes and bibliographies or digital tools such as OPACs and CD-ROMs. However Nicholas et al. (2006) emphasize a further revolution, or 'big bang' in information access and use as a result of the Internet revolution. In doing so, they coin the phrase 'the digital information consumer' and argue that this revolution can be characterized by five major changes. These merit consideration.

1. *From control to no control.* Searching was largely undertaken in controlled contexts; that is to say, it was usually in libraries or information centres. The searches were often mediated by information professionals and if they were not the searchers then they were not far away if help or advice was required. Now searchers are largely on their own; whether in home, office, library or, increasingly, using mobile devices whilst on the move.

2. *From bibliographic services to full-text, visual and life-critical services.* There has been a major change in the available resources. Where once it was almost exclusively a matter of searching bibliographic data via OPACs or databases such as ERIC or INSPEC, now it is a matter of full texts, still and moving images, downloadable music and more. Not withstanding the phenomenal success of Google, the available services increasingly have origins in the media world rather than in information retrieval.

3. *From niche to universal systems.* There has been a shift from targeted systems such as a directory or handbook or a bibliographic database to the vast array of information sources and services which are available on the Web in all its glorious chaos.

4. *From a few searchers to everyone.* For many years information seeking was the preserve of the few – essentially information professionals searching on behalf of a relatively small number of privileged individuals. From the mid-1980s there was a surge of end-user searching, encouraged by the widespread emergence of OPACs and CD-ROMs. The emergence of the Web has brought information seeking to the truly mass market. It is no longer the preserve of professionals and the curious few but within the grasp of millions of people of all types, from all walks of life and from all over the world, who are using the Web to seek for information.

5. *From corner store to megastore/shopping mall.* The situation has changed from one in which there was a restricted number of essentially targeted information

resources available to one in which searchers are faced with a veritable cornucopia of potential information resources from which to choose. For the information seeker, it is as though the corner shop has been replaced by the megastore or even a shopping mall. There are, of course, many critics of megastores and shopping malls who claim that the vast array of choice is illusory and that the service element of the corner shop has been lost. Whether or not this applies to the digital information consumer in the Web world remains to be seen.

As a result of these major changes, they argue that we should stop referring to end-users and rather consider them as information consumers. Indeed, in an era where we are all users of information it makes little sense to refer to end-users. We should consider these notions of digital information behaviour not because we argue that they make the need for 'conventional' knowledge systems such as catalogues redundant but to make it clear that there have been significant shifts in the tools available to users; accordingly their information behaviour has changed. Knowledge systems need to change to account for that behaviour. Nielsen reminds us that 'users spend most of their time on *other* websites' (Jakob's Law of Web User Experience). From this he draws the conclusion that it makes sense to ensure that a website is as similar as possible to sites with which users and potential users are likely to be familiar.

INFORMATION BEHAVIOUR

The somewhat curious term information behaviour (information does not behave!) has been coined recently to emphasize the fact that information seeking is not an end in itself but rather that it is sought in a context to solve a problem or make sense of a situation: the information seeker does not simply decide to seek information for its own sake. As we have moved through the notions of user studies to information-seeking behaviour to information behaviour, various researchers have sought to develop models or theories which help describe and predict information-seeking behaviour.

An abstract or conceptual model is a structure which helps us to think about something, whilst a theory is a generalized description based upon a large number of observations which has the power to predict future behaviour. In this academic sense it is much more than the common usage of the word where it is used to represent conjecture, opinion or speculation. Various social scientists make a distinction between what Merton termed 'grand theories' and more modest 'middle-range' theories. He saw grand theories as those which explained large segments of human behaviour whilst middle-range theories deal with more limited settings. As far as information behaviour is concerned, it can be said that there are numerous models which represent information seeking and which are useful to enable us to improve our understanding; there is considerably less that can be considered as theory, even on the scale of middle-range theories, which can be used to predict future behaviour. Indeed, it is more appropriate to refer to them as theoretical perspectives rather than theories.

From the many models of information-seeking behaviour which exist, we have chosen to explore four important ones: those attributed to Ellis (1989), Kuhlthau (1993), Wilson (1999) and Dervin (1992). We also introduce Chatman's theory of information poverty. Further models can be found from the writings of Case (2002) and Spink and Cole (2006).

ELLIS'S MODEL OF INFORMATION SEEKING

The widely quoted Ellis model consists of six cognitive stages in the search process which he refers to as: starting, chaining, browsing, differentiating, monitoring and extracting. Whilst this model was developed through a detailed investigation of the information seeking of social scientists, it has subsequently formed the basis of a range of investigations. The stages are outlined in Figure 4.1 and discussed below.

Stage	Activity
Starting	Activities characteristic of the initial search for information
Chaining	Following chains of citations or other forms of connections between information objects
Browsing	Semi-directed searching in an area of potential interest
Differentiating	Using differences between sources as filters on the nature and quality of the material examined
Monitoring	Maintaining awareness of developments in an area of interest by monitoring particular information sources
Extracting	Systematically working through a particular information object to extract material of interest to the problem in hand

Figure 4.1 Ellis's six-stage model of information seeking

Ellis argued that these six stages characterize information-seeking behaviour, though the interrelationship between these stages will obviously vary with every unique information-seeking episode and will depend upon the unique characteristics of the information need, information seeker and context.

1. *Starting* refers to the characteristics of starting a search for information; for example, when a researcher is starting a new project or is new to a particular subject area. Typical behaviours include attempting to locate a relevant reference which can serve as a starting point; this might include systematic use of library catalogues, abstracts, indexes, search engines and, particularly, review articles.

2. *Chaining* is the process whereby the information seeker makes use of references in information objects discovered in the previous stage of the process. This might be backward chaining by following up references in an information object, or forward chaining by using a given information object as the source of a search within Web of Science or a similar citation database.

3. *Browsing* has come to be recognized as an important part of information seeking though for many years it was somewhat disparaged. It is considered here to refer to forms of semi-structured searching rather than totally random browsing. Typical forms of this type of information seeking include browsing through the contents pages of relevant journals, whether on library shelves or (increasingly) those to which electronic access is available. Whilst browsing is principally about locating information for a particular problem, especially in the case of the information seeker, delving into a new topic area is also concerned with improving familiarity with the information sources relevant to that topic.

4. *Differentiating* refers to the process of using the characteristics of information sources as a means of filtering the retrieved information. Researchers and practitioners in a given field of study frequently have an acute awareness of the status of specific journals and information sources. This might refer largely to the perceived ranking of the journal in its field but it might also relate to its perceived area of specialization: does it concentrate mainly on theoretical approaches or it is it more interested in methodological approaches? The reputations of authors and their areas of expertise are also used as means of filtering the retrieved information. Finally, the approaches or perspectives taken by a particular research group might be used as means of filtering retrieved information.

5. *Monitoring* newly available information in a given field of study is important for researchers and many other professionals. It is important for these people to be aware of recent developments within their specializations. This is achieved through regularly checking the contents pages of relevant journals, use of alerting and announcement services such as ZETOC, and informally through colleagues and discussion lists. The precise nature of the monitoring varies between individuals and depends on the field of study.

6. Finally, *extracting* refers to the process of interacting with located information objects to acquire the information which is specifically relevant to the task in

hand. This will include going through journal papers, reports, books and even sources such as reliable blogs and wikis to extract pertinent information.

KUHLTHAU'S MODEL OF INFORMATION SEEKING

Kuhlthau developed her model of information seeking from studies of library users. She considers that information seeking distinguishes between information sought, search methods and relevance judgements. The search starts when an individual becomes aware of an information need, or an anomalous state of knowledge (ASK), as Belkin (1980) has termed it – that is, a knowledge gap. At this early stage in the information-seeking process, the information seeker concentrates efforts on understanding what is sought and relating this to existing knowledge. The next step, selection, requires the selection of a topic to be investigated. This is followed by the gathering of information on the general subject area so that the information seeker has sufficient information about the topic area to be able to focus on the exact information need required to resolve the anomalous state of knowledge. In these early stages, as the information seeker still seeks to understand the subject area it may well be difficult to present a query in a manner with which an information retrieval system can cope. Eventually the information seeker has sufficient knowledge of the topic and its general area to be able to formulate an information need. He or she will have an appreciation of the required information and will concentrate on its collection. At this stage effective interaction between information seeker and information source should take place, provided that there is a reasonable match between the user's formulation of their information need and the system design. Finally the presentation stage is where the retrieved information and it used for the necessary task.

WILSON'S MODEL OF INFORMATION-SEEKING BEHAVIOUR

Arguably the person who has developed and extended most models of information seeking is Tom Wilson, who has developed a series of increasingly refined models of information behaviour over the last 25 years. Wilson criticized his initial models on the grounds that they were little more than maps of the area of information behaviour and indicated gaps in research. As such, they neither suggested causes for particular information behaviour nor offered hypotheses for testing. His later model is presented in Figure 4.2. This model has its focus on the person seeking information on a particular context. It recognizes that information seeking may be of different types which are specified as passive attention, passive search, active search and ongoing search. Further it recognizes that there is a feedback loop which is based upon the processing and use of information, a fact which relates clearly to the notion of ongoing search. This serves to recognize that

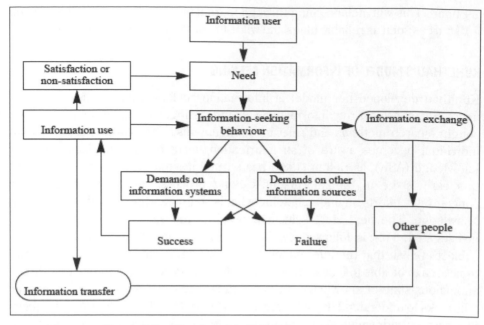

Figure 4.2 Wilson's model of information-seeking behaviour

an information-seeking episode is not necessarily a one-off completed activity but rather the searcher may continue the search at a later date. It further recognizes that, whilst it is often implicit that information seeking is an active process, there can also be passive acquisition of pertinent information. Early work on information seeking frequently referred to barriers to information access. In this model the term 'intervening variables' is coined. It is done to emphasize that their impact may be positive as well as the negative impact on information seeking suggested by the term 'barriers'. It can be seen from the diagram that these variables can be of several types relating to the source, the searcher and the context. Case (2002) suggests that the term 'activating mechanisms' can be viewed as motivators of the information-seeking process. Importantly this model introduces theories from outside library and information science which may explain information seekers' behaviour. It is proposed that the psychology theory of stressing/coping may offer a means of explaining what some information needs prompt information seeking more than others. It is argued that risk/reward theory (from consumer research) may explain why some information sources are more used than others and finally social learning theory (again from psychology) may be used to explain why people may or may not seek information successfully.

DERVIN'S PERSPECTIVE ON INFORMATION SEEKING

Finally, we consider briefly the model associated with Brenda Dervin. This model makes a bridge between models and theories since there are some who view her 'sense making' as a theory rather than a model. Dervin herself refers to this as a set of assumptions, a theoretical perspective and a methodological approach which is designed so that information can be perceived as a tool to enable humans to make sense of a particular reality. Sense making is implemented through four components, namely situation, gap, outcome and bridge. A situation in time and space defines the context within which information is sought to help resolve a problem. The gap refers to the distance between contextual situation in which the information seeker finds themselves and the desired outcome. The outcome is the result of the sense-making process and the bridge is the means by which the information seeker closes the gap between current and desired situation. This highly generalized view of information seeking has been developed by Dervin over a number of years as a result of numerous studies of information seeking by differing groups of users in different contexts. Subsequently it has served as the basis for information-seeking behaviour research by many other researchers.

CHATMAN'S THEORY OF INFORMATION POVERTY

Most of the theories applied to information behaviour have been borrowed from one or other of sociology, psychology or communication studies. One theory which has emerged within the field itself is the theory of information poverty developed by Chatman. Whilst it has emerged from within the field, it has clearly borrowed from elsewhere. This theory provides an interesting illustration of a middle-range theory inasmuch as, rather than seeking to provide a grand theory of all information behaviour, it offers an explanation of the information behaviour of people from information-poor communities, namely janitors, prisoners, single mothers undergoing work training and occupants of a retirement home. Her theory of information poverty consists of the following six propositions:

1. People who are defined as information-poor perceive themselves to be devoid of any sources that might help them.
2. Information poverty is partially associated with class distinction. That is, the condition of information poverty is influenced by outsiders who withhold privileged access to information.
3. Information poverty is determined by self-protective behaviours which are used in response to social norms.
4. Both secrecy and self-deception are self-protecting mechanisms due to a sense of mistrust regarding the interest or ability of others to provide useful information.

5. A decision to risk exposure about our true problems is often not taken due to a perception that negative consequences outweigh benefits.
6. New knowledge will be selectively introduced into the information world of poor people. A condition that influences this process is the relevance of that information in response to everyday problems and concerns.

Whilst the theory was derived from observations of the information seeking of markedly different groups of information-poor people, it is not without its critics who argue that the theory is not transferable to other information-poor groups, either in other countries or in the US where this work was undertaken.

CONCLUSION ON INFORMATION-SEEKING BEHAVIOUR

It has been pointed out by numerous authors that Zipf's Principle of Least Effort might function as a paradigm within which research into information-seeking behaviour might be undertaken. Zipf was a philologist who analysed the statistical distribution of words within texts. Unsurprisingly, he showed that some words were more heavily used than others. In part he explained this by arguing that authors used words which were at hand (in other words, had been used recently); that is, they were the words which could be used with least effort, there was no need to think of alternatives. Case argues that this principle of least effort is seen in various places in the information world and cites the so-called '80–20 rule' by which 20 per cent of books account for 80 per cent of loans from libraries. Further, he reminds us that another expression of the Principle of Least Effort is Mooers' Law, that:

> An information retrieval system will tend not to be used whenever it is more painful and troublesome for a customer to have information than for him not to have it.

This serves as a powerful reminder that IR systems must be made as simple to use as possible.

THE PROCESSES OF INDEXING AND SEARCHING

These processes are generally performed by people, though computers are playing an increasingly important part in both; indexers are guided by systems developed to improve the consistency of indexing whilst search systems may contain some automatic processing intended to aid the searcher. It has long been the case that some indexing is done entirely automatically, whether it is the straightforward generation of computer-generated (see Chapter 11) or more complex automatic indexing algorithms. The role of humans in both indexing and searching can be thought of as involving the three stages:

Familiarization → Analysis → Translation

INDEXING

Indexing is the process whereby subject metadata can be added to information objects or their surrogates to support more effective and efficient retrieval.

The only totally adequate indication of the content of a document is the document in its entirety. Any other indications of document content, such as classification notation or alphabetical subject terms are partial representations of content; they are surrogates for document content.

The aim of the three stages of indexing is to represent the subject content of a document as accurately as possible within the indexing language(s) of the particular knowledge system, bearing in minds the needs of the projected users of the system. Different users will have different needs; for example a health knowledge system developed for use by health professionals such as doctors and nurses will probably use a different indexing language from one designed for use by the general public. Whilst the doctor might refer to 'rubella', it is more likely that a member of the general public will refer to 'German measles'. The representation of document content might be referred to by different authors as a *document profile* or a *document surrogate*. The steps in the creating the document surrogate are now examined.

Step 1 – Familiarization

The first step involves the indexer becoming conversant with the subject matter of the document to be indexed. Documents are composed of words, and indexers and searchers use words to represent or convey concepts. However, at this stage it is important for the indexer to identify the concepts that are represented by the words. In order to achieve good consistent indexing, the indexer must have a thorough appreciation of the structure of the subject and the nature of the contribution that the document is making to the advancement of knowledge within the particular discipline. From time to time the indexer may need to consult external reference sources in order to achieve a sufficient understanding of the document for effective indexing. Certainly it will always be necessary for the indexer to examine the document content, concentrating particularly on those parts of the document which offer clues about its content; title, contents page, chapter and section headings, introduction, conclusions, abstracts and author-assigned keywords.

Step 2 – Analysis

The second step towards constructing the representation of document content involves the identification of the concepts within the documents which are sufficiently important to the document to merit indexing. For example, consider a book entitled *Wills and Probate* which has sections on making a will, executors, administration of an estate, pension, tax, house ownership, grants and intestacy, amongst others. Usually it is possible to identify a central theme in a document and produce a document summary based upon this central theme. Frequently, but not always, the author will have attempted to do this when writing the document title, which is why the title is often useful to the indexer. However, the indexer must be aware of the author or editor who uses an attention-seeking or amusing title; well-known examples include articles on catalogues with the titles 'How golden is your retriever?' and 'On the care and construction of white elephants'! Clearly the indexer must represent the central theme of the document in its surrogate but the extent to which subsidiary themes are to be presented in the surrogate will vary depending upon both the intended group of users and the particular environment. In determining whether or not to include a particular concept in the surrogate, the indexer will often find it useful to ask the question, 'Would a searcher find this document useful if seeking information on this concept?'

It is helpful to have such guidelines concerning the types, range and number of concepts to be indexed but often this will be left to the discretion of the indexer. Many traditional indexing approaches have sought to find an indexing term which is co-extensive with the document being indexed; that is, the scope of the indexing term and the document are similar. For example for the book on wills and probate, it would not be adequate to index the book with the term 'wills' alone as the book is also about probate.

Note that the term 'analysis' has been used here in its restrictive meaning. Some authors use 'analysis' to apply to all processes associated with the construction of a document surrogate of any kind. In this definition analysis subsumes all of the processes associated with indexing, cataloguing, classification and abstracting.

Step 3 – Translation

Having determined the concepts chosen to represent the document, these concepts must be translated into the controlled index language(s) used in the system. This involves representing the chosen concepts in the terminology of the appropriate subject headings, thesaurus and classification scheme in use in the given retrieval system. For example, if it had been decided that the subject of a document is 'Social conflict and educational change in England and France between 1789 and 1948', then it might be decided that this is represented by a classification number such as 942.073 or the terms:

Education
History
Social conflict
England
France

As another example, if it has been determined that the document is about 'Radioactivity in surface and coastal waters of the British Isles', this might be translated into the thesaurus terms:

Water pollutants
Radioactive materials
British Isles

or the classification number 629.1680941.

It must be remembered that the indexing takes place with a particular user population in mind and this is taken into account both by the indexer and by the creator(s) of the controlled vocabulary which has been created for use in the particular system. Thus it is quite possible that the same document will be indexed with different terms for different audiences. This does not mean that one or other indexer is right or wrong; it simply means that the concept of 'user warrant' is at play.

Finally, it should be noted that there are many different approaches to indexing. This is inevitable not only for reasons of history, indexer preference and organizational procedures but also because different situations require different approaches.

SEARCHING

Indexing and searching are complementary. The searcher uses the document surrogate created by the indexer as a basis for searching but the searcher does not come to the search process with any knowledge of specific document surrogates. Nevertheless, the search process involves the same three steps as the indexing process, as shown below.

Step 1 – Familiarization

As far as possible the searcher should have a clear view of the objective of the retrieval process. Whilst this seems an obvious statement, there are instances when the searcher is not fully aware of what can or might be retrieved. Two common examples are where:

1. The searcher is an information professional seeking to identify information or documents on behalf of someone else. Here, familiarization can be partially achieved by conducting a reference interview with the end-user. The reference interview should ascertain a clear subject profile and also other characteristics of the required information, such as constraints of language, time period and intellectual level. The intermediary also needs to be conversant with the sources to be searched.

2. The searcher is an information consumer, possibly approaching the search in some ignorance of their real needs or the literature that might be available. Some degree of ignorance or uncertainty of this type is not unusual; indeed it could be argued that it is the norm, otherwise why would the searcher be seeking the information in the first place? Belkin has referred to this as the searcher having an 'anomalous state of knowledge'; that is to say that the searcher is aware of the need for some information but is not exactly able to specify what that information is.

Step 2 – Analysis

When the aim of the search is as clear as possible the next step is to analyse the concepts in the information need. Sometimes, particularly for a straightforward search in a printed index, it will be sufficient to establish these concepts in the searcher's mind. On other occasions, where the search must be specified with a number of interacting concepts and other parameters, it will be necessary to write the concepts down. For example, if information is required on 'primary education' and this is a search term in a database, then the search profile merely involves the term 'primary education'. If, however, the searcher seeks information on 'Recovering hydrogen from coal tar in a continuous electrofluid reactor' and is only interested in reports, books or periodical articles that provide a review of the subject since 1990 and are written only in English, then the search profile will be much more complex. Building a search profile has much in common with building a document surrogate when indexing. The search profile will comprise a series of search keys representing subjects and other characteristics of the search requirements that together indicate the scope and nature of the search.

Step 3 – Translation

Translation of the concepts in a search profile will involve reference to a thesaurus, classification scheme or list of subject headings which has been used in the indexing of documents in the collection to be searched. Many computer-based systems make this process semi-automatic and terms can be selected from online search aids. If such tools are not available, consultation of the inverted file of the database may be a useful source of potential search terms. Alternatively it would be helpful to use reference tools within the discipline as a source of potential search terms. The quality of translation depends considerably on the support that is available in the system being searched. In a printed index, guidance on indexing practices is useful. In computer-based systems, there will be a range of facilities which support searching of different parts of the records, including assigned subject terms, abstracts and the natural language text of the document. The development of a search profile is often an evolutionary process and some of the approaches are described in the next section of this chapter.

Finally, it is essential to remember that successful information retrieval not only depends upon the effectiveness of indexing and searching in a single source. Most searchers need to use multiple information sources and knowledge structures to locate the required information and documents. This means that, even if individual sources have been carefully indexed, through the use of controlled vocabularies, a searcher using several sources (each of which has been indexed using a different controlled vocabulary) still has to negotiate a complex maze of different subject terms and subject relationships. Selection of the appropriate sources is key: no amount of searching a source that does not provide access to the information sought will produce a positive outcome.

INFORMATION SEEKING

Information seeking is frequently characterized as being either browsing or searching. Borgman et al. (1995) define browsing as an interactive process of skimming over information and selecting choices. Browsing is the ability to navigate through information space looking for information of interest. It relies upon recognition of patterns of words rather than the matching of search terms against the documents or document surrogates in a database. Browsing is likely to be particularly effective in seeking information when the topic sought is ill-defined. Browsing has increased in importance with the emergence of the Web, which, through its links between pages, has facilitated browsing. Browsing is generally preferred to information searching when:

- the information need cannot be clearly defined
- the cognitive burden of browsing is less than that of searching
- the system facilitates browsing through its available features.

The focus of this book is on the structuring of knowledge for targeted retrieval and so browsing is not considered further. A brief introduction to types of browsing and tools which support browsing is provided in Chapter 7 of Large, Tedd and Hartley (1999). It must also be acknowledged that users will browse in

113

systems that are designed for targeted information retrieval and that many episodes of information seeking utilize a mixture of both browsing and seeking.

INFORMATION SEARCHING

In contrast to browsing, information searching requires the more structured and targeted search for information which meets pre-determined criteria. These criteria are determined through the process outlined in the previous section of this chapter. Targeted information searching can be seen as consisting of one or other of three types of search, namely known-item searches, factual searches and subject searches. A *known-item search* is one where the searcher requires the location of an already-known item; typically this might be a search in an OPAC for a book of which the author and/or title are known. A *factual search* is a search for a piece of factual information such as the time of trains from Manchester to London or the boiling point of ethyl alcohol. A *subject search* is a search for information on a particular topic which the searcher may be able to define only partially. Typically the last type of search is the most complex, not only because it is one in which the exact requirements may not be specified but also because the searcher is unlikely to know exactly what is there to be retrieved and consequently cannot be certain how successful a search has been. With a subject search, the searcher is aiming to:

- retrieve sufficient relevant information

and avoid:

- retrieving too much information
- retrieving too much irrelevant information
- retrieving too little information.

REFINEMENT OF SEARCH STRATEGIES

Whilst all too many searchers simply enter a few keywords and assume the results are the best available, an important feature of information searching in an electronic environment is the interactive nature of the searching; that is to say that the searcher can amend the search in the light of results achieved. Frequently this will involve broadening the scope of the search if insufficient information is retrieved or narrowing the search if the initial foray into the database has retrieved too much information.

Search-broadening tactics seek to maximize the amount of relevant information retrieved without increasing too much the amount of irrelevant material which is retrieved; this is referred to as increasing the recall (see Chapter 10). Search output can be increased by replacing one or more search terms with a more general term or even by removing a term from the search criteria. Search criteria can be made less constraining by reducing the requirements for items to be retrieved in which the search terms are present close to each other. Finally, the number of information objects retrieved can be increased by removing any search criteria such as language constraints.

Search-narrowing tactics seek to reduce the amount of information retrieved. Ideally this is achieved by reducing the number of irrelevant items retrieved and thereby increasing the precision of the search (see Chapter 10 for details on search precision). Search output can be reduced by replacing a search term with a more specific term, by placing limits such as language or time period on the search or by making the search criteria more demanding by requiring that search terms are closer together; for example, replacing a search for items containing the terms 'information' and 'retrieval' with a search for items containing the phrase 'information retrieval'. Finally, a search might be narrowed by requiring a sought term to appear in a specified part of the retrieval item; for example, the title, the descriptor or the URL.

Five types of search strategies have been proposed:

1. *Briefsearch* – a 'quick and dirty search' – is a single-search formulation, normally a Boolean combination of terms, to retrieve a few relevant items (see Figure 4.3). It is the fastest and simplest strategy. This strategy is used to:
   - retrieve a particular document known to be relevant to the problem
   - get a rough idea of what a database contains on a given topic
   - retrieve a few items to examine the index terms which may later be used to formulate a search profile for a more precise search.
2. *Building blocks* – the most commonly used approach to searching, as shown in the example in Figure 4.4. Each of the concepts of a search profile are represented by a series of synonyms, near-synonyms, narrower terms from a hierarchy or appropriate related terms. The terms representing each concept are grouped by Boolean OR and then the sum totals of each facet are linked together by Boolean AND. The relevance of the retrieved material is examined and the search profile amended, using the tactics noted above to achieve an acceptable outcome.
3. *Successive facets strategy* constructs each facet one at a time, successively as needed, as shown in Figure 4.5. At each step each new facet is intersected with the previous result. This approach can be used:
   - if you suspect that ANDing all the facets will retrieve too few or no items
   - if you suspect that one facet is ambiguous in meaning.
4. *Pairwise facets* – the facets are ANDed a pair at a time instead of all together, as illustrated in Figure 4.6. Consider this approach:

– if it is thought that all facets are well defined, each with a sizeable literature, roughly equivalent in relevancy and specificity of definition of the search problem

– if it is considered that the intersection of all the facets will result in zero postings.

5. *Citation pearl growing* moves from high precision towards increasing the number of items retrieved in the search (see Figure 4.7). A known highly pertinent document is used to select search terms to be formulated into a search profile. (This can often be achieved using Briefsearch.) The resulting set is examined and further search terms identified and added to the search profile and the search repeated. This process can be cycled until sufficient information has been retrieved. This can be a fairly complex and time-consuming process but it may be useful when:

– the terminology of the subject is not well known

– the searcher cannot use a thesaurus or other word list to help create the search profile.

Search topic: Chinese blue and white porcelain

ss Chinese and blue and white and porcelain
1 2763 chinese
2 6539 blue
3 9734 white
4 538 porcelain
5 2 chinese and blue and white and porcelain

Figure 4.3   Briefsearch

INFORMATION CONSUMERS AND SEARCHING

In line with the information consumer perspective and taking a lead from consumer behaviour models, Rowley proposes a typology of information searching based on the level of involvement in the search task, and the balance between habit and decision making in a given context, as shown in Figure 4.8. This model suggests an alternative way of categorizing search approaches, each of which might be effective for specific contexts. Importantly, this model rejects the notion that there is one best practice model of searching, and argues that the most appropriate approach to searching depends on the purpose of the search.

Search topic: Redundant churches in East Anglia

   ss redundant or disused
1   22 redundant
2   35 disused
3   43 redundant or disused

   ss church? or chapel?
4   165 church?
5   54 chapel?
6   187 church? or chapel?

   ss east(w)anglia or norfolk or suffolk or cambrid? or esssx
7   5634 east
8   15 anglia
9   18 east(w)anglia
10 68 norfolk
11 57 suffolk
12 155 cambrid?
13 96 essex
14 284 east(w)anglia or norfolk or suffolk or cambrid? or essex

   3 and 6 and 14
15 3 and 6 and 14

Notice particularly the third block, a topic – East Anglia and its constituent counties. Listing them all in a search is laborious, and often overlooked by inexperienced searchers. The truncation of Cambridgeshire cuts down both the drudgery and the chance of error. 'East' could probably have been omitted without ill-effect, as Anglia is not often used except in this combination.

Figure 4.4 Building blocks strategy

Search topic: Sheltered housing for old people

   ss sheltered(w)housing
1   44 sheltered
2   3166 housing
3   34 sheltered and housing

   ss old or elderly
4   5054 old
5   654 elderly
6   5233 old or elderly

   3 and 6
7   22 3 and 6

However, it is only the old and the disabled, and predominantly the former, who need sheltered housing. Examination of the results of set 3 (i.e. omitting old and elderly from the search) should reveal that most of the titles will be potentially relevant to some extent. The second facet would therefore be better omitted from the search specification.

Figure 4.5 Successive facets strategy

Search topic: Satellites in weather forecasting

   ss satellite? and weather
1 264 satellite?
2 756 weather
3 16 satellite? and weather

   forecasting
4 538 forecasting

   1 and 4
5 11 1 and 4

   3 and 4
6 11 3 and 4

The first pair of facets (satellite? and weather) gives slightly higher recall than the second pair (satellite? and forecasting).

Figure 4.6 Pairwise facets strategy

A Briefsearch has retrieved from ERIC the following item, which is known to be relevant:

EJ521883 PS524404
The Role of Emotion in Children's Understanding and Emotional Reactions to Marital Conflict.
Crockenberg, Susan; Forgays, Deborah Kirby
Merrill-Palmer Quarterly; v42 n1 pp. 22–47 Jan 1996
Theme issue topic: 'Conflicts in Families and Between Children; Advances in Theory and Research.'
ISSN: 0272-930X
Available from: UMI
Language: English
Document Type: RESEARCH REPORT (143); JOURNAL ARTICLE (080)
Journal Announcement:CIJAUG96
Abstract: Tested a process model for the impact of children's exposure to marital conflict on their behavior and children's negative emotional reactions to fathers independently predicted children's behavioral adjustment. (MDM)
Descriptors: *Adjustment (to Environment); *Child Behavior; Conflict Resolution; *Emotional Response; *Family Problems; *Models; Predictor Variables; Sex Differences; *Young Children
Identifiers: Marital Discord

Selected major (starred) descriptors can be used as the basis for further searches. By checking them against the ERIC Thesaurus, additional semantically related terms will be suggested for building blocks.

Figure 4.7 Citation pearl growing

CURRENT AWARENESS AND RETROSPECTIVE SEARCHES

An important distinction in subject searches is between those which are undertaken to update knowledge on a topic (current awareness searches) and retrospective searches which seek to find out sufficient information to solve a problem. Current awareness searches involve the updating of a person's

	High-involvement search task	Low-involvement search task
Decision making (the choice of source and strategy)	*Complex searching* – uses range of sources and search strategies; for example, bibliographic search, when a comprehensive collection of literature is required from across the Web, or the compilation of a bibliographic database, etc.	*Limited* searching – explores some alternatives; for example, keeping up to date, as in scanning electronic and print sources for new developments at work, or finding new products for leisure purposes
Habit (the use of frequently consulted or convenient sources)	*Quality searching* identifies one tried and-tested source the searcher must be convinced that this is right; for example, a search for facts, addresses, etc. (as a quick reference source) or for a database of artefacts in a museum	*Lazy searching* – takes what the searcher finds first – no evaluation; for example, browsing, talking to friends, using an available and simple public access terminal

Figure 4.8 **Typology of information seeking**
Source: Rowley, 1999

knowledge by regularly running the search profile against known relevant sources, whilst retrospective searches are undertaken when a person wishes to acquire knowledge on a given topic. Various commercial databases allow a searcher to store a profile (that is, a search statement) of their subject interests. Each time the database is updated, the profile is run against the newly added material and the searcher is notified of items which match the profile. A variant on this is the ZETOC service offered from MIMAS (<http://zetoc.mimas.ac.uk/>). ZETOC is based on the content pages of the 16,000 journals received by the British Library. A ZETOC user can specify those journals of interest. When a new issue is received by the British Library, the ZETOC service ensures that those users who have indicated an interest in that journal receive an e-mail of its contents page. A more recent variant of current awareness is offered by RSS feeds. RSS stands for Really Simple Syndication – a family of web-feed formats which provides a means of keeping abreast of developments by arranging for news feeds to be sent to a piece of software on a PC/laptop known as a 'newsreader' or 'aggregator'.

USABILITY

The term 'user-friendly' is overworked and now rendered almost meaningless. Its sole value is to remind us that, as well as being effective, it is important that a system is as easy to use as is possible for the intended audience. It is important not to forget Mooers' Law which tells us that:

119

An information retrieval system will tend not to be used whenever it is more painful and troublesome for a customer to have information than for him not to have it.

(Chu, 2003, p. 10)

It is more useful to think in terms of the usability of an information retrieval system. The International Standards Organization (ISO), in a document on software quality, suggests that usability is:

A set of attributes that bear on the effort needed for use, and on the individual assessment of such use, by a stated or implied set of users.

(ISO, 1991)

Whilst more recently in its guidance on usability, it has defined usability as:

The extent to which a product can be used by specified users to achieve specified goals with effectiveness, efficiency and satisfaction in a specified context of use.

(ISO, 1998)

The web usability expert, Jakob Nielsen, tells us that usability is a 'quality attribute that assesses how easy user interfaces are to use'. He then elaborates by arguing that usability has five components, namely:

1. *learnability* – how easy is it for users to accomplish basic tasks the first time they encounter the design?
2. *efficiency* – once users have learned the design, how quickly can they perform tasks?
3. *memorability* – when users return to the design after a period of not using it, how easily can they re-establish proficiency?
4. *errors* – how many errors do users make, how severe are these errors, and how easily can they recover from the errors?
5. *satisfaction* – how pleasant is it to use the design?

(<http://www.useit.com/alertbox/20030825.html>)

There are various guidelines intended to promote good interface design and usability. The best known are those of Schneiderman and Nielsen, respectively. Schneiderman's eight golden rules are:

1. *Strive for consistency* – Consistent sequences of actions should be required in similar situations; identical terminology should be used in prompts, menus and help screens; and consistent commands should be employed throughout.
2. *Enable frequent users to use shortcuts* – As the frequency of use increases, so do users' desires to reduce the number of interactions and to increase the pace of interaction. Abbreviations, function keys, hidden commands and macro facilities are very helpful to the expert user.

3. *Offer informative feedback* – For every operator action, there should be some feedback. For frequent and minor actions, the response can be modest, while for infrequent and major actions, the response should be more substantial.

4. *Design dialogues to yield closure* – Sequences of actions should be organized into groups, with a beginning, middle and end. The informative feedback at the completion of a group of actions gives the operators the satisfaction of accomplishment, a sense of relief, the signal to drop contingency plans and options from their minds, and an indication that the way is clear to prepare for the next group of actions.

5. *Offer simple error handling* As far as possible, design the system so the user cannot make a serious error. If an error can be made, the system should be able to detect the error and offer simple, comprehensible mechanisms for handling the error.

6. *Permit easy reversal of actions* – This feature relieves anxiety, since the user knows that errors can be undone; it thus encourages exploration of unfamiliar options. The unit of reversibility may be a single action, a data entry, or a complete group of actions.

7. *Support internal locus of control* – Experienced operators strongly desire the sense that they are in charge of the system and that the system responds to their actions. Design the system to make users the initiators of actions rather than the responders.

8. *Reduce short-term memory load* – The limitation of human information processing in short-term memory requires that displays be kept simple, multiple page displays consolidated, window motion frequency reduced, and sufficient training time allotted for codes, mnemonics, and sequences of actions.

(Schneiderman and Plaisant, 2005)

Nielsen refers to his 10 usability heuristics, or rules of thumb. These offer the following guidance:

1. *Visibility of system status* – The system should always keep users informed about what is going on, through appropriate feedback within reasonable time

2. *Match between system and real world* – The system should speak users' language, with words, phrases and concepts familiar to the user rather than system-oriented terms. Real-world conventions should be followed, making information appear in a natural and logical order.

3. *User control and freedom* – Users often choose system functions by mistake and will need a clearly marked 'emergency exit' to leave the unwanted state without having to go through an extended dialogue. Support undo and redo.

4. *Consistency and standards* – Users should not have to wonder whether different words, situations, or actions mean the same thing. Follow platform conventions.

5. *Error prevention* – It is important to have helpful error messages but it is even better to have a careful design which prevents a problem from occurring in the first place. Either eliminate error-prone conditions or check for them and present users with a confirmation option before they commit to action.
6. *Recognition rather than recall* – Minimize the user's memory load by making objects, actions and options visible. The user should not have to remember information from one part of the dialogue to another. Instructions for use of the system should be visible or easily retrievable whenever appropriate.
7. *Flexibility and efficiency of use* – Accelerators, unseen by the novice user, may often speed up the interaction for the expert user such that the system can cater for both inexperienced and experienced users. Allow users to tailor frequent actions.
8. *Aesthetic and minimalist design* – Dialogues should not contain information which is irrelevant or rarely needed. Every extra unit of information in a dialogue competes with the relevant units of information and diminishes their relative visibility.
9. *Help users recognize, diagnose and recover from errors* – Error messages should be expressed in plain language (no codes), precisely indicate the problem and constructively suggest a solution.
10. *Help and documentation* – Even though it is better if the systems can be used without documentation, it may be necessary to provide help and document-ation. Any such information should be easy to search, focused on the user's task, list concrete steps to be carried out and not be too large.

(Nielsen, n.d.)

These guidelines and heuristics provide a framework both for good design and for testing systems. The importance of usability is emphasized by some recent research concerning OPACs. Fast and Campbell have demonstrated that users prefer the familiarity of search engines over OPACs even though they are well aware of the superior quality control associated with resources located via OPACs rather than on the Web (Fast and Campbell, 2004). Similarly Hartley and Booth (2006) have reported that users who cannot master a new system rapidly will soon revert to a familiar system.

SUMMARY

Knowledge is organized so that it can be located, retrieved and used when needed as easily as possible; that is to say that the entire purpose of the techniques explored in this book is to enable users of IR systems to retrieve required knowledge as readily as possible. In this chapter, we have considered the users of these systems. In particular, we have explored some of the many models of information seeking which researchers in this area have developed. These include the models and theories attributed to Ellis, Kuhlthau, Wilson and Dervin. The processes of indexing and searching both have the three stages of familiarization, analysis and translation. A section on information seeking outlines different search strategies, and suggests that the most appropriate search strategy may be dependent on the context. The final section discusses the importance of the usability of a system and reviews some guidelines for how the usability of information retrieval systems can be enhanced.

REVIEW QUESTIONS

1. In what ways has information access changed in the last 10 years according to Nicholas et al. (2006)?
2. What are the 10 myths of information-seeking research?
3. What are the six steps in the Ellis model of information-seeking behaviour?
4. Explain the Wilson model of information behaviour.
5. What do you understand by the term 'sense making'? How does sense making contribute to our understanding of information seeking?
6. Outline the similarities between the processes of indexing and searching.
7. What are the five well-known approaches to search strategy?
8. Outline Rowley's typology of information-seeking behaviour.
9. What do you understand by the term 'usability'?
10. What are Schneiderman's eight golden rules for maximizing usability of a system?

REFERENCES AND FURTHER READING

Belkin, N.J. (1980) Anomalous states of knowledge as a basis for information retrieval. *Canadian Journal of Information Science*, 5, 133–43.

Borgman, C., Hirsch, S.G., Walker, V.A. and Gallagher, A.L. (1995) Children's search behavior on browsing and keyword online catalogs: the Science Library Catalog Project. *Journal of the American Society for Information Science and Technology*, **46** (9), 663–84.

Case, D.O. (2002) *Looking for Information: A survey of research on information seeking, needs and behaviour.* 2nd edn 2007, London: Academic Press.

Chatman, E.A. (1996) The impoverished life-world of outsiders. *Journal of the American Society for Information Science*, **47** (3), 193–206.

Chu, H. (2003) *Information Representation and Retrieval in the Digital Age.* Medford NJ: Information Today for the American Society of Information Science and Technology.

Dervin, B. (1992) From the mind's eye of the user: the sense-making qualitative-quantitative methodology. In J.D. Glazier and R.R. Powell, *Qualitative Research in Information Management*, pp. 61–84. Englewood CO: Libraries Unlimited.

Ellis, D. (1989) A behavioural approach to information retrieval system design. *Journal of Documentation*, **45** (3), 171–212.

Fast, K.V. and Campbell, D.G. (2004) 'I still like Google': university student perceptions of searching OPACs and the Web. In L. Schamber and C.L. Barry, *ASIST 2004, Proceedings of the 67th ASIST Annual Meeting*, pp. 138–46.

Hartley, R.J. and Booth, H. (2006) Users and union catalogues. *Journal of Librarianship and Information Science*, **38** (1), 7–20.

International Standards Organization (ISO) (1991) *Software Engineering Product Quality* (ISO 9126). Geneva: ISO.

International Standards Organization (ISO) (1998) *Guidance on Usability* (ISO 9241-11). Geneva: ISO.

Kuhlthau, C. (1993) *Seeking Meaning*. Norwood NJ: Ablex.

Large, A., Tedd, L.A. and Hartley, R.J. (1999) *Information Seeking in the Online Age: Principles and practice*. London: Bowker Saur. (See Chapter 2 on information-seeking behaviour and Chapter 7 on browsing.)

Nicholas, D., Huntington, P., Williams, P., and Dobrowski, T. (2006) The digital information consumer. In A. Spink and C. Cole (eds) *New Directions in Human Information Behaviour*, pp 203–28. Dordrecht: Springer.

Nielsen, J. (n.d.) *Jakob's Law of the Web User Experience*. Available at <http://www.useit.com/alertbox/9605.html> [accessed 11 November 2006].

Nielsen, J. (n.d.) *Ten Usability Heuristics*. Available at <http://www.useit.com/papers/heuristic/heuristic_list.html> [accessed 26 December 2006].

Rowley, J.E. (1999) Towards a consumer perspective on information behaviour research. *Information Services and Use*, **19**, 289–98.

Rowley, J.E. (2006) *Information Marketing*, 2nd edn. Aldershot: Ashgate.

Schneiderman, B. and Plaisant, C. (2005) *Designing the User Interface: Strategies for effective human–computer interaction*, 4th edn. Boston MA and London: Addison-Wesley.

Spink, A. and Cole, C. (eds) (2006) *New Directions in Human Information Behaviour*. Dordrecht: Springer.

Wilson, T.D. (1999) Information behaviour models. *Journal of Documentation*, **55** (3), 249–70.

5   Subjects as access points

INTRODUCTION

The primary focus of this chapter is on indexing languages that are used to represent subjects. Accordingly the chapter starts by exploring the concept of a subject. Next, the types of indexing languages and some of the key features of indexing languages are introduced. Several significant sections then explore the construction of controlled indexing languages and thesauri. Finally, the chapter presents a review of the searching facilities that support subject access to information. At the end of this chapter you will:

- recognize the complexities associated with deciding what a document is 'about'
- understand the difference between natural and controlled indexing and searching languages
- be able to explain the key features of information retrieval systems such as specificity and exhaustivity
- be aware of the challenges associated with using words to represent subjects
- be aware of how relationships between terms and concepts can be represented in thesauri
- be familiar with the commonly available facilities embedded in online searching systems and search engines.

APPROACHES TO SUBJECT RETRIEVAL

Users often approach information sources not with names in mind, but with a question that requires an answer or a topic for study. Users seek documents or information concerned with a particular subject. This is a common approach to information sources and, in order to provide for it, the document or document representation must include enough data to ensure that items on specific subjects are retrieved.

What is a specific subject? A rabbit is a rabbit; but is it? Europeans will have in mind the European rabbit, Americans the cottontail; they belong to different genera. A rabbit is a concrete entity – that is, we can see it and pick it up (preferably not by its ears) and define it by its physical characteristics (long ears, furry, weighs around a kilogram) and behaviour (hopping movement, digs burrows, breeds freely). Abstract concepts can be more difficult to pin down. Some are fairly straightforward, like 'music' (encyclopaedia definition: 'the organized movement of sounds through a continuum of time'); some, like 'geography' ('the science that deals with the distribution and arrangement of all the elements of the earth's surface') look straightforward until we think of the vast scope of the subject; while the concept of 'games' defies definition – the philosopher Wittgenstein concluded after a long study that the subject could only be defined through its examples. Not only may subjects be in themselves difficult to define, we must remember that they do not exist in isolation in the way that named entities do. If we are looking for information on William Shakespeare, Mount Everest or Microsoft, we can be sure when we have found it that we have come to the right place as these are all 'classes of one'. Common subjects, on the other hand, form networks of conceptual relationships with other subjects. A student seeking information on sustainability may not be sure whether they are seeking information in the business or the environmental science literature. An amateur photographer seeking information on flash guns may search under either of the terms 'photography' or 'cameras'. Any system of subject retrieval must then have a mechanism for directing users to other, closely related subjects.

'ABOUTNESS'

Information retrieval is in general concerned with what an information object is *about* rather than what it *means*; whilst this is important for texts it is even more important in the context of images, such as paintings.

What is meaning? One point of view holds that that meaning is inferential: a scientific paper may be *about* a statistical correlation between tobacco smoking and lung cancer; what it *means* is that the one may cause the other. Another argument states that indexers should adopt a neutral position and not attempt to impose upon the reader their views on what a document means. There is also the point of view – grounded in literary theory – that meaning is interactive (and to that extent subjective), the result of the interaction between the text and the individual reader. Perhaps the most powerful argument against indexers attempting to represent the meaning of documents is economic: it would simply take too long to do. A trained indexer can grasp what a document is about by scanning it rapidly. The algorithms for computer searching can use combinations of the words used in a document, a citation or an abstract to achieve an adequate representation of what it is about. To attempt to extract the meaning of a document would involve close and expert analysis.

What a document is about can certainly be established by a human indexer, but now that cheap online storage and retrieval of full text are commonplace, the value of human indexing has been questioned. We shall revisit the debate about the difference between computer-based indexing and searching and human indexing later, but at this point it is useful to observe that a key element in this debate is the extent to which the words in a document can be taken as a representation of what the document is about. Fairthorne offered the following example that illustrates this issue:

> *Moby Dick* is about a whale, *Othello* is about a handkerchief, and about other things. The difficulties are to identify which of the things mentioned refer to relevant topics, and how to deal with topics of the document that are not mentioned explicitly ...
>
> Parts of the document are not always what the entire document is about, nor is a document usually about the sum of the things it mentions.
>
> (Fairthorne, 1969, p. 79)

In other words, this paragraph has just mentioned a whale and a handkerchief, but nobody would suggest that it is *about* those things. It is the human indexer's job to ensure that a document's overall topic and, perhaps, its major constituent themes are adequately represented. Some argue that even this is not straightforward, and that there are a number of different ways of understanding 'aboutness'. Some writers suggest that it is easier to consider the question: 'What is the document for?'. In addition, determination of the subjects of non-textual information packages can pose even more difficulties, and the challenges vary from one medium to another. For example, for a film, the title may provide a clue as to what the film is about. With art works another option is to identify the theme (for example, a country garden) or to enumerate objects or scenes within the work (such as the Tower of London, or elephants).

In recent years there has been a considerable growth of interest in image retrieval (see Chapter 9). Image retrieval can be based on metadata (such as the creator, date or locations), associated text, including human-assigned descriptors, or image characteristics such as colour, texture, and shape. Image retrieval systems are used to create records about images, and often include subject keywords drawn from a controlled language. Content-based image retrieval systems seek to achieve automatic indexing of images based on attributes of the images that can be used for retrieval, such as the depiction of a particular event, the presence of one or more persons or objects, and the presence of a specific location.

TYPES OF INDEXING AND SEARCHING LANGUAGES

An indexing language can be defined as the terms or codes that might be used as access points in an index. A searching language can be defined as the terms that are used by a searcher when specifying a search requirement. If the terms or codes are assigned by an indexer when a database is created, then the indexing language is used in indexing. The same terms or codes may also be used as access points to records during searching. While the indexing language may be distinct from the searching language, clearly, if retrieval is to be successful, the two must be closely related. Indexing languages may be of two different types: controlled indexing languages (or assigned-term systems) and natural indexing languages (or derived-term systems). Each of these is briefly discussed below.

CONTROLLED INDEXING LANGUAGES (ASSIGNED-TERM SYSTEMS)

With these languages a person controls the terms that are used as index terms.

Controlled indexing languages may be used for names and other labels but much emphasis is placed upon languages with terms that describe subjects. Normally an authority list identifies the terms that may be assigned. Indexing involves a person assigning terms from this list to specific documents on the basis of subjective interpretations of the concepts in the document; in this process the indexer exercises some intellectual discrimination in choosing appropriate terms.

There are two types of subject-based controlled indexing languages: alphabetical indexing languages and classification schemes. In alphabetical indexing languages, such as are recorded in thesauri and subject headings lists, subject terms are the alphabetical names of subjects. Control is exercised over which terms are used, and relationships between terms are indicated, but the terms themselves are ordinary words. In classification schemes each subject is represented by a code or notation. Classification schemes are particularly concerned to place subjects in a framework that crystallizes their relationships, one to another. More generally though, classification is implicit in all indexing. A document in which content is wholly or partially specified in the index term RABBITS is thereby classed with other documents to which the same specification has been applied. Controlled indexing languages take the process of classification one stage further, by displaying semantic links – between rabbits and hares, for example. Formal enumerative bibliographic classification schemes, such as the Dewey Decimal Classification and the Library of Congress Classification, display

128

these relationships in a systematic manner. They are able, in addition, through their notation to exclude particular connotations of meaning: thus DDC's 599.322 denotes rabbits as zoological entities, but not as pets (which would be 636.9322).

Thesauri have always been features of the document management systems and bibliographic databases that have been designed to manage larger collections. They are increasingly featuring in a wide range of database and networked applications. Thesauri typically show the controlled indexing term, with related, narrower and broader terms, as shown in Figure 5.5. They may be displayed in a window during search strategy formulation, to aid a user in the selection of terms. Often terms can be selected from the thesaurus listing simply by clicking on them. Hypertext links in thesauri listings can be used to move between different occurrences of the same term in the list. Another application of thesauri is as a basis for automatic indexing. Related applications of thesauri are in the creation of semantic nets and semantic knowledge bases.

NATURAL INDEXING LANGUAGES (UNCONTROLLED OR DERIVED-TERM SYSTEMS)

These languages are not really a distinct or stable language in their own right, but rather are the 'natural' or ordinary language of the document being indexed. Strictly, natural language systems are only one type of derived-term system. A derived-term system is one where all descriptors are taken from the document being indexed. Thus, author indexes, title indexes and citation indexes, as well as natural language subject indexes, are derived-term systems. Any terms that appear in the document may be candidates for index terms. Emphasis has traditionally been on the terms in titles and abstracts, but increasingly the full text of the document is used as the basis for indexing. Natural language indexing using the full text of the document may be very detailed, and in some systems some mechanism for deciding which terms are the most important in the indexing of a given document may be appropriate. Such mechanisms are often based upon statistical analysis of the relative frequency of term occurrence.

Natural language indexing can be executed by a human indexer, or automatically by the computer. The computer might index every term in the document, apart from a limited stop-list of very common terms, or may only index those terms that have been listed in a computer-held thesaurus.

Natural language indexing and controlled language indexing are used extensively in many information retrieval applications. The dilemma facing systems designers is that to offer anything other than natural language indexing in the context of the huge databanks available through the Internet would be prohibitively expensive. On the other hand, controlled language indexing is seen as valuable in a supportive environment for inexperienced users because they do not need to navigate all the variations inherent in natural language. Significant effort is being directed towards the development of system interfaces that manage this variability, either implicitly or explicitly, on behalf of the user. Many databases include terms from controlled indexing languages (often including both alphabetical indexing languages and classification schemes) and also support searching on the text of the record, thus covering all options.

The relative merits of controlled and uncontrolled indexing languages are summarized in Figure 5.1.

Advantages of uncontrolled indexing languages

- Low input cost
- Full database contents searchable
- No human indexing errors
- No delay in incorporating new terms
- High specificity gives precision. Excels in retrieving individual terms – names of persons, organizations, etc.
- Exhaustivity gives potential for high recall. Does not apply to title-only databases

Disadvantages of uncontrolled indexing languages

- Greater burden on searcher, particularly with terms that have many synonyms and several species
- Information implicitly but not overtly included in text may be missed
- Absence of specific to generic linkage
- Vocabulary of discipline must be known
- Syntax problems. Danger of false drops through incorrect term association
- Exhaustivity may lead to loss of precision

Advantages of controlled vocabulary indexing languages

- Eases searching through:
  - control of synonyms and near-synonyms
  - qualification of homographs
  - provision of scope notes
  - display of broader, narrower and related terms
  - expresses concepts elusive in free text
- Overcomes syntax problems with compound terms and other devices
- Normally avoids precision loss through over-exhaustivity
- Maps areas of knowledge

Disadvantages of controlled vocabulary indexing languages

- High input cost
- Possible inadequacies of coverage
- Human error in interpretation and application of index terms can occur
- Possibly out-of-date vocabulary
- Difficulty of systematically incorporating all relevant relationships between terms
- Lack of specificity
- Lack of exhaustivity
- The searcher needs to become acquainted with the language

Figure 5.1 Comparison of uncontrolled and controlled indexing languages
Based on: Mulvaney, 1994

FEATURES OF RETRIEVAL SYSTEMS

This section explains some fundamental concepts that are central to the design and application of indexing languages; an understanding of these concepts is an essential basis for the further development of our discussion of indexing languages; these concepts also impact on searching options and strategies. These features need to be considered alongside other aspects of interface design that contribute to the usability of information retrieval systems, as discussed in Chapter 4.

EXHAUSTIVITY AND CONTENT SPECIFICATION

It was suggested above that indexes attempt to specify content by means of single words or phrases. Clearly, the whole of the subject content cannot be specified by anything less than the complete text. Indexing has to try to sum up the salient points, while ignoring the non-essentials. This can be done at a number of levels, which, even though they are presented here as distinct strata, form a continuum. Exhaustivity of indexing is the name given to the depth of indexing which it is the policy of a given indexing system to employ. Exhaustivity is therefore a management decision. The level of exhaustivity at which a system operates can either be built into the system (for example, by restricting the number of fields available for index terms), or it can be controlled operationally, by giving instructions to indexers.

Summarization refers to the process of conveying the overall subject content of a document in a single word or a short phrase or structured heading: for example, Rabbits, or Breeds of Rabbits or Rabbits – Breeds. Indexing at the level of summarization is commonly applied to graphic material – photographs and the like – which convey information perceptually; and also, particularly, to books, which normally have their own detailed indexing systems in the form of back-of-book indexes and contents lists. Library catalogues and published bibliographies are nearly always indexed at the level of summarization.

A second level of exhaustivity is found in many databases that are indexes to collections or to journal literature, and select the most significant subjects in the text – often around six to twelve controlled descriptors. In addition, the words in the title and abstract are available for searching. Contents lists operate at this level.

Even more exhaustive are back-of-book type indexes: indexes to individual documents, which should list every subject discussed in the text (Figure 5.2). The ultimate level of exhaustivity is provided by the text itself. In full-text retrieval systems any word or phrase is potentially available for searching. (Most systems have a stop-list of very common words that have not been indexed and cannot therefore be retrieved.) At this point we have a concordance rather than an index.

131

1. Summarization

Subject heading: Indexing (supplied by the Library of Congress)
Title: Indexing books
Series title: Chicago guides to writing, editing and publishing

2. Most significant subjects

Chapter headings:
    1. Introduction to book indexing
    2. The author and the index
    3. Getting started
    4. Structure of entries
    5. Arrangement of entries
    6. Special concerns in indexing
    7. Names, names, names
    8. Format and layout of the index
    9. Editing the index
    10. Tools for indexing

3. Detailed subject specification

Index (part):
    abbreviations
        alphabetizing, 130
        of company names, 177, 180–81
        cross-references to and from, 102, 128–29
        double-posting, 130
        explaining, 12, 70
        spelling out, 128–29
        for states in U.S., 175–76
    access points
        converting subentries to main headings, 219
        main heading as primary, 77, 217
        multiple, with double posting, 75, 76, 221
    accuracy of entries, assessing, 230
    acronyms
        alphabetizing, 130

4. The full text

Text: Alphabetizing of abbreviations and acronyms

Abbreviations and acronyms should be alphabetized in the same way as the other entries in the index, whether letter-by-letter or word-by-word. They are not usually alphabetized as if they were spelled out. An exception that many publishers allow is that the abbreviation U.S. may be alphabetized as though spelled out. This allows a term like U.S. Bureau of Reclamation to interfile with other entries such as United States Coast Guard.

Figure 5.2   **Levels of exhaustivity within a single work**
Based on: Mulvaney, 1994

SPECIFICITY

Specificity is an aspect of controlled language systems. It refers to the vocabulary of the system, and denotes the extent to which we are able to specify subject content when indexing. The Dewey Decimal Classification, for example, specifies rabbits as domestic animals at class 636.9322. This class is, however, unable to specify individual breeds of rabbit: there are no subclasses for lop-eared or angora rabbits or any other breed. Neither can this class distinguish between rabbits kept as pets and rabbits grown for meat or for their fur. A specialist manual on keeping pet angora rabbits has to be classed with all other works on rabbits as domestic animals. This clearly makes searching less precise, as the searcher has to sift through a number of marginally relevant items all classed in the same category. A higher level of specificity thus improves the precision of a search; that is, its ability to sift out unwanted material. Special systems (that is, systems confined to one subject area or other field) often use differential levels of specificity. Topics that are central to the subject field are indexed at a higher level of specificity than peripheral subjects. For example, if Domestic Animals is a system's principal subject field, it would be quite likely to make specific provision for the various breeds of rabbit. If the subject field is something remote, however, there might be no specific provision even for rabbits: we might have to include them under a more general term, like Pets.

Specificity and exhaustivity are related to the extent that in practice greater exhaustivity needs to be matched by greater specificity in the indexing terms. Most book indexes, for example, are both specific and exhaustive. The combination of specificity and exhaustivity is often referred to as *depth of indexing*.

COMPLEX TOPICS

A final set of definitions concerns the way in which complex topics are handled. A document may not be simply about a single subject such as rabbits or apples or chess; it may very well deal with some more precise aspect, like breeds of rabbits, or the effect of pre-storage heat treatment on the shelf life of apples. The traditional method of dealing with complex topics has been to encapsulate as much of the topic as possible into a single subject string or heading; *Rabbits – Breeds* for example, or *Apples – Shelf Life – Effect of – Heat Treatment*. Indexes that make use of these types of subject access strings are known as *pre-coordinate indexes*, because the concepts that comprise a heading are strung together or coordinated by the indexer in advance of any searches that may be carried out. Due to their multiple components, these indexes require elaborate rules for the consistent construction of the subject strings; the use of pre-coordination in subject headings is discussed further in Chapter 7. Because of this lack of flexibility many systems employ a quite different method of handling complex topics. The alternative is to represent the subject of a document by a number of one-concept terms and the searcher is able to combine as many or as few of them as are required, using Boolean or other search logic: for example, Child Attitudes and Marital Conflict. Systems employing this method of indexing and searching are known as *post-coordinate* systems. The earliest of these systems were card-based, using specialized stationery and other equipment, but nearly all systems in use today are computerized. Because the coordination of search terms is conducted by the searcher, the support for such coordination, as embedded in the search facilities offered in different information retrieval contexts, needs to be considered alongside any indexing that is based on the human or computer assignment of terms.

THE FUNDAMENTALS OF CONTROLLED INDEXING LANGUAGES

As discussed above, human indexing is normally executed with the aid of a list of indexing terms, or an indexing language. This list controls the terms that indexers are permitted to apply to a document, and offers guidance on the forms of terms, the conceptual relationships between terms, and the scope and meaning of specific terms. These lists are described as thesauri or subject headings lists. Both of these types of tools are important in searching. If a database has been indexed using a controlled indexing language then using index terms from that language in the search process is likely to enhance the quality of the search output. Further, thesauri may also be used in various ways in computer-based indexing.

This section discusses the fundamentals of vocabulary control, relying heavily on *BS 8724-2: 2005 Structured Vocabulary for Information Retrieval – Guide – Part 2: Thesauri*. This guide offers significant practical advice in the creation of thesauri, but in doing so it also implicitly identifies the issues that need to be addressed in vocabulary control. Thus whilst, much of the section that follows provides information on the way in which index languages can be designed, it also indicates many of the problems that arise with uncontrolled languages. The issues that are addressed here, in relation to thesauri, also need to be considered, variously, in the context of classification schemes, ontologies and lists of subject headings, as discussed in later chapters in this part of the book.

How does vocabulary control work in practice? Consider the term wagon. The word has a plural, *wagons*, as well as an alternative spelling, *waggon(s)*, so we must opt for one or other spelling, and have some means of alerting those who use other forms of the word. A wagon is a wheeled vehicle for transporting freight; but it can denote a range of specific vehicles, according to whether the transport is by rail or by road and, if the latter, whether it has an engine or is drawn by a horse or tractor. So for indexing purposes we may well wish to limit our definition to just one of these. If road vehicles, they are often known by their manufacturer's name and perhaps the name of the model. Finally, there are other words or phrases whose meaning is synonymous or nearly so (*cart, truck, lorry*), or which belong to the same category but have a wider or narrower meaning (*road vehicle, pick-up truck*), or which, while not strictly belonging to the same category, are an essential part of the definition of a wagon (*freight, goods*).

From this example it is possible to see that there are four key ways in which the terms used in indexing can be usefully controlled:

1. the form of a term (such as its grammatical form and spelling) is controlled
2. a choice is made between two or more synonyms or near synonyms to express the same concept
3. a decision is made on whether to admit proper names
4. a term may be deliberately restricted in meaning to the most effective meaning for the purposes of the thesaurus.

In addition, the semantic relationships between terms may be defined for the purpose of the indexing language.

At its simplest, a controlled language is a list (known as a *thesaurus*) of permitted terms and terms which are semantically related. All controlled languages have an alphabetical display sequence. There may also be a *systematic* (classified) sequence, either as the principal display or as an adjunct to the alphabetical display. The fundamental aim of a thesaurus is to guide the indexer and searcher to choose the same term for a concept.

The vocabulary of a controlled language comprises the available terms used for indexing. Such terms describe the content of a document, and so are called *preferred terms* or *descriptors* or *controlled terms*. These may be words, or they may be coded into the notation of a classification schedule, where the notation translates the concepts behind the words. In either case, any relationships between the terms are fixed and permanent.

CONSTRUCTION OF DESCRIPTORS

Each preferred term included in a thesaurus should represent a single concept (or unit of thought). A concept may be expressed by a single-word term or a multi-word term.

The concepts represented by preferred terms are likely to fall into one of the following categories:

1. things and their physical parts: *birds, documents, mountain regions*
2. materials: *rubber, plastic, paint*
3. activities or processes: *glaciation, hairdressing, lubrication*
4. events or occurrences: *natural disasters, funerals, exhibitions*
5. properties of persons, things, materials or actions: *stability, confidence, speed*

6. disciplines or subject fields: *philosophy, medicine, business studies, archaeology*
7. units of measurement: *minutes, kilometres*
8. types of people and organizations: *adults, nations, financial service organizations, nurses.*

Proper names may also be used where they are used for records about a place, object, person or organization.

If a candidate term does not conform to one of these types, it should not be used as it stands. In many cases, a term can be made to conform by being modified in accordance for controlling word forms. These rules are:

- Avoid **verbs**: use *cookery, opposition* not *cook, oppose.*
- Do not use attributes (**adjectives** or **adverbs**) on their own, but only to help define an entity: *yellow fever, fast food*; but not *yellow* or *fast* on their own.
- Very occasionally an attribute may be found on its own as a descriptor, if a noun is implied; for example, *baroque [style].*
- Avoid adjectives or adverbs of **degree**, unless they have a technical meaning: *small firms, very high frequency.*
- Use **nouns** and **noun phrases**, including adjectival and prepositional phrases as appropriate: *women workers, prisoners of war.*
- Use the **plural** number for 'count' nouns (how many?): *buildings, paintings*; also for substances or materials treated as a class with more than one member: *Plastics, Poisons.*
- Use **singular** for non-count nouns (how much?): *Snow, Painting* (notice that it is possible to use both singular and plural if their meanings are distinct), *physics* (which is not a plural!); also for parts of the body which occur singly: *mouth, respiratory system,* but *lips, lungs.*
- Use the most widely accepted **spelling**: *Romania,* not *Roumania.* However, 'widely accepted' begs the question: by whom? Some readers will already have noticed the UK (rather than US) English spellings of *archaeology* and *kilometres* above.
- Use **slang** or **jargon** only if well established and there is no acceptable alternative: *hippies* have been with us for long enough to become established (except that they now seem to be transforming themselves into *New Age travellers*).
- Use **abbreviations** and **acronyms** only if they are unambiguous and in common use within the subject field. Words like *radar* have ceased to be regarded as acronyms, and it saves space and time to list bodies such as *UNICEF* as acronyms; but *WHO* or *BP* can only lead to ambiguity and misunderstanding. Again, there are grey areas: *CD-ROMs? URLs?*
- Differentiate **homographs** by a qualifier within parentheses: *cranes (lifting equipment); cranes (birds).* Homographs have the same spelling but different

meanings. In a specialist thesaurus only one meaning might apply, and will be clear from the context.

- Use a **scope note (SN)** to exclude possible alternative meanings or where the meaning is not immediately apparent, or to instruct indexers how a term is to be used. A scope note clarifies the intended use of the term within the thesaurus. For example, for the term 'illuminations' the **SN** includes both the ornamental decoration and the illustrations in manuscripts, as well as in some early printed books, if done by hand.

- Do not **invert** phrases: *storage batteries* not *batteries, storage*. (This particular example also carries the risk of ambiguity.) The inversion rule is quite explicit. Compound terms, that is, multi-word concepts, have for many years been the bugbear of controlled language systems. The problem is whether to invert phrases and, if so, to what extent. In manually searched indexes, inversion brings a useful collocation, as the eye can run down a list from (say) *dogs* to *dogs, gun, dogs, sporting* or *dogs, working*. The problem is that this construction could be extended to *dogs, hot,* which would benefit nobody. Inverted headings are inherently unpredictable, and a distraction to searching. Today's rules of thesaurus construction presuppose computer-searched indexes, which with keyword access are indifferent to word order and are not intended for sequential searching.

Compound terms then should not be inverted. Other restrictions also apply, notably that they are to be avoided altogether if a noun phrase can be factorized down:

Garage doors	use instead	*Garages* AND *Doors*
Coal mining	use instead	*Coal* AND *Mining*
Animal behaviour	use instead	*Animals* AND *Behaviour*

Factorizing is used when each separate word retains its original meaning. Factorizing should not be used for terms where the original meaning has been lost (*Deck chairs*), where a different type of entity is denoted (*silk flowers*), where one term is used metaphorically (*elbow joints*) or where one or both terms are semantically empty on their own (*family problems*). Where compound topics like *coal mining* are admitted, they are in effect pre-coordinated terms, and are described as having a high *pre-coordination level*. Normal principles of thesaurus construction require compounds to be reduced to their constituent elements (for example, *coal mining* is retrieved by a Boolean search on *Coal* AND *Mining*).

Occasionally a single descriptor may pre-coordinate two or more concepts, as with *life satisfaction* (a search on *Life* AND *Satisfaction* would be likely to generate all manner of false coordinations); or *student evaluation of teacher performance* (to make it clear who is evaluating whom). *Child behaviour* is another instance. It could be factorized into *Children* AND *Behaviour* without loss of meaning; but the phrase is one that is widely used and understood, so that the convenience and precision of having a ready-made phrase could be considered to outweigh the disadvantage of making the vocabulary larger than is strictly necessary.

SEMANTIC RELATIONSHIPS

Next, semantic relationships must be considered. Semantic relationships between terms are, as their name implies, built into the meanings of the terms. They are permanent, in that they do not change according to whatever document is being indexed or searched. Semantic relationships are stable; that is, they remain constant within an indexing language and do not change to accommodate the indexing requirements of particular documents. In theory, they ought to be transferable between indexing languages, but in practice other considerations (for example, disciplinary bias and the degree of specificity required) often militate against this. The rules govern the relationships in meaning between pairs of terms (for example *seas/oceans, legs/knees, food/diet*) – or more precisely how the meaning of the second word relates to the first. There are three basic types of relationship: equivalence, hierarchical and associative.

Equivalence relationships

Such a relationship exists where two or more terms are regarded as having the same meaning. One is the preferred term (descriptor); all others are non-preferred terms (non-descriptors). Non-preferred terms are indicated in a thesaurus by the instruction:

> *Non-preferred term* USE *Preferred term*
> Asses USE Donkeys

Under the preferred term is placed the reciprocal of this instruction (UF stands for 'use for'):

> *Preferred term*
>   UF *Non-preferred term*
> Donkeys
>   UF Asses

which serves as a check for both indexers and searchers.

The following subcategories of equivalence relationship have been distinguished:

1. *Synonyms.* These are terms that can be used interchangeably for indexing and searching purposes, even if they do not quite mean the same thing. There is a range of different kinds of synonyms. Some examples are:

Variant spellings, including stem variants, inverted word order and irregular plurals

Rumania USE Romania   Romania UF Roumania
Ground water USE Groundwater   Groundwater UF Ground water
Mouse USE Mice   Mice UF Mouse

Singulars and plurals are distinguished if the plural is irregular and would file a considerable distance away from the singular.

Selling USE Sale   Sale UF Selling
Sea food USE Seafood   Seafood UF Sea food

Variant names for emergent concepts

Notebook computers USE Laptop computers   Laptop computers UF Notebook computers

Popular names and scientific names

Rock roses USE Cistus   Cistus UF Rock roses

Common nouns and slang or jargon terms

Psychiatrists USE Shrinks   Shrinks UF Psychiatrists
Soluble coffee USE Instant coffee   Instant coffee UF Soluble coffee

2. *Quasi-synonyms.* These are terms whose meanings are different but overlap in ordinary usage, but are treated as synonymous for indexing purposes.

Deceleration USE Acceleration   Acceleration UF Deceleration
Softness USE Hardness   Hardness UF Softness

The above two examples are antonyms: they represent different viewpoints of the same property continuum. The following two examples might or might not be regarded as equivalent, depending on subject field:

Fostering USE Adoption   Adoption UF Fostering
Barley USE Cereals   Cereals UF Barley

These would only be regarded as synonymous if they were on the fringe of the subject field of the thesaurus, where the generic level is set rather higher than for central themes. A thesaurus on social welfare would almost certainly have *fostering RT adoption* (an associative relationship, RT standing for 'related term'), and one on agriculture would have *barley BT cereals* (a hierarchical relationship, BT standing for 'broader term'.) In these instances specific terms are being subsumed under a broader concept. This is known as 'upward posting': treating a narrower term as if it were equivalent to, rather than a species of, its broader term.

3. *Representation of complex concepts by a combination of terms*. Where a multi-word term is deemed to be unsuitable as a preferred term, but might be sought by some users, it may be represented by a combination of two or more preferred terms.

> Coal mining USE Coal + Mining
> B2B Marketplaces USE Internet + Trading

In a classification schedule synonyms are often shown in parentheses; for example, DDC's 796.334 Soccer (Association football). Quasi-synonyms may be shown by an inclusion note; for example, 796.33 Inflated ball driven by foot. Example: pushball – where Pushball is not given a specific place in the classification.

Hierarchical relationships

Here both terms are preferred terms and the scope of one of them falls completely within the scope of another. Indexers are able to select the most specific term available to index concepts within the document. Searchers can extend a search by transferring from a first access term to a broader (more general) or narrower (more specific) term. Hierarchical relationships are indicated by BT (broader term) and NT (narrower term); for example:

> Sparrows BT Birds   Birds NT Sparrows

There are three subcategories of hierarchical relationship:

1. *Generic* relationships identify the link between a class or category and its members or species; for example: *some* As are B; *all* Bs are A:

> Protest NT Rebellion   Rebellion BT Protest
> Reptiles NT Snakes   Snakes BT Reptiles

but not:

> Pets NT Budgerigars

Why does this not qualify? Because not all budgerigars are pets. Most hierarchies are unique (a snake is a reptile and not any other kind of living creature), but the next example is a *polyhierarchy* (as is the Brain example below).

Rocks NT Coal	Coal BT Rocks
Fossil fuels NT Coal	Coal BT Fossil fuels

2. *Hierarchical whole–part relationship*. This applies when the name of the part implies the name of its possessing whole:

Science NT Chemistry	Chemistry BT Science
Head NT Brain	Brain BT Head
Central nervous system NT Brain	Brain BT Central nervous system
Canada NT Ontario	Ontario BT Canada

but not:

Buildings NT Doors

A door is a necessary part of any building, but cars, railway carriages, etc., also have doors.

3. *Instance* (class-of-one) identifies the link between a general class of things or events and an individual instance of that class, often represented by a proper name.

Mountain regions NT Alps	Alps BT Mountain regions

Hierarchical relations *modulate*; that is, they move a step at a time through their hierarchy; for example:

Science NT Chemistry	Organic chemistry BT Chemistry
Chemistry NT Organic chemistry	Chemistry BT Science

and not, for example, Science NT Organic chemistry. If an intermediate step is omitted, there is a very real likelihood that a search will skip over potentially useful material.

In a classification schedule indentation is used to indicate hierarchical relationships, often with different typefaces. There may be a corresponding lengthening of the notation for more specific terms; but many bibliographic classification schemes either do this inconsistently (for example, DDC) or do not set out to do it at all, as with the LCC and Bliss Bibliographic Classification (BC2).

Associative relationships

This relationship is not easy to categorize. BS 8723-2: 2005 (p. 27) suggests:

The associative relationship covers associations between pairs of preferred terms which are not related hierarchically or by equivalence, but the terms are semantically or conceptually associated to such an extent that the link between them needs to be made explicit in the thesaurus, on the grounds that it may suggest additional or alternative terms for use in indexing or retrieval.

As with hierarchical relationships, both terms are descriptors. As already noted, *RT* (related term) is the thesaural symbol, and its reciprocal is the same. The following are typical:

Buildings RT Doors   Doors RT Buildings

This is the more usual kind of partitive relationship, where the part is not unique to the whole, and is therefore regarded as an associative relationship rather than as hierarchical.

One key kind of associative relationship is where there are two preferred terms with overlapping meanings, such that the terms are used interchangeability in some contexts, but not in others.

Boats RT Ships   Ships RT Boats

Other examples of associative linkage include:

- a discipline or field of study and the objects or phenomena studied:
  Forest RT Forestry
- an operation or process and its agent or instrument:
  Midwife RT Birth
- an action and the product of the action:
  Ploughing RT Furrows
- an action and its patient or target:
  Harvesting RT Crops
- a concept and its unit of measurement:
  Electrical power RT Watt

Classification schedules are by their nature set out hierarchically. There may occasionally be found references to associated topics in other parts of the schedule; for example, in DDC:

790   Recreational & performing arts
      Class the sociology of recreation in 306.48

There is often a temptation to enter RTs as BT/NT (broader term/narrower term). In some cases it is very difficult to determine whether a relationship should be entered as BT/NT or RT/RT. A rule of thumb is to check whether both terms belong to the same basic type (abstract or concrete entities). If they do not, the relationship cannot be hierarchical, and must be associative (if it is to be admitted at all): for example, Entomology is a discipline or science (an abstract entity), and cannot therefore belong to the same hierarchy as Insects (which are concrete entities).

Another temptation is to make RTs indiscriminately. The principle of RTs is that there must be an immediate and necessary relationship between the two terms. If the relationship is not direct or not necessary, then the terms either should not be related at all, or at best should be linked indirectly, through a third term. Consider the following:

Authors
 RT Books
  Publications
  Textbooks

Books and Textbooks are hierarchical to Publications. It would be enough therefore to make the one reference.

 Authors RT Publications

and let users find their own way if they wish to pursue the references through Publications NT Books and Books NT Textbooks. It is also tempting to link topics that are only indirectly connected; for example, by sharing a common BT. So there is little point in links such as Mice RT Hamsters, simply because they share the common BT Rodents.

USING FACET ANALYSIS TO ANALYSE AND REPRESENT RELATIONSHIPS

The simplest way to present a thesaurus is to arrange all the descriptors with their relationships into a single alphabetical sequence. Many thesauri are of this kind. However, much of the effectiveness of a thesaurus is lost if this alphabetical display is not backed up by means of some kind of systematic display. Because alphabetical order scatters subjects indiscriminately, it is not possible to obtain an overview of the way the subject matter of the thesaurus is structured. The most widely used technique for creating systematic displays is *facet analysis*. The resultant faceted classification can also be displayed to support indexing and searching.

Facet analysis involves:

1. A set of terms representing simple concepts; that is, the descriptors created by applying the rules of thesaurus construction.

143

2. The grouping of the terms into a number of mutually exclusive categories, called *facets*, using just one characteristic of division at a time.

3. Organizing the facets into a limited number of *fundamental categories*. These are generalized categories which can be adapted to any subject field, and define the role of a term within the overall scheme of the thesaurus. Some examples of fundamental categories are given in Figure 5.3.

In a working thesaurus these categories will inevitably be heavily adapted to the subject-matter in hand. The *Art and Architecture Thesaurus* (<www.getty. edu/vow/AATsearchpage.jsp>), for example, calls Concrete entities its Objects facet, and Time its Styles and Periods facet. The *Multilingual Egyptological Thesaurus* (213.132.220.88/ccer/apps/thesaurus) has an even more specialized list of facets: Acquisition; Present Location; Category; Provenance; Dating; Material; Technique; State of Preservation; Description; Language; Writing; Category of Text; Text Content; Divine Names; Royal Names.

4. In many cases, a notation will be required to fix the filing value of each term in a systematic sequence.

Entities
Abstract: *Archaeology, Kilometres, News*
Concrete:
    Naturally occurring: *Titanium*
    Living: *Birds*
    Man-made: *Paintings*
    Complex: Buildings
Properties (Attributes): *Speed, Elasticity*
Materials, Constituents: *Adhesives*
Parts: *Limbs, Doors*

Actions
Processes (internal, intransitive): *Glaciation*
Operations (external, transitive): *Marketing, Cookery*

Place (location, environment): *London*

Time: *Nineteenth century, Summer*

Figure 5.3   Examples of fundamental categories

DISPLAYING THE THESAURUS

The principal symbols denoting functions and relations have been described and used above. To recap, they are:

- SN: Scope note, defining or restricting the meaning of a word within the indexing language
- USE: The term preceding this symbol is a non-preferred term. The preferred term follows this symbol.
- UF: The reciprocal of USE. The term that follows this symbol is a non-preferred term.
- BT: The term that follows is a broader term – another preferred term, but having a more general meaning.
- NT: The term that follows is a narrower term – another preferred term, but having a more specific meaning.
- RT: The term that follows is a related term – another preferred term, having a meaning that is associated with the term preceding the symbol, but not one of the types described above.

By convention, the symbols are listed after each term in the above order. BS 8723-1: 2005 permits other symbols in addition to BT/NT if finer distinctions are considered necessary for denoting hierarchical relations:

- TT: the term that follows is the top term in the hierarchy to which the term preceding this symbol belongs
- BTG: broader term (generic)
- NTG: narrower term (generic)
- BTP: broader term (partitive)
- NTP: narrower term (partitive).

The use of language-free symbols, such as < for BT and > for NT, is also another option.

Figure 5.4 shows a typical thesaurus record according to BS 8723-2: 2005.

THESAURUS USE

As discussed earlier in this chapter, a controlled indexing language (such as that codified in a thesaurus) can be used in both indexing and searching. There are three basically different ways in which a thesaurus can be used:

1. *In indexing but not in searching*: this is the 'indexing thesaurus', where the database is mostly used for simple searching, often by less expert searchers. Retrieval is helped if the user is prompted for potentially relevant search terms. Some electronic systems will automatically map a user from the 'unpreferred' to the preferred term.
2. *In searching but not in indexing*: this is the 'searching thesaurus'. The thesaurus assists the searching of a free-text database by suggesting

Camera accessories

    CC: H002
    BT: photographic equipment
    NT: flash guns
              light meters
              tripods
    RT: cameras

Camera components
    CC: H006
    BT: cameras and camera components
    NT: camera lenses
              camera viewfinders

Camera lenses
    CC: H007
    BT: camera components

Camera viewfinders
    CC: H008
    BT: camera components

Cameras
    CC: H009
    BT: cameras and camera components
    NT: digital cameras
              film cameras
              instant picture cameras
              plate cameras
              reflex cameras
              special-purpose cameras
    RT: camera accessories
              photography

Colour
    CC: A204
    BT: optical properties

Contrast
    CC: A205
    BT: optical properties

Figure 5.4   Thesaurus entry consistent with BS 8723-2: 2005

additional search terms. This can be done automatically ('query expansion') if the thesaurus is available online. A searching thesaurus tends to provide a wider set of terms as entry vocabulary than a traditional thesaurus, and make greater use of automatic construction techniques. Many experienced searchers use a thesaurus when carrying out natural language searches, especially on full-text files. The thesaurus is used, not as a source of indexing terms, but as a reminder of semantically related terms to be added to a building block for searching.

3. *In both indexing and in searching*: this is the traditional way in which a thesaurus is used. The same thesaurus is used for indexing (by the database compilers) and for searching (by users who know how to use a thesaurus and have one available). This kind of use presumes expert searchers. In indexing or in searching, terms may be added to the descriptor list or to the search statement without the explicit knowledge of the indexer or searcher.

A thesaurus must be integrated into the systems in which indexing and searching take place. This is relatively straightforward in a printed thesaurus, in which the indexer or searcher simply consults the printed alphabetical or other displays of the thesaurus. However, most thesauri are used in electronic systems, and there are special considerations as to how this might be achieved. First and foremost, the thesaurus needs to be exported from the thesaurus management system that will be used for its creation and maintenance into the information retrieval system. In such applications there is a need both to be able to browse and search the thesauri and also to be able to use the thesaurus in a search. In order to be able to browse the thesaurus it is necessary to be able to:

- search for terms containing any word or character string
- move between related terms using hyperlinks
- switch between alternative display modes of the thesaurus.

In order to be able to use the thesaurus in the search, it is necessary to be able to:

- select one or more terms from a thesaurus for use in a search
- build a search statement by copying terms from the thesaurus
- select sub-trees from the thesaurus to be used in the search
- rely on the system substituting a preferred term when the searcher enters a non-preferred term.

In order to be able to use a thesaurus in indexing it is necessary to be able to:

- copy terms directly into an indexing form
- enter non-preferred terms and have them automatically converted to the corresponding preferred term, with a notification to the indexer
- submit possible new terms to the thesaurus editor.

Figure 5.5 shows extracts from searching under the term 'adolescents' in three different thesauri that are used to search various databases made available through CSA (the electronic collections resource, recently merged with the similar resource Proquest). The on-screen display invites the searcher to:

147

- *select thesaurus* – to specify the thesaurus that they wish to use
- *browse thesaurus* for – to indicate the search term
- *select display* – to choose between alphabetical index, hierarchy, and rotated index as the display format for the thesaurus.

There is also an option to mark terms in the display, and to combine them using either AND to narrow, or OR to broaden. Note, in particular, that the terms included in the three thesauri are different, and derive from the literature and subject discipline in which the concept of an 'adolescent' is being considered. Also note that the networks of relationships between terms are different. Note also that two of the listings give additional 'maintenance' information, such as when the term was added, and earlier terms that have been superseded. There is also a variation in the extent of use of scope notes between the different listings.

ASSIA Thesaurus
Adolescents [+]
    Use For
        Teenagers
    Broader Terms
        Children [+]
    Narrower Terms
        Autistic adolescents
        Behaviour disordered adolescents
        Blind adolescents
        Conduct disordered adolescents
        Deaf adolescents
        Developmentally disabled adolescents
        Disadvantaged adolescents
        Emotionally disturbed adolescents
        Gifted adolescents [+]
        Hearing impaired adolescents
        Hyperactive adolescents
        Learning disabled adolescents
        Low intelligence quotient adolescents
        Reading disabled adolescents [+]
        Runaway adolescents [+]
        Sexually abused adolescents
        Sick adolescents
        Special needs adolescents
        Violent adolescents
        Visually impaired adolescents
    Related Terms
        Students [+]
        Young people [+]

Sociological Indexing Terms
Adolescents
    Persons aged 13 to 17

Formerly (1963–1985) DC 014600, Adolescence/Adolescent/Adolescents
Use For
Teenage/Teenagers (1963–1985)
Teenage/Teenagers
Broader Terms
Age Groups [+]
The narrower terms listed below refer to groups with fixed age ranges, which are specified in their scope notes.
Added, 1986
Related Terms
Adolescent Development
The physiological, psychological, cognitive, and social growth of the individual from age 13 to 17
Adolescent Parents [+]
Parents aged 13 to 17 years
Added, 1992
Adolescent personality
Added, 2003
Children[+]
Persons aged 24 months to 12 years
Dating (Social)
Family Planning [+]
Family Relations
High School Students
Junior High School Students
Juvenile Delinquents
Juvenile Offenders
...

ERIC Thesaurus
Adolescents
Approximately 13–17 years of age
Use For
Adolescence
Teenagers
Broader Terms
Age groups
(Note: see also list of age-levelling Descriptors)
Related Terms
Adolescent attitudes
Attitudes of, not toward, adolescents
Adolescent behaviour
Behaviour of adolescents (Note: do not use for immature behaviour by those older than adolescents)
Adolescent development
Adolescent literature
Any reading material written primarily for, or read widely by, youth of secondary school age
Children
Aged birth through approximately 12 years
...

Figure 5.5 Comparison of extracts from three online thesauri

149

SEARCH FACILITIES

The first part of this chapter has examined the challenges associated with using subjects to access information and documents. We have observed that information retrieval systems have both natural language (based on the words in the document itself, including in electronic systems the metadata added by, for example, the web page creator, but sometimes selected automatically with the aid of a thesaurus) and controlled language indexing (based on words chosen to represent the document by human indexers). The relatively detailed consideration of the functions and design of thesauri, as a major category of controlled indexing and searching languages, has illustrated the challenges embedded in using words as subject access points. There are significant complexities in forms of words, meanings of words, and relationships between words and their underlying concepts to navigate. A key issue in such contexts is that the user does not know what documents are available and/or does not know the terms by which records can be retrieved. This complexity has led to the development of search engines and other online information retrieval systems that exhibit a number of search facilities designed to optimize the efficiency and effectiveness of searching processes. Although there are variations between systems, there is a standard range of search facilities that are used widely in many search engines, such as those used to search the Web (for example, Google and Yahoo!), the search engines in the websites of organizations (such as government agencies and on line retailers), and the search engines on the websites of electronic journal publishers, aggregators and abstracting and indexing services. Most of these facilities are used in the context of a web-based interface, although they were developed in the days of command-based online information retrieval systems, where the user needed to know the commands and to type them in as a series of instructions in order to make any progress whatsoever. Since these search facilities are fundamental to the experience of information searching they are reviewed here. First we briefly review the difference between basic and advanced search options, and then progress to consider search logics, and finally explore specific search facilities that support searching in text-based and networked environments.

BASIC AND ADVANCED SEARCH OPTIONS

Most organizations offer two different levels of search to support navigation of their websites and databases: basic search and advanced search. Figure 5.6 shows examples of basic search and advanced search for Blackwell's Synergy electronic journal collection, whilst Figure 5.7 (which we shall discuss in more detail later) shows the advanced search options for Google. These two figures show some basic differences between basic and advanced search options.

Basic or easy search

This invites the searcher to enter a word or a phrase, and then to click the Go or Search button. Sometimes the searcher is also invited to limit the search to certain categories of documents. For example, IngentaConnect's basic search allows the searcher to restrict the search to one of the following: electronic content; fax/Arial content; or journal or book title. On eBay the basic search can be restricted by location (countries in the European Union, or items within a specified distance of a given postcode), or by 'Show only' options (such as: Items listed with PayPal, Buy It Now Items, Item condition, and type of seller). Once some words are entered the search engine performs, using those words and applying one of the search logics discussed below, and any other algorithms built into the search engine. Basic search has three main functions:

- to support simple, novice searching
- to do a 'quick and dirty' search that pulls up some relevant documents
- to support browsing.

Advanced search

This typically prompts the user to enter a much wider range of criteria. For example, on the screen in Figure 5.6, it is possible to enter specific details of the journal article that is being sought, or to differentiate between searching for words in titles, abstracts or the full text of the document. There are also options for date limiting results, and formatting the display of results. Figure 5.7 shows that Google Advanced Search also allows a wide range of search options to be specified, including specifying precise combinations of words to be searched for, language, file format, location of occurrence of search terms within a web page, and usage rights. Significantly, the criteria that can be specified vary with the nature of the database being searched, although many of the search options outlined below are applicable in a wide variety of contexts. Advanced Search looks more complex than Basic Search, and the searcher normally has to choose to open the Advanced Search page. On first appearance the range of options available under Advanced Search can be daunting, but the application of just one or two criteria may be all that is necessary to achieve a much more targeted retrieval. Further, as with the Blackwell Synergy Advanced Search, if the searcher is conducting a 'known-item' search (say for a specific journal article, or for the web page of a specific organization), Advanced Search supports the rapid location of such an item.

Blackwell Synergy - My Synergy - Journals - Mozilla Firefox

File   Edit   View   History   Bookmarks   Tools   Help

Restore Down

GO ⊙

OCDE / OECD   **User name:**
Password:

Register | Forgotten Password | Athens/Institution Login

Synergy Home | Browse | Search | My Synergy | Books Online | Resources | About | Help

Blackwell
Synergy

Blackwell Synergy
Online journals for
learning, research
and professional
practice

Using Synergy

Welcome to *Blackwell Synergy*, the home
of over 1 million articles from over 850
journals.

Blackwell Publishing is now part of Wiley. For
more journals, online books and databases in
your subject area go to **WileyInterscience**.

Sign up for e-mail alerts

Should you ever require help please contact
the **helpdesk**.

Journals

Show: All Journals By Subject   ∨   Save settings

✚ Premium + Backfiles   ⦿ Premium access   ⦿ Partial access   [free] Free content
✔ Favorite Journal   ⬚ OnlineOpen

All Journals by Subject

⊞ **Business, Economics, Finance and Accounting**
⊞ **Construction, Engineering, Computing and Technology**
⊞ **Health Sciences**
⊞ **Humanities**
⊞ **Law and Criminology**
⊞ **Life and Physical Sciences**
⊞ **Mathematics and Statistics**
⊞ **Medicine**
⊞ **Social and Behavioral Sciences**
⊞ **The Arts**
⊞ **Veterinary Medicine, Animal Sciences, Agriculture and Aquaculture**

Quick Search

Search in all journals:

GO ⊙

▶ Advanced search
▶ Saved searches

Quick Link

Select a journal   ∨

Vol: **Issue:**   **Page:**

GO ⊙

▶ Try CrossRef search

Privacy Statement | Terms & Conditions | Contact | Help

Technology Partner — Atypon Systems, Inc.

Blackwell   Blackwell Synergy® is a Blackwell Publishing, Inc. registered trademark
Publishing   Partner of CrossRef, COUNTER, AGORA, HINARI and CARE

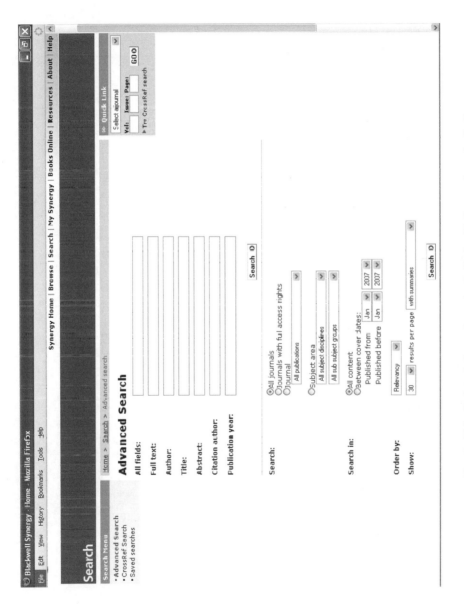

Figure 5.6 Basic and advanced searches in Blackwell's Synergy journal collection

Google Advanced Scholar Search - Mozilla Firefox

File Edit View Go Bookmarks Tools Help   scholar.google.com

Google
Scholar BETA

Advanced Scholar Search

Advanced Search Tips | About Google Scholar

Find articles

with **all** of the words

with the **exact phrase**

with **at least one** of the words

without the words

where my words occur   anywhere in the article ▸

10 results ▸   Search Scholar

Author   Return articles written by   e.g., "PJ Hayes" or McCarthy

Publication   Return articles published in   e.g., J Biol Chem or Nature

Date   Return articles published between   ____ — ____   e.g., 1996

Subject Areas

◉ Return articles in all subject areas.

○ Return only articles in the following subject areas:

☐ Biology, Life Sciences, and Environmental Science
☐ Business, Administration, Finance, and Economics
☐ Chemistry and Materials Science
☐ Engineering, Computer Science, and Mathematics
☐ Medicine, Pharmacology, and Veterinary Science
☐ Physics, Astronomy, and Planetary Science
☐ Social Sciences, Arts, and Humanities

©2007 Google

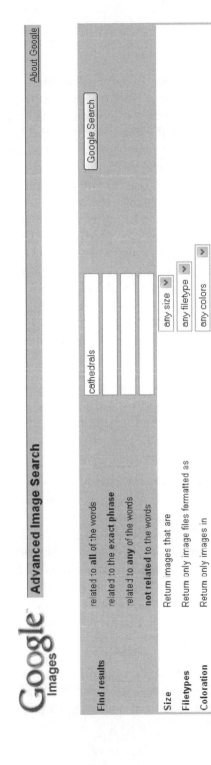

Figure 5.7   Advanced search in Google

155

SEARCH LOGICS

BOOLEAN SEARCH LOGIC

Search logic is the means of specifying combinations of terms that must be matched for successful retrieval. Boolean search logic is employed in searching most systems. It may be used to link terms from either controlled or natural indexing languages, or both. The logic is used to link the terms that describe the concepts present in the statement of the search. As many as 20 to 30 or more search terms may be linked together by search logic in order to frame the search statement. Search logic permits the inclusion in the search statement of all synonyms and related terms, and also specifies acceptable and unacceptable search-term combinations. Search strategies often need to be more complex with natural language terms, in order to accommodate all the potential spelling variations and near-synonyms. In an online search the search statements are evolved one at a time, and feedback is available at each stage. The searcher specifies a search statement and the computer responds with the number of relevant records. With this type of search facility, the search strategy can be refined to yield a satisfactory output.

The Boolean logic operators are AND, OR and NOT.

AND reduces the number of items retrieved:
    Children AND *Parents* retrieves items in which *both* terms occur.
OR increases the number of items retrieved:
    Children OR *Parents* retrieves items in which *either* term occurs.
NOT subtracts the second term from the first.
    Children NOT *Parents* retrieves items in which *only the first term* occurs.

The operators are subject to some variation. A few systems use AND NOT or ANDNOT. Also, operators may often be abbreviated, so that on Dialog and asterisk (*) can be used to represent AND and a plus sign (+) for OR.

It is common to use more than one operator in a search statement, as in for instance: *Children* AND *Parents* AND *Conflict* OR *Discord*. Once more than one operator has been introduced, the priority of execution needs to be considered. In the example above it is necessary to specify whether the search should be conducted as (*Children* AND *Parents* AND *Conflict*) OR *Discord* or as *Children* AND *Parents* AND (*Conflict* OR *Discord*). This latter is the expected order of execution, and must be specified by the use of parentheses.

The use of parentheses in formulating a search statement is often known as *nesting*. Each software package (or search service) has its own priority rules (for example, it may be stipulated that AND is always processed before OR), and successful searching depends on heeding these rules, and making appropriate use of parentheses. Nesting forces priority, and offers a clear specification from the searcher's perspective.

RELEVANCE RANKING AND BEST MATCH SEARCH LOGIC

A weakness of Boolean searching used on its own is that it returns straight hit-or-miss responses, and items that partially fulfil the search specifications are excluded. For example, a search on *Children* AND *Parents* AND (*Conflict* OR *Discord*) would not return items containing the terms *Parents* AND *Conflict* but not *Children*. Many search systems now relevance rank results by relevance, listing items matching any of the search terms, with the best matches first. This can be done in a variety of ways, for example:

> *Children* AND *Parents* AND *Conflict*
> *Children* AND *Parents* AND *Discord*
> *Children* AND *Conflict*
> *Children* AND *Discord*
> *Parents* AND *Conflict*
> *Parents* AND *Discord*
> *Children* AND *Parents*
> *Children*
> *Parents*
> *Conflict*
> *Discord*

A variation common in Web search engines is to use *implicit OR*, then relevance rank the results so that AND combinations are ranked before OR combinations, and adjacency before either. (This is one reason for the huge search sets generated by many simple Web searches.) The user could, for example, simply enter *Children Parents Conflict Discord*.

In most search statements it is possible to designate certain concepts as being more significant than their neighbours. In its role in formulating search profiles, weighted-term logic may be introduced either as a search logic in its own right, or as a means of reducing or ranking (relevancy ranking) the search output from a search whose basic logic is Boolean.

In an application where weighted-term logic is the primary search logic, each search term in a search profile is allocated a weight. These weights can be allocated by the searcher, but more commonly are allocated automatically. Automatic allocation of weights is usually based on the inverse frequency algorithm which weights terms in accordance with the inverse frequency of their occurrence in the database. Thus common words are not seen to be particularly valuable in uniquely identifying documents. A further refinement considers both the frequency and the positioning of the terms – that is, words in important positions (titles, headers, early in the document) are given a higher ranking than words appearing elsewhere. If the weights are assigned by the searcher, they are associated with a relevance rating on a document which is found containing that term as a search term. Search profiles combine terms and their weights in a simple sum, and items rated as suitable for retrieval must have weights that exceed a specified threshold weight. A simple Selective Dissemination of Information (SDI)-type profile showing the use of weighted-term logic is shown below:

Search description: The use of radioactive isotopes in measuring the productivity of soil.
A simple search profile (which does not explore all possible synonyms) might be:

8 *Soil*	4 *Plants*
7 *Radioisotopes*	3 *Food*
7 *Isotopes*	2 *Environment*
6 *Radioactive*	2 *Agriculture*
5 *Radiation*	1 *Productivity*
5 *Agricultural chemistry*	1 *Water*

A threshold weight appropriate to the specificity of the searcher's enquiry must be established. For instance, a threshold weight of 12 would retrieve documents with the following combinations of terms assigned, and these documents or records would be regarded as relevant:

Soil and *Plants*
Soil and *Radioisotopes*
Soil and Agricultural chemistry
Radioisotopes and *Agricultural chemistry*
Soil and Food and *Agriculture*

Documents with the following terms assigned would be rejected on the grounds that their combined weights from each of the terms identified in the records did not exceed the pre-selected threshold:

Productivity and *Water*
Food and *Soil*
Radioactive and *Agriculture*

Alternatively no threshold weight may be used, and then users will simply be presented with records in ranked order, and can make their own choice as to how far down the list they choose to scan.

Weighted-term search logic may also be used to supplement Boolean logic. Here weighted-term logic is a means of limiting or ranking the output from a search that has been conducted with the use of a search profile that was framed in terms of Boolean logic operators. In the search, and prior to display or printing, references or records are ranked according to the weighting that they achieve, and records with sufficiently high rankings will be deemed most relevant, and be selected for display or printing. In this application, relevancy ranking is most often achieved through an analysis of the number of occurrences of search terms or hits in the document.

The inverted indexes that need to be created to support Boolean searching and relevance ranking, respectively, are different. An inverted index may be stored in the form of a large matrix, with each row corresponding to an individual term, and each column to an individual record. A Boolean search simply requires that each of these cells in the matrix have a value of 1 or 0. A mechanism that uses some type of term-weighting scheme will require the cell of the matrix to have a value n, where n is the result of a more complicated function of a number of variables. These values may be calculated on the basis of term occurrences. Each record may be considered as a vector or sequence of values.

Automatic ranking can be achieved using one or more of a number of different algorithms. Traditional information retrieval systems variously use:

- *word document frequency* – the relative frequency of a query term in a document
- the *position of the query terms* within the document, such as their distance apart, and their order, whether they appear in key places such as the title or in headings, and how close they are to the beginning of the document.
- *inverted document frequency* – based on the relative frequency of a term in all documents – such that rarely occurring terms in the document set are preferred.

Web search engines use all of the above ranking algorithms, but also make use of a range of additional query-dependent factors and, also some query-independent factors. Query-dependent factors include:

- *emphasis on anchor text* – with terms in the anchor text being counted higher
- *language* – matching the language of the document to that of the query
- *geotargeting* – taking into account the location of the user and the pages.

Query-independent factors are used to determine the quality of a particular document. These include:

- *link popularity* – whereby the quality or authority of a document is measured according to its linking within the Web graph
- *directory hierarchy* – in which documents higher in a hierarchy are preferred
- *number of incoming links* – more incoming links mean that the document is treated as more important
- *click popularity* – in which documents visited by many users are preferred
- *up-to-dateness*, so that more current documents are preferred
- *document length* – such that documents that are neither too short or too long are preferred
- *file format* – such that there is a differentiation between, say, HTML, PDF and DOC documents
- *size of the website* – such that documents from a larger website are preferred.

OTHER COMMON SEARCH FACILITIES

Standard retrieval facilities are available in most information retrieval applications. These facilities cater for the uncertainty in document-based systems. In Web and Windows-based systems the options are likely to be embedded in pull-down menus, dialogue boxes and screen forms, with their boxes, buttons and check boxes. Command-based systems need a set of commands and the searches are executed through the use of these commands.

SET-UP FACILITIES

These facilities set up the environment in which the search will proceed and are therefore environment-dependent. Help and news are common, as well as connection facilities including logon and logoff facilities and security and user authentication (to restrict access to databases to users having access rights). Also, on the main menu at the start of a search there may be options to allow the searcher to control the screen display, to inform the user of any costs that they are incurring during the search, and to remind the user of any saved searches or alerts that have been set up. There may also be information about the search service, its databases and help and customer service arrangements. The selection of database may be a further preliminary, and information may be available on the databases, including content, pricing and update frequency. Navigation buttons are also important in supporting navigation between the different screens displayed during a search session.

SELECTING SEARCH TERMS

Identification of search terms can be assisted by the display of search-term, thesaurus or index listings. The display may show index or search terms and, sometimes, their number of postings.

ENTERING SEARCH TERMS

Once a search term has been selected it must be entered. This may merely involve clicking on the term in a search-term listing, typing the term in, or using the term as a component in a more complex search statement. The system responds by creating a set of 'hits' relating to documents indexed by those terms that have been entered, displaying brief details for each of those hits, as discussed below, and illustrated in Figure 5.8.

COMBINING SEARCH TERMS

Search terms may be combined into search statements with the aid of a search logic, as discussed earlier in this chapter. Figure 5.7, which shows advanced search options, illustrates some ways in which such logic may be embedded in a screen form. Boolean search logic or relevance ranking is common.

ENTERING PHRASES

Many search engines allow the user to enter a search phrase, such as *Purchasing Books on the Internet*. As discussed above the system will often treat this as an implicit OR search, although some search engines may process phrases as if each of the terms were linked together with AND. Thus the above phrase would be searched as: *Purchasing and Books and Internet*. Notice that this search statement assumes that 'linking' words such as *on* and *the* are automatically excluded from the search statement.

SPECIFYING SECTIONS OF DOCUMENTS OR FIELDS IN RECORDS TO BE SEARCHED

The ability to search for the occurrence of terms in a specific section of a document or in specific fields in a record facilitates more precise searching. For example, through the specification of whether a search might be conducted on a subject field or author field it may be possible to differentiate between documents on a person (say, *Shakespeare*) as subject and as author. In order to be able to specify appropriate field labels, it is necessary to know the fields in a given database and which fields are indexed for successful field-based searching. Often it may be possible to search on a combination of fields or sections.

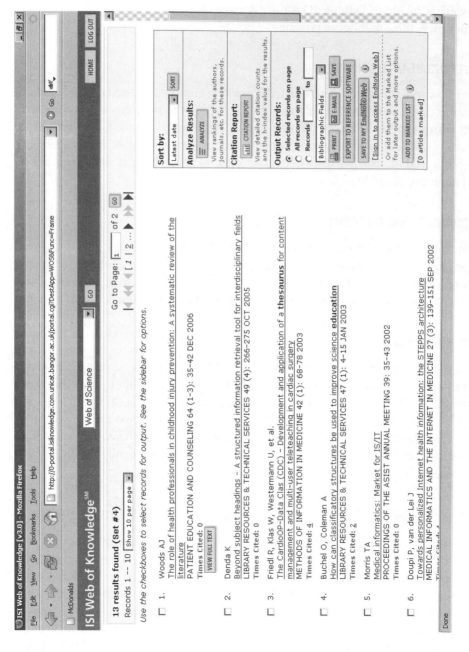

Figure 5.8 Output from a search on Web of Knowledge

TRUNCATION AND SEARCH-TERM STRINGS

Truncation supports searching on word stems. By using the truncation character at either end of a word, the system can be instructed to search for a string of characters, regardless of whether that string is a complete word. For example, if the user asks for a search on *Countr** this would retrieve records including words such as Country, Countries, Countryside and Countrywide. The use of truncation eliminates the need to specify each word variant, and thus simplifies search strategies. This is particularly useful in natural language information retrieval systems where word variations are uncontrolled.

The most basic truncation is right-hand truncation where characters to the right of the character string are ignored. Left-hand truncation can be useful in circumstances where a variety of prefixes might occur. This is particularly useful in searching chemical databases. For example, **Chloride* might retrieve records of 'chloride' with various prefixes. Truncation, or masking as it is called in this context, is sometimes also available in the middle of words. Here truncation can be useful to cater for alternative spellings. So, for example, *Na*ional* will search for records with National and Nacional. In order to control the array of word variants that might be retrieved as the result of a truncation, in some systems it is possible to specify the number of characters that are to appear after the truncated string. For example, *Employ???* might select terms with a maximum of three additional characters.

PROXIMITY, ADJACENCY AND CONTEXT SEARCHING

Often a subject is best described by a phrase of two, three or more words. Subjects such as Information Retrieval and Competitive Advantage need two words to describe them. It is useful if a search can be performed for such phrases. One obvious option is to search for the two words ANDed together; for example, *Information* AND *Retrieval*. This should retrieve records containing the phrase but will also retrieve other records where these two words appear, but where they do not appear next to each other. This method, then, only allows crude phrase searching.

Another option is to store such terms as phrases, possibly by inserting hyphens to mark phrases. Then, for example, *Information-Retrieval* would be stored as one term in the inverted file. This method is satisfactory but is primarily applicable to controlled indexing; phrases must be marked at input, and searchers must enter the term in exactly the form in which it was originally entered.

A more flexible option is the use of proximity operators. There are various different kinds of proximity operators. These can require that:

- two words appear next to each other; for example, *'Information Retrieval'*, *Information and Retrieval, Information* (N) *Retrieval*, depending on the search system

- two words appear within the same field, sentence or paragraph; for example, *Browser* SAME *Microsoft**
- two words be within a specified distance of one another; for example, *Information* (W.3) *Retrieval*
- two words be within a specified distance of one another, with the maximum number of words to come between the two words set by the system: for example, in Dialog DataStar, *Peanuts* NEXT *Asthma* will find the two terms within a five-word range of each other. The operator NEAR is found on many Web search engines.

RANGE SEARCHING AND LIMITING

Range searching is particularly useful when selecting records on the basis of numeric or date fields. They might, for instance, be used to select records according to a price field or publication date field. Fairly common range operators are:

EQ equal to	LT less than
NE not equal to	NL not less than
GT greater than	W within the limits
NG not greater than	OL outside the limits.

There are also a number of other ways in which the search output can be limited; by, for example, specifying searching in a specified field, or in a given language or type of document format.

DISPLAYING SEARCH OR RESULTS SETS

The display shows the user how many documents, search terms and references were found, and thereby indicates whether it might be appropriate to further refine the search (see Figure 5.8).

DISPLAYING RECORDS

Once a successful search has been performed, details relating to each hit are displayed. The format for the display may be quite different for different types of search engines. For example, for Web search engines the elements of the display mainly show the context in which the search words have been located and the Web address of the page that has been identified by the search. For bibliographic databases a short record which includes identified fields, such as the author, article title and citation will typically be displayed. OPACs often first display one-line records and then allow the user to display the full record. Some systems offer options for display formats, such as 'full', 'short' or 'custom'. In addition there may be opportunities to select and mark records for saving, printing or e-mailing, and, in bibliographic databases, to display a fuller version of the record, often including an abstract and a summary and, where appropriate, the full text of a document in different formats. With a more complete record displayed, there may also be opportunities to search for related documents (in terms of shared subjects or authors) and citing documents (document citing the current document); these support further 'cycling' of the search.

SEARCH HISTORY AND SEARCH SETS

Many systems will show the search history, or the stages in the search. This allows the searcher to return easily to previous search outputs and, if appropriate, to further develop an earlier search. Some systems assign a number to each search set created so that the sets can then be re-used within the same search session. This permits the user to construct the search in stages, combining search sets by number:

Set 1:	CONFLICT
Set 2:	DISCORD
Set 3:	1 OR 2
Set 4:	CHILDREN
Set 5:	PARENTS
Set 6:	4 AND 5
Set 7:	3 AND 6

This may look long-winded, but it reduces typographical errors and gives the searcher the opportunity to re-use any of the terms in different combinations in order to refine the search. A search statement in the form *Children* AND *Parents* AND (*Conflict* OR *Discord*) will generate only one search set, and the terms cannot be re-used in other combinations.

With systems that do not store search sets, a search has to be entered as a single statement, and once the user moves on to the next search the old search is lost. There may be a facility for refining a search (by performing a search on the set of search results instead of on the whole database), or for storing searches for re-use.

SEARCH MANAGEMENT

Search management includes opportunities to review the search strategy that has been adopted and, permanently or temporarily, to save a search profile for subsequent use. Search profiles may be saved temporarily or permanently. Temporary saves are useful for searches where a searcher might wish to reflect on a search, or otherwise come back and complete the search at a later point in time. Permanent saving of the search profile is usually associated with current awareness or alerting services. The search profile will be run on behalf of the user at regular intervals in order to identify new material, and this will be sent to the user as a current awareness notification. Intelligent agents and other push technologies that refine profiles over a period of time are a recent innovation in this area. A recent innovation is RSS ('Really Simple Syndication') news feeds which notify the user when websites have added new content.

MULTI-FILE SEARCHING

Where, as with the online search services, there are a number of databases that might generate relevant records in response to one search, multi-file search facilities are beneficial. The most user-friendly multi-file search option is when other databases can be searched without reformulating the strategy. This requires the system to make the appropriate adjustments in search terms and fields to be searched. The most refined multi-file searching then goes on to produce an integrated set of records drawn from several databases, and with duplicate records eliminated. For example, in Dialog DataStar the Repeat command allows the previous search history to be viewed to create a new search which can be run in other databases. If the searcher wishes to conduct a multi-file search from the beginning, then there are two different options in Dialog DataStar, one through Easy Search in which the search is managed for the searcher, the other in Advanced Search in which the searcher has the opportunity to adjust the search to accommodate the differences between the databases being searched (such differences might relate to the controlled indexing languages and the record format). When the sets from the different databases are combined, duplicates can be removed. Many online search services have a database of databases, such as Dialog's Dialindex (File 411). Available databases are grouped by subject. The searcher specifies a subject group to be searched and enters a search specification. The system returns the number of hits for each database.

DISPLAYING THE THESAURUS

As discussed earlier, where a controlled indexing language has been used to provide index terms, a thesaurus will often be available in both printed and online formats. This thesaurus displays the controlled vocabulary used and relationships between terms, and is therefore a useful tool in narrowing or broadening searches. It is useful if the thesaurus can be displayed in a window to assist users as they attempt to develop a search strategy.

HYPERMEDIA

Many systems, including the WWW, offer hypermedia searching. True hypertext searching relies upon an indexer establishing conceptual links between documents. Creators of web pages often do this when they indicate which terms are to be used as links to other pages. However, in a large database this is very labour-intensive. An alternative is to rely upon the content, including the text and other objects in the record, and use the occurrence of objects or terms as the basis for hypermedia links. Thus, if the same term or object appears in two records or documents, the user may move from one record to another by, say, clicking on the term or object and without explicitly returning to the index.

Characteristic	Web IR	Traditional IR
Document		
Language	Documents in many languages	Documents often in one language
File types	Several file types	Usually all documents in same format
Document length	Wide range, with longer documents divided into parts	Length varies, but often to a lesser extent than with Web documents
Document structures	Depend on file format and mark up	Structured documents that support advanced field searching
Spam	Search engines have to select documents suitable for indexing	Suitability of documents is designed in the database design stage
Hyperlinks	Documents are heavily linked to each other and the links can be used in retrieval	Documents are usually not connected, citation data is used for this purpose
Database		
Amount of data, size of databases	Size of the Web is unknown: the whole Web can not be indexed	Exact amount of data can be determined when using formal criteria
Coverage	Unknown-only estimates are possible	Complete coverage according to the defined sources
Duplicates	Many documents exist in many copies or versions	Duplicates do not enter the database, and there is only one version for each document
User		
User interests	Heterogeneous	Clearly defined user group with known information needs
Type of queries	Very short, quick queries	Users may have more subject knowledge and formulate more complex query statements
IR system		
User interface	Easy to use interfaces	More complex interface
Ranking	Relevance ranking is the norm	Search outputs are more restricted and ranking is less important

Figure 5.9 Differences between Web IR and traditional IR

Source: developed from Lewandowski, 2005

DIFFERENCES BETWEEN WEB INFORMATION RETRIEVAL AND TRADITIONAL INFORMATION RETRIEVAL

Most of the search facilities discussed in this chapter were in use in online information retrieval systems before the advent of the Web. This leads to the notion of traditional information retrieval. Such information retrieval is concerned with the retrieval of documents or document surrogates all of which are in the same record format, and which are within one database or a series of linked databases that have been compiled to cover a specific subject or to meet the needs of a specific audience. Information retrieval on the Web operates across boundaries of document type, user group and user interest. Figure 5.9 summarizes some of the differences between Web IR and traditional IR in terms of document, database, user and IR system characteristics respectively.

SUMMARY

This chapter has explored issues associated with subjects as access points. It has introduced the different types of indexing and searching languages; the two main kinds of indexing languages are controlled and natural language. Systems designers need to decide when to use each of these, taking into account the consequences for the other features of retrieval systems, exhaustivity and content specification, specificity, and the way in which complex topics are represented. By exploring in some detail the features of thesauri this chapter has demonstrated many of the challenges of the use of subjects as access points and how these can be resolved using alphabetical indexing languages. The next chapter takes this discussion further by exploring the context of classification, which focuses more directly and specifically on the nature of relationships between subjects.

Another way to explore the complexities of subject searching and access is to review the extensive range of search facilities embedded in the interfaces to online and web-based databases. The chapter has reviewed different search logics that provide the overall framework for search strategies. Next, a range of specific search facilities that can variously be used to refine and hone a search are introduced. These include: truncation, proximity searching, range searching and search sets, as well as options for managing the search development, and the display of 'hits' and links to other related records and the full text of documents.

REVIEW QUESTIONS

1. What do you understand by the term 'aboutness'? Why is it an important concept?

2. In general terms discuss the difference between controlled indexing languages and natural indexing languages.
3. Define and explain each of the following features of information retrieval systems: exhaustivity, specificity and complex topics.
4. What are the basic types for preferred terms? How may candidate terms that do not conform to one of these types be modified by controlling the word form?
5. What are the main categories of semantic relationships? Using examples, discuss why each of these is important in indexing and searching.
6. Explain facet analysis and discuss how it can be used to analyse and represent relationships.
7. Explain the different contexts in which thesauri are used.
8. Discuss the idea of a search logic and, with the use of examples, demonstrate how search logics can be used in the searching process.
9. In addition to search logics, what are the other features that a search system often offers to make searching more efficient and effective?
10. Deconstruct a recent information search that you have conducted and demonstrate the relevance of each of the topics addressed in this chapter.

REFERENCES AND FURTHER READING

Aitchison, J., Gilchrist, A. and Bawden, D. (2000) *Thesaurus Construction and Use. A practical manual.* London: Europa Publications.

Armstrong, C.J. and Large, J.A. (2001) *Manual of On-Line Search Strategies*, vol. 1. Aldershot: Gower.

Bell, S.S. (2006) *Librarians' Guide to Online Searching.* Westport CT: Libraries Unlimited.

Bradley, P. (2004) *Advanced Internet Searcher's Handbook*, 3rd edn. London: Facet.

Brenner, E.H. (1996) *Beyond Booleans: New approaches to information retrieval.* Philadelphia PA: National Federation of Abstracting and Indexing Services.

Broughton, V. (2006) *Essential Thesaurus Construction.* London: Facet.

Chang, S.J. and Rice, R.E. (1993) Browsing: a multi-dimensional framework. *Annual Review of Information Science and Technology*, **28**, 231–76.

Chowdhury, G.G. (2003) *Introduction to Modern Information Retrieval.* London: Facet.

Chowdhury, G.G. and Chowdhury, S.S. (2007) *Organizing Information: From the shelf to the web.* London: Facet.

Chu, H. (2003) *Information Representation and Retrieval in the Digital Age.* Medford NJ: Information Today for the American Society for Information Science and Technology.

Cousins, S.A. (1992) Enhancing subject access to OPACs: controlled vocabulary versus natural language. *Journal of Documentation*, **48** (3), 291–309.

Dalmau, M., Floyd, R., Jiao, D. and Riley, J. (2005) Integrating thesaurus relationships into search and browse in an online photograph collection. *Library Hi-Tech*, **23** (3), 425–52.

Ellis, D. (1996) *Progress and Problems in Information Retrieval.* London: Library Association Publishing.

Fairthorne, R.A. (1969) Content analysis, specification and control. *Annual Review of Information Science and Technology*, **4**, 71–109.

Foskett, A.C. (1996) *Subject Approach to Information*, 5th edn. London: Facet.

International Standards Organization (1986) *Documentation – Guidelines for the Establishment and Development of Monolingual Thesauri*. ISO 2788: 1986. Geneva: ISO.

Khan, K. and Locatis, C. (1998) Searching through cyberspace: the effects of link display and link density on information retrieval from hypertext on the World Wide Web. *Journal of the American Society for Information Science*, **49** (2), 176–82.

Lancaster, F.W. (2003) *Indexing and Abstracting in Theory and Practice*. London: Facet.

Lewandowski, D. (2005) Web searching, search engines and information retrieval. *Information Services and Use*, **25**, 137–47.

McCulloch, E. (2005) Thesauri: practical guidance for construction. *Library Review*, **54** (7), 403–9.

Milstein, S., Dornfest, R. and Biersdorfer, J. (2006) *Google – The Missing Manual*. Cambridge MA: O'Reilly.

Mulvaney, N.C. (1994) *Indexing Books*. Chicago IL: University of Chicago Press.

Nicholson, S. (1997) Indexing and abstracting on the World Wide Web: an examination of six Web databases. *Information Technology and Libraries*, **16** (2), 73–81.

Rowley, J.E. (1994) The controlled versus natural indexing languages debate revisited: a perspective on information retrieval practice and research. *Journal of Information Science*, **20** (2), 108–19.

Schlein, A.M., Newby, J.J. and Weber, P.J. (2004) *Find It Online: The complete guide to online research*. Tempe AZ: Facts on Demand Press.

Schwartz, C. (2001) *Sorting Out the Web: Approach to subject access*. Norwood NJ: Ablex Publishing.

Shiri, A., Revie, C. and Chowdhury, G.G. (2002) Thesaurus assisted search term selection and query expansion: review of user-centred studies. *Knowledge Organisation*, **29** (1), 1–19.

Wellisch, H. (2000) *Glossary of Terminology in Abstracting, Classification, Indexing and Thesaurus Construction*. Medford NJ: Information Today.

6 Classification and order

INTRODUCTION

Classification and the creation of structure through categorization of knowledge is one of the most fundamental of human learning activities. In organizing knowledge in order to make it accessible to a wide range of different people it is necessary to establish and use classification schemes or taxonomies that are:

- explicit
- available to both indexers and users
- designed to mirror the cognitive structures of potential users
- designed to encompass the literature, information or knowledge base with which they will be used.

As discussed in the previous chapter, all subject access – whether it uses controlled language or natural language, or wherever in the process the control is exercised – needs to concern itself with both concepts and their labels, and the relationship between these concepts. This chapter focuses on the principles associated with defining relationships between concepts. After a brief introduction on the nature of systematic arrangement, the chapter discusses classification from the perspective of bibliographic classification schemes. Whilst these schemes and the approaches to classification and organizing knowledge that they adopt have their roots in a print rather than a digital environment, there are a number of good reasons for examining such schemes:

- Some of the major bibliographic classification schemes, most notably the Dewey Decimal Classification Scheme and the Library of Congress Classification Scheme, have had a significant impact on the development of classification practices for documents in both traditional and digital libraries.
- Classification data is one type of metadata often included in bibliographic records.

- Unlike many special-purpose (in terms of their subject coverage or the literature to which they are intended to be applied) or community-specific taxonomies, the major bibliographic classification schemes seek to cater for all knowledge.

The following chapter explores other aspects of classification and subject authority tools, including both some of the long-standing and widely used bibliographic tools, and taxonomies and ontologies developed mainly for use in digital environments to support the structuring of knowledge for a wide range of different purposes.

At the end of this chapter you will:

- be aware of the importance of systematic arrangement in the organization of knowledge
- understand the nature and functions of bibliographic classification
- be able to explain the functions of the different components of a bibliographic classification scheme: schedules, notation and index.

CATEGORIES, HIERARCHIES AND SYSTEMATIC ARRANGEMENT

The formation of categories is one of the most fundamental of human learning activities. Many of us have observed small children in their attempts to categorize the everyday world, and can supply instances – a typical one being the two-year-old who classified birds as pigeons if they were flying and ducks if they were walking or swimming. It is by classifying the objects and activities of the everyday world that children develop their world-knowledge, and this process is constantly being added to and fine-tuned throughout life.

Chapter 5 discussed the categorization of pairs of terms in three basic ways: where term A is considered equivalent to term B; where A and B are in a hierarchical relationship; and where there is such a close association between A and B that the one forms part of the definition of the other. The skills we acquire in recognizing these relationships are essentially classificatory skills. We use these skills, often unconsciously, in a number of ways when accessing information.

Classifications of the objects of the everyday world are often known as taxonomies. Their archetype is Linnaeus's systematic ordering of the world of botany. Such classifications work by grouping things together on the basis of their similarities and dissimilarities. Thus onions, leeks, shallots, chives and garlic are grouped together under the family name of Alliaceae.

The systematic arrangement of knowledge, or of the documents in a collection or index, has two important functions:

1. it gives us an overview of the subject field covered

2. it makes it possible for information on a subject to be retrieved without having to search the whole file.

Most contents pages of books are effectively classifications of their contents. *Encylopaedia Britannica* has a classification of the whole of knowledge to introduce readers to its scope and organization. Other classifications are not hard to find. Governments maintain official classifications of occupations and industries; educationalists have classifications of schools and of exceptional children; supermarkets group their wares on their shelves, and so on.

Information professionals use classification or systematic arrangement in many ways. The longest-established use of classified order is for the arrangement of the stock of libraries. A number of classification schemes have been devised for this purpose. Taxonomies or classification schemes are also used in the design of knowledge transfer in expert systems, and in the design of searching algorithms and systems to search the Web and other collections of digital documents. In turn, such implementations mean that information users often make use of classification either consciously or unconsciously in:

- menu-based user interfaces which are hierarchically organized: we start with a broad area, and narrow it down in hierarchical steps to find the required information
- traditional alphabetical indexes, where the reference structure does not give any help in expanding a search to a term that is hierarchically broader: we have to think of the broader term ourselves
- online searching, where if we wish to search on terms that are hierarchically narrower, we *may* be able to make use of an online thesaurus or other taxonomy, but more usually have to enter the narrower terms individually and OR them together.

Library classifications have much in common with the taxonomic groupings of the everyday world, but there are important differences:

- Taxonomic groupings of the everyday world are limited to generic relationships.
- Documents, as we have seen in Chapter 5, deal with combinations of topics; for example, a *report* on the *prevention of diseases* in *onions*.
- The classification of documents is governed by *literary warrant*: the actual or probable existence of documents that are about the topic for which a class has been defined.
- Documents can only be arranged in a one-dimensional, linear order. This makes it possible for shelf arrangement to show only one kind of relationship at a time.

FUNCTIONS OF BIBLIOGRAPHIC CLASSIFICATION

Traditionally, bibliographic classification has two functions:

1. Linking an item on the shelves with its catalogue entry. An item's class mark forms part of its shelf mark (also known as call number and book number), which enables items located within a library catalogue to be retrieved from the shelves.
2. Direct retrieval by browsing. If we know where a subject is classed, we can locate it without having to search the whole collection; and can moreover expect to find related subjects nearby. However, because of the limitations of linear order, not all like subjects can be collocated. It is the function of a classification to group together the topics that the users of the collection are most likely to want grouped together (both on library shelves and in digital collections).

These two functions taken together are sometimes referred to as marking and parking. The qualities that a bibliographic classification requires in order to achieve these ends are a helpful collocation and sequence, and a brief and memorable notation. Alphabetical subject access to documents organized by a classification scheme is achieved through access based on an alphabetical indexing language, such as natural language keywords, or terms from a controlled indexing language. As discussed in the previous chapter such controlled indexing languages also have structure and indicate relationships between terms. This has led to work on the design of special classification schemes that seek to align structures and terminology to generate integrated classification and alphabetical subject lists or thesauri. Thus classification can be viewed as having a third function, generating the structure that underlies alphabetical indexing languages. Thesauri, subject headings and classifications may all be viewed as manifestations of the same 'deep' index language structure (which, broadly, is the position taken by this book).

A classification may be *general* or *special*. A general classification covers all subjects. A special classification concentrates on a narrower range of topics, typically the goods manufactured or services provided by the organization for which it has been developed. Some general classifications, notably UDC and BC2, have been developed in sufficient depth to enable them to be adapted to special collections.

Why classification *scheme*? A classification is simply a systematically arranged list. To be of practical use a classification needs additional features, and these are what make it into a scheme. A classification scheme has three components:

1. the *schedules*, in which subjects are listed systematically showing their relationships: the ordering of subjects in these schedules is not self-evident, and therefore requires:

2. a *notation*, a code using numbers and/or letters that have a readily understood order which signals the arrangement of the schedules; and

3. an *alphabetical index* to locate the terms within the schedules.

It is often stated that a classification requires a fourth component: an *organization* to develop it and maintain its currency. This is true, but such a mechanism is not unique to classification; it is a feature of all controlled language systems.

SCHEDULES

Classification schedules comprise the following elements:

- the division of classes by a single characteristic at a time
- main classes
- facets, generated by facet analysis (as described in Chapter 5)
- sub-facets (arrays), formed by the subdivision of the facets by a single characteristic at a time.

These will now be described in turn.

DIVISION OF CLASSES

Division of classes must be by one principle (characteristic) of division at a time; that is, all the subclasses have the same attribute. For example, garments can first be divided according to function (for example, overcoats, dresses, underwear), and then within these functional groups, or classes, there will be further principles of division, such as size or material. Failure to observe this principle (see Figure 6.1) reduces the predictability of the system and can lead to cross-classification, which could be problematic if you know of a tame stray dog or an embalmed sucking pig. More plausibly perhaps, DDC's Architecture class (720) has subdivisions 722–724 for schools and styles, and 725–728 for types of structure. Ancient Egyptian architecture is at 722.2, and Temples and shrines at 726.1. Where does one class a book on ancient Egyptian temples? The schedules have a clear instruction to use the latter number and, provided we know that types of structure take precedence over schools and styles, all is well.

There are two approaches to the division of classes: *enumerative*, and *analytico-synthetic* or *faceted*. Historically, bibliographic classifications have followed Linnaean principles. Linnaeus divided the plant kingdom into Orders: flowering and non-flowering plants; and then proceeded by successive subdivision to enumerate the various genera and species of plants in their classes and subclasses. Such a top-down, deductive procedure applied to documents results in an *enumerative* classification. Both LCC and DDC are essentially enumerative classifications.

An extreme example, from an old Chinese encyclopaedia, shows the confusing result of the simultaneous application of more than one principle of division. Animals are classed as:

(a) belonging to the Emperor
(b) embalmed
(c) tame
(d) sucking pigs
(e) sirens
(f) fabulous
(g) stray dogs

(h) included in the present classification
(i) frenzied
(j) innumerable
(k) drawn with a very fine camel hair brush
(l) et cetera
(m) having just broken the water pitcher
(n) that from a long way off look like flies

Figure 6.1   An idiosyncratic set of principles of division

Example from DDC showing enumeration of different types of relationship

628.16833 Protection of the water supply from pollution by oil spills

600 Technology (Applied sciences) [*Discipline facet*]
620 Engineering and allied operations [NT]
628 Sanitary and municipal engineering. Environmental protection engineering [NT]
 .1 Water supply [RT of Sanitary engineering. *Key system facet*]
 .16 Testing, analysis, treatment, pollution countermeasures [*Operations facet*]
 .168 Pollution countermeasures [NT]
 .1683 Countermeasures for industrial wastes [*Agents facet*]
 .16833 Oil spills [NT]

This is a typical DDC chain, comprising four facets, and with the class mark including both semantic and syntactic relations in a single seamless whole. The same class mark could be represented thus, with hierarchical (semantic) relationships represented vertically, and syntactic relationships horizontally.

Discipline	Key system	Operation	Agent
Technology			
Engineering		Testing, etc.	Countermeasures for industrial wastes
Sanitary engineering	Water supply	Pollution countermeasures	Oil spills
628	.1	68	33

Figure 6.2   Enumerative classification: example 1

176

The enumerative method of compiling a classification brings with it a number of problems:

1. Successive subdivision of classes can only properly cover one kind of relationship – the hierarchical. Other semantic relationships, and all syntactic relationships, have to be assimilated as best they can. This in practice means that relationships of different types are listed in the schedules in a way that makes them look hierarchical when they are not. Figure 6.2 shows how a single DDC class can include associative as well as hierarchical relationships, together with a range of syntactic relationships.
2. Successive subdivision of classes carries the temptation to continue subdividing for the sake of it, ignoring literary warrant.
3. Another problem with enumerative classification is that of repetition. Subordinate topics have to be enumerated every time, which bulks out the schedules (see Figure 6.3).
4. Enumerative classifications behave in a very similar way to enumerative subject headings lists, in that they may permit only a limited amount of pre-coordination. Just as a work on the architecture of wooden church buildings would carry the LCSH headings *Church architecture* and *Wooden buildings*, so

---

Example from DDC showing (a) enumeration of complex topics, and (b) repetition of data

370 Public policy issues in education
.1 Specific elements
.11 Support of public education
.112 Support of public elementary education
.113 Support of public secondary education
.114 Support of public adult education
.118 Support of public higher education
.119 Support of public special education
.12 Support by specific level of government, international support
.121 Support by national governments
.1212 National support of elementary education
.1213 National support of secondary education
.1214 National support of higher education
.1215 National support of adult education
.1216 National support of special education
.3 Public policy issues in private education
.32 Public support of private education
.322 Public support of private elementary education
.323 Public support of private secondary education
.324 Public support of private higher education
.326 Public support of private adult education
.328 Public support of private special education

Figure 6.3 Enumerative classification: example 2

the best that an enumerative classification like DDC can offer is 721.0448 Architectural structure – Specific materials – Wood, and 726.5 Buildings associated with Christianity (class here church buildings), with no provision for combining the two. So, for physical items such as books, in the classing of works on the same subject at two different places we are forced to make a choice between two non-specific class marks, and there is a very real danger of cross-classification. On the other hand, for digital objects there is the additional flexibility of the option of assigning two or more class marks.

In contrast, *faceted* classifications are constructed in an inductive, bottom-up manner, as was described in Chapter 5. Figure 6.4 shows the principal features of a faceted classification:

- Compound topics are formed by synthesis.
- The classification is infinitely hospitable to new compounds. All facets can be expressed. Suppose, for example, someone made a study of resistance to change in the power structure of small groups. There is no problem: simply alter the final facet to KCT X Resistance to change, giving KMD GMR CTX.

The topic of **Stability and power structure in small groups** can be analysed into three facets: (1) Small groups [*Key system*]; (2) Power structure [*Property*]; Stability [*Property*].

The topic in DDC (an enumerative classification)
300 Social sciences
301 Sociology and anthropology
302–307 Specific topics in sociology and anthropology
302 Social interaction
.3 Social interaction within groups
.34 Social interaction in primary groups

This shows the principal features of an enumerative classification:

1. Compound topics are enumerated in the schedules.
2. Only those compounds that are enumerated can be classed specifically. The concept 'Power structure' has to be subsumed under the more general Social interaction. The third facet – 'Stability' – cannot be expressed at all.

The topic in BC2 (a faceted classification)
BC2 analyses the topic into three facets, shown here with their hierarchies and notations:

1. Social units – Individuals in society – Collectivities – Groups – Primary groups – Small groups: KMD
2. Social processes – Social action – (Special forms of behaviour) – Social interaction and social relationships – Social relationships – Power and influence – Power structure: KGM R
3. Social processes – (Types of processes) – (Change and equilibrium) – Equilibrium, social equilibrium, stability: KCS

These three notations are combined according to the rules of the scheme to give: KMD GMR CS.

Figure 6.4   Enumerative and faceted classifications compared

178

Enumerative classification – summary

- DDC and LCC have a long lineage and are widely used. On the other hand, they incorporate a legacy of an approach to knowledge organization that has roots in the nineteenth century, which can lead to them being seen as antiquated and inflexible. Counterbalancing this legacy is their persistence, which is based in solid organizational support and regular revision. DDC, in particular, has been gradually and carefully updated, with the piecemeal incorporation of faceted features. These vary in extent: 780 Music is fully faceted, but 150 Psychology has very few such features. Edition 22 of DDC was published in 2003, in both print and electronic form, and consolidates the regular updates issued through WebDewey (<www.oclc.org/dewey>).
- Perhaps the strongest inherent advantage of enumerative classification is that it is constructed and displayed in a way that can be intuitively understood. If we take a topic like 'Stability and power structure in small groups' we think of it like that: as a phrase, not as three facets to be stuck together. And if we cannot find the precise topic, we look for the nearest match, in the spirit of compromise that is part and parcel of everyday life. In spite of its many faceted features, and sometimes labyrinthine instructions, DDC can be picked up and understood in its main features with little preliminary training, and LCC is even more thoroughly enumerative than DDC.
- Enumerative classification is incapable of the depth of pre-coordination (or 'hospitality in chain' – see next major section) of faceted classification. This is not often a problem provided a generally helpful sequence of topics is maintained, and the system is not used in the compilation of verbal subject indexes.
- Synthesis is unevenly developed, and methods vary from class to class.
- Enumerative schemes are more difficult to revise, because enumerated compounds have to be relocated.
- Schedules tend to be bulky, because the enumeration of compound topics leads to much repetition of data. This, however, is becoming less of a practical (that is, weight!) problem now that electronic access to schedules is available.

Faceted classification – summary

- Faceted classification has largely been developed since the 1950s.
- Schemes can be daunting on first acquaintance, as the construction of compound subjects requires both knowledge of the methods of synthesis used and the ability to look up two or more places in the schedules.
- Schedules are compact, as only simple topics are listed, with little repetition of data.
- Application is systematic and predictable. With familiarity, the classifier can work with speed and confidence.

- Schemes can be more easily kept up to date.
- Faceted classification has had an incalculable influence on the development of controlled languages over the past half-century, but the schemes themselves are largely confined to a few specialist applications. DDC and LCC have an iron grip on general libraries, and BC2 has been developed too late and with insufficient resources to make a significant impact.

MAIN CLASSES

General classifications, whether enumerative or faceted, must have an initial system of broad classes, called the *main classes* or *primary facets*. All current classifications base their main classes on disciplines. Disciplines are ways of looking at the world. The narrowest definition of disciplines postulates a small number – perhaps six or seven – of fundamental *disciplines*, and contrasts them with *phenomena*, the objects of the world, any of which can be studied from more than one disciplinary viewpoint. Many of the traditional disciplines of professional and academic life are, according to this perspective, subdisciplines: a fundamental discipline applied to a particular group of phenomena. So biology is science applied to living organisms, social science is science applied to human groups, and so on. Bliss Bibliographic Classification, second edition, is constructed in this way (see Figure 6.5).

The use of disciplines raises a number of questions and problems:

- There is a large body of literature, often but by no means exclusively written for children, the focus of which is a phenomenon treated from a range of disciplinary viewpoints: water, colour, life underground, and so on. (BC2 reserves class 3 for such topics.)
- There needs to be provision for topics that are too general in scope to fall within the disciplinary structure. Traditionally, such topics have been placed in a main class labelled Generalia. These may include:
  - the vehicles for communicating information: books, journals and so on
  - documents with no subject limitation, which may be classed by their format or arrangement: encyclopaedias, general newspapers and the like
  - the tools of knowledge: systems, computers
  - the disciplines associated with any of these: publishing, information science, librarianship, bibliography.
- Not all disciplines are clear-cut. Geography, for example, is a loose aggregate of topics.
- Disciplines are by no means static, but are constantly evolving and being added to, often by the fusion of distinct fields of study, as with biochemistry or psycholinguistics.

180

2	Generalia: physical forms and forms of arrangement
4/6	Phenomena: objects of knowledge. Attributes, activities, entities
7/9	Knowledge, information, communication
A/Z	Disciplines: forms of knowledge
A	Philosophy
AM	Mathematics
AY	Science
B	Physical sciences
E	Biological sciences
H	Human sciences and human studies
	Physical anthropology, health and medicine, psychology
J/Z	Social sciences and humanities

Figure 6.5   Order of main classes in BC2

The number and order of main classes are determined by:

- Philosophical and scientific considerations – Bliss studied for 40 years to find a 'scientific and educational consensus' on which to base his classification. Francis Bacon and Hegel are both said to have influenced Dewey in his choice of main classes.
- The practicalities of the notation – in theory, anyone constructing a classification should determine the number and order of the classes first, and then apply a notation; but Melvil Dewey thought of the notation first and adapted the schedules to it.
- Other considerations, from the pragmatic to the ideological – for example, the Library of Congress's primary function is to serve Congress, and a basic function of government is national defence. The LCC accordingly has a main class for military science. Or take Colon Classification (CC): to its deviser Ranganathan, mysticism was the pinnacle of human experience, so he created a main class for it, gave it a suitable notational symbol – the Greek letter delta (Δ) – and located it at the very centre of his classification.

FACETS

A vocabulary of terms organized into *broad facets* is the defining structural feature of a faceted classification. The terms are derived from the literature, using the technique of facet analysis outlined in Chapter 5. An important difference between the terms of a classification schedule and a verbal system is that the terms of the former represent the *concepts* defining each class, whereas the terms in the latter are *labels* for retrieval. In many cases these are identical. Where they are not so, classes can be defined by means of headings such as Secondary forms of energy,

Persons by miscellaneous social characteristics, or Postage stamps commemorating persons and events, which would be unacceptable (except as node labels) in a verbal system. As they are collected, many of the terms will tend to organize themselves into groups. These are the broad facets of the classification. A facet is the total subset of classes produced when a class is subdivided by a single broad principle or characteristic.

SUBFACETS AND ARRAYS

Once the broad facets have been determined, each must be examined to see if it can be further subdivided by a more specific principle into *subfacets*, or *arrays*. The order of classes within an array can often be determined intuitively, the guiding principles being that (a) any hierarchies must be indicated, and (b) alphabetical order is used only as a last resort. More specifically, the following arrangements have been found useful:

- Chronological, for example for history and literature; also for operations carried out sequentially, such as the sequence of agricultural operations from ploughing to harvesting.
- Evolutionary, such as the stages in the life cycle.
- Increasing size or complexity, for example for musical ensembles.
- Spatial, with the proviso that classification is one-dimensional, making it impossible to maintain full geographic contiguity. Thus, in DDC's Table 2 (Geographic areas), the first area enumerated under -4 Europe is -41 British Isles, from where the table crosses the North Sea to Germany and tours the central European states as far as Hungary (-439); after which it skips to France (-44), Italy (-45), Iberian Peninsula (-46); then an even greater leap to Eastern Europe and Russia (-47).

Enumerative systems such as DDC also recognize subfacets. For example, 011 Bibliographies has these divisions:

.1 Universal bibliographies
.2 General bibliographies of works published in specific languages
.3 General bibliographies of works published in specific forms
.4 General bibliographies of works exhibiting specific bibliographic characteristics other than form [e.g. rare books, reprints]
.5 General bibliographies of works issued by specific kinds of publishers
.6 General bibliographies of works for specific kinds of users and libraries
.7 General bibliographies of works having specific kinds of content.

However, whereas a faceted classification would be able to express as many of these characteristics as required (for example, serial publications from underground presses, or rare books in microform), with DDC it is only possible to express one characteristic.

Unless a classification is intended for in-house use only, it is helpful to allow alternative locations where user feedback suggests that other collocations might be preferred.

CITATION ORDER

The principles are precisely the same as for pre-coordinate systems generally (see Chapter 7) except that, in general, in classification discipline forms the primary facet.

Alternative citation orders are sometimes offered. An example from DDC is subject bibliographies (016), where the preferred citation order is Bibliographies – Subject, as in 016.61 for a bibliography of medicine. The alternative treatment scatters subject bibliographies by topic instead of keeping them all together, as 610.16.

FILING ORDER

This is the actual sequence of books on shelves, citations in bibliographies, etc. There is an apparent paradox here. Schedules are arranged from general to specific, which means that the *least* significant facet is listed first and the most significant last. In other words, filing order is the *reverse* of the citation order. This is known as the *principle of inversion*, and maintains the principle of filing general topics before special in syntactic as well as in semantic relationships (see Figure 6.6). In DDC the principle is seldom specifically acknowledged, but often followed in practice, in 'class elsewhere' and 'preference' instructions. For example, when classifying the book on ancient Egyptian temples referred to earlier, there is an instruction at 722–724 to 'class specific types of structures regardless of school or style in 725–728' – that is, at the *later* class.

NOTATION

Notation is a code applied to topics in order to fix their arrangement. Thus, notation or code may be used in organizing books on shelves, files in a filing cabinet, entries in a catalogue or bibliography, or electronically held resources or their representations. The term 'notation' is generally used for document arrangement for shelf retrieval and for manually searched files. The more general term 'code' is used in machine retrieval.

Notation fixes a pre-existing arrangement; that is, it is applied to the schedules

Citation order:
Literature by origin – Periods – Authors – Literary forms – Literary movements

Schedule – *inverting* the citation order

B Literary mov'ts	D Literary forms	F Authors	H Periods	K Lit. by origin
B2 Naturalism	D2 Poetry	Arrange	H2 Classical	K2 English
B4 Romanticism	D4 Drama	*alphabetically*	H4 Modern	K4 French
D42 Comedy	*within facets*	H41 15th century	K6 Classical	
D44 Tragedy	K and H	H45 19th century	K61 Greek	
K62 Latin				

Filing order, showing general-to-special order:

Romanticism in literature	B4
Poetry	D2
Romanticism in poetry	D2B4
Nineteenth-century literature	H45
Nineteenth-century poetry	H45D2
English literature	K2
Romanticism in English literature	K2B4
Romanticism in nineteenth-century English literature	K2H45B4
Romanticism in nineteenth-century English poetry	K2H45D2B4
The poetry of John Keats	K2H45FKeats
Romanticism in the poetry of John Keats	K2H45FKeatsB4

Figure 6.6 Citation order and filing order

of a classification system *after* the subjects to be included, and their order, have been settled. It is necessary because systematic order is not self-evident.

After fixing the order of classes, the next important function of notation is hospitality – the ability to accommodate new subjects. For manual searching, a notation should be easy to use. Finally, there is the question of expressiveness: it must be open for a notation to express the hierarchical structure of the classification, and also to express the facet structure of compound topics. These considerations will now be discussed in turn, together with a brief consideration of shelf notation.

SHOWING THE ORDER OF CLASSES

The purpose of notation is to give each class an address that fixes its order within the classification. The ordinal values of Arabic numbers and roman letters are widely understood and form the basis of all notations. Where more than one kind of symbol is used – a *mixed notation* – filing precedents may have to be set, and here the ASCII sequence of numbers – upper case/lower case – is used. Where non-alphanumeric characters are used, they are assigned arbitrary ordinal values.

HOSPITALITY

Notation must be hospitable to the insertion of new subjects. There are two methods by which this can be achieved:

1. Unassigned notation within an array. If the new topic is coordinate, all is well if a suitable gap has been provided. DDC20 classed Roller skating at 796.21, with 796.22 unused; DDC21 appropriated 796.22 for Skateboarding.
2. Subdivision of the notation. If the notation is hierarchical and the new topic is by nature subordinate, it can be slotted in naturally. DDC20 used 004.67 for wide area networks (WANs), and DDC21 inserted a class for the Internet at 004.678. However, if the array of subordinate topics has a larger number of classes than the notational base can accommodate, then the hierarchical nature of the notation is inevitably compromised.

EASE OF USE

A notation should be easy for users to remember, copy, and shelve books by.

To a large extent this is a function of *brevity*: the shorter the notation the easier it is to remember. Length of notation is determined by the following factors:

- The *notational base* – there are over twice as many letters as numbers, so a lettered notation will be shorter than one that uses numbers alone.
- The *allocation* of notation to the literature – this particularly affects established classification schemes, whose main classes may have been established for a century or more, and where the original allocation becomes less balanced with time and the emergence of new subdivisions. Growth subjects like Electronic engineering tend to have long notations (621.38 in DDC), which gives all topics within that class even longer notations: 621.389334 is the number for Stereo systems. Conversely, some subjects have little or no growth: the classic instance is Logic (160 in DDC).
- Provision for *synthesis* – the more facets, the longer the notation. In DDC this can lead to some very long notations, especially in classes such as 338 Production, where the synthesis of Topic + Industry + Place leads to prodigious notations: a history of the Merseyside ship repair industry is classed at 338.4762382002094275. Where synthesis is systematic, as in faceted classifications, the notation for a facet will be consistent. In BC2, for example, 28 introduces Place, so that 28S will always denote Japan. In DDC synthesis is anything but systematic: Africa is often denoted by -096, but 344.096 denotes Laws relating to religion; a class mark ending in -03 often denotes a dictionary or encyclopaedia, but 697.03 denotes central heating.
- *Mnemonics,* where the same notational symbol is consistently used to denote

185

the same topic, is properly an aspect of synthesis. Occasionally a classification having a lettered notation may be able to use *literal mnemonics* based on the initial letter of a subject. BC2 has AL Logic, AM Mathematics, C Chemistry, among others. There is, however, a temptation on the part of the designer of classifications to allow literal mnemonics to distort the order of the schedules; and they can raise false expectations among users – for example, that B should denote Biology. (In BC2 B is Physics, and Biology is E.) At worst, it can lead to the use of alphabetical order as a lazy substitute for classification.

- *Chunking* – long notations are more memorable if broken up into shorter groups in the manner of telephone numbers. Many classifications (DDC, UDC, BC2) use groups of three symbols separated by spaces or points.

EXPRESSIVENESS

The notation *may* express the hierarchy of classes, and if it is intended for digital manipulation, this is a requirement. With manual systems, anyone familiar with DDC tends to expect this: there is an intuitive satisfaction in observing that, say, 636 denotes animal husbandry, 636.1 horses, and 636.12 racehorses. However, maintaining hierarchical expressiveness has certain problems:

- it can lead to excessively long notations
- it is impossible to maintain if the number of terms in an array exceeds the notational base
- human perspectives on hierarchical structures can change over time: also, relationships between subjects change as knowledge develops.

The notation *may* also express the facet structure of classes. In a faceted classification, there is often an expectation that this will be achieved. Even DDC makes some use of facet indicators, both generally throughout the scheme; for example, where 09 often (but by no means invariably) introduces place or time, and in individual classes, notably 780 Music, where both 0 and 1 are used only as facet indicators. A few classifications, notably UDC and CC, use non-alphanumeric symbols to introduce particular facets. UDC, for example, encloses places between parentheses and uses the colon to introduce a whole range of relationships. This complicates filing, as it is not self-evident whether, say, 63:31 Agricultural statistics will file before or after 63(31) Agriculture in ancient China. Another drawback is that facet indicators make the notation longer. A simple way to avoid both problems is to use a lettered notation, the initial letter of each class being in upper case and the rest in lower case; for example, TjgLmEs for a (hypothetical) notation containing three facets.

SHELF NOTATION

The notation inscribed on the back of books may usefully be shorter than that used in catalogues and other indexes. DDC notation supplied by central bibliographic agencies is often segmented; that is, one or two points are shown at which the notation could be cut off. So the 21-digit class appearing above could be shortened to 338.4762382 or even 338.4 (the maximum allowed in the Abridged DDC).

The notation forms the basis of an item's *call number* or *shelf mark*, the actual symbol on the spine of the item which determines its place on the shelves and which the catalogue uses to locate it. This has three elements:

● a symbol denoting any special shelving sequence, such as oversize items (usually omitted for items within the main sequence)
● the class mark proper (full length or shortened)
● a device to denote the item's position within that class: this may be a Cutter number – a letter followed by one or more numbers as a coded representation of the author's name – or some other (usually simpler) device.

Cutter numbers are used by LC to arrange books alphabetically within a class number (see Chapter 7 for more detail). They consist of the initial letter of the main entry heading followed by one or two numbers that represent the second or subsequent letter of the name. The precise distribution of the numbers depends on the initial letter. For most names beginning with a consonant the second letter is replaced by a number according to a set process:

a e i o r u y are represented respectively by the numbers: 3 4 5 6 7 8 9.

So the name Davidson might be represented by .D3, Deakin by .D4, and so on. The numbers may be expanded decimally, using the third letter of the name, so Dean might be .D42. Further expansion is applied as required. The system is collection-specific: two libraries applying Cutter numbers independently would be likely to assign different numbers to the same work so there is a tendency to rely on numbers supplied by LC. Cutter-Sanborn Author Tables are a modification, using three digits. For large collections, Cutter numbers provide a better collocation than systems based on the first three letters of the heading, or on the initial letter followed by a running accession number.

ALPHABETICAL INDEX

The index to the classification schedules has two purposes:

187

- to locate topics within the classification
- to bring together related aspects of a subject which appear in more than one place in the schedules. (Indexes to classification schemes are sometimes known as relative indexes.)

Faceted classifications need only index the simple concepts appearing in the schedules. Related aspects are uncommon, but do occur (essentially they reflect polyhierarchies): for example, the index to class K Society of BC2 gives two locations for Ethnomethodology. Enumerative classifications must show enumerated compound subjects: examples from DDC were given in Figures 6.2 and 6.3. Additionally, DDC's index also includes a selection of synthesized compounds: Pines, Elms and Eucalyptus, for example, have subheadings for Ornamental arboriculture, whereas Apples, Firs and Yews do not.

REVISION

Bibliographic classifications are inherently out of date. In part this is due to the tendency of all controlled language systems to lag behind the times. Additionally with classification:

1. Classifications are necessarily *closed* rather than open systems. The *ordering* of a new topic is not automatic, as it is with verbal systems: only a controlling organization can determine the correct placing of a new topic within the schedules.
2. Any revision of the order of topics typically involves the physical removal of books from shelves, the altering of their shelf numbers, and their replacement – a far more labour-intensive operation than the altering of surrogate records.

So classification schemes tend to be revised on the principle of doing only as much as the market will bear. The point is stressed here to explain how it is that, even though modern faceted principles have been shown to be far superior to traditional enumerative classifications, the great majority of libraries use enumerative classifications. LCC is almost entirely enumerative. DDC is largely enumerative but with variable proportions of faceted features. UDC is a faceted system grafted on to an enumerative base. BC, second edition, is thoroughly faceted, but is incomplete and little-used. CC, the original faceted classification, has few users outside its home country.

THE CLASSIFICATION PROCESS

These guidelines are based on DDC, but can be adapted to apply to any classification.

ANALYSE THE SUBJECT

- Use *title* and *subtitle*, *contents list* and scan the *author's introduction* for any paragraph describing the purpose of the book. Treat *blurbs* with caution – their primary objective is to sell the book.
- In working situations you have *outside sources*: reviews, bibliographies (such as *BNB*, MARC records), subject experts, etc.
- Make a mental note of the word or phrase which most precisely describes the subject; for example, if it is on combine harvesters, note it as such, not as agricultural machinery.

NOW GO TO THE CLASSIFICATION SCHEDULES

The most reliable way to classify is to start at the most appropriate discipline in the *summary tables* and work downwards through the schedules.

WHAT IS THE DISCIPLINE?

If the work appears to fall between two (or more) main classes, then:

- class at the discipline which receives the greater emphasis
- watch the schedules for instructions on classing interdisciplinary works
- check the DDC *index*: if the first index entry has a class mark on the same line (and not after an indented subheading), that is probably the place to classify a topic covering more than one discipline (but check the schedules).

WHICH ASPECT OF THE SUBJECT FIRST?

- Check the schedules carefully for any *table of precedence*, *class here* note, or *class elsewhere* note. If necessary, check the broader containing headings for your subject (for example, for 305.4 check 305, 302–307, and 300 – this is why it is always best to work downwards from the main class whenever you can).
- In any given subject, there is an expectation that the more important facets of a subject will be listed *after* the less important: for example, class Norman castles at 728.81 Castles rather than at 723.4 Norman architecture.
- Class at the *passive* system; that is, at whatever is at the receiving end of any

process or operation: for example, a book on bovine medicine with cattle (636.2) rather than veterinary medicine (636.0896).

- Follow any *add* instructions (for example, to give 636.20896), but *never* try to combine two numbers from the schedules if there is no specific instruction to do so.
- Anything normally falling within the scope of DDC's *standard subdivisions* is classed last; that is, common subject aspects, such as historical aspects of X; also biography, management, philosophy, psychology, psychology, statistics, computer applications, and so on:
  - the subject in relation to a particular *place*
  - the subject written for a class of users who would not normally be the target readership; for example, Anatomy *for nurses*
  - the way the subject is arranged or presented; for example, dictionary, humorous treatment.

MORE THAN ONE SUBJECT

When classifying a work with two or more independent themes, the following would be possible options:

- if one is clearly subordinate, ignore it (for example, Chess and draughts)
- if the two subjects are treated equally, class the work by the earlier one, unless there are contrary instructions
- if three or more themes fall within the same general subject field, class at the first more general class that will accommodate all of them
- if necessary, apply a combination of these rules.

FINAL CHECK

Always check a class mark upwards through every stage of its hierarchy. If doing so leads to a heading that is irrelevant or misleading, there is a strong possibility that you have selected an inappropriate number (another reason for starting with the main class and working downwards).

SUMMARY

This chapter has led us from a discussion of classification as a fundamental human activity to an introduction to the theoretical features of a bibliographic classification and some practical hints on how to apply a classification scheme. Our account is necessarily brief, and should be supplemented by at least a selection of the fuller studies listed below.

In studying a construct as complex, abstract and highly organized as bibliographic classification, it is all too easy to lose sight of the principles among the plethora of detail. Much of this chapter has elaborated principles introduced in Chapter 5. It may help to keep the following three principles from Chapter 5 firmly in mind:

1. Bibliographic classification is not something apart, but is in essence a means of organizing a controlled vocabulary. Turn back to the principles of language control section in Chapter 5, as a reminder of how the trio of basic semantic relationships – equivalence, hierarchical, associative – are displayed in classification schemes.
2. Facet analysis, introduced in Chapter 5, lies at the core of modern classification theory.
3. The systematic display that forms the most obvious feature of a bibliographic classification indicates its main purpose: to achieve the sequence of topics that is most helpful to the users of the system. The section 'Displaying the thesaurus' in Chapter 5 took us in steps from a simple alphabetical display to systematic displays which are at the threshold of bibliographic classification.

REVIEW QUESTIONS

1. Discuss the everyday use of categories, hierarchies and systematic arrangement.
2. What are the functions of bibliographic classification schemes?
3. Explain the difference in fundamental design between the schedules of enumerative classification schemes, and those of faceted classification schemes.
4. What are the key features of the notation of a bibliographic classification scheme?
5. Outline the stages in the classification of an information object when performed by a human indexer.

REFERENCES AND FURTHER READING

Batley, S. (2005) *Classification in Theory and Practice: Sorting out your library*. Oxford: Chandos.

Beghtol, C. (1998) Knowledge domains: multidisciplinary and bibliographic classification systems. *Knowledge Organization*, **25** (1/2), 1–12.

Broughton, V. (2004) *Essential Classification*. London: Facet.

Chan, L.M. and Mitchell, J.S. (2003) *Dewey Decimal Classification: A practical guide*, 3rd edn. Dublin OH: OCLC.

Chowdhury, G.G. (2003) *Introduction to Modern Information Retrieval*. London: Facet.

Dewey Decimal Classification and Relative Index (2003) 22nd edition, 4 vols. Albany NY: Forest Press.

Foskett, A.C. (1996) *The Subject Approach to Information*, 5th edn. London: Library Association.

Foskett, D.J. and Foskett, J. (1974) *The London Education Classification: A thesaurus/classification of British educational terms*, 2nd edn. London: University of London Institute of Education Library.

Hunter, E. (2002) *Classification Made Simple*. Aldershot: Ashgate.

Joachim, M.D. (2003) *Historical Aspects of Cataloguing and Classification*. Binghamton NY: Haworth Press.

Lancaster, F.W. (2003) *Indexing and Abstracting in Theory and Practice*, 3rd edn. London: Facet.

Library of Congress *Classification Web*. Available (by subscription) at <http://classweb.loc.gov/>.

Library of Congress (2006) *Classification Web*. Available at <http:/classificationweb.net/tutorial> [accessed 15 June 2006]

McIlwaine, I.C. (2000) *The Universal Decimal Classification: A guide to its use*. The Hague: UDC Consortium.

Marcella, R. and Maltby, A. (2000) *The Future of Classification*. Aldershot: Gower.

Mills, J. (1969) Bibliographic classification. In *Encyclopedia of Library and Information Science*, vol. 2, pp. 368–80. New York: Dekker.

Mills, J. and Broughton, V. (1987) *Bliss Bibliographic Classification*, 3rd edn, vol. titled *Introduction and Auxiliary Schedules*. London: Bowker.

OCLC (2006a) *Using OCLC Web Dewey: An OCLC tutorial*. Available at <www.oclc/dewey/resources/tutorials> [accessed 15 June 2006].

OCLC (2006b) *Introduction to the Dewey Decimal Classification*. Available at <www.oclc.org/dewey/versions/ddc22print/intro.pdf> [accessed 15 June 2006].

Palmer, B. (1971) *Itself an Education: Six lectures on classification*. London: Library Association.

Scott, M.L. (2005) *Dewey Decimal Classification, 22nd edn – A study manual and number building guide*. Westport CT: Libraries Unlimited.

Spärck Jones, K. (2005a) Revisiting classification for retrieval. *Journal of Documentation*, **61** (5), 598–601.

Spärck Jones, K. (2005b) Some thoughts on classification for retrieval. *Journal of Documentation*, **61** (5), 571–81.

Taylor, A.G. (2004a) *The Organization of Information*, 2nd edn. Westport CT: Libraries Unlimited.

Taylor, A.G. (2004b) *Wynar's Introduction to Cataloguing and Classification*. Westport CT: Libraries Unlimited.

Taylor, A.G. (2006) *Introduction to Cataloguing and Classification*, 10th edn. Westport CT: Libraries Unlimited.

7 Further concepts and tools for subject access

INTRODUCTION

The previous two chapters have explored the principles of subject access to information and documents by examining, in turn, alphabetical controlled indexing languages, with their focus on the use of words and terms to represent subjects, and classification, with its focus on the relationships between subjects. In order to illustrate key principles in each of these approaches, the chapters have examined, respectively, the key features of thesauri and classification schemes. This chapter develops that discussion by exploring further concepts and tools that are used to support subject access. The origins of several of these tools pre-date the digital age, but they continue to be developed, adapted and applied for use in a range of digital and non-digital contexts. This chapter gathers together a range of significant tools. At the end of this chapter you will:

- understand the nature and role of pre-coordination in subject descriptors and headings
- be aware of subject heading theory and practice, and the main features of the Library of Congress Subject Headings
- be aware of the major bibliographic classification schemes, and the criteria for their selection
- understand the nature and application of taxonomies and ontologies in accessing digital resources.

PRE-COORDINATION

In Chapter 5 we suggested that a person's natural inclination is to describe subjects in documents by means of title-like phrases: Laboratory techniques in organic chemistry, Skin diseases in dogs, and the like. These are examples of compound concepts: in the language of information retrieval, they are pre-coordinated. In contrast, thesauri as described in Chapter 5 deal in simple concepts only – Laboratory techniques; Organic chemistry; Skin; Diseases; Dogs – and are designed for use with post-coordinate indexing and searching methods. There are a number of contexts in which pre-coordinated, title-like subject phrases are used for indexing purposes. Subject headings used in catalogues and catalogue databases, such as the Library of Congress Subject Headings (LSCH) includes a number of concepts in the same heading; for example, *Drug-abuse – Treatment – Great Britain*. Such 'strings' are also displayed by search engines to assist users in the navigation of web-based databases. Although, in a digital world, post-coordination is the predominant approach, both subject headings and bibliographic classification schemes are pre-coordinate and are well embedded in the metadata used by libraries, publishers and other agencies. In addition, from a theoretical perspective an awareness of the alternative to post-coordination enhances our appreciation of the nature of post-coordination.

Chapter 5 offered some basic definitions of the difference between post-coordination and pre-coordination. This section develops the discussion of pre-coordination more fully through discussion of the nature of subject headings. The subsequent section expands on this theme with reference to a specific set of subject headings that has played an important role in the development of subject access, the LCSH.

THE NATURE OF PRE-COORDINATION

To re-cap, pre-coordination is the combination of index terms at the *indexing* stage. The indexer constructs a heading containing as many terms as are required to summarize as much of the subject content of the document as the indexing system permits, and the searcher has to accept this heading in its entirety. This reflects and systematizes our natural tendency to think of subjects as phrases, like 'Drug abuse treatment in Britain'. The LCSH for this topic is: *Drug abuse – Treatment – Great Britain.*

A pre-coordinate indexing system is one which, like LCSH, sets out to create *compound* headings – that is, headings which may contain two or more elements or facets. In addition to this use of pre-coordination in alphabetical subject headings, it is important to recognize that library classification schemes are also pre-coordinate systems.

Pre-coordinate indexing languages were originally designed to support searching in printed indexes and catalogues. However, by the time online searching became the norm, and post-coordinate searching became the more usual way of accessing databases, pre-coordinate indexing systems were deeply and permanently embedded into many of the largest and most highly institutionalized bibliographic databases. Machine-searchable indexes (with a few exceptions) use inverted files to decompose subject headings, titles, etc., into their constituent keyword elements. These can then be searched individually, using the standard techniques of post-coordinate searching. For example, a record carrying the subject heading *Drug abuse – Treatment – Great Britain* would be retrieved by a search on any Boolean combination of individual words: *Abuse* AND *Britain*, and so on.

After specificity, pre-coordination is the most powerful device for improving the precision of a search – far more precise than the crude AND of Boolean searching. A few systems (MeSH, Compendex) permit limited pre-coordination in a Boolean search. The method typically consists of applying a subheading to the descriptor for a system or organ (for example, *Kidneys – Lesions*). In natural language searching, phrase searching and the use of adjacency and proximity operators, as discussed in Chapter 5, are forms of pre-coordination.

SYNTAX, SIGNIFICANCE ORDER AND REFERENCES

There are two key aspects of pre-coordinate indexing systems:

1. syntax and its associated significance order, and
2. references.

Pre-coordination is an aspect of the wider field of *syntax*: the study of the way we put words together to make sentences. Formally, syntax comprises the rules defining valid constructions in a language. These include rules for such elements as word order and punctuation, neglect of either of which reduces intelligibility. In the English language, a great deal of syntax is about word order: alter the order of 'Dog bites man' and you either reverse its meaning or create something unintelligible. The same happens with an indexing language. Here are two typical subject headings:

History – Teaching
Teaching – History

Anyone familiar with the English language coming across either would intuitively understand its meaning: the teaching of history, and the history of teaching.

The significance order, or the order of terms in a multi-concept subject heading, is seen to be of particular importance in ensuring appropriate user interpretation of the heading. Significance order is the basis on which index terms are combined. In printed indexes or on-screen lists, the significance order determines the filing order. Thus, if, for example, a document were given the subject heading

Soccer – Cup Competitions, it would generally be far more useful if it could be sought in a filing sequence which included:

> *Soccer – Cup Competitions*
> *Soccer – Friendly Matches*
> *Soccer – Leagues*

and so on, than in a filing sequence which looked like this:

> *Cup Competitions – Golf*
> *Cup Competitions – Netball*
> *Cup Competitions – Rugby League Football*
> *Cup Competitions – Soccer*
> *Cup Competitions – Tennis*

and so on.

This proposed significance order implies that the indexer expects that a person is more likely to be interested in soccer in all its aspects than in cup competitions across a range of sports. Also, anyone searching library shelves or 'one place' indexes, having noted the sequence *Soccer – Cup Competitions*, would reasonably expect the same pattern to be observed for items on cup competitions in other sports.

Significance order cannot be left entirely to intuition. The intuitions of two cataloguers in the Library of Congress, presumably working separately and at different times, gave the world not only the heading *Drug abuse – Treatment – Great Britain, but also Drug abuse – Great Britain – Prevention*. A more systematic set of syntactic rules is needed if this kind of inconsistency is to be avoided. These rules are known as *citation order*.

Citation order is the order in which the facets of a compound subject are set down (that is, cited) in a pre-coordinate system. The elements may combine to make up a verbal subject heading or a classification notation. Traditionally, citation order has always been based on significance order. In making up a subject heading, as many of the facets are used as are required, or as the system permits; for example:

> *Soccer – Refereeing*
> *Soccer – Cup Competitions*
> *Soccer – Cup Competitions – Refereeing*

The principles of citation order were largely evolved in the 1960s, and are based on the fundamental categories of facet analysis described in Chapter 6. Citation order also underpins the construction and use of library classification schemes.

The intention of 'standard' citation order was to form a set of readily understood and generalizable principles for determining facet sequence across all subjects. The elements of citation order are shown in Figure 7.1.

196

```
[Discipline – in bibliographic classification only]
   Key system (things acted on, objectives, end products)
      Kinds (in verbal systems, often forms a phrase with key system)
         Parts (of key system)
            Materials (recursion is possible from here on)
               Properties (of key system)
                  Processes (from within key system)
                     Operations (from outside)
                        Agents
                           Common facets: subject
                                          place
                                          time
                                          form
```

Figure 7.1   Standard citation order

The following notes and comments are to be read in conjunction with Figure 7.1.

- *Discipline.* General classification schemes all use discipline as their primary facet: for example, in DDC the topic *Horses* is expressed as Zoological sciences – horses (599.725), Animal husbandry – horses (636.1), etc. The descriptor in a verbal system (such as LCSH) would be, simply, *Horses*.
- *Key system.* A question-begging term for 'whatever seems most significant'. Often it conveys the idea of *purpose*, *end product*, etc. Key systems are always passive, and represent what is being influenced or acted upon. Examples might include: Testing the hardness of *metals*; Software packages for *machine knitting*; or *Road* construction in developing countries. A key system in one context may not be so in another; for example, *Maps* is the key system of the topic The cataloguing of *maps*; but if the topic had been The cataloguing of maps in *university libraries*, then the key system would be *University Libraries*, and *Maps* would be Materials.
- *Kinds.* Whatever differentiates a term (focus); for example, *Portable Printers* where *Portable* differentiates such printers from other printers. Most alphabetical systems now treat these semantically; that is, they would use the single heading *Portable Printers*. (Technically, *Printers* is known as the *focus* and *Portable* the *difference*.) A classification system, on the other hand, would differentiate printers by establishing subfacets:

Printers		
(by portability)	*(by method of operation)*	*(by colour)*
fixed	ink-jet	monochrome
portable	laser (etc.)	colour

197

- *Parts*. These are often treated semantically (that is, using BT and NT). Here we are concerned with those instances where the part is not unique to the whole, and so has to be entered syntactically in pre-coordinate systems; for example, *Garages – Doors*. As well as physical parts, this category includes constituent parts; for example, Recruitment of *personnel* to the Civil Service.
- *Materials*. These are fairly self-explanatory (for example, *Glass* for windows), though in practice this category is often subsumed under Kinds or Parts, and in verbal systems is often treated as a phrase (*Steel Doors*). It is possible to have *kinds* of materials (*Galvanized Steel Doors*), parts of materials, etc.; and the same applies to the facets which follow: for example, an agent (see below) can have kinds, parts, etc.
- *Properties*. Whatever qualities a key system possesses; for example, Testing the *hardness* of metals; The development of *reading skills* in children.
- *Processes*. These occur *within* the key system, and do not require any external agency; for example, *Diseases* of mice; *Development* of reading skills in children.
- *Operations*. These imply an agent (which need not always be named); for example, *Coaching* children in reading; The *conquest* of California by the USA; Road *construction* in developing countries.
- *Agents*. The agent or instrument which carries out an operation; for example, *Roundworms* as vectors of virus diseases in potatoes; The marketing of prepackaged consumer goods by *multinational companies*; The conquest of California by the *USA*.
- *Common facets* are concepts that are applicable to a wide range of topics. Most pre-coordinate indexing systems have lists of such concepts, so they can be tacked on to the end of a heading. They may be:
  - *subjects* like Research or Psychology, which exist as disciplines in their own right, but are also applicable to any subject;
  - *places*, where they limit the context of a topic (for example, Road construction in *developing countries*);
  - *time*, often a more restricted view of the common subject History (for example, The conquest of California by the USA, *1846–1850*), but sometimes including other temporal concepts (for example, *weekly*);
  - *form*, a catch-all which includes physical form (such as *videos*), literary form (for example, *poetry*), and form of presentation (for example, *manuals*) or arrangement (such as *dictionaries, tables, programmed texts*): they are most closely associated with headings for use in library catalogues and bibliographies of books.

As with fundamental categories, citation order often has to be adapted to the subject in hand, particularly within the humanities and social sciences. For example, in Education it is generally agreed that the key system is the Educand – the person being taught. However, in the literature of education it is not always easy to distinguish the Educand from the schools and colleges where education takes place. Some systems regard them as one; others distinguish them. The next most important facet concerns what is taught; that is, Curriculum subjects which correspond nearly enough to the generalized Materials facet. Under Processes we can subsume Student learning, but Teaching implies an Agent (the Teacher), so it is more properly an Operation; but teaching and learning are not always distinguishable in the literature.

EVALUATING PRE-COORDINATION

There are six possible ways to arrange a subject string containing three elements; a five-element string can be arranged in 125 different ways. Therefore, in pre-coordinate systems, strings become exponentially more difficult to handle as the number of elements in them increases. More generally, they require more intellectual effort at the input stage, and are therefore costly to produce. Also, they make for bulky indexes, as they create cumbersome networks of references; and unless the index is 'articulated' (that is, includes linking words such as 'for', 'in', 'of', etc, to clarify relationships), a long subject string can be difficult to interpret. Thus the exhaustivity possible with pre-coordinate systems is low, and they can only operate at the level of summarization. In practice, many systems limit the amount of pre-coordination they permit.

Another inherent problem with pre-coordination is that the searcher has to make do with the sequence of topics imposed by the system's citation order. To some extent, multiple entry indexing systems, as discussed in Chapter 11, can alleviate this problem. These, however, are inherently bulky, and unsuited to all situations – in particular they cannot be applied to shelf classification.

A summary of the relative merits of pre-coordinate and post-coordinate techniques is given in Figure 7.2. This figure also acts as a summary of the key differences between the major post-coordinate indexing languages, thesauri and the main exemplars of pre-coordinate indexing languages – that is, classification schemes.

SUBJECT HEADINGS LISTS

ORIGINS AND PRINCIPLES

Alphabetical subject headings began to be systematized well over a century ago, in 1876, when Charles Ammi Cutter published his *Rules for a Dictionary Catalog* (Cutter, 1904). Originating in that era and drawing on Cutter's work, *Library of*

Pre-coordination:
- improves the precision of searching
- makes for indexes that are familiar to users, in that they present a more-or-less complete statement of the subject
- is traditionally used for user-conducted searches in manual systems
- is available in well-tried, 'standard' systems (particularly LCC, DDC and LCSH in MARC records)
- in A–Z order makes one-stage 'dictionary' indexes, which can be used with little or no training
- a classification system which is the only practical way to arrange the stock of open-access libraries

BUT:
- a fixed citation order leads to complications in collocation and searching
- pre-coordinate indexes are only effective at summarization level, because large numbers of terms in a string become very difficult to handle
- indexing in controlled language systems is slow and costly.

Post-coordination:
- permits indexing to any level of exhaustivity
- accommodates different kinds of searching pattern
- makes it easy to add or discard terms when searching
- is syntax-free (i.e., has no citation order), and so indexing is faster and therefore cheaper
- is the dominant method of computer-based searching

BUT:
- it cannot be used for shelf arrangement
- a limited range of syntactic relationships is shown, and false coordinations are difficult to avoid when searching
- the searcher has to input terms individually, and does not see a full statement of the subject
- indexing to higher levels of exhaustivity can lead to an excess of recall, with large numbers of marginally relevant items being retrieved
- formulating Boolean searches, and the protocols of computer searching, can be complicated, even in menu-driven systems
- command-driven online systems are user-unfriendly, and may require an intermediary.

Figure 7.2 Summary of pre-coordination and post-coordination

Congress Subject Headings (LCSH) is the pre-eminent authority list for subject headings. First published in 1909, and at the time of writing (2006) in its 29th edition, it is used not only by the Library of Congress but widely throughout the English-speaking world. The headings form the alphabetical subject approach in a wide range of MARC records.

Around the start of the twentieth century, the Library of Congress thoroughly reorganized its cataloguing procedures, adopting and developing Cutter's *Rules*, and inaugurated its printed card distribution service. Its dictionary catalogue, based on Cutter's principles, was quite simply the best available at the time. LCSH has continued with only evolutionary alterations (most of them since 1975) until the present day.

LCSH is based on the principles laid down by Cutter:

- Subject entry under the most specific word or phrase expressing the subject. In Cutter's words: 'Put Lady Cust's book on "The cat" under *Cat*, not under *Zoology* or *Mammals*, or *Domestic Animals*.' This establishes the principle of alphabetico-direct as opposed to alphabetico-classed entry; alphabetico-classing is where subject entries display two or more hierarchical levels, a broad topical heading with a specific subheading; in this case, *Domestic Animals – Cats*.
- A work may have two or more subject entries if the subject cannot be fully specified in one. Cutter did not recognize subheadings: a work on social conditions in rural England might have entries under *Social Conditions*, *Rural Conditions* and *England*. This principle is still to be found in LCSH: while subheadings are permitted, such a work would now have the headings *England – Rural Conditions* and *England – Social Conditions*.
- The wording of subject headings must reflect usage. Cutter selected headings on the basis that they should be terms in general usage and accepted by educated people. In addition to problems with new subjects that lacked accepted or established names, this guiding principle engendered inconsistency in the form of headings. Equally, Cutter's devotion to natural language posed problems with multi-word terms. Direct order was preferred, but inverted phrases were acceptable when it could be established that the second term was definitely more significant, leaving it to the individual to judge when to apply this. The well-intentioned vagueness of these rules has been inherited by LCSH.
- A uniform heading for each subject, with references from synonymous terms. This technique states for once and for all the guiding principle of vocabulary control and, together with specific entry, is Cutter's most lasting contribution to indexing theory and practice.
- *See also* references linking related subjects. While Cutter's system of references has been refined, the main features of semantic relations are clearly laid down.

LCSH embeds Cutter's principles as outlined above, with the major exceptions that subdivisions are widely used. Also, in recent years, aspects of the thesaurus approach have been incorporated, including improvements in the consistency of the form of headings and the use of the thesaurus conventions BT, NT, etc., to express semantic relationships. Nevertheless, LCSH is still full of inconsistencies, but, together with DDC, it is well entrenched in cataloguing practice, and therefore remains important. Paradoxically, some of these inconsistencies are less significant in online search systems, because with keyword access the order of terms in headings is much less important.

TYPES OF HEADING

Most headings are mapped to their equivalent LCC class numbers. The simplest form of heading is a single noun; for example, *Advertising; Heart; Railroads; Success*. A heading may be followed by a *parenthetical qualifier*, usually to distinguish homographs; for example, *Cold (Disease)*; or to explain terms not widely known; for example, *Dodoth (African tribe)*. Some qualifiers simply limit or qualify their heading by discipline; for example, *Divorce (Canon law)*; *Bread (in religion, folklore, etc.)* – the precise form of the qualifier can vary. A few, like *Cookery (Chicken)*, are idiosyncratic forms of pre-coordination.

Phrase headings will usually be in direct order, often in the form of adjective plus noun; for example, *Nuclear physics; American drama; Mining machinery*. There are some inverted headings, such as: *Education, secondary*, and *Functions, Abelian*, but editorial policy is to reduce the number of inverted headings, and many have been eliminated; for example, *Gas, natural* has become *Natural gas*.

Conjunctive phrase headings link overlapping topics by means of 'and' or 'etc.'; for example, *Literary forgeries and mystifications; Mines and mineral resources; Law reports, digests*, etc. As well as being used for the conjunction of A and B, this type of heading can also be used to express a relationship between A and B topics; for example, *Good and evil; Television and children; Literature and society*. Because of their inherent looseness, this type of heading has now been discontinued and some headings simplified; for example, *Cities and towns, Ruined, extinct, etc.*, is now simply: *Extinct cities*.

A final form of heading is the *prepositional phrase heading*; for example, *Fertilization of plants; Radar in speed limit enforcement; Automobile driving on mountain roads*.

Headings for *named entities* – persons, families, places, corporate bodies – are established where possible in accordance with AACR2, and can usually be checked in the Name Authority File.

Many headings have scope *notes*. These usually start with the formula 'Here are entered works ...', and go on to define or explain the heading, indicate its application, and often to indicate the line of demarcation with related headings.

A heading may be a *topical heading* (what the work is about) or a *form heading* (indicating the work's physical form or its form of presentation and arrangement). A heading such as *Short stories* might apply to a collection or to a work of criticism. In some but not all cases a subdivision may clarify which is which.

SUBDIVISIONS

The subdivision of headings greatly increases the precision of headings. Subdivisions are introduced by a hyphen. A large number of subdivisions are

enumerated under their headings, but many more are designated *free-floating*. These are commonly used subdivisions which can be added to headings as required, and do not appear specifically after their headings in LCSH. They can be of general or restricted application: there are around 40 different categories of the latter. They are controlled by *pattern headings* (that is, representative headings for personal names, other proper names, various ethnic and national topics and certain everyday objects, which then serve as a pattern for all entries of the same type). Subdivisions are of four types: topical, form, geographic and period.

1. *Topical* (that is, subject) *subdivision*, often follows standard citation order; for example, *Heart – Diseases; Herbicides – Research – Technique; Shakespeare, William, 1564–1616 – Characters – Children.*
2. *Form subdivisions* are the everyday common facets denoting common subject or form; for example, *Engineering – Dictionaries; Mathematics – Study and teaching; France – History – Revolution, 1789–99 – Fiction.*
3. *Geographic subdivisions* are the common facets of place; for example, *Probation – Northern Ireland; Geology – England – Peak District.*
4. *Chronological subdivisions* are the common facet of time. Mostly, however, they are not free-floating but are tailored to their topic; for example, *Great Britain – History – to 1485; Great Britain – History – Victoria, 1837–1901; France – Politics and government, 1589–1610; English drama – Restoration, 1660–1700.* Occasionally, period is expressed in ways other than by a subdivision; for example, *Art, Renaissance.*

It will be seen from the above examples that more than one subdivision may be applied. There are usually specific instructions for particular combinations, to maintain control over the use of subdivisions. Recent policy has been to replace subdivisions with a phrase heading if possible; for example, *Railroads – Stations* has become *Railroad stations*. In the application of subdivisions the following should be noted:

- *Order of heading and subdivision.* Most headings conform to standard citation order (Entity – Action or process) (for example, *Kidneys – Diseases*) but with occasional exceptions (for example, *Advertising – Cigarettes*, which places the process before the product, presumably on the grounds that advertising is advertising, whatever the product).
- *Topic versus place.* Usually topic comes first, but there are many occasions, particularly in the social sciences, where place takes precedence. To confuse matters further, cities are treated differently from regions; for example, *Nottingham (Notts) – Hospitals*; but *Hospitals – Nottinghamshire.*
- *Geographic names* may serve as headings, as part of a heading, as a subdivision, or as a qualifier; for example, *Manning Provincial Park, BC*;

Jamaica – description and travel; *Paris in literature*; *Building permits –
Belgium*; *Japanese in San Francisco*.

The filing sequence of headings and subheadings in card indexes and printed lists
can be complex. An example appears in Figure 11.4.

Editorial policy has always been to create new headings as needed. Because of
varying editorial policies stretching back for nearly a century, there are many
inconsistencies in the formulation of headings. Where there has been a change of
policy, normal practice has been to leave existing headings alone, and apply the new
policy only to headings established after the change of policy; retrospective revision
was undertaken only when the pressure to change became intolerable, as when
Negroes was changed to *Blacks*, or *Electronic calculating machines* to *Computers*.
This conservatism was understandable and indeed necessary with card catalogues.
Now that, increasingly, software is able to accommodate global changes to the
catalogue database, current practice is to replace headings systematically.

REFERENCES IN LCSH

The former reference symbols *See*, *x*, *sa* and *xx* have, since 1988, been replaced
with the thesaurus conventions:

USE
UF   Used for
BT   Broader topic
NT   Narrower topic
RT   Related topic

The symbols denote equivalence, hierarchical and associative relationships (as
already described in Chapter 5). Note, however, the subtle use of *topic* (acknowl-
edging that some headings are pre-coordinate) instead of *term* (which in a
thesaurus normally indicates a simple concept). Figure 7.3 shows an example of
their effect.

The abbreviation *sa* (*see also*) is still used, but is limited to general references.
The following general reference appears under the heading Bibliography:

sa names of literatures, e.g. *American literature*; and subdivision *Bibliography*
under names of persons, places and subjects; also subdivision *Bibliography –
Methodology* under specific subjects, e.g. *Medicine – Bibliography –
Methodology*; and subdivision *Imprints* under names of countries, states, cities,
etc.

References are used in two ways. The *cataloguer* uses the references in the List to
help locate the correct heading. References to headings in a catalogue or

bibliography are interfiled with the headings. The *catalogue user* uses the references to help locate the correct heading for a topic, also as a means of moving between related topics. This use of references is becoming obsolete. It was normal usage with card and printed catalogues and bibliographies; but it is very unusual to include references in computerized catalogues and bibliographies.

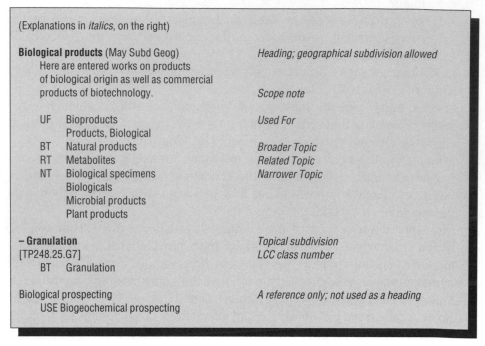

(Explanations in *italics*, on the right)

Biological products (May Subd Geog)   *Heading; geographical subdivision allowed*
    Here are entered works on products
    of biological origin as well as commercial
    products of biotechnology.   *Scope note*

    UF   Bioproducts   *Used For*
         Products, Biological
    BT   Natural products   *Broader Topic*
    RT   Metabolites   *Related Topic*
    NT   Biological specimens   *Narrower Topic*
         Biologicals
         Microbial products
         Plant products

− **Granulation**   *Topical subdivision*
[TP248.25.G7]   *LCC class number*
    BT   Granulation

Biological prospecting   *A reference only; not used as a heading*
    USE Biogeochemical prospecting

Figure 7.3   LCSH heading with its references

ASSIGNING SUBJECT HEADINGS

As subject headings are pre-coordinated, and can often be used as they stand, it is easy to think that assigning them is simply a matter of picking from a list. In reality there are a number of issues to be considered. These include:

1. Policy issues:
   – Are subject headings to be assigned:
     ○ only to complete works?
     ○ to partial contents, where a substantial part of a work deals with a distinct topic?
     ○ to individual chapters, articles, etc.?
     ○ to parts of a work, as analytical entries, where a work consists of a small number of discrete items?

- What is the maximum number of subject headings that can be assigned to a work?
- Are there any categories of work to which no subject headings are to be assigned? (Possible examples include fiction and general periodicals.)
- If a specific heading is not available, is there a mechanism for creating a new heading?
- If keyword access is also available, do the subject headings complement the keywords available elsewhere in the record, or are they searchable independently of them?

2. In working situations, headings and their references are recorded in a Subject Authority File (see Chapter 12).
3. Specific entry: use the most specific heading that will accommodate the subject content of the work. If there is no specific heading, and a new heading cannot be created, use the nearest broader heading.
4. Multiple headings: consider whether more than one subject heading is needed to cover the major aspects of the subject content. Occasionally, depending on policy, additional subject headings may be assigned to express subordinate themes within the work.
5. Multi-topical works: if a work deals separately with two or three distinct topics, assign separate subject headings to each topic, provided that the topics do not together constitute a more general topic (for example, a work dealing with inorganic and organic chemistry is assigned the single heading *Chemistry*).
6. Follow any *scope notes* governing correct usage.
7. Apply subdivisions judiciously, paying attention to LCSH's often subtle rules governing their application and sequencing (where more than one subdivision applies). Again, check any scope notes, as distinctions between subdivisions (for example, between *Social conditions* and *Social life and customs*) can be fine.

BIBLIOGRAPHIC CLASSIFICATION SCHEMES

INTRODUCTION

Chapter 6 explored the principles of classification as they apply to the components of a classification scheme: schedules, notation, index and revision. In particular, in the context of schedules, issues associated with the development of classes, and the differentiation between enumerative and faceted classification, were reviewed, using examples from a specific classification scheme. This section briefly reviews some of the key features of some significant bibliographic classification schemes. The three major general classification schemes are DDC, its offspring UDC, and

LCC. Since, like LCSH these are used variously, both for the more traditional shelf arrangement, but also in a variety of catalogue and indexing databases, these will be described in some detail in this section. Two other schemes that have made important contributions – BC (and its successor BC2) and CC – will be discussed briefly because of their influence on current theory and practice. The section concludes with a brief discussion of special classification schemes.

The three major schemes were all introduced before the ideas of facet analysis were developed. They are thus basically enumerative schemes, though all have some analytico-synthetic features. In the case of UDC these are very extensive, less so with DDC, although the latter has embraced the principles of facet analysis and is incorporating more synthetic features. With LCC they are a minor feature.

THE DEWEY DECIMAL CLASSIFICATION

Normally abbreviated to DDC, this is the most widely used classification in the world. It is used in over 135 countries and in the national bibliographies of more than 60 countries, and is translated into 30 languages. Libraries of every type apply Dewey numbers on a daily basis, and share these numbers through a variety of channels. Dewey is also used as a browsing mechanism for resources on the Web. The current edition, DDC21, was published in 2003; the most recent Abridged edition is edition 14, published in 2004. WebDewey and Abridged WebDewey provide flexible digital access to the scheme.

In 1876 Melvil Dewey, a 25-year-old college librarian, published anonymously *A Classification and Subject Index for Cataloguing and Arranging the Books and Pamphlets of a Library*, with 12 pages of introduction, 12 pages of tables and 18 pages of index. It had three novel features which are still important in classification schemes today:

1   Books were to be shelved by relative instead of fixed location. With fixed location, books were given a fixed place on a numbered shelf, and any new books on the subject represented by that shelf had to be filed at the end. When the shelf became full, a new sequence had to be started elsewhere. With relative location, the books were now numbered in relation to each other and not to the shelves. The whole collection could grow as required, and a more detailed subject specification became possible – Dewey's 999 classes were a great advance on anything that had gone before.
2. It employed a simple decimal notation instead of the cumbersome notations (often involving roman numbers) previously used. The notation was an important factor in the early and continued success of the scheme.
3. A detailed subject index, made necessary by the detail of the classification.

The second edition of 1885 established three further principles:

1. Decimal subdivision – this greatly increased the ability of the scheme to support specific detail.
2. Integrity of numbers – Dewey made some quite sweeping relocations in the second edition, and to sugar the pill announced that future editions would expand but not relocate – a policy that was followed until 1951. This policy, however reassuring to users and convenient for librarians, inevitably meant that the structure of the scheme became more and more outmoded over time.
3. Synthesis – this was in the form of: (a) a table of 'form divisions' representing some of the common facets, which could be appended to any number; and (b) 'divide like' instructions, the forerunner of the present 'add' instructions, where all or part of one number may be added to another in order to specify an extra facet.

Schedules

With DDC the notation is everything; the evidence is that Dewey fitted his classification to the notation rather than the other way round. The magnificent simplicity of a pure numeric notation is achieved at the cost of the most tightly constricted notational base of any classification. Each stage in the subdivision of the universe of knowledge permits only nine divisions. A three-digit notation allows for only 999 classes, and Dewey used them all. As the universe is not organized on regular decimal lines, it is inevitable that each 1–9 subdivision will, more often than not, include topics from more than one facet or subfacet. With very few exceptions, classes are divided top-down on the enumerative principle. This again has resulted in many classes being divided according to more than one principle of division at a time. This is further discussed below.

Another way of saving notational space is the use of pseudo-hierarchies. One class is used as an umbrella heading for a miscellaneous collection of loosely associated topics. Some examples are:

380	Commerce, communications, transportation
387	Water, air, space transportation
646	Sewing, clothing, management of personal and family living
646.7	Management of personal and family living. Grooming
629.28	[Vehicle] tests, driving, maintenance and repair.

In a few places the original division of classes omitted steps in hierarchies and left no space in the notation for a necessary broader term to be added later. One instance is the sequence 385–388, which denoted rail, canal, sea and land transport without providing a place for transportation generally. Recently, transportation generally has been classed at 388, sacrificing general-to-special in order to keep the subject together.

Figure 7.4 lists the main classes in DDC. The classes are based on disciplines, with occasional exceptions, notably 770 Photography, which includes both technical and artistic aspects.

000	Computers, information & general reference
100	Philosophy & psychology
200	Religion
300	Social sciences
400	Language
500	Science
600	Technology
700	Arts & recreation
800	Literature
900	History & geography

Figure 7.4 DDC main classes

Synthesis

The scheme is essentially enumerative, and originally had a very inconsistent facet structure, but revision in recent editions has aimed, wherever feasible, to adopt a structure that better reflects the faceted approach. This is achieved both through the arrangement of classes in the schedules and also though the use of synthetic devices, such as the tables and the 'Add to' instructions. Accordingly, within the schedules there are now examples of both consistency and inconsistencies in facet structure. For example, in 370 Education we find:

371	Schools and their activities [itself a hotchpotch of assorted facets with Special education tagged on at the end]
372, 373, 374	Stages of education: elementary, secondary, adult [with Higher education separated from these at 378]
375	Curricula
379	Public policy issues in education.

Yet careful inspection of the class 624.1, as shown in Figure 7.5, reveals relatively close adherence to the identification of a facet structure and to standard citation order.

'Add' instructions also make the citation order clear. For example, the class for elementary education for specific objectives, 372.011, has an 'add' instruction to add to this number the subdivisions of 370.11. Thus, 370.115 denotes Education

624.1 Structural engineering and underground construction
  .15 Foundation engineering and engineering geology [Key system]
  .151 Engineering geology [NT Properties, processes, operations]
  .152–.158 Foundation engineering [*Centred heading*][NT]
  .152 Excavation [Operations]
  .153 Foundation materials [Materials]
  .154–.158 Specific types of foundations [*Centred heading*][Kinds]
  .16 Supporting structures other than foundations [Key system]
  .17 Structural analysis and design [Operations]
  .171 Structural analysis [Operations]
  .172–.176 Loads, stresses, strains [*Centred heading*] [Processes]
  .177 Structural design and specific structural elements
  .1771 Structural design [Operations]
  .1772–.1779 Specific structural elements [Parts]
  .18 Materials [in structural engineering][Key system, Materials]
  .19 Underground construction [Key system]

Figure 7.5   Facet structure and centred headings in DDC class 624.1

for social responsibility, and Elementary education for social responsibility will be classed at 372.0115.

Preference instructions, indicate which facet is to be preferred and which is to be ignored are another way of making the citation order explicit. For example, in 624.1 (see Figure 7.5), 624.17723 is Beams and girders, and 624.1821 Iron and steel. There is an instruction at 624.182: Class specific structural elements in metal in 624.1772–624.1779, so that Structural steel girders would be classed at 624.17723.

Further synthesis is provided through the tables. Except for T1, which can be added in many places, table notation may only be added as instructed in the schedules and tables. The tables are:

- T1: Standard subdivisions: this is the oldest of the tables, covering the common facets of form and subject
- T2: Geographic areas, historic periods, persons: this is the longest by far of the tables; typically (but not invariably) applied after -09 from Table 1
- T3: Subdivisions for the arts, for individual literatures, for specific literary forms
- T4: Subdivisions of individual languages and language families
- T5: Ethnic and national groups
- T6: Languages.

DDC has an alphabetical index that covers all of the schedules, and which is updated with each new edition. In addition, there are three summary tables of the whole classification, that aid navigation.

Organization and use

Control of the scheme was assigned by Dewey himself to the Lake Placid Club Educational Foundation, a not-for-profit body. The club owned Forest Press, DDC's publisher, which gave the scheme a sound financial footing. An editorial office was established within the Library of Congress, ensuring both literary warrant for the scheme and the inclusion of DDC class numbers in USMARC records. In 1988 the Forest Press was sold to OCLC, and editorial work is now done by the Library of Congress under contract with OCLC Forest Press. There is a broadly based Editorial Policy Committee, which includes members from Canada, Australia and the UK, and advises the editorial team. Other experts are also consulted as required. Dewey Decimal Classification's literary warrant has been improved through becoming part of OCLC, as OCLC's Online Union Catalog is now accessed electronically as part of the revision process. This, being based on a very wide range of working collections, gives a better idea of the range of titles that libraries actually acquire than could be obtained from a single legal deposit collection.

New editions are published every seven years. One or two major divisions are recast completely, with piecemeal alterations elsewhere. A single-volume abridged edition is published alongside every full edition. WebDewey and Abridged WebDewey are updated on a quarterly basis. WebDewey also includes:

- mappings between LCSH and Dewey numbers
- additional index terms
- links to LCSH authority records
- selected mapping from Medical Subject headings (MeSH).

Although libraries may classify new stock by the latest edition of DDC, earlier editions remain important because many libraries are reluctant to reclassify, and thus leave stock classified by earlier editions long after they have been superseded.

THE LIBRARY OF CONGRESS CLASSIFICATION

The detailed classification scheme of the Library of Congress was occasioned by the library's removal to new premises in 1897. The scheme consists of 21 main classes set out in over 50 volumes. Publication began in 1899 and was virtually complete by 1910 – apart from class K Law, publication of which did not commence until 1969 and was not completed until 1993. There are revised editions of most classes. Recent editions are published in the USMARC format for classification data, and the full schedules, together with LCSH, are available on Classification Web.

The scheme's name describes it precisely: it is the classification of the Library of Congress. It exists to serve the needs of that body. It was, and is, an in-house classification. However, as the classification of the world's largest library, its suitability to other large academic and research collections was soon recognized, and was greatly advanced by the library's decision in 1901 to make its printed catalogue cards available for sale to other libraries.

Schedules

The scheme was based on the long-defunct *Expansive Classification* of Charles Ammi Cutter. Its main classes (see Figure 7.6) are clearly tailored to the needs of the LC, as they were perceived a century ago. Like everything else about LCC, the order of the main classes is thoroughly pragmatic; every class exists because subject specialists have perceived the need for it, and the order and detail of the classes have been developed, again by specialists, to meet the requirements of an exceptionally large working collection operating under exacting conditions.

Each class was compiled separately, and could be used independently. It follows that the classification is almost entirely enumerative, with much repetition of detail, making the schedules very extensive. Classes are divided in a broadly hierarchical manner; but as the scheme was compiled piecemeal at a time when classification theory barely existed, there is little consistent application of either hierarchies or a facet structure, even within a single class.

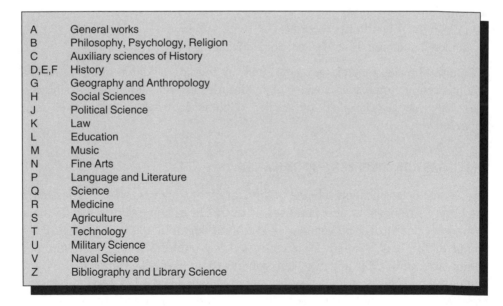

A	General works
B	Philosophy, Psychology, Religion
C	Auxiliary sciences of History
D,E,F	History
G	Geography and Anthropology
H	Social Sciences
J	Political Science
K	Law
L	Education
M	Music
N	Fine Arts
P	Language and Literature
Q	Science
R	Medicine
S	Agriculture
T	Technology
U	Military Science
V	Naval Science
Z	Bibliography and Library Science

Figure 7.6 LCC main classes

There are a number of recurring themes, including:

- A tendency to file common form and subject facets before general works on a topic. A common sequence is:
  - Periodicals, Societies
  - Collections, Dictionaries
  - Theory, Philosophy, Congresses
  - History
  - General works
- Alphabetical subdivision – which purists would object is the negation of classification – is frequently used, in the form of Cutter numbers. For example, class HJ4653 Income tax – United States – Special, A–Z has subdivisions that include .C3 Capital gains and .E75 Evasion.
- A variable amount of ad hoc synthesis, which is specific to each main class.

Notation

The general pattern of LCC's notation can be observed in the examples above: one or two (very occasionally three) capital letters followed by up to four digits used numerically rather than decimally. Hospitality is achieved by leaving gaps in the notation (see Figure 7.7). Where these have been filled, the notation is then expanded decimally. It is all very clear and workmanlike, like the number plate of a car. The use of Cutter numbers adds to the complexity of the notation.

H Social sciences
HM–HX Sociology
HV Social pathology. Social and public welfare. Criminology
HV 6001–9920 Criminology
HV 6254–6773 Special crimes
HV 6435–6402 Offenses against the public order
HV 6435–6453 Illegal organizations
HV 6441–6453 Outlaws. Brigands. Feuds

Figure 7.7   LCC notation

For many years there was no official comprehensive alphabetical index, but only the indexes to each volume. LCSH served as a rough and ready index, as many headings have relevant LCC class marks. Today, cataloguers can make use of Classification Web which offers sophisticated navigation tools for the location and verification of class numbers as discussed below.

Organization and use

As the in-house classification of a huge legal deposit library, LCC assigns new class marks as the need arises. Previously various lists and updates were published. Now, the weekly updates of Classification Web ensure easy access to recent changes. Revision, and notification of revision, is thus continuous. Radical revision of individual classes is very much the exception. A range of official manuals and documents are published as part of the Cataloguers' Reference Shelf (<www.itsmarc.com>).

Classification Web offers the following features that make the schedules easier to use:

- dynamic classification through weekly updates
- browse screens and search screen to navigate the schedules
- hierarchy browser
- subject correlations – to find matches between LCSH and class numbers
- notes function for the cataloguer's own notes
- search of LC subject authority records.

The scheme is primarily used by LC itself and by other extensive research collections such as large academic libraries, mainly North American but also in other English-speaking countries, including many UK university libraries. The resources behind the scheme, and the size of the collections that currently use LCC and its inclusion in MARC records, are sufficient to ensure its stability and continuation throughout the foreseeable future.

THE UNIVERSAL DECIMAL CLASSIFICATION

Usually abbreviated to UDC, this emerged from an attempt in 1894 by two Belgians, Paul Otlet and Henri LaFontaine, to commence the compilation of a 'universal index to recorded knowledge'. A classified rather than an alphabetical approach was necessary in the index because of the many languages involved, and because an internationally acceptable notation was important. The DDC was already in its fifth edition, and Melvil Dewey's permission was obtained to extend the scheme. A conference in 1895 established the Institut International de la Bibliographie (IIB) to be responsible for the index. The first edition of UDC was published in French between 1904 and 1907.

The First World War and the unfavourable climate after it led to the demise of the index, but UDC continued with a second edition in French and a third in German. The IIB eventually became the Fédération International d'Information et de Documentation (FID). The British Standards Institution, the official English editorial body, published an abridged English edition in 1961. Publication of a full

English edition had begun in 1943 but was not completed until 1980. Since 1992 all rights and responsibilities for UDC have been vested in the UDC Consortium, representing various international and national organizations. The machine-readable Master Reference File (MRF) contains the UDC schedules, together with the records needed for administration, maintenance and archiving. As of 2005, the MRF contained some 66,000 classes (compared with 220,000 classes in the full editions). The main source for the MRF was the International Medium Edition, in English. Although there are some entries in French and German, the output from the MRF continues to be distributed in English. There are also editions in various combinations of Full, Medium and Abridged in around 20 other languages – French, German and English are UDC's official languages.

Schedules

The overall outline of the schedules follows DDC. The schedules and notation are largely hierarchical, though hierarchies are less clearly indicated than in DDC. In the Medium edition many classes have headings describing aggregates of topics; thus:

675.25 Mechanically treated leathers. Including: Embossed leather. Buff. Perforated, punched leather.

The Full edition provides subclasses for each of these. The schedules include some pre-coordinated classes, for example:

341.345	Internment of military personnel in neutral countries
551.588.5	Influence of ice on climate
664.71	Milling of wheat and rye
664.782	Processing of rice. Rice milling
664.784	Processing of maize. Maize milling (corn milling)
664.785	Processing of oats. Oat milling

Synthesis

While many enumerated compounds do occur, the principal means of pre-coordination is by synthesis. Within the schedules, 'special auxiliary subdivisions' are frequently to be found. These often indicate a Processes or Operations facet, and are introduced by .0 (less frequently by a hyphen or an apostrophe). They apply only to their class. For example, under 636 Animal husbandry, 636.082 is the special auxiliary for the breeding of animals. 636.1 denotes Horses, and 636.16 Ponies, which would give 636.1.082 and 636.16.082 for the breeding of horses and ponies respectively. In a few places an equivalent of DDC's 'Add' instructions is to be found, indicated by ≞; for example, 378.18 Student life, customs, etc. ≅ 71.8 –

classifiers have to work out for themselves which part of the number to bring across. There are also ten common auxiliary tables (see Figure 7.8).

+	Coordination	622+669 Mining and metallurgy
/	Consecutive extension	643/645 The home and household equipment (*the same as 643+644+645*)
:	Simple relation	17:7 Ethics in relation to art
[. . .]	Subgroup	31:[622+669](485) Statistics of mining and metallurgy in Sweden (*to remove ambiguities from certain combinations*)
::	Order-fixing	77.044::355 War photography (*for use in machine retrieval systems, where retrieval of the subordinate concept is not required*)
These five are purely linking devices. The other auxiliaries have their own classes, and could in certain circumstances be used as the primary facet:		
=	Languages	61=161.1 Medical documents in Russian
(0 ...)	Form	61(031) A medical encyclopaedia; also common subjects: 7(091) History of art
(1/9)	Place	7(450.341) Venetian art
(= ...)	Ethnic grouping and nationality	7(=72) Australian aborigine art
'...'	Time	61'16' Seventeenth-century medicine
The following are dependent common subdivisions and can only be used as suffixes:		
.00	Point of view	7.000.28 The Christian outlook on art
-03	Materials	645.13-037.87 Linoleum floor coverings
-05	Persons	7-053.2 Children's art

Figure 7.8 UDC common auxiliary tables

Most of the auxiliaries can, if required, be repeated or combined with one another, so a high degree of synthesis is possible. The colon is the general-purpose relational indicator: when UDC was used to compile subject indexes, before machine retrieval became the norm, it was common to find hugely lengthy notations containing four or more facets strung together with colons. Uniquely among general classifications, UDC allows the individual user a large degree of autonomy in selecting the citation order. Standard citation order is officially recommended, however, and in many places it is built into the schedules through the special auxiliaries.

Notation

Though based on DDC, UDC's notation is far more complex, thanks to its non-alphanumeric auxiliaries. The notation is completely hospitable through the use of decimal expansion.

As UDC has been largely developed for use in scientific and technical contexts, the allocation of the notation is even more skewed than DDC's, and classes 5 and 6 comprise almost two thirds of the schedules. For more specific subjects the notation can be extremely long.

UDC's filing order is complicated by the range of non-alphanumeric characters in the notation, and by the possibility of many auxiliaries being used independently, so that a class number could conceivably begin with a bracket, equals sign or double-quote.

Organization and use

UDC's revision structure has in the past been notoriously slow and this has been one of its main limitations. In addition, computer-based indexing systems have largely rendered obsolete UDC's detailed indexing function. UDC remains very popular for shelf classification, particularly in the libraries of continental Europe. It is also used to arrange various bibliographies and indexing services.

OTHER GENERAL CLASSIFICATION SCHEMES

There are two other general classification schemes that merit a mention: the Colon Classification, and the Bliss Bibliographic Classification. Despite some useful full or partial implementations, these two schemes are of more interest for their contribution to theory (and thereby their influence on the schemes discussed earlier in this section, on some of the approaches used in the design of thesauri, and on the ontologies discussed later in this chapter) than as practical working classification schemes.

Colon Classification (CC)

Devised by S.R. Ranganathan, this is chiefly of historical interest for its development of facet analysis. First published in 1933, subsequent editions have introduced quite drastic changes.

CC's facet formula is simple: PMEST, which stands for Personality, Matter, Energy, Space and Time. Personality is (broadly) Key system; Matter is Materials; Energy is Processes and Operations; and Space and Time are two of the common facets. Aligning these with standard citation order gives:

Key system	Personality
Kinds	
Parts	
Materials	Matter
Properties	
Processes	Energy
Operations	
Agents	
Common facets	Space
	Time

Bliss Bibliographic Classification (BC)

This was the outworking of the lifelong study of classification by Henry Evelyn Bliss (1870–1955), and was published in stages between 1940 and 1953. Though published in the US its major impact was in the UK and elsewhere, particularly in the specialist fields of education, social welfare and health. A Bliss Classification Association was formed in the UK to sustain and develop the classification, and the decision was made to undertake a major revision on analytico-synthetic principles, using and developing the work of the Classification Research Group towards the elusive goal of a completely new general classification scheme. In reality this goal proved very elusive and the main contributions of the schemes have been to advance theory and support the development of a number of specialist classification schemes. Bliss's original classification had many synthetic features, but was essentially enumerative in structure, and chiefly notable for the care taken over the order of classes. The revision (BC2) was to retain much of this macrostructure, but otherwise is effectively a new classification.

The key features of BC2 are as follows:

1. As BC2 is entirely faceted, only simple concepts appear in the schedules. The schedules are rigorously hierarchical (see Figure 7.9).
2. While the notation is not hierarchical, hierarchies are clearly indicated by indentation and by summaries at the head of every column. Subfacets are shown within parentheses.
3. BC2's basic citation order is Disciplines – Phenomena. Phenomena that are treated in a non-disciplinary manner are given a numbered notation, to make them file *before* the disciplines. The main classes are little changed from BC, and continue to embody Bliss's principles of following the 'educational and scientific consensus', placing general before special, 'gradation in speciality', and the collocation of related subjects.
4. BC2's notation uses both numbers and letters. Numbers and letters are used together in the listing of main classes. Otherwise, numbers are used only as

facet indicators for the common subdivisions: the standard method of building class marks is by retroactive notation. The notation is remarkably brief, and can pack a goodly number of facets into a small compass. Brevity is assured by means of:

- a long notational base
- sensible allocation of notation to the classes
- a non-hierarchical notation
- absence of facet indicators.

5. BC2's indexes show simple concepts only. Each volume of the schedules has its own index: there is no general index.

```
K        Society
KC       Social processes
KCY      Social action
(Types of action by consequences for society)
KIB      Divisive processes
KIC      Conflict
(Types of conflict)
(By instruments used)
KII X    Force
KIJ      Violence
KIJ V    Feuds and vendettas
KIJ X    Vendettas
```

Figure 7.9   BC2's hierachy for 'Vendettas'

Both BC and BC2 have been dogged throughout their lives by a chronic lack of resources. Their intrinsic qualities may make them the benchmark by which other classifications may be judged, but quality is not in itself enough to attract users and ensure its future. Paradoxically for a classification calling itself Bibliographical, it may be that BC's future is to be used predominantly not as a library classification but as a quarry for others to mine. More than any other general classification, BC2 resembles the systematic display of a thesaurus. Its specificity is such that the great majority of its headings can be used as they stand as thesaurus descriptors, and reorganizing the semantic relationships for a thesaurus is relatively straightforward. More generally, the study of classification schedules is recognized to be an excellent starting point for anyone who needs to learn how a subject is structured, and the detail and rigorous analysis of BC2's schedules make it especially useful in this respect.

TAILORING CLASSIFICATION SCHEMES IN USE

Whilst the general classification schemes discussed above and, in particular, DC and LCC have had a significant effect on cataloguing and classification practice, these schemes do not always meet the requirements for specific collections or databases. Accordingly, over the years there has been considerable attention directed towards each of the following two options:

- modifying published classification schemes to suit the requirements of a special documents collection or application
- developing a special classification scheme, typically to organize a collection for a specific use, organization, or with a specific subject focus.

In addition, there has been increasing interest in the development of ontologies and taxonomies to support access to Web databases and organization-based document collections and knowledge resources. This topic can be viewed as a development of work on the theory of classification in the field of librarianship and information science (and specifically work on special classification schemes), but with the increasing awareness of the strategic importance of knowledge to organizations and societies, and the increased complexity of document and information formats, work on ontologies is also informed by a number of other disciplinary contributions.

Modification of an existing classification scheme may be undertaken when the overall structure and approach of the scheme is suitable, but it has some specific limitations. Reasons for modifying a scheme may include:

- providing extra specificity for applying a general classification to a special collection
- giving a special collection a shorter base notation
- altering the citation order, to bring together distributed relatives (for example, in DDC in an academic library, to bring together all aspects of Geography, or to arrange literary works by Language – Period – Author instead of DDC's preferred Language – Form – Period – Author)
- to simplify the classification.

Modifications are of two kinds:

- making use of one or more of the scheme's own published alternatives: for example, DDC has an option that permits literary works to be classified at -8 under each language irrespective of literary form
- buying in or developing an unauthorized modification.

In either case, the implications must be carefully considered:

- Many libraries use centrally produced bibliographic records that include DDC and/or LCC class numbers. Resources must be allocated to identify records whose class numbers require modifying, as well as to apply the local modification.

- If there is pressure from users to modify parts of the scheme (for example, the better to reflect patterns of academic study), can the objective be met by other means; for example, by guiding or user education?
- Are the publishers of the scheme preparing an official revision? Local alterations to individual classes can be overtaken by a future edition of the classification.
- Have identical or similar problems been encountered elsewhere? If so, how have they been addressed?

Another option is to design a special classification scheme to suit the specific application. Examples of contexts in which special classification schemes have been developed and continue to be used are:

- Bibliographies, indexing and abstracting services and their associated databases.
- Shelf arrangements of special collections. These may be business, industrial and research libraries, specialist government libraries, organizations within the voluntary sector, or special collections within general libraries, especially local studies collections in public libraries. Special classifications for these purposes were often devised with indexing as an additional objective.
- Shelf arrangement of a particular class within a general classification: for example, Elizabeth Moys's (1982) *Classification Scheme for Law Books*, originally to stand in for LCC's then-unpublished class K Law.
- Thesaurofacets – a thesaurus having its systematic display developed with notation and rules for pre-coordination, enabling it to be used as a shelf classification as well as for post-coordinate retrieval. The eponymous original was the English Electric *Thesaurofacet* of 1969.
- Records management systems where files are stored in a topic-related order.

In general, schemes aim to cover just one subject area, or to meet the interests of one user group. More specifically, their types include:

- schemes restricted to a conventional subject area or discipline; for example, music, insurance, chemistry
- schemes devised for other associations of topics; for example, local collections, industrial libraries, archives
- schemes for a certain type of user; for example, children, general browsers
- schemes for documents in a particular physical form; for example, pictures, sound recordings; or restricted to a certain form of publication; for example, patents, trade catalogues
- schemes for classifying the subject content of works of the imagination; for example, fiction, paintings: conventional classification schemes classify these only by non-subject characteristics.

221

The heyday of special classification schemes was in the 1960s and 1970s. Today library or database managers would be well advised to contemplate using an existing special classification only when satisfied that none of the major general classifications is viable, and to construct a special classification as an absolute last resort. The focus of activity has moved: in many cases it will be found that a thesaurus, locally maintained as an authority file, and perhaps based on a published thesaurus, will be all that is required for specific subject retrieval, and a published classification scheme will suffice for shelf arrangement. In some contexts such schemes have also been an important input into the development of taxonomies and ontologies discussed below.

TAXONOMIES AND ONTOLOGIES

These can be seen as developments of controlled indexing languages such as thesauri and classification schemes. Or, to put it another way, thesauri, subject headings lists and classification schemes can be viewed as well-established exemplars of taxonomies and ontologies. In common with these earlier tools, taxonomies and ontologies are concerned with identifying and mapping the relationships between the terms and concepts in a subject area or documentation relevant to a specific community. But they are designed for use in a wider range of contexts than the traditional domains of the librarians and information scientists, although information professionals have often been prominent in their development. Taxonomies have been generated by a combination of information technologies and systems developers, together with software vendors. Ontologies have their roots in the disciplines of philosophy and artificial intelligence. The confluence of these various disciplines in this area has led to some lack of clarity in the use of terminology, leading (for example) to the terms taxonomy and ontology sometimes but not always being used interchangeably, and to multiple definitions of both terms.

Accordingly, it is difficult to propose definitions that accommodate all of the different meanings associated with the terms ontology and taxonomy, but the following definitions provide a basis for further discussion and development later in this section. Gruber (1993) defines ontology as:

... a formal, explicit specification of shared conceptualization ...

An ontology is therefore a 'knowledge map' or 'knowledge organization system'. Each of us has different knowledge maps of the same subject, depending on the scope and depth of our engagement with the subject. In an organization or information retrieval system which will be shared by many individuals it is important to identify a 'knowledge map' that will support information organization and management that is effective for the community of users, hence Gruber's notion of a 'shared conceptualization'. Such an ontology includes (in common with a classification scheme) the key concepts in the knowledge domain, identified with names, and an indication for the relationships between those concepts. The term 'ontology' is used with varying degrees of precision. For example, in the context of the Semantic Web it may be applied loosely to any knowledge organization system, whereas in artificial intelligence applications ontology has a formal meaning as discussed in the section below.

Again, the term 'taxonomy' has multiple meanings and uses, but in general a taxonomy is also a 'knowledge map'; however, in this case the nature of the relationships between terms is clearly and explicitly defined and is typically characterized by hierarchical relationships of the type discussed in the section on thesauri. A taxonomy can be seen as the operational conceptualization of a domain embedded in a specific system, or adopted by a chosen user.

This section first explores the nature of taxonomies and ontologies, respectively, and then moves on to explain the approach to generating ontologies. After a brief section of folksonomies a final subsection discusses the concept of semantic interoperability and the Semantic Web.

TAXONOMIES

Taxonomies typically provide a set of categories with hierarchical and other relationships specified between the categories; they typically support classification or categorization. 'Taxonomy' is a loose term with a wide range of different uses. Gilchrist (2003) suggests that the word is being used with at least five different meanings, although there is some overlap between these proposed categories. Reiteration of these meanings serves to exemplify the nature and contexts of use of taxonomies. The term 'taxonomy' is used in the following contexts:

1. *Web directories*, often implemented through menus in the user interface. The user is presented with a list of terms; clicking on a given term displays a second-level list of terms, and so on. Each level is not necessarily hierarchical, and terms may be repeated at different places in the structure to provide for alternative pathways for the searcher. The Open Directory Project is a significant exemplar of this approach (<www.dmoz.com>).
2. *Taxonomies to support automatic indexing*, in which the user is presented with a controlled list of possible search terms. The user does not see the taxonomy behind these terms; for each term displayed in the classification there is an algorithm comprising a set of words and phrases, synonyms and syntactic variations, weights and instructions. This rule base is used to automatically

223

extract appropriate index terms (see <www.factiva.com> and <www.lexisnexis. com>). The classification and taxonomy, which is akin to an expanded thesaurus, are manually constructed, but the algorithms guide their application.

3. *Taxonomies created by automatic categorization.* There are software packages available that automatically create categories from text analysis, and then classify the analysed documents using the categories created (<www.gammasite.com>). These categories are displayed for the user in a similar format to Web directories (that is, menu-type options) or as two-dimensional maps which show related terms. The software algorithms are typically based on the statistical analysis of the occurrence and co-occurrence of terms in the database.

4. *Front-end filters.* Here the taxonomy is available for the user to apply in query formulation. Homographs can be disambiguated and synonyms clustered, and related terms can be identified. The selected search terms are then submitted. Front-end filters are essentially a thesaurus which is easy to use and navigate.

5. *Corporate taxonomies.* These are somewhat different from the previous four categories. A corporate taxonomy is the basis for a high-level map on an enterprise portal that guides the user through the intellectual capital of the organization. Through this portal, users can access information about the organization, such as its business processes, methods, guidelines and standards, its people and its documents. Or to quote Gilchrist (2001, p. 101):

> A taxonomy aspires to be: a correlation of the different functional languages used by the enterprise ... to support a mechanism for navigating, and gaining access to, the intellectual enterprise ... by providing such tools as portal navigation aids, authority for tagging documents and other information objects, support for search engines, and knowledge maps ... and possibly ... a knowledge base in its own right.

> One major initiative of this kind involved the creation of a 'megathesaurus' from a number of pre-existing thesauri; each term in the megathesaurus carries the addresses of any corporate information repositories that use that term; software supported the assimilation of thesauri into a megathesaurus.

An interesting example of the involvement of information professionals in the development and use of a taxonomy is that of government librarians in the UK. Over a period of years they have developed a taxonomy which has been through several iterations and has now stabilized as the Integrated Public Service Vocabulary (IPSV). The driving force behind the creation of IPSV has been the UK government's determination to provide electronic access to government information and to encourage UK citizens to interact with government via the Web. This led to a recognition that, in order to organize government information across departments, there was a need for a standardized vocabulary so that each department was using the same language in the same way. IPSV is intended to be the top-level language used for creating the subject element in the metadata associated with government websites in order to ease the interaction with government websites for UK citizens. Details about the Integrated Public Service Vocabulary can be found at <http://www.govtalk.gov.uk/schemasstandards/gcl.asp> [accessed 7 December 2006].

ONTOLOGIES

Recently, ontologies – explicit formal specification of the terms in a domain and the relationships between them – have been developed for a wide range of different applications in machine translation, enterprise modelling, knowledge management and information retrieval. Within knowledge management, ontologies may be used to support knowledge sharing, creation/innovation, information and knowledge retrieval, and knowledge elicitation (capture and monitoring of knowledge). In addition ontologies are widely used on the WWW. This is further discussed below in the section on the Semantic Web. The growing interest in ontologies is driven by:

- the huge amount of information now available, and therefore needing management
- the availability of relatively inexpensive computing power, the Web and large numbers of networked resources
- a growing trend within organizations to seek to collate external and internal information, and information from a wide range of different document and data types.

An ontology defines a common vocabulary for researchers and practitioners who need to share information in a domain. It includes machine-interpretable definitions of basic concepts in the domain and the relationships amongst them. In general ontologies can be used to:

- share common understanding of the structure of information among people or software agents
- enable re-use of domain knowledge
- make domain assumptions explicit
- separate domain knowledge from operational knowledge
- analyse domain knowledge.

The typical components of an ontology are:

- *Classes*, which define the concepts in the domain; for example, in an ontology on food and wine, one class may be 'wines'.

- *Instances*; for example, the class 'wines' may have a number of specific instances, which are the different types of wines.
- Classes may also have *subclasses*, that represent concepts that are more specific than the class. For example, the class of 'wines' can be divided into red, white and rosé. Alternatively, the class of 'wines' can be divided into sparkling and non-sparkling. Which of these processes of division is most helpful depends upon the intended use of the ontology.
- *Slots* (also known as roles or properties) which describe the various features and attributes of both classes and instances, and thereby the *relations* between them. For example, Château Lafite Rothschild Pauillac has a full body (the body slot) and it is produced by the Château Lafite Rothschild winery (the maker slot). At the class level, instances of the class 'wines' will have slots describing their flavour, body, sugar level, make, etc.
- *Facets* (sometimes called role restrictions) that are restrictions on slots.

Figure 7.10 shows some classes, instances and relations amongst them in the wine domain. Italics are used for instances, and normal type for classes. Boxes on arrows indicate slots. All instances of the class 'wines', and its subclass 'Pauillac' have a slot 'maker', the value of which is an instance of the class 'winery', signified by the 'io' box on the arrows in the figure. All instances of the class 'winery' have a slot 'produces' that refers to all wines (instances of the class 'wines' and its subclasses) that the winery produces.

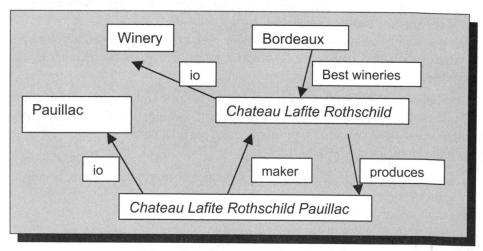

Figure 7.10 Some classes, instances and the relations amongst them in the wine domain

Source: Noy and McGuinness, n.d.

226

It is important to recognize, however, that ontologies come in different forms. Some ontologies are taxonomies, such as classification of hierarchical listings of terminology in a specific subject area. Others, such as metadata schemas, are sets of conceptual characteristics, and specify the elements to be used, what those elements mean, and what kinds of attributes and values those elements have (see Chapter 2). Yet other ontologies provide a semantic analysis of words, including variant word forms such as nouns, verbs, adjectives and adverbs (rather than just nouns as are used in thesauri). The Unified Medical Language System (UMLS) is a good example of a system that exhibits many of the characteristics of an ontology. The UMLS is composed of three 'knowledge sources': a 'meta-thesaurus', a lexicon and a semantic network. The metathesaurus pulls together terminology from many other biomedical vocabularies and classifications, linking many terms for the same concepts. The lexicon contains syntactic information for words, including verbs that do not appear in the metathesaurus. The network contains information about the categories to which the metathesauus concepts have been assigned and describes the relationships amongst them.

Ontologies are often part of a bigger system. Artificial intelligence applications such as problem-solving methods, domain-independent applications and software agents use ontologies and knowledge bases built using ontologies as data to run their processes. For example, an ontology of wine and food and of appropriate combinations of wine with meals could be used for various applications in a suite of restaurant-managing tools. One application could create wine suggestions for the menu of the day or answer queries from waiters and customers. Another application could analyse an inventory list of a wine cellar and suggest which wine categories to expand and which partial wines to purchase for upcoming menus or cookbooks.

GENERATING ONTOLOGIES

An ontology is a representation of a domain of knowledge or other objects. As such, it must reflect the concepts in this domain. On the other hand, there are always numerous different ways in which a domain can be modelled. Ontology design starts with an appreciation of what the ontology is going to be used for. This will influence which concepts are included and which are excluded and the granularity of the ontology. Identifying the purpose of the ontology involves answering questions such as:

- What is the domain that the ontology will cover?
- What is the ontology going to be used for?
- What types of questions will be asked of the system in which the ontology is embedded?

- Who will use the ontology?
- Who will maintain the ontology?

Another preliminary consideration in ontology design is whether there are existing ontologies that can be re-used. This issue of re-using existing schemes has already been discussed earlier in this chapter. Most importantly, in the context of semantic operability (see below), there is a considerable advantage associated with re-using existing ontologies in terms of the potential for interaction with other applications and, say, integration into a digital library. The Ontolingua ontology library (<www.ksl.stanford.edu/software/ontolingual>) and the DAML ontology library (<www.daml.org/ontologies/>) are libraries of ontologies. There are also a number of publicly available commercial ontologes, such as RosettaNet (<www.rosettanet.org>) and DMOZ (<www.dmoz.org>). Such ontologies may not provide the complete solution but can be imported into an ontology development environment and adapted or modified (but see the next sectionon semantic interoperability for further comments on possible difficulties in this approach). In addition to such externally produced taxonomies, for many applications the documents, data or objects to be organized by a proposed taxonomy are likely to have been organized previously, and this earlier taxonomy, set of file categories, thesaurus or classification scheme can often provide a valuable starting point.

The steps in ontology development depend upon the complexity of the proposed ontology and, significantly, on whether the ontology development involves human assignment of terms or is automatic (computer-based). Automatic generation of ontologies has the particular advantage that ontologies can be automatically updated but, as discussed below, automatic ontology generation tools have some limitations.

The following stages are one example of the steps in the creation of an ontology:

1. Determine the domain and scope of the ontology (as discussed above).
2. Identify any existing ontologies for evidence of the concepts in the domain.
3. Build the ontology, including:
   - identifying key concepts and terms
   - defining class, the class hierarchy, subclasses, relations, slots and facets
   - choosing a representation language, or writing the code and coding the ontology
   - creating instances of classes
   - establishing naming conventions.
4. Evaluate the ontology, through both system and user testing.
5. Document the ontology and generate user guidelines.
6. Revise and update the ontology, to ensure that the ontology continues to reflect the objects in the real world effectively.

Ontology generation technologies or classification tools operating with good-quality data can generate comparable levels of accuracy to systems based on human intervention. Many such tools use seed words provided by domain experts as a basis for ontology generation. Concepts are extracted from raw data using some of the established techniques of natural language indexing, such as:

- part-of-speech (POS) tagging to extract high-frequency words or phrases that could be used to define concepts
- word sense disambiguation to extract relations such as 'is a' and 'associated with' where the distinction lies in the linguistic property of the nouns
- tokenizers – to break strings into a series of tokens between two delimiting characters (such as the spacing between works) and determine the length of each string
- pattern matching – using, for example, a semantic lexicon of paired words with their meanings which provides the ability to extract phrase-meaning pairs from a document.

The further development of such tools is still an active area of research. Machine learning is being developed to assist in the differentiation between different phrases that refer to the same concept, and to eliminate the masking effect of 'shallow semantics'.

FOLKSONOMIES

These have gained in popularity in recent years. A folksonomy is a loose form of language control which has emerged in the Internet era. The term refers to an open-ended list of terms which has been generated collaboratively by members of a community to index, or in their terminology to tag, information objects available on the Internet. Since the vocabulary is generated within and shared by the community which creates it, the process is often referred to as 'social tagging'. The term 'folksonomy' has been generated by the merging of the terms 'folk' and 'taxonomy' and so literally is taxonomy or classification by the people. In terms of metadata creation for information objects on the Web, folksonomies have two advantages. Firstly, they are created by the members of a community and so are likely to reflect the terminology used within that community rather better than a terminology created from outside the community. Secondly, given that folksonomies have none of the hierarchical structures and term relationships associated with conventional controlled vocabularies, they are much cheaper to create and maintain. The weakness, of course, is that the list is open-ended, continually changing, and has none of the features of conventional controlled vocabularies in terms of controlling synonyms and homonyms and displaying term relationships. Folksonomies can be seen as a means of attempting to overcome the shortcomings of search engines without adopting the more formal approaches to subject representation developed by information professionals and described in detail throughout this book. The Internet has seen the widespread emergence of tools developed by and for the community and a culture of sharing as exemplified by open source software and Wikipedia; in a sense folksonomies are the information retrieval equivalent of this somewhat anarchic approach. Hammond et al. (2006) provide a review of folksonomies and some of the available social tagging tools and approaches, whilst some theoretical concerns regarding folksonomies are discussed by Petersen (2006). To date there has been no comparison of the retrieval performance of folksonomies and conventional controlled vocabularies and so it is too early tell whether folksonomies will survive to make a lasting contribution to information retrieval or whether they are simply a passing fad.

SEMANTIC INTEROPERABILITY AND THE SEMANTIC WEB

One of the big challenges in the use of ontologies is that they need to be dynamic in order to accommodate the changes in the domain to which they are being applied. Such changes may be associated with changes in the knowledge base of a subject field or, in organizational contexts, may arise from changing structures within an organization, and between an organization and other organizations. This need to adapt and evolve ontologies has led to a considerable focus on ontology mapping. There are a number of ways to merge ontologies:

- re-using available ontologies to link different domains
- aligning ontologies by establishing links between them through some form of translation function using agent technology
- merging ontologies to create a single ontology
- integrating ontologies through clustering on the basis of similarities.

In all of these situations there are significant challenges associated with semantic inconsistencies and difference in knowledge formats. Semantics is concerned with the meaning individuals or groups give a particular term or concept. Confusion can arise from different communities associating different meanings or nuances of meaning to the same term. For example, the term 'groups' means one thing to a management scientist, and quite another to a mathematician. As discussed in Chapter 2, interoperability between two metadata systems needs to be managed at three different levels: semantic, structural and syntactic. In other words, semantic interoperability is only part of a wider picture. Developments in semantic interoperability need to be embedded in systems in which metadata standards are in use to also support the other levels of interoperability. Hence, standards to support these different aspects of interoperability have advanced in tandem.

Once we move outside the orbit of a specific organization or a specific subject area and start to examine the access and retrieval issues associated with all of the resources on the Web, the scale of the problem becomes even more daunting. The section on taxonomies above discussed some of the partial solutions to this problem, and there has been some considerable work on taxonomies and ontologies to aid in retrieval and navigation in relation to Web resources in specific disciplines (for example, social science, medicine).

The World Wide Web Consortium (W3C) (<www.w3c.>) has been responsible for the development of schemas or ontologies such as the Resource Description Framework (RDF) and the Web Ontology Language (OWL) with a view to supporting interoperability across applications. Such schemas are components toward the implementation of the Semantic Web.

The Semantic Web is an important concept which seeks to provide a common framework that allows data to be shared and re-used across application, organizational and community boundaries. It is essentially a language for recording how data relates to real-world objects, thus allowing a person, or a machine, to start in one database and then move through many other databases which are connected by being about the same thing – in other words the databases are connected through their semantic links. The Semantic Web is a kind of 'global' ontology which makes explicit the semantics underlying all resources on the Web. This is a very complex issue in a context in which it is necessary to accommodate multiple languages (such as French, Spanish, Japanese, Arabic, etc.), scripts and communities.

The Semantic Web is concerned with the establishment and use of common formats for interchange of data; this improves on the original Web, based on XML for syntax and URL for naming, which only offered interchange of documents. We must now revisit the two important components of the Semantic Web already mentioned – RDF and OWL. RDF is used to represent information and to exchange knowledge on the Web. OWL is used to publicize and share ontologies, thereby supporting Web searching, software agents and knowledge management. Whilst the RDF is a universal format for data on the Web that provides interoperability between applications that exchange machine-understandable information, ontologies are essential for ensuring that information has an explicit meaning. Ontologies are the building blocks for the Semantic Web: they manage the different meanings ascribed to terms in different contexts and by different communities. OWL seeks to standardize the means of representing ontologies in the Web context.

SUMMARY

This chapter started with discussion of some long-established tools that continue to be used to support subject access in a range of different contexts; it briefly visited the topic of special classification schemes, and concluded with an introduction to ontologies and taxonomies as they are currently being developed to support access to digital resources. In time we have travelled from the late 19th century to the beginning of the 21st century. In some ways there is an enormous disparity between the topics covered by this chapter. Long-established classification schemes (such as DDC and LC) and subject headings lists (such as LCSH) remain important for at least four reasons:

1. They are metadata standards that are embedded in other standards (such as MARC) and thereby within systems.
2. Large existing bibliographic databases make use of these schemes and lists. In the case of classification schemes, the notation also provides a link to printed objects, such as books, maps and other documents.
3. They encapsulate a lot of theory, practice and learning about the nature of, challenges associated with, and potential solutions in subject access.
4. They are a rich 'knowledge base', showing terms and their relationships, that can be mined in other ontologies.

On the other hand it is important to acknowledge that their contribution for the future has the potential to be impeded by:

1. legacies in structures, terminologies and organization that sometimes act as a major hindrance to their application in digital and networked environments
2. the origins within, and ownership by, only one of the main professional communities that is concerned with building ontologies and systems for the future.

Some would argue that taxonomies and ontologies are no more than enhanced classification schemes or thesauri, designed for use in specific applications. Others would suggest that the semantics embedded in such tools are very differently represented from those adopted by traditional controlled language tools. No doubt the truth lies somewhere between these two opposing pole positions. Ontologies are being developed for a wide range of different applications in artificial intelligence, knowledge management and Web searching. Given the wide range of applications for which ontologies are developed it is not surprising that there are a range of different types of ontologies, and that there is some terminological confusion associated with even basic terms, such as taxonomy and ontology. On the other hand, one might wonder, if the ontologists cannot arrive at a consensus as to the meaning or meanings of the word ontology, how successful are they likely to be with other semantic endeavours?

REVIEW QUESTIONS

1. Explain what is meant by pre-coordination, and discuss why it is important.
2. Outline the principles underpinning the design of traditional subject headings lists. Discuss the types of headings to be found in the Library of Congress Subject Headings.
3. What types of subdivisions are used in the Library of Congress Subject Headings? Outline some of the main challenges that the management and use of such subdivisions pose.
4. Compare and contrast DDC and LCC in terms of their schedules and notations.
5. Review and evaluate the different approaches to synthesis used in DDC. Compare these with the approaches used in UDC.
6. Discuss the contributions made to the theory and practice of classification by the Bliss Bibliographic Classification and the Colon Classification, respectively.
7. Why is it necessary to tailor classification schemes to suit specific collections or communities? Discuss the different kinds of special classification schemes.
8. Discuss what you understand to be the meaning of the terms ontology and taxonomy.
9. Outline how an organization might go about generating an ontology, indicating the key decisions that it will need to make in the process.
10. What is the Semantic Web and why is it important?

REFERENCES AND FURTHER READING

Aitchison, J. (1986) A classification as a source for a thesaurus: the Bibliographic Classification of H.E. Bliss as a source of thesaurus terms and structure. *Journal of Documentation*, **42** (3), 160–181.

Aitchison, J., Gilchrist, A. and Bawden, D. (2000) *Thesaurus Construction and Use: A practical manual*, 4th edn. London: Aslib.

Bater, B. (2007) *Practical Taxonomies*. London: Facet.

Bates, M.J. (1989) Rethinking subject cataloging in the online environment. *Library Resources and Technical Services*, **33** (4), October, 400–412.

Bellomi, F., Cristani, M. and Cuel, R. (2005) A cooperative environment for the negotiation of term taxonomies in digital libraries. *Library Management*, **26** (4/5), 271–80.

Berners-Lee, T., Hendler, J. and Lassila, O. (2001) The Semantic Web. *Scientific American*, **284** (5), 34–44.

Berry, M. (2003) *Survey of Text Mining: Clustering, classification, and retrieval*. New York: Springer-Verlag.

Broughton, V. (2004) *Essential Classification*. London: Facet.

Chan, L.M. (1990) Subject analysis tools online: the challenge ahead. *Information Technology and Libraries*, **9** (3), September, 258–62.

Chan, L.M. (2005) *Library of Congress Subject Headings: Principles and practice*. Westport CT: Libraries Unlimited.

Chan, L.M. and Mitchell, J.S. (2003) *Dewey Decimal Classification: A practical guide*, 3rd edn. Dublin OH: OCLC.

Coates, E.J. (1960) *Subject Catalogues: Headings and structure*. London: Library Association.

Cutter, C.A. (1904) *Rules for a Dictionary Catalog*, 4th edn. Washington DC: Government Printing Office (and later reprints).

Dewey Decimal Classification and Relative Index (2003), 22nd edn, 4 vols. Albany NY: Forest Press.

Ding, Y. (2001) A review of ontologies with the Semantic Web in view. *Journal of Information Science*, **27** (6), 377–84.

Ding, Y. and Foo, S. (2002a) Ontology research and development. Part 1 – a review of ontology generation. *Journal of Information Science*, **28** (2), 123–36.

Ding, Y. and Foo, S. (2002b) Ontology research and development. Part 2 – a review of ontology, mapping and evolving. *Journal of Information Science*, **28** (5), 375–88.

Doerr, M. (2001) Semantic problems of thesauri mapping. *Journal of Digital Information*, **1** (8). Available at <http://jodi.ecs.soton.ac.uk/articles/v01/i08/editorial/> [accessed 15 June 2006].

Drabenstott, K.M. and Vizine-Goetz, D. (1994) *Using Subject Headings for Online Retrieval: Theory, practice, and potential*. San Diego CA: Academic Press.

Fensel, D. (2001) *Ontologies: A silver bullet for knowledge management and electric commerce*. Berlin: Springer.

Foskett, A.C. (1996) *The Subject Approach to Information*, 5th edn. London: Library Association.

Franklin, R.A. (2003) Re-inventing subject access for the Semantic Web. *Online Information Review*, **27** (2), 94–101.

Gilchrist, A. (2001) Corporate taxonomies: report on a survey of current practice. *Online Information Review*, **25** (2), 94–102.

Gilchrist, A. (2003) Thesauri, taxonomies and ontologies – an etymological note. *Journal of Documentation*, **59** (1), 7–18.

Gilchrist, A. and Kibby, P. (2000) *Taxonomies for Business: Access and connectivity in a wired world*. London: TFPL.

Gruber, T.R. (1993) A translation approach to portable ontology specifications. *Knowledge Acquisitions*, **5**, 199–220.

Gruber, T. (n.d.) *What is an Ontology?* Available at <www-ksl.Stanford.edu/kst/what-is-an-ontology.html> [accessed 15 June 2006].

Hammond, T., Hanny, T., Lund, B. and Scott, J. (2006) Social bookmarking tools!: a general review. *D-Lib Magazine*, **11** (4) [accessed 3 December 2006].

Hunter, E. (2002) *Classification Made Simple*. Aldershot: Ashgate.

Jashapara, A. (2004) *Knowledge Management: An integrated approach*. Harlow: FT Prentice Hall.

Joachim, M.D. (2003) *Historical Aspects of Cataloguing and Classification*. Binghamton NY: Haworth Press.

Kaiser, J. (1911) *Systematic Indexing*. London: Pitman.

Kremer, S., Kolbe, L.M., and Brenner, W. (2005) Towards a procedure model in terminology management. *Journal of Documentation*, **61** (2), 281–95.

Lancaster, F.W. (2003) *Indexing and Abstracting in Theory and Practice*, 3rd edn. London: Facet.

234

Library of Congress Classification Web. Available (by subscription) at <http://classweb.loc.gov/>.

Library of Congress (2004) *Subject Cataloging Manual: Subject headings. 2004 cumulation*. Washington DC: Cataloging Distribution Service, Library of Congress.

Library of Congress (2006a). *Library of Congress Subject Headings – Principles of structure and policies for application*. Available at <www.itsmarc.com/crs/shed0014.htm> [accessed 15 June 2006].

Library of Congress (2006b) *Classification Web*. Available at <http:/classificationweb.net/tutorial> [accessed 15 June 2006].

McIlwaine, I.C. (2000) *The Universal Decimal Classification: A guide to its use*. The Hague: UDC Consortium.

Mills, J. and Broughton, V. (1987) *Bliss Bibliographic Classification*, 3rd edn, vol. titled *Introduction and Auxiliary Schedules*. London: Bowker

National Library of Medicine, *Unified Medical Language System (UMLS)*. Available at <http://nlm.nih.gov/research/umls>.

Nicholson, D. and Shiri, A. (2003) Interoperability in subject searching and browsing. *OCLC Systems and Services*, **19** (20), 58–61.

Noy, N.F. and McGuinness, D.L. (n.d.) *Ontology Development 101: A guide to creating your first ontology*. Available at <http://protege.stanford.edu/publications/ontology_development> [accessed 15 June 2006].

OCLC (2006a) *Using OCLC Web Dewey: An OCLC tutorial*. Available at <www.oclc/dewey/resources/tutorials> [accessed 15 June 2006].

OCLC (2006b) *Introduction to the Dewey Decimal Classification*. Available at <www.oclc.org/dewey/versions/ddc22print/intro.pdf> [accessed 15 June 2006].

Petersen, E. (2006) Beneath the metadata: some philosophical problems with folksonomy. *D-Lib Magazine*, **12** (11) [accessed 3 December 2006].

Saeed, H. and Chaudhry, A.S. (2002) Using the Dewey Decimal Classification scheme (DDC) for building taxonomies for knowledge organization. *Journal of Documentation*, **58** (5), 575–83.

Shiri, A., Nocholson, D. and McCulloch, E. (2004) User evaluation of a pilot terminologies server for a distributed multi-scheme environment. *Online Information Review*, **28** (4), 272–83.

Soergel, D. (1999) The rise of ontologies or the re-invention of classification. *Journal of the American Society for Information Science and Technology*, **50** (12), 119–120.

Studwell, W.E. (1991) Of eggs and baskets: getting more access out of LC subject headings in an online environment. *Cataloging and Classification Quarterly*, **13** (3/4), 91–6.

Svenonius, E. (2000) *The Intellectual Foundation of Information Organization*. Cambridge MA: MIT Press.

Taylor, A.G. (2004) *The Organization of Information*, 2nd edn. Westport CT: Libraries Unlimited.

Tuhope, D., Koch, T. and Heery, R. (2006) *Terminology Services and Technology: JISC state of the art review*. Bristol: JISC.

Vickery, B.C. (1997) Ontologies. *Journal of Information Science*, **23** (4), 277–86.

Wang, J. (2003) A knowledge network constructed by integrating classification, thesaurus, and metadata in digital library. *International Information and Library Review*, **35**, 383–97.

Warner, A.J. (2002) *A Taxonomy Primer. Lexonomy*. Available at <http://www.lexonomy.com/publications/aTaxonomyPrimer.html> [accessed 15 June 2006].

8 Access through author names and titles

INTRODUCTION

This chapter draws together strands from earlier chapters. Chapter 3 examined document *representation*, including record formats, bibliographic description and the structure of the MARC record. This chapter examines document *access* in the context of catalogues and bibliographies Many of the principles associated with the selection of author access points and the control of forms of names are relevant in a wide range of indexing and searching contexts. Access points, called *headings*, in catalogues and bibliographies use a special kind of controlled language – one that is confined to proper names and is governed not by a thesaurus but by cataloguing rules. In most of the world there is just one cataloguing code: the *Anglo-American Cataloguing Rules*, first published in 1967, extensively revised in 1978 (AACR2), and reissued with revisions in 1988, 1998, 2002 and 2005. As was explained in Chapter 3, Part I of AACR2 addresses document description. Part II, entitled 'Headings, Uniform Titles, and References', addresses document access. This chapter is based on the recommendations provided by the latest version of AACR2, the 2005 revision. By making specific reference to AACR2 rules and recommendations throughout, this chapter achieves two objectives:

- for those interested in the details of cataloguing practices, it acts as an informative general guide
- for those more interested in other indexing and searching environments it offers a structured discussion of the issues associated with handling authors and titles as access points in information retrieval situations.

This chapter aims to give you a critical awareness of cataloguing rules governing access points. At the end of the chapter you will:

- be able to explain the functions of catalogues
- appreciate issues associated with the choice of access points and the concepts of main, added and alternative entries
- understand how headings for persons, corporate bodies and uniform titles are chosen and structured
- make and use references in catalogues.

CATALOGUES AND THEIR FUNCTIONS

In order to understand the approach taken by AACR2 to author and title access, it is necessary to understand the nature of catalogues and their functions, and indeed, to delve a little back into the historical context which has a major impact on current practices. A catalogue is a list of the documents in a library, with the entries representing the documents arranged for access in some systematic order. Catalogues, today, are often held as a computer database, and accessed through online public access catalogue (OPAC) interfaces.

A catalogue comprises a number of entries, each of which is an access point for a document. A document may have several entries, or just one. Figure 8.1 shows a mini-catalogue, based on the examples in Figure 3.10. Entries are shown with both author and titles as headings, and most works are represented by more than one entry. In this example, main and added entries are distinguished, as added entries have shorter (Level 1) descriptions. Traditionally cataloguers, in general, and AACR2, in particular, have distinguished between main and added entries; the idea being that for each work there should be one main or chief entry (showing all cataloguing details), supplemented, as appropriate by added entries for other access points that might be useful to users. More recently, AACR2 has acknowledged that in electronic databases the concept of alternative entries is more appropriate. Alternative entries are a series of equivalent entries supporting access to the representation of a work through different access points.

The functions of a catalogue were systematically defined over a century ago by Charles Ammi Cutter, whose *Rules for a Dictionary Catalog* (fourth edition, 1904) is one of the seminal works of the information and library profession. Cutter's is the classic analysis, and is still widely accepted as the starting point for a definition of the functions of a catalogue:

1. To enable a person to find a book of which either

the author
the title **is known**
the subject

Cutter oversimplifies. No single one of these attributes (except sometimes the

Castles and palaces map of the British Isles. – Edinburgh: Bartholomew, [198-]. – 1 wall chart: col.; 101 × 75 cm (fold to 26 × 16 cm) 728.810941

English madrigals / The King's Singers. – HMV Classics, c1995. – 1 sound disc. + 1 leaflet. – Compact disc. – HMV 5 69009 2 782.543

Frink / Edward Lucie-Smith and Elisabeth Frink. – Bloomsbury, 1994. – 138p. – ISBN 0-7475-1572-7. 730.92

Geoff Hamiltons [sic] 3D garden designer. – Computer program. – St Ives, Cambs: GSP, c1998. – 1 computor optical disc; 4¾ in. – System requirements: Windows 95 or higher. – Summary: Plant encyclopedia and graphic editor producing plans for gardens and parks. – GSPCD125 712.6

Hamilton, Geoff Geoff Hamiltons [sic] 3D garden designer. – Computer program. – GSP, c1998. – 1 computer optical disc; 4¾ in. – System requirements: Windows 95 or higher. – GSPCD125 712.6

King's Singers English madrigals / The King's Singers. – [London]: HMV Classics, c1995. – 1 sound disc (73 min.): digital, stereo.; 4¾ in. + 1 leaflet (6p.: col. ill.; 13 cm.). – (HMV Classics; 145) . – Compact disc. – 'The principal composers in this collection are Thomas Morley and Thomas Weelkes' – accompanying notes. – HMV 5 69009 2 782.543

Lucie-Smith, Edward Frink: a portrait / Edward Lucie-Smith and Elisabeth Frink. – London: Bloomsbury, 1994. – 138p., [16]p. of plates: ill. (some col.) ports; 22 x 23 cm. – Ill. on lining papers. – ISBN 0-7475-1572-7. 730.92

Frink, Elisabeth Frink / Edward Lucie-Smith and Elisabeth Frink. – Bloomsbury, 1994. – 138p. – ISBN 0-7475-1572-7. 730.92

Markova, Meg see Mystic Meg

Meg, Mystic see Mystic Meg

Morley, Thomas English madrigals / The King's Singers. – HMV Classics, c1995. – 1 sound disc. + 1 leaflet. – Compact disc. – HMV 5 69009 2 782.543

Mystic Meg Mystic Meg's lucky numbers: for life, love and the lottery / illustrations by Caroline Smith. – London: Warner, 1996. – 289p.; ill.; 18 cm. – ISBN 0-7515-1875-1 133.335

Mystic Meg's lucky numbers. – Warner, 1996. – 289p. – ISBN 0-7515-1875-1 133.335

Smith, Edward Lucie – see Lucie-Smith, Edward

Weelkes, Thomas English madrigals / The King's Singers. – HMV Classics, c1995. – 1 sound disc. + 1 leaflet. Compact disc. – HMV 5 69009 2 782.543

Figure 8.1 Mini author/title catalogue

title) can be relied upon to find a book. In practice, two are needed: author + title, or author + subject, or title + subject. With the increased availability of keywords as identifying elements in online searches, it is no longer necessary to know the first word of an author, title or subject heading. Otherwise, Cutter's basic definition of the catalogue as a finding list to the contents of a library or library system still holds good, but with the reservation that in recent years attitudes to retrieval have become access-based rather than collection-based, so that many catalogues range more widely than their own collections. Also, most library catalogues now include not only books but other materials as well, particularly audiovisual materials (films, videos, tapes, slides, etc.); only occasionally are there separate catalogues for these. Catalogues did not and do not normally list the contents of books or serials. For serials normally only the title of the serial as a whole is catalogued, and other indexes identify the individual articles.

The catalogue is primarily a finding list for known-item searches. It gives direct access to a specific document, details of which are known to the searcher, and in the past often constituted a library's administrative record of its stock. This type of catalogue has been variously labelled a *direct* catalogue, *finding-list* catalogue or *inventory* catalogue. This group of functions is valid for card and printed catalogues as well as OPACs. The latter usually offer extended facilities for known-item searches (for example, author/title acronym; title keywords; control number).

2. To show what the library has:
by a given author ...

This has caused, and continues to cause, endless confusion in catalogues. Many authors use or are known by variants on their name (George Bernard Shaw; Bernard Shaw; G.B. Shaw; even G.B.S.) or even by two or more completely different names (Anthony Eden; Earl of Avon). Cutter implies that all the works of a given author must appear in a catalogue under a single unique and uniform heading.

A catalogue that sets out to fulfil these functions is called a *collocative* or *bibliographic* catalogue. This group of functions has long been recognized as being far subordinate to the *finding-list* function. Advances in bibliography over the past century have meant that there is now far less need for a catalogue to provide this kind of service than there was in Cutter's time. However, much networked catalogue copy is produced by national bibliographic agencies (such as the British Library), whose primary function is to produce a national bibliography which will correctly and uniquely ascribe each work to its author. Current cataloguing rules (AACR2) try to reconcile this tension but essentially the bibliographic tail continues to wag the finding-list dog in the majority of our catalogues.

... on a given subject ...

Nearly all catalogues offer a subject approach. 'On a given subject' is a delightfully simple phrase, implying that the subject of a published item can be adequately summed up in a single word or short phrase. This might have sufficed a century ago, but it is ill-equipped to express the complexities of current publishing and scholarship. However, such is the weight of tradition that it is largely through Cutter's influence that the subject approaches available in library catalogues today are simplistic, crude and superficial. (Notice, again, that AACR2 does not deal with the subject approach.)

... in a given kind of literature.

Catalogues are mostly well equipped to tell the user if a book is prose or poetry, or even (say) German poetry. In other respects (say, all books written in German; all humorous books; all biographies) catalogues today are less helpful. The MARC record format does however provide for these (and other) approaches.

3. To assist in the choice of a book:
as to its edition ...

It is basic to the function of a catalogue to be able to identify each item uniquely, and the need for catalogues to indicate the edition of a work is undisputed. Beyond this, full descriptive cataloguing (AACR2's Levels 2 and 3) provides for considerably more detail than is needed for identification. Such elements as subtitle, series title, physical description (pagination, etc.) and (usually) notes serve to characterize rather than to identify, and some library catalogues exclude them as a matter of policy.

... as to its character (literary or topical)

Cutter had annotations in mind when he wrote this. A century ago, libraries kept their stock on closed access, and every item had to be individually requested. Under these conditions, suitably annotated catalogue entries were considered well worthwhile in giving readers some better idea of what they were requesting, and so saving the time and shoe-leather of library clerks scurrying to and fro in the stacks. Open access and plastic jackets have removed the need to annotate catalogue entries routinely, although annotation can still be useful in catalogue entries for DVDs, CD-ROMs and similar non-browsable materials.

Access to items of information by the names of the persons responsible for their intellectual content has a long and complex history. The need for a code of practice was powerfully established a century and a half ago by Antonio Panizzi, who, as Keeper of Printed Books in the British Museum Library, had to persuade the trustees of the need for the complex rules he was proposing to introduce. This he did by sending each of them off separately with copies of the same books, to catalogue them; and on their return he pointed out to them how each of them had done it quite differently.

The problems of personal names, as of corporate bodies, are, as Panizzi told his trustees, essentially two: agreeing on the name to be used, and establishing its entry element and other factors affecting its filing position in an alphabetical list. (In these respects the rules governing the author approach are the standard thesaural rules of vocabulary control extended to proper names.) These problems are as real today as they were in Panizzi's day, though societal and technological changes have emphasized different aspects of them. With personal names, the

241

problems addressed by Panizzi and his successors as compilers of catalogue codes for a full century were predominantly historical: what name to use for a nobleman; how to enter classical writers; whether to use the vernacular or Latinized form of name of writers like Linnaeus, and so on. Today we tend to be more occupied with the problems of reconciling all the varied traditions of contemporary personal names in the global society. In the case of factors affecting filing, technology has removed many of the old problems. With keyword access, the filing element of Muhammad Ali or Chiang Kai-shek is no longer an issue.

While the author approach is traditionally associated with library catalogues, listings other than author indexes or catalogues also involve the arranging of entries according to the names of persons or organizations. Telephone directories are an obvious example, and there are many trade directories and similar publications that are alphabetically arranged. Even in this era of computer-based searching, there is still a significant place for manually searched, alphabetically arranged databases.

THE STRUCTURE OF AACR2 PART II

As discussed in Chapter 3, AACR2 has two parts. Part I deals with Description, whilst Part II focuses on Headings, Uniform Titles and References. Part II deals broadly with the following three themes:

1. *Choice of access points*. An access point may be a person, a corporate body, or a title. A work is likely to have more than one access point, typically two or three.
2. *Headings*. The cataloguer may have to choose between different names, or variant forms of the same name, or between different entry (filing) elements for any of the chosen access points. This establishment of standard names and forms of names is known as authority control. Cataloguing agencies often have lists showing previous decisions, authority lists, which inform subsequent decisions.
3. *References*. Finally, references are needed for the guidance of catalogue users who approach the catalogue under a name or filing element other than the one that has been used.

The following sections cover these three themes. It is anticipated that RDA will have a different structure (see Figure 3.7), but it will continue to cover resource description and access point control. In the area of access point control it is likely that many of the principles embedded in AACR2 will be reviewed and re-interpreted, although it is not envisaged that RDA will be as prescriptive because it will seek to accommodate a wider range of application environments.

CHOICE OF ACCESS POINTS

The general principle is to provide access points under the significant persons and corporate bodies, and under titles, shown in the description. This principle of identification of a specific set of access points remains relevant in electronic databases where a controlled language is used. Recently AACR2 has termed this 'alternative heading entries'. It contributes to the control of the level of exhaustivity of the indexing, and thereby impacts on search performance.

The concept of one primary or main access point or heading which underlies AACR's approach to the choice of headings has its origins in manually searched indexes. Additional entries are made as shorter, added entries. The original concept of main entry was partly administrative, partly intellectual. Administratively, the main entry in a card catalogue might carry 'tracings' – notes at the foot, or on the reverse, of the card, showing where the added entries were filed, so that the catalogue could be properly updated whenever a work was discarded or its catalogue entry amended. Intellectually, main entry was selected on the basis of the author 'chiefly responsible for the creation of the intellectual or artistic content of a work' (21.1A1). This principle is extended to works of corporate bodies. For the great majority of items, the main entry consists of a single personal author, which in a catalogue entry is followed immediately by the title – which follows our normal everyday practice of citing a work by its author and title.

The idea of main entry is thus deep-rooted, and, even though there is general acceptance that it has little relevance to modern cataloguing practice, it survives largely through being built into the structure of the MARC record. In most libraries, however, the main entry heading does have one persisting role – it determines the shelving position of an item, as some kind of abbreviation (such as a Cutter number) forms part of the shelf mark.

Most of Chapter 21 (that is, 21.1–21.28) is concerned with establishing main entry and distinguishing it from added entries. Sections 29 and 30 deal specifically with added entries, as the rules for main entry include instructions for added entries only where these are specifically covered by the rule.

GENERAL RULE: 21.1

Main entry under a personal author or corporate body has to be justified on criteria of responsibility for the existence of the work; otherwise main entry is under title.

WORKS FOR WHICH A SINGLE PERSON OR CORPORATE BODY IS RESPONSIBLE: 21.4

Single person 21.4A
Single corporate body 21.4B
Problems and special cases 21.4C–D

Personal authors are straightforward to define; corporate bodies ('no body to kick, no soul to be damned') are more elusive. AACR2 defines a corporate body as 'an organization or a group of persons that is identified by a particular name and that acts, or may act, as an entity'. The designation of corporate *author* is studiously avoided. Instead, works are described as 'emanating from' one or more corporate bodies – the desperate verb, with its connotations of spiritualism and drains, warns of the many hair-splitting and sometimes arbitrary distinctions that are inevitably associated with corporate bodies. The general intention of rule 21.1B (main entry under corporate body) is clear enough: works dealing with the policies, procedures, operations or resources of the body, or which record or report its collective thought or activity. The specific rules on the other hand are fraught with provisos and special cases, making their consistent application very difficult in practice.

Here, as throughout AACR2, the examples are essential reading, and demonstrate the need not just to establish principles, but to share examples and to be consistent with prior practice. They show how the problem or condition set out in the rule is applied to individual cases.

WORKS OF UNKNOWN OR UNCERTAIN AUTHORSHIP, OR BY UNNAMED GROUPS: 21.5

Main entry is under title. The second example under 21.5A (*A Memorial to Congress against an increase of duties on importations/by citizens of Boston and vicinity*) illustrates the definition of a corporate body: the group acted as an entity, but is not identified by a particular name.

WORKS OF SHARED RESPONSIBILITY: 21.6

Shared responsibility is where two or more persons (or occasionally corporate bodies) have performed the same kind of activity. In cases where principal responsibility is indicated (usually by layout or typography), main entry is straightforward. Otherwise, an arbitrary rule is applied: if there are two or three contributors, main entry is under the first named, with added entries for the second and/or third. If there are four or more authors, main entry is under title, with an added entry for the first named person or body only.

Citation practice is to name two authors; for example, Aitchison, Jean and

Gilchrist, Alan. Headings of this kind are not authorized by AACR2 and are not found in modern catalogues. The main entry would be under Aitchison, Jean with an added entry under Gilchrist, Alan.

COLLECTION OF WORKS BY DIFFERENT PERSONS OR BODIES: 21.7

Editors of works consisting of contributions by different hands, and compilers of collections, are not regarded as having sufficient responsibility for their works to warrant main entry. In all cases, main entry is under title, with an added entry for the editor. If, however, a collection does not have a collective title, then main entry is made under the heading appropriate to the first contribution.

MIXED RESPONSIBILITY : 21.8–21.27

Notice the spread of rules; unusually, AACR2 takes a case-by-case approach in this section. Mixed responsibility covers works to which different persons or bodies have contributed different kinds of activity. Two types of mixed responsibility are distinguished: works that are modifications of other works (for example, adaptations, revisions and translations) and new works (such as collaborations between artist and writer, interviews, and – wondrously, but such works exist – communications 'presented as having been received from a spirit' through a medium). Principal responsibility is usually assigned to the person or body (or spirit!) named first. However, at 21.10A, covering adaptations of texts, main entry is under the heading for the adapter, to the annoyance of children's librarians everywhere.

RELATED WORKS: 21.28

We now come to the sixth and last condition of authorship. Related works are separately catalogued works that have a relationship to another work. These include continuations and sequels, supplements, indexes, concordances, scenarios and screenplays, opera librettos, subseries and special numbers from serials.

A related work is entered under its own appropriate heading, with an added entry under the work to which it is related. In some cases 'name-title' added entries are prescribed. These consist of the author and the title of the related work, for example,

Homer: Odyssey

for an adaptation that has a different main entry heading and title.

ADDED ENTRIES: 21.29–21.30

The rule for added entries consolidates and expands on all the previous rules in Chapter 21. Added entries, under headings for persons, corporate bodies and titles, are made to provide a further access point. Added entries are to be applied judiciously and sparingly – the rules are almost as much concerned with when not to make an added entry as when to make one – there is though a splendid catch-all at 21.29D: 'If ... an added entry is required under a heading or title other than those prescribed in 21.30, make it.'

The specific rules at 21.30 cover:

- Two or more persons or corporate bodies involved. These include collaborators, editors, compilers, revisers and so on; also performers, and other related persons or bodies, such as the addressee of a collection of letters, or a museum where an exhibition is held. Corporate bodies warrant an added entry unless they function solely as distributor or manufacturer.
- Two or more persons or bodies sharing a function. Entries are made under all of them if there are no more than three. If there are four or more, an added entry is made only under the first.
- Related works (which may need a name/title heading).
- Other relationships if needed, unless the relationship between the name and the work is that of a subject. The example given is that of an art collection from which reproductions of art works have been taken.
- Titles (with a few exceptions); today's automated catalogues will provide these automatically.
- And, if thought appropriate, translators, illustrators, series title and analytical added entries (entries for separate works contained within the item being catalogued – a collection of plays, for example); guidance is given on this.

HEADINGS FOR PERSONS

The process of choosing headings for persons is designed to instil consistency into the names and forms of names used for a given person. This process is also referred to as authority control. Chapter 22 is set out step by step. First, a choice may have to be made between different names by which the same person may be known. Second, once the name has been decided, the entry element must be decided. Finally, it may be necessary to make additions to names, to clarify the person's identity or to distinguish the name from other similar names.

CHOICE OF NAME: 22.1–22.3

Many people use more than one name. They may be completely different names, as with authors who change their names on marriage, or who use pseudonyms, or are known to their friends and to posterity by a soubriquet or nickname, as with the Venetian painter Jacopo Robusti, whose father was a dyer and so was called Tintoretto. Or the names may be variants, as with Tony (for Anthony) Blair, or Ovid (Publius Ovidius Naso), or W(illiam) Somerset Maugham. The general rule is to use 'the name by which a person is commonly known from the chief sources of information of works by that person issued in his or her language'; otherwise one should work from reference sources in his or her language or country.

The principle that a person can appear under only one form of heading is broken only in the case of pseudonyms (22.2B). This complex rule tries to allow for the fact that nobody can be certain how many authors are lurking in catalogues under one or more pseudonyms (Stendhal is said to have used 71). Established writers may have two or more separate bibliographic identities, as with Charles Lutwidge Dodgson the mathematician and Lewis Carroll the author of *Alice in Wonderland*; AACR2 allows such writers to retain their separate identities. In the case of contemporary authors, the basis for the heading is the name appearing in each work, with connecting references where two or more names are known to belong to the same person.

ENTRY ELEMENT: 22.4–22.11

Once the name has been established, it is time to decide on the order of the components of the name in the heading. The general rule is to follow national usage, unless a person's preference is known to be different. In most cases the surname is the entry element. Problems occur with compound surnames (Lloyd George) and names with prefixes (it Van Gogh, why not Van Beethoven?). AACR2 lists the commoner national usages; the International Federation of Library Associations (IFLA, 1996) publication *Names of Persons* may be consulted for others.

The section tails off in an entertaining miscellany, including persons who are to be entered under a title of nobility (Lord Byron becomes Byron, George Gordon Byron, *baron*); under a given name (Leonardo, *da Vinci*); or under initials etc., or under a phrase: the name of lottery winners' friend Mystic Meg should surely have been inverted according to 22.11B; and the 1920s book *Memoirs of a Flapper/by One*, is solemnly entered under the heading One.

ADDITIONS TO NAMES: 22.12–22.20

In some instances AACR2 calls for additions to names. They may be needed for identification purposes (Francis, *of Assisi, Saint*; Moses, *Grandma*; Elizabeth I, *Queen of England*; or even Beethoven, Ludwig van (*Spirit*)). Often, though, they serve the collocative function, distinguishing names that would otherwise be identical (Smith, John, 1924–; Smith, John, 1837–1896); Murray, Gilbert (Gilbert George Aimé); Murray, Gilbert (Gilbert John). There are also a number of special rules for names in certain languages, which cover a small number of Asiatic languages only. *Names of Persons* examines a wider range.

REFERENCES TO PERSONAL NAME HEADINGS

References generally are used to make different approaches to a heading. In this they differ from added entries, which make different approaches to a document or its representation. References are made from a form of name that might reasonably be sought to the form of name that has been chosen as a heading. References therefore should not be made to non-existent headings, and there must be a mechanism (normally through authority control; see Chapter 12) to record under every heading which references have been made to it.

Chapter 22 gives some specific instances of the use of references. The conventional symbol × introduces the name from which reference is to be made, thus

Leonardo, *da Vinci*
× Vinci, Leonardo da

is an instruction to make the reference

Vinci, Leonardo da *see* Leonardo, *da Vinci*

References are treated in full in Chapter 26. *See* references are made as necessary from different names, from different forms of a name, and from different entry elements of a name. Two examples of each type follow:

Barrett, Elizabeth *see* Browning, Elizabeth Barrett
Konigsberg, Allen Stewart *see* Allen, Woody

Ovidius Naso, Publius *see* Ovid
Nanaponika, Thera *see* Nyanaponika, Thera

Dr Seuss *see* Seuss, Dr
James, Anne Scott- *see* Scott-James, Anne

In the case of pseudonyms, *see also* references are made to link the different headings used for the same person, for example:

Innes, Michael *see also* Stewart, J.I.M.
Stewart, J.I.M. *see also* Innes, Michael

A variant is the explanatory reference, typically for contemporary authors appearing under several pseudonyms:

Plaidy, Jean. *For this author under other names, see*
Carr, Philippa; Ford, Elbur; Holt, Victoria; Kellow, Kathleen; Tate, Ellalice

CORPORATE BODIES

Before rules for headings for corporate bodies are given, AACR2 has a short chapter on geographic names. Geographic names are not used as such, but may constitute, or be added to, a heading for a corporate body. Specifically, they are used:

- as the names of governments and communities
- to distinguish between corporate bodies with the same name
- to add to some corporate names (particularly names of conferences).

They have their own chapter in AACR2 because of their pervasive nature. The chapter is, however, little more than an appendix to Chapter 24 (Corporate bodies). The rules are uncomplicated (but note the international emphasis: country is almost always added to the names of places smaller than a country).

AACR2's definition of a corporate body was given earlier in this chapter: 'an organization or a group of persons that is identified by a particular name and that acts, or may act, as an entity'. From a cataloguer's viewpoint, the principal differences between a person and a corporate body are that:

- Persons are unique and indivisible. A corporate body may have subordinate or related bodies whose names require the parent body's name for proper identification. (This can include government departments.)
- A person who changes their name remains the same person. Change of name in a corporate body normally denotes a change of purpose or scope, so that the body under its new name is a different body from the old.

ESTABLISHING THE NAME OF A CORPORATE BODY

Rule 24.1, the General rule – 'Enter a corporate body directly under the name by which it is commonly identified' – was quite revolutionary when introduced in 1967. The examples are worth studying by anyone involved with manually searched indexes, since 'directly' is rigorously applied and often conflicts with telephone books and other everyday reference tools. Thus Colin Buchanan and Partners files under letter C, not at any inversion of the name under B; the University of Oxford is to be sought under U and not O; and so on.

The name by which a body is 'commonly identified' is to be determined if possible from items issued by the body in its language. When this condition does not apply, reference sources (including works written about the body) are to be used.

The rules for variant names broadly follow personal authors. For the most part they prescribe what most people would intuitively choose:

UNESCO
not United Nations Educational, Scientific and Cultural Organization

Society of Friends
not Quakers, or Religious Society of Friends

Additions, in 24.4, are prescribed for names which do not convey the idea of a corporate body. Study the examples: Bounty (*Ship*) and Apollo 11 (*Spacecraft*) help to illustrate the breadth of definition of a corporate body. Ships have a name and may act as an entity – the Bounty's logbook is a famous example. (Spacecraft, one assumes, qualify only if they are manned?) Rock groups and the like often require this kind of parenthetical qualifier.

Omissions, 24.5, do not require much attention; in the main, they codify common-sense omissions of initial articles, citations of honour and terms indicating incorporation, etc.

There are a number of special rules prescribing additions for specific types of body: governments and conferences are the most important of these. Additions for governments (24.6) are needed when governments at different levels share the same name, as with New York city and New York state. In the case of conferences (24.7) AACR2 comes very close to prescribing a 'structured' form of heading. We are instructed to omit from the name any indications of number, frequency or year(s). These are to be tacked on to the end of the heading, together with the date and location of the conference. The resulting headings take the following pattern:

International Congress of Neurovegetative Research (*20th: 1990: Tokyo, Japan*)

How does one retrieve such a heading? With keyword access all is well; but in manually searched indexes, the slightest error in transcription ('Congress' misremembered as 'Conference', or even the substitution of 'on' for 'of') can make headings of this type well-nigh irretrievable. Experienced searchers faced with this type of situation will have other search strategies to hand, such as a keyword search or some other subject search.

SUBORDINATE AND RELATED BODIES

These are to be entered directly under their own name whenever possible (24.12); that is to say, when the name does not necessarily imply subordination. Thus the Bodleian Library belongs to the University of Oxford, but it is to be entered directly under its name, even though the format may be inconsistent with other university libraries.

Bodies to be entered subordinately (24.13) include:

- a body that is subordinate by definition (for example, Department, Division, Committee), provided it cannot be identified without the name of the higher body
- a name that is so general that it requires the parent body for proper identification
- a name that does not convey the idea of a corporate body
- university faculties, institutes, etc., where the name simply denotes a field of study
- a name that includes the entire name of the higher or related body.

As always, AACR2's examples should be studied carefully.

In many cases with subordinate bodies there is a hierarchy of subordination. Where there are three or more levels of subordination, cataloguers are instructed to omit intermediate elements in the hierarchy unless this might result in ambiguity. This rule had some purpose in manually compiled and searched indexes, in preventing headings from becoming unnecessarily long. However, it necessitates some complex references (as well as being difficult to apply consistently); and in the context of online retrieval, it has been argued that it would be simpler either to use the subordinate body on its own as a heading, or to set down the complete hierarchy once and for all, allowing each searcher to home in on whichever part of it they wish.

GOVERNMENT BODIES AND OFFICIALS

Governments form one of the most important categories of corporate body. They operate at many levels: international, national, regional, local. Mostly, a government is entered under its conventional name, which is the geographic name of the area governed (rule 24). Essentially governments are treated in the same way as any other corporate body, but because of their complexity AACR2 devotes a section (24.17–24.26) to them.

National governments have three traditional areas of responsibility: the legislature, for which the agency is the country's legislative body (for example, Parliament, Congress); the executive, which consists of the government and its various departments, ministries, etc., and also its armed forces; and finally the judiciary, or courts of law. Governments also have ambassadors and other agencies to represent their interests abroad. Much of the complexity of headings for governments derives from the tendency of modern government to pervade and regulate more and more areas of everyday life. The range of government agencies today is such that AACR's general rule (24.17) and its default condition is that a body created or controlled by a government is to be entered directly under its name, with a reference from the agency as a subheading of the name of the government, thus:

Heading: Arts Council of Great Britain
Reference: Great Britain. Arts Council *see* Arts Council of Great Britain

The agencies performing the central functions of government are entered as a subheading of the name of the government according to rule 24.18, which somewhat paradoxically forms an exception to the general rules for governments. The proliferation of government agencies today is such that an official publication is to be assumed not to be concerned with one of the central functions of government. Rule 24.18 lists 11 types of government agencies to be entered subordinately. As a further exception, there are special rules for government officials, legislative bodies, constitutional conventions, courts, the armed forces, embassies and consulates, and delegations to international or intergovernmental bodies – all of which are entered subordinately. Where there are degrees of subordination, the general rules – 24.14, elaborated at 24.19 – apply. The special rules have some exceptions, however: the heading for the US Senate is United States. *Congress. Senate* and not simply United States. *Senate*. A similar construction is prescribed for other legislative bodies, and for armed forces.

AACR2 also devotes three pages to special rules for religious bodies and officials (24.27).

REFERENCES TO HEADINGS FOR CORPORATE BODIES

The principles for making references to corporate bodies are similar to those for personal names. The following are some typical instances, covering different names, different forms of a name and different entry elements:

Deutschland (Bundesrepublik) *see* Germany (Federal Republic)
Friends, Society of *see* Society of Friends
International Business Machines Corporation *see* IBM
Quakers *see* Society of Friends
Religious Society of Friends *see* Society of Friends
Roman Catholic Church *see* Catholic Church
RSPB *see* Royal Society for the Protection of Birds
United Nations Educational, Scientific and Cultural Organization *see* UNESCO

Subordinate bodies lead to complications not found with personal names:

> University of Oxford. *Bodleian Library see* Bodleian Library

and for more than one degree of subordination:

> United Kingdom. *Department of Energy. Energy Efficiency Office see*
> United Kingdom. *Energy Efficiency Office*

Change of name in corporate bodies can give rise to more insidious complications:

> Great Britain. *Board of Education*
>   *see also*
> Great Britain. *Ministry of Education*
> Great Britain. *Department of Education and Science*
> Great Britain. *Department for Education and Employment*

with similar references under the three other bodies. In such cases an explanatory reference is often recommended, giving the dates between which each name applied. Rule 26.3C has some even more complex examples.

UNIFORM TITLES

Covered by AACR2's Chapter 25, uniform titles are filing titles supplied by the cataloguer, and are used optionally. They have two functions:

1. to bring together entries for different editions, translations, etc., of the same work, appearing under different titles
2. to provide identification for a work when the title by which it is known differs from the title of the item in hand.

Function 1 is typical of collocative catalogues. It belonged originally to manually searched files: a uniform title such as:

> Dickens, Charles
> [Martin Chuzzlewit] The Life and Adventures of Martin Chuzzlewit

could be retrieved electronically by keyword access even without the uniform title. Function 2, however, is a finding-list function and is valid irrespective of the mode of searching. A person searching for an edition of Swift's *Gulliver's Travels* could conceivably have problems retrieving this without its uniform title:

> Swift, Jonathan
> [Gulliver's Travels] Travels into Several Remote Nations of the World / by Lemuel Gulliver

and a work such as this:

[Arabian Nights] The Book of the Thousand and One Nights

could be completely irretrievable.

There are a number of special categories of works that might carry a uniform title. They include:

- *Collections*: a uniform title may be used to collocate complete or partial collections of an author's works, where these appear under different titles; for example:

   Maugham, W. Somerset
   [Selections] The Somerset Maugham Pocket Book

   Specific uniform titles are prescribed for use as appropriate, for example: [Works], [Poems], [Short stories], [Poems. Selections], [Short stories. Spanish. Selections].

- *Sacred scriptures*. Uniform titles for the more logical arrangement and retrieval of the Bible and other sacred scriptures are well established. The method is reminiscent of subject retrieval with its fixed citation order:

   Bible. Testament. Book or group of books. Language. Version. Year.
   For example:
   Bible. N.T. Corinthians. English. Authorized.
   Bible. English. Revised Standard. 1959.

- *Music*. This often requires a uniform title, especially in the case of classical works, as the international nature of music publishing often results in editions of works having title pages in a variety of languages. They are best explained by examples:

   Handel, George Frederick
   [Messiah. Vocal score]
   Rossini, Gioacchino
   [Barbiere di Siviglia. Largo al factotum]
   Schubert, Franz
   [Quintets, violins (2), viola, violoncelli (2), D. 956, C major]

CITATIONS, CATALOGUE ENTRIES AND METADATA

This chapter opened by referring to earlier chapters where document representation was described. AACR2 is unusual in its careful separation of

Citations	Catalogue entries	Metadata
Based on tradition of scholarly acknowledgement of predecessor's work	Strongly influenced by tradition of historical bibliography: the identification of individual copies of hand-printed books. Often based on information used in compiling national bibliographies	Recently developed from first principles
Single entry only, under author or author substitute	Multiple entries for responsible persons, corporate bodies, titles; one of these being the point designated the main entry and the rest added entries. In an OPAC these produce a range of access points. Also include references from different approaches to names	One record with embedded keys to provide multiple access points
May include both monographs and papers that form part of a larger unit (journal articles, conference papers, etc.)	Items forming part of a larger unit are excluded (with few exceptions)	Indexer defines unit or document
Form short, single-purpose lists in both manual and computer-held files	In manual files, form long multi-purpose lists	Access is via search keys
Do not normally give physical locations, but should include enough information to enable an item to be traced or a resource to be accessed	Give locations (shelfmark)	Give location based on URL
Good quality control. Inclined towards academic publications, often reports of research by individuals or small teams	Quality mediated by considerations of commercial publishing and acquisition by libraries	Material accepted on 'common carrier' basis. Some validated material, but no systematic quality control. Includes promotional materials and worse
Representation and access combined. Give sufficient information for identification purposes only	Representation and access separated. Identify and may often additionally characterize as an aid to selection	Representation and access combined. Direct access to resource

Figure 8.2 Citations, catalogue entries and metadata

representation (description) and access. While Chapter 3 did not discuss document access as such, it did discuss citations, where the document representation has its own built-in access point. Also, in Chapter 2 we looked at metadata, a mechanism for both representing and accessing networked electronic resources. Citations, catalogues and metadata have evolved through quite different traditions. Figure 8.2 summarizes some points of similarity and contrast.

SUMMARY

This chapter started by visiting the fundamental objectives and functions of catalogues. This provides a useful backdrop for consideration of the use of authors' names (including those of corporate bodies and governments) as access points in information retrieval systems. By using AACR2 as a basis for its structure, this chapter has rehearsed many of the difficulties in achieving consistency in the choice of author, choice of name and form of name that arise when names are used in cataloguing and information retrieval; it has also explained AACR2's recommendations in response to these challenges. The use of added entries and references has also been discussed. The concepts of uniform title and its application were also introduced. A final section summarized the differences between citations, catalogue entries and metadata.

REVIEW QUESTIONS

1. Outline Cutter's rules for a dictionary catalogue and explain why they are still relevant to cataloguing and indexing over 100 years after they were originally formulated.
2. Make a list of the key decisions that a cataloguer needs to make in the choice of author headings and access terms for a document.
3. Identify the six different authorship conditions used in AACR2 and explain when each of them applies.
4. When selecting a heading to represent a person, AACR suggests that it is necessary to consider the choice of name, the entry element, any additions to names and any references. Taking the perspective of a searcher, explain why it is useful for cataloguers to consider each of these issues.
5. Explain why corporate body names cause difficulties for both cataloguers and searchers. Include reference to subordinate and related bodies, and to government bodies.
6. Why are references necessary for corporate body headings? Using examples, demonstrate some of the complexities of references to support access to corporate body headings.
7. What is a uniform title? Using examples, illustrate when a uniform title might be useful.
8. Explain the relationship between catalogue entries and metadata.
9. Discuss why an information professional would benefit from acquaintance with AACR2's guidelines on author names and titles.

REFERENCES AND FURTHER READING

Anglo-American Cataloguing Rules (AARC2) (2004), 2nd edn, rev. 2002, 2004. London: Library Association.

Baughman, B. and Svenonius, E. (1984) AACR2: main entry free? *Cataloging and Classification Quarterly*, **5** (1), 1–15.

Bowman, J.H. (2003) *Essential Cataloguing*. London: Facet.

Carpenter, M. and Svenonius, E. (eds) (1986) *Foundations of Cataloging: A sourcebook*. Littleton CO: Libraries Unlimited.

Cutter, C.A. (1904) *Rules for a Dictionary Catalog*, 4th edn. Washington DC: Government Printing Office (and later reprints).

Dowski, C.A. (2005) Cataloguing at the crossroads; now that we have AACR2 revised chapter 12, where do we go from here? *Technical Services Quarterly*, **23** (1), 75–86.

Fattahi, R. (1995) Anglo-American Cataloguing Rules in the online environment: a literature review. *Cataloging and Classification Quarterly*, **20** (2), 25–50.

Fritz, D.A. (1998) *Cataloging with AACR2 and USMARC: For books, computer files, serials, sound recordings, video recordings*. Chicago: American Library Association.

Gorman, M. (1978) The Anglo-American Cataloging Rules, second edition. *Library Resources and Technical Services*, **22** (3), 209–26.

Gorman, M. (2004) *The Concise AACR2*, 4th edn. London: Facet.

IFLA (1996) *Names of Persons: National Usages for Entry in Catalogues*, 4th edn. Munich and London: K. G. Saur.

Joint Steering Committee for the Revision of AACR (2002) *Anglo-American Cataloguing Rules*, 2nd edn, rev. 2002, updated 2004. Chicago and London: CILIP.

Joint Steering Committee for Revision of AACR (2005) RDA: resource description and access. Available at <www.collectionscanada.ca/jsc/rdapresentations.html> [accessed 18 October 2006].

Jones, W. (2002) *Cataloguing the Web: Metadata, AACR and MARC21*. Lanham MD: Scarecrow.

Library of Congress, Network Development and MARC Standards Office (2003) *MARC21 Concise Format for Bibliographic Data*. Library of Congress. Available at <http://lcweb.loc.gov/marc/bibliographic> [accessed 18 October 2006].

Lubtezky, S. (1953) *Cataloging Rules and Principles*. Washington DC: Library of Congress.

Madison, O.M.A. (1992) The role of the name main-entry heading in the online environment. *Serials Librarian*, **22** (3/4), 371–91.

Maxwell, R.L. (2004) *Maxwell's Handbook for AACR2: Explaining and Illustrating the Anglo-American Cataloguing Rules through the 2003 update*. Chicago: American Library Association.

Medeiros, N. (2005) The future of the Anglo-American cataloguing rules. *OCLC Systems and Services: International digital library perspectives*, **21** (4), 261–3.

Svenonius, E. and McGarry, D. (2001) *Seymour Lubetzky: Writing on the classical art of cataloguing*. Greenwood Press.

Taylor, A.G. (2000) *Wyner's Introduction to Cataloguing and Classification*, 9th edn, with D.P. Miller. Englewood CO: Libraries Unlimited.

Taylor, A.G. (2004) *The Organization of Information*, 2nd edn. Westport CT: Libraries Unlimited.

257

Part III
Systems

9 Organizing knowledge in the digital environment

INTRODUCTION

In the early chapters of this book, we introduced a range of techniques which are used in the organization of knowledge or, more accurately, metadata about information objects containing knowledge so that they can be retrieved, or as many writers now say, discovered and used. In a previous chapter we considered the users of organized knowledge and paid attention to the interface with knowledge retrieval systems. In this chapter we explore the range of systems which are available to enable different users in different situations to access organized knowledge. In recent years, the idea of the portal as the means of accessing knowledge organization systems and a range of other services has become important. Closely associated with the portal is the notion of personalization of access to digital systems and services. There is an ever-increasing number of systems available for knowledge organization. In the following pages we explore numerous long-standing tools for knowledge organization, including abstracting and indexing databases, citation indexes and OPACs. We also consider more recent developments, in the shape of digital libraries, institutional and subject repositories, Internet search engines, records and content management systems, image retrieval systems and social networking tools such as wikis and blogs.

At the end of this chapter you will:

- understand what is meant by a portal
- appreciate how the concept of personalization relates to portals and knowledge organization systems
- be aware of the range of different types of digital system through which organized knowledge can be accessed, including OPACs, digital libraries, institutional and subject repositories, search engines and directories, databases

261

of abstracts and indexes and citation indexes, content management systems and records management systems, image retrieval systems, wikis and blogs.

WHAT IS A PORTAL?

As its name implies, a portal offers access to a range of information resources and other services. Some indication of what is meant by a portal can be gained from a number of definitions. For example, IBM define a portal as:

> ... a single secure point of interaction with diverse information, business processes and people personalised to a user's need and responsibilities.
>
> (IBM, 2003)

Many authors use the terms 'gateway' and 'portal' interchangeably whilst others make a clear distinction between the two. For example, Brophy (2001) advises us that the UK Joint Information Systems Committee draws a distinction between a gateway and a portal, as follows:

> A gateway should be regarded as a virtual place that provides signposts to resources. The user enters the gateway, is assisted to select the most useful pointers and then follows them to locate resources themselves. Typically, a gateway would consist of an ordered list of URLs; when the user clicks on a URL he moves to the site where the resource itself is to be found. The user is a temporary visitor to the gateway, moving rapidly on – but of course quite possibly returning again and again to find more useful resources.

By comparison:

> A portal is a more sophisticated resource. The user sends a query to the portal which examines it, reformats it and uses it to query a series of other resources that may contain content of relevance. The results from these searches are then concatenated and otherwise processed by the portal (e.g. to remove duplicates) before being presented to the user. In essence the user, having entered the portal, never leaves – the portal goes out into the information universe on his or her behalf.
>
> (Brophy, 2001)

Whilst these definitions show clear differences, they give a flavour of a portal as being a single point of access to a range of resources and services. The value of a single point of access to organized knowledge and to other services has obvious advantages for the user, given the complex information environment, but it also has advantages for the supplier. Rowley (2000) has pointed out that an organization providing a portal acquires the following advantages:

- strong visibility in cyberspace, coupled with a more high-tech image
- the opportunity to create a community of consumers who identify with the portal
- control in strategic alliances with partners with whose sites links are made; mutual links might represent a collaborative arrangement, but organizations without such ready access to an online consumer community may be at a disadvantage in strategic alliances in virtual business networks
- the ability to collect data about consumer choices, search paths and interests: this allows the organization to create a profile of its community which relates to elements of the latter's behaviour as consumers.

Given the lack of agreement on a definition of a portal, examination of the features offered by portals provides a useful means of improving our understanding of what they do. Butters (2003) has undertaken an extensive analysis of portals produced by a range of different suppliers, including search engines, information service providers (ISPs) and universities. Inevitably, not every portal provider offers all these facilities but the range gives a useful indication of how portals seek to be a one-stop shop for their users. Butters identifies:

- a wide range of utilities; for example, e-mail, address book, bookmarks, calendar, currency calculator, maps and many more
- personalization (see below)
- resource discovery, including access to quality-assured resources, to bibliographic databases, citation databases and electronic journals, the ability to search local OPACs and tables of contents, and the facility of searching the Web
- news feeds on a whole range of topics (see RSS feeds in Chapter 4)
- community communication; for example, chat, bulletin boards, collaborative working and newsgroups.

Pearce (2003) undertook a sizable survey of user requirements from institutional portals. The top ten requirements in rank order are presented in Figure 9.1.

Whilst the Butters survey analysed features offered by all portals and not just those in education, it is very noticeable that the users in Pearce's survey placed far greater emphasis on access to knowledge than some of the portal providers appear to be offering. In order to illustrate features offered by via a portal, the Association for Computing Machinery portal (as shown in Figure 9.2) provides access to details of forthcoming conferences, access to full text of some publications, access to a bibliographic database of some 450,000 items, access to online learning materials for personal development and press releases. Some of the material is available to anyone who registers whilst other material is available only on a subscription basis.

Rated	Feature
1st	Search your favourite resources
2nd	Library administration
3rd	Access or update teaching materials
4th	Personal information
5th	Library and quality Internet resources alerts
6th	Access your institutional e-mail
7th	Handbook
8th	Deadline alerts
9th	Access or update reading lists
10th	Campus news

Figure 9.1 The top ten rated features for institutional portals
Source: Pearce, 2003

WHAT IS PERSONALIZATION?

Personalization is the attempt to deliver content and services to a system user. It requires the collection of information about an individual's use of the system such that the system can attempt to deliver relevant content to the individual. Personalization is an attempt in the digital world to offer individualized service in an attempt to build customer loyalty.

An obvious example of personalization is the manner in which Amazon makes recommendations based upon a combination of previous purchases and items about which information has been sought by an individual. This attempt at an individualized service in the digital world has both advantages and disadvantages as Amazon itself clearly demonstrates. Whilst it may be acceptable to receive recommendations based upon previous behaviour and this can lead to notification of possible purchases of which the individual is unaware, it can also lead to frustration. As soon as a user purchases items for other people, the system's 'understanding' of interests becomes distorted.

There is a generally accepted distinction between personalization (where the system gathers information about one's behaviour and uses that as a means of providing personalized service) and customization. Services which offer the latter enable users to build an individualized service through the configuration of an interface and the services offered by taking choices from the services available. The creation of My Yahoo! offers a good example of customization.

The term 'personalization' hides the obvious fact that the service might not be aimed at a single individual but in some cases might be offered to a work group such as a research team.

264

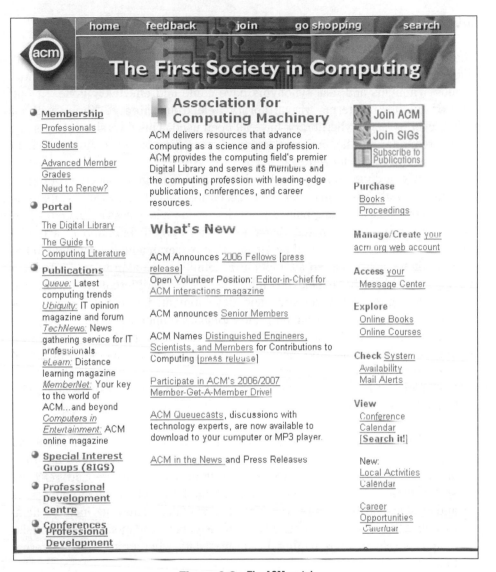

Figure 9.2 The ACM portal

Whilst personalization has become relatively commonplace in the commercial environment, it is much rarer in the library and information world. There might well be many users who would appreciate automatic notification of new books added to a library where the notification was based upon past library use. The concept of personalization is explored further by Bonnett (2001).

DIGITAL LIBRARIES

These have been an area of constant research and development since about 1990. Whilst the term 'digital libraries' has become standard in that period of time, various synonyms and near-synonyms have come and effectively gone. At one time or another the terms 'virtual library', 'electronic library', 'library without walls', 'cybrary' and 'cyberlibrary' have all been used. This diversity of terms is a timely reminder of the limits of keyword searching and the importance of organizing knowledge for retrieval.

Put simply, a digital library can be viewed as a managed collection of digital information with associated services, accessible via a network. Whilst this definition provides a starting point for our discussion it is necessary to go further. Numerous authors have noted that there is no agreed definition of a digital library. This might be explained by the fact that research and development in the field continues apace and so attempts at a definition are akin to trying to hit a moving target. A further explanation might be that many different professions are involved in digital library research and development; interest is certainly not confined to library and information professionals. Computer scientists have long been active in digital library research and many other professionals with an interest in ICT have become involved in the creation and operation of digital libraries within their own particular fields.

One lengthy and widely used definition is that of Borgman (2000), as quoted by Tedd and Large (2005):

> Digital libraries are a set of electronic resources and associated technical capabilities for creating, searching and using information. In this sense they are an extension and enhancement of information storage and retrieval systems that manipulate digital data in any medium (text, images, sounds ...) and exist in distributed networks. The context of digital libraries includes data, metadata that describe various aspects of the data ... and metadata that consist of links or relationships to other data or metadata, whether internal or external to the digital library.
>
> Digital libraries are constructed – collected and organized – by [and for] a community of users, and their functional capabilities support the information needs and uses of that community ... In this sense they are an extension, enhancement and integration of a variety of information institutions as physical places where resources are selected, collected, organized, preserved and accessed in support of a user community. These information institutions include, among others, libraries, museums, archives and schools, but digital libraries also extend and serve other community settings, including classrooms, offices, laboratories, homes and public spaces.

A number of points from this extended definition are worth emphasis. Firstly, a digital library contains digital objects which have been *selected* as being of importance to the particular group of users for whom the library is intended. Secondly, and importantly for readers of this book, access to the objects is *organized* in some way that is logical to the purpose of the digital library. In these respects they share features with traditional libraries. Thirdly, the library contains *metadata* about the objects within the library. In this case there are similarities and differences between traditional libraries and digital libraries. Although traditional libraries also contain metadata about their collections in the form of catalogue records, the metadata in a digital library may need to be more extensive than that in a traditional library. The differences between metadata in a digital library and catalogue data in a traditional library were explored in Chapter 2. Fourthly, digital collections are made available by a wider range of organizations. Professional societies often provide access to their journals and sometimes their textbooks in a form which is referred to as a digital library; for example, the American Society for Information Science and Technology offers its members a digital library. Museums make digital libraries available; for example, the Hermitage Museum in St Petersburg, Russia. Figure 9.3 shows the digital collections page of the museum.

A clear difference between traditional and digital libraries is the provision by the latter of facilities with which to manipulate the digital data. For example, the digital library Perseus (<http://www.perseus.tufts.edu/>) provides an extensive collection of digital materials relating to the ancient world. This is supported by a range of tools which are available for use in conjunction with the resources in the library. As well as a browser and a collection summaries (in effect a table of contents), Perseus offers a tool for drawing digital maps of the world, various language tools relating to terms in English, Latin and ancient Greek, an atlas of London from 1780 to the present day and a virtual reality tool. In part these additional facilities are illustrated by the extract from the Perseus home page which is presented as Figure 9.4.

Finally, the users, or more accurately the potential users, of a digital library are distributed worldwide and in many cases it will be impossible for the creators of the library to be aware of the information needs of users in the way that librarians in many traditional libraries would be expected to be able to achieve. Whilst this may be a problem for the 'digital librarian', it is clearly an advantage for the user, who can access remote materials without leaving home or office. There are two ways in which digital libraries differ from traditional libraries which are especially important to users and creators alike. Creation of a digital image of a fragile object enables its use without endangering its existence. Furthermore it is possible in a digital library to create a virtual collection by bringing together digital versions of objects which are intellectually related but currently geographically scattered.

Some further examples of digital libraries will serve to demonstrate the range of

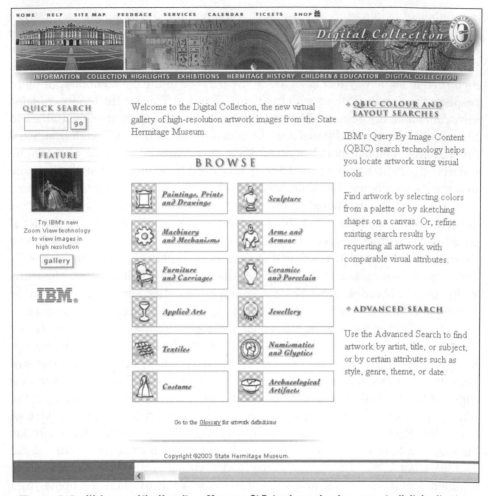

Figure 9.3 Web page of the Hermitage Museum, St Petersburg, showing access to digital collections

both materials and suppliers. An interesting example of a digital library which offers access to a wide range of material is the New Zealand Digital Library developed and maintained at the University of Waikato (<*http://nzdl.sadl. uleth.ca/cgi-bin/library*>). This offers access to a range of collections, including a facility for user-created collections, collections from the United Nations and on humanitarian topics such as a world environment library and a humanitarian development library. The New Zealand Digital Library was developed by the team which developed the Greenstone Digital Library software and so, in addition to collections of materials, this library also provides access to demonstrations relating to software and a number of topics in the creation and provision of electronic services such as the open access initiative (see below).

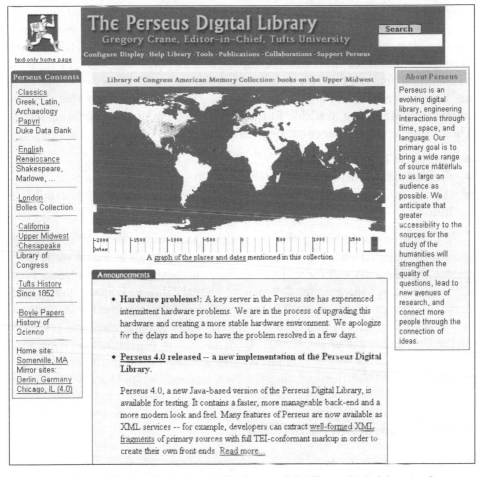

Figure 9.4   Clip from the home page of the Perseus digital library of materials concerning the ancient world

Especially in the UK, many writers have referred to the concept of a hybrid library; that is, a library which is a mixture of digital and print resources. The reasoning for this approach is that in organizational contexts such as universities, there would be a need for many years to have access to both print and digital resources. For a short period of time, a series of specific hybrid libraries were developed, such as HyLife at the University of Northumbria and Builder at the University of Birmingham. Whilst these were specifically research projects which are no longer available, it is certainly fair to say than many university libraries today are strictly hybrid libraries: they offer integrated access to both print and electronic resources. Certainly the library of Manchester Metropolitan University (MMU) fits this description, as it provides access through its catalogue to a wide

269

range of print books and e-books, print and electronic journals, bibliographic databases and links from bibliographic citations to full texts (<http://www.library. mmu.ac.uk>). National libraries have a responsibility to preserve the cultural heritage of the nation. Inevitably this means that for some time to come they will be collecting both print and digital material. Even the most cursory examination of the home page of the national libraries in the UK make it obvious that they are collecting and making available to their users both print and digital materials. Their respective home pages can be seen as follows:

- the British Library (<http://www.bl.uk>)
- the National Library of Scotland (<http://www.nls.uk>)
- the National Library of Wales (<http://www.llgc.org.uk/drych/index_s. htm>).

Finally, it is worth noting that in addition to a wide range of commercial software, the digital library movement has created and made available some 'open source' digital library software. The best known of these are probably DSpace and EPrints Archive Software and Greenstone Digital Library. DSpace and EPrints Archive Software are widely used in the creation and management of institutional repositories (see later in this chapter). Greenstone Digital Library was produced by the University of Waikato, New Zealand, and is now distributed in cooperation with UNESCO. It is widely established and has been used in the creation of a number of digital libraries, including the New Zealand Digital Library.

OPEN ACCESS AND REPOSITORIES

The emergence of the Web is producing profound changes in the way which scholarly information is being made accessible. Since the middle of the 17th century, the subscription-based academic journal has been the pre-eminent means of communicating new information and interpretations of existing information. However the open access movement is rapidly providing an alternative means of providing access to material. Put simply, open access is free access to digital content via the Internet. One aspect of this is the publishing of an increasing number of electronic journals, such as *Ariadne, DLib Magazine* and *Information Research* within the information field. However, of increasing importance and closely related to digital libraries is the concept of open archiving, by which authors of scholarly works deposit their work in one or more open archives: these are of two types – institutional repositories and subject-based repositories. The open access movement is steadily gaining in importance – a development which has been aided by the support given by various government bodies which fund research, both in North America and Europe.

An institutional repository is a digital archive of the intellectual output of a particular university. However, whilst it is clear that such a repository is a logical home for the research output of the given university, there is as yet no agreement on the complete content of these repositories. Amongst the content proposed for inclusion in institutional repositories are:

- pre-prints of articles or research reports submitted for publication
- the text of journal articles accepted for publication
- revised texts of published work with comments from academic readers
- conference papers
- teaching materials
- student projects
- doctoral theses and dissertations
- datasets resulting from research projects
- committee papers
- computer software
- works of art
- photographs and video recordings.
    (<http://www.arl.org/SPARC/> and <http://www.sparceurope.org/>)

Whilst the presence of the first two items in this list is understandable, there is less agreement in either principle or practice about some of the other items. At the time of writing (late 2006), there are areas of uncertainty concerning the relationship between institutional repositories and other locations for digital objects, notably institutional virtual learning environments.

In addition to institutional repositories, there is an increasing number of subject-based repositories which provide access to digital objects which have been deposited with them; also on the increase are the offers of access to the metadata of objects deposited in other repositories. A typical example within the field of library and information science is DLIST (Digital Library of Information Science and Technology) hosted at the University of Arizona. DLIST describes itself as:

> ... a cross-institutional, subject-based, open access digital archive for the Information Sciences, including Archives and Records Management, Library and Information Science, Information Systems, Museum Informatics, and other critical information infrastructures.

Established in 2002, it has as its vision:

> ... to serve as a dynamic archive in the Information Sciences, broadly understood, and positively impact and shape scholarly communication in our closely related fields.

    (<http://dlist.sir.arizona.edu/>)

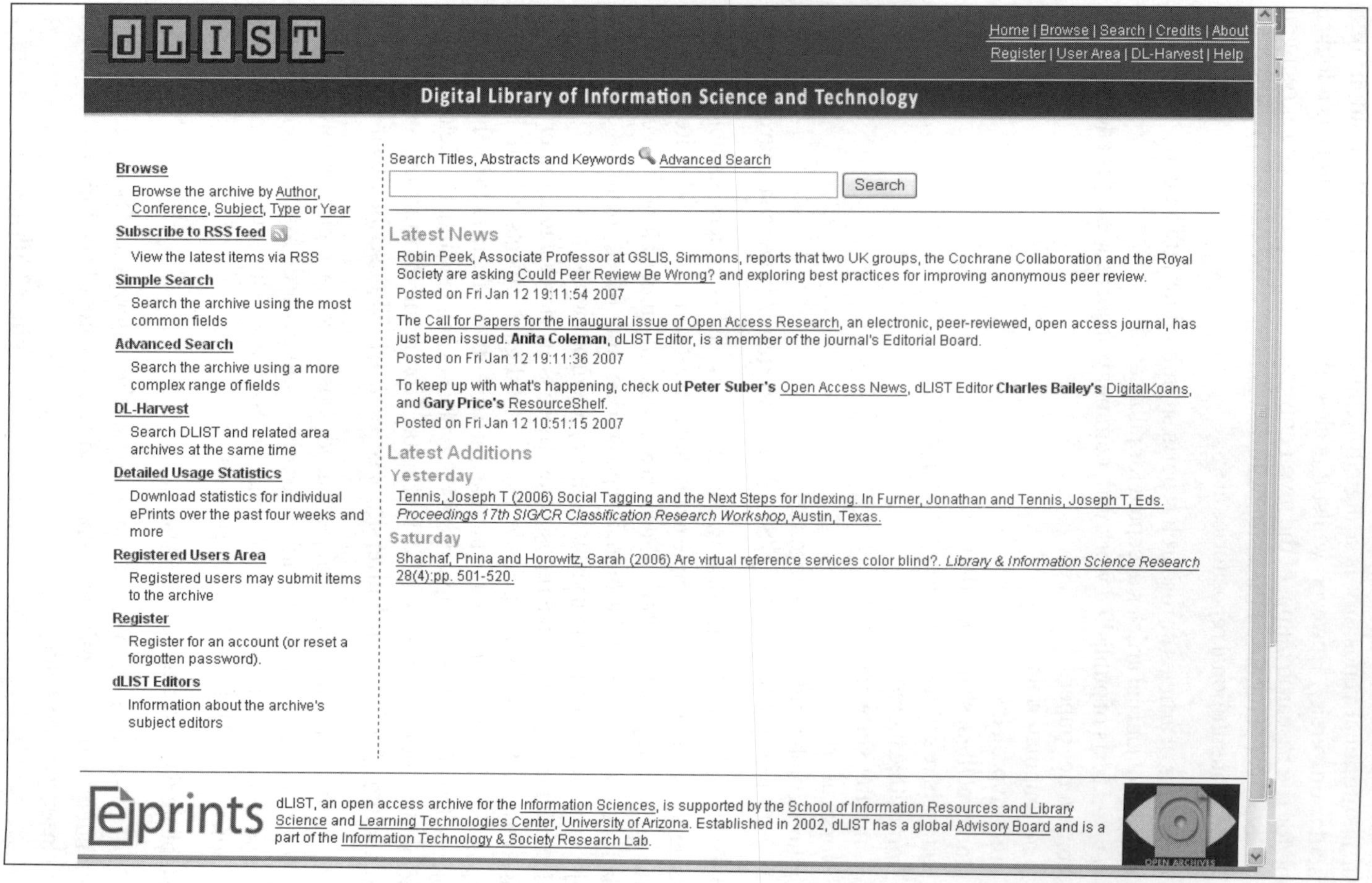

Figure 9.5   Home page of DLIST, a subject-based repository for materials in information science and technology

The home page of DLIST is shown in Figure 9.5. Important subject repositories in other disciplines include:

- arXiv – an open access archive of research papers in mathematics and physics (<http://arxiv.org/>)
- CogPrints – an open access archive in the cognitive sciences (<http://cogprints.org/>), and
- CiteSeer – an open access archive for computer science which has been harvested from distributed websites (<http://citeseer.ist.psu.edu/>).

The creation of an ever-increasing number of repositories led to the need for a means of searching multiple overlapping information stores. This led to the invention of the Open Archives Initiative Protocol for Metadata Harvesting (OAI-PMH). The philosophy behind OAI-PMH is not one of distributed search as adopted by InforM25 (see section on OPACs below); rather it assumes that it is preferable for the information seeker to search a single source. To this end, it defines a minimum standard to which repositories should conform in their metadata to enable that metadata to be automatically captured, or harvested, by software. It also defines a series of commands to allow that harvesting to take place; these are based upon a simple http-based request-response framework. A non-technical framework is provided by Lynch (2001) and a detailed exposition of version 2.0 can be obtained from the Open Archives website (Open Archives Initiative Protocol for Metadata Harvesting, 2006).

SEARCH ENGINES AND DIRECTORIES

The term 'search engine' is now often applied to any information retrieval system, whether publicly accessible or confined to access within an organization. However, its original use referred to the publicly available search engines which enable anyone to search the Web – an arena which is currently dominated by Google. It is in this latter context of searching the Web that the term 'search engine' is used here. Whilst each Web search engine keeps the exact details of its search algorithms secret, they all operate in a similar manner. The starting point is a piece of software known as a Web crawler or spider which trawls the Web on a regular basis and follows links which it finds to other websites. The located web pages are then analysed and automatically indexed so that a huge index of the Web is created. When the searcher enters a keyword or keywords into a search engine, the word or words are checked against this index and a list of websites containing the term(s) are presented to the user. Usually this list is ranked by expected relevance to the user. The ranking is based on a number of features such as whereabouts in the web page the terms appear and how often they appear. The

273

revolution which occurred with the appearance of Google was the use of the links which appear on a website to aid in the relevance ranking. The idea behind Google is that the ranking of a particular website is increased if it has a large number of links to well-established and reliable websites such as the BBC. The ideas behind the Google approach have been outlined by the creators of the search engine, Larry Page and Sergey Brin (Brin and Page, 2006).

Most search engines will include an advanced search facility which enables the searcher to specify search criteria using the Boolean operators AND OR NOT and by specifying the presence in particular parts of the web page items such as the URL or the title; a few may offer word proximity searching.

Search engines in general and Google in particular have taken information retrieval away from being the preserve of librarians, information scientists and computer scientists and placed it in the lives of millions and millions of people worldwide. Unsurprisingly, the leading search engines such as Google, Alta Vista, Yahoo and MSN offer an increasingly bewildering array of additional services. Whilst adding little to the understanding of the organization of knowledge, the books by Battelle and by Vise provide fascinating explanations of how search engines are making waves far beyond the confines of the organization of knowledge. Vise (2005) outlines how Page and Brin transformed information retrieval and in the process became multi-millionaires through their creation of Google. Battelle (2005) explains how search engines have become big business and are making major impacts on business and culture.

QUALITY-CONTROLLED RESOURCES: INTUTE

The vastness of the Internet is both its strength and its weakness. Whilst there is clearly a wealth of high-quality material accessible via the Web, there is also a huge amount of dross. Intute is a national Internet service aimed at the higher and further education communities in the UK (<http://www.intute.ac.uk>). It consists of a database of descriptions of a limited number of websites which have been selected by a network of subject experts. Web resources accessed via Intute have been assessed for both their relevance to the HE/FE communities and for their quality and reliability. The database is divided into four major sections, namely:

1. science and technology
2. arts and humanities
3. social sciences
4. health and life sciences.

They can be searched either separately or as a single database. In order to develop them, various in-house controlled vocabularies have been developed.

ONLINE PUBLIC ACCESS CATALOGUES (OPACs)

These are an important means of gaining access to organized knowledge. Most OPACs provide access to the material held in a single library. Whilst a number of libraries have attempted to include in their catalogues items from the Web, most libraries focus on providing access to the materials within their organization. In most public and academic libraries and in many commercial and government organizations, the OPAC is the public face of an integrated library management system which contains modules such as circulation control and serials control. In most cases at the heart of this library management system is a database of bibliographic records which have been created according to AACR2 and stored in the MARC format which were discussed in Chapter 3. Some libraries provide access through the OPAC to holdings of journals and increasingly the journal holdings are extended to provide direct access to the full text of journals when the library has negotiated that access.

More recently, union OPACs have become available. These provide access to all the documents in a consortium of libraries. Examples of the latter include COPAC – the OPAC of the Consortium of University Libraries (in the UK). COPAC provides a single union catalogue of 27 major university and national libraries available as a single merged database (<http://copac.ac.uk>). The simple, clear COPAC search page is shown in Figure 9.6. Another example is InforM25, which provides access to the materials held in a number of libraries in London and environs; it is a virtual union catalogue which is created 'on the fly' using the Z39.50 protocol (<http://www.inform25.ac.uk/Link/>). The InforM25 search interface is presented in Figure 9.7.

In a small number of cases it is possible to search both the local OPAC and a remote union OPAC simultaneously; a facility which is available via MMU library which enables concurrent searching of its own OPAC and COPAC.

ABSTRACTING AND INDEXING DATABASES

The process of indexing was discussed in Chapter 4. The outcome of that process is a series of subject- or mission-specific bibliographic databases which record the publications within the discipline of the mission area and make them available for future searching. Well-known examples include Chemical Abstracts for chemistry, Biological Abstracts (BIOSIS) for life sciences and Psychological Abstracts (PsycInfo) for psychology. These, and many other bibliographic tools, make extensive use of the subject access tools which are described in this book. For example, the educational database ERIC (Educational Information Resources Center), a sample record of which is shown in Figure 9.8, has its own thesaurus.

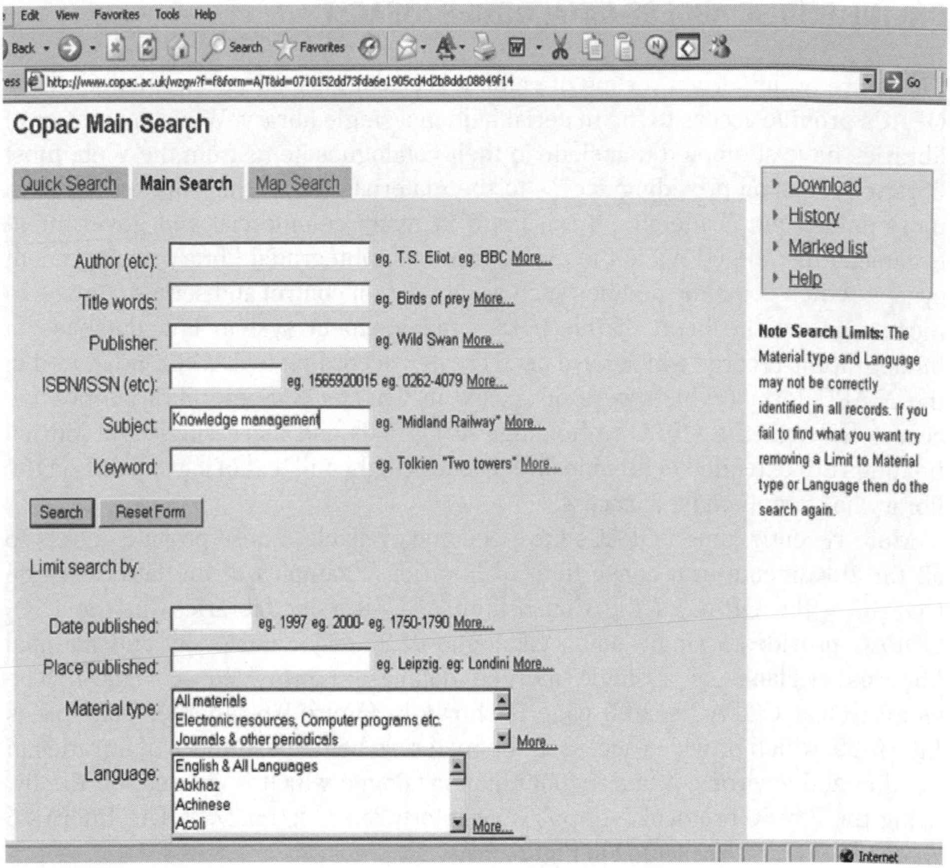

Figure 9.6 The author/title search page of the COPAC system

The index terms from the thesaurus are presented in the field labelled 'Descriptors'. INSPEC is the major bibliographic database for the fields of physics, electronics and computer science. A typical record is presented in Figure 9.9. This record has been enhanced by the addition of terms from the INSPEC thesaurus. These are listed in the field 'INSPEC controlled terms'. The field 'INSPEC classification codes' shows appropriate classifications from that specially devised classification scheme. The field 'Uncontrolled terms' is an interesting example of the addition of natural language terms by the indexer to aid retrieval. Many major abstracting databases will regularly check terms added in this field as a source for candidate terms to add to a system's thesaurus. As a final example, PsycInfo is the major bibliographic database for research material in psychology. The sample record displayed in Figure 9.10 shows the use of both a specific alphabetical vocabulary in the field labelled 'Subject heading' and a subject-

InforM25
M25 CONSORTIUM Search Catalogues
OF ACADEMIC LIBRARIES

InforM25 home | New search | Help

9901650 1

Step 2. Search the selected catalogues

2a: Search Type

- ◉ Author / Title
- ○ Periodical title
- ○ Identifier (e.g. ISBN, ISSN)
- ○ Subject
- ○ Keyword anywhere

2b: Search Terms

Author (e.g. Woolf, Virginia)

Title (e.g. To the lighthouse)

When you have entered an author or title, or both:

[search catalogues]

You have selected: University of the Arts London; Birkbeck, University of London; University of Brighton, Brunel University; Buckinghamshire Chilterns University College; Canterbury Christ Church University; City University; University of East London; Goldsmiths, University of London; University of Greenwich; Imperial College London; Institute of Education; University of Kent; Royal Botanic Gardens, Kew; King's College London & Courtauld Institute of Art; Kingston University; London Business School; London Metropolitan University; ULRLS - Senate House Library/Heythrop College/Sch. Advanced Study; London School of Economics and Political Science; London School of Hygiene & Tropical Medicine; London South Bank University; Middlesex University; Natural History Museum; The Open University; School of Pharmacy; Queen Mary, University of London; University of Reading; Roehampton University; Royal College of Art; Royal Holloway, University of London; School of Oriental & African Studies; St.George's University of London; St Mary's University College, Twickenham; University of Surrey; University of Sussex; Thames Valley University; UCL (UCL Library Services); Victoria and Albert Museum /National Art Library); The Wellcome Library; University of Westminster; Institute of Contemporary History & Wiener Library;

To change catalogue selection, go to: [select catalogues from list]
To make a new selection by geographical zone, start again.

If you have any queries about or difficulties using this service, please consult staff at your local library.
© M25 Consortium, 2006

Figure 9.7   Search page of the InforM25 virtual union catalogue

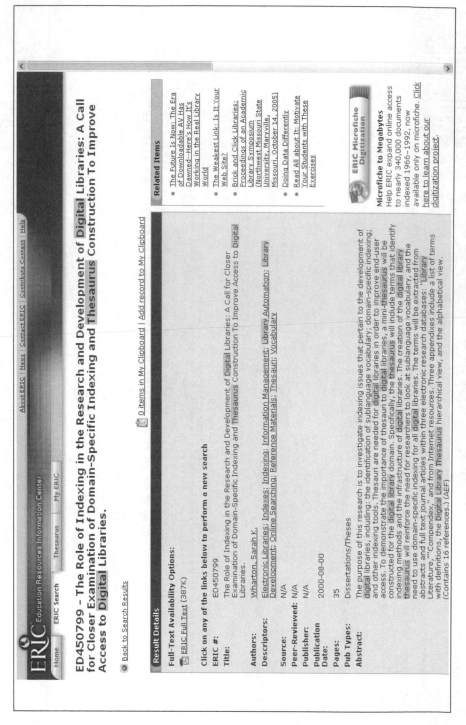

Figure 9.8   A sample record from the ERIC database

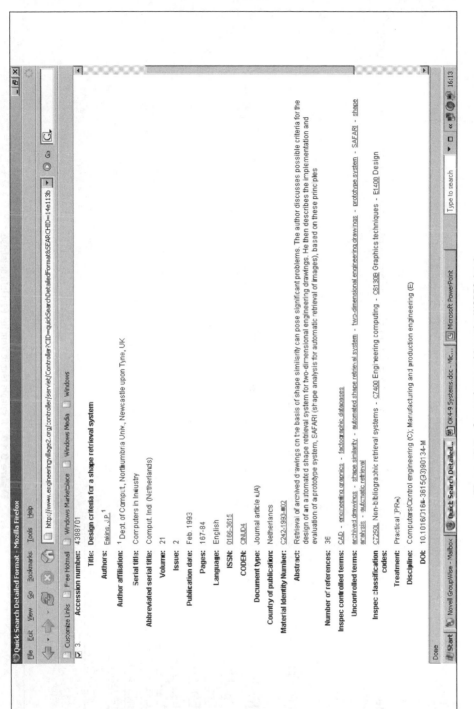

Figure 9.9   A sample record from the INSPEC database

Peer Reviewed Journal: 2005-02830-009.

Maternal use of physical punishment in response to child misbehavior: Implications for child **abuse** prevention. [References].

2005

Ateah, Christine A; Durrant, Joan E.

Child Abuse & Neglect. Vol 29(2) Feb 2005, 169-185.

physical punishment, child misbehavior, child **abuse** prevention, mothers, cognition, affect, discipline

*Child Discipline
*Cognition
*Emotional States
*Mothers
***Punishment**
Behavior Problems
Child **Abuse**
Prevention

Childrearing & Child Care [2956]

Figure 9.10   A sample record from the PsycInfo database

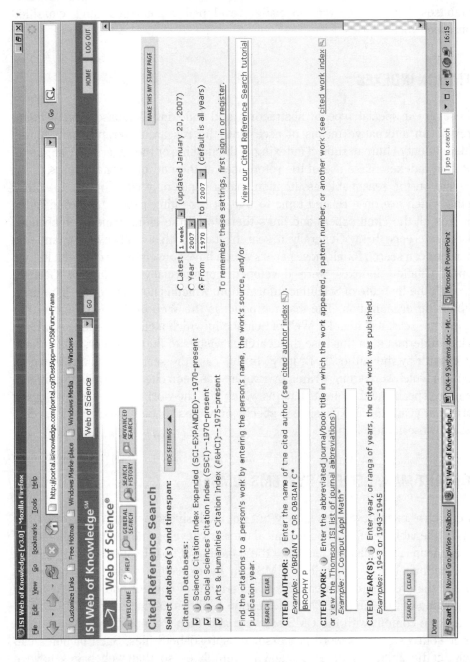

Figure 9.11 The cited reference search page of ISI Thomson's Web of Science search page

specific classification scheme in the field labelled 'Classification code'; both have their own detailed thesaurus to aid indexing and retrieval. Many other abstracting databases have their own specially developed alphabetical and classified controlled vocabularies.

CITATION INDEXES

These are a special type of abstracting and indexing database developed to provide an alternative means of accessing the research literature which was independent of human subject indexing of documents or the vagaries of language. Citation indexes make use of the references at the end of journal papers. They operate on the reasonable assumption that a paper only cites (refers to) other items which are on a related topic to that of the citing paper. A citation index records all the cited papers and links them to all the citing papers which have made reference to it. Generally a search starts with a known paper and the searcher can search for all those papers which have subsequently cited the known paper. Citation indexes were developed commercially by Eugene Garfield through the Institute of Scientific Information, which is now part of the Thomson publishing organization. The major product is the Web of Science. Figure 9.11 shows the search screen for Web of Science in which a cited reference search is being undertaken; in this case the searcher wishes to find all papers which have cited work by the author 'P. Brophy'. In this case the searcher has requested all items in which something written by Brophy has been cited. It is quite possible to be more specific and request all items which cite the work of a named author in a particular year. It is also possible to specify only those papers which cite a specific paper by the named author.

CONTENT MANAGEMENT SYSTEMS (CMSs)

These have been developed largely but not exclusively for the Web world; their aim is to enable relatively non-technical users to develop and manage websites or other means of publishing, enabling the handling of text, images and multimedia information objects. Typically a CMS can be expected to contain facilities to enable the creation of content, the management of content and the delivery or publishing of that content. Content creation facilities might include the ability to create the content with the CMS software and then to import information from other sources such as word processor or spreadsheet files. Such facilities can include the ability to develop standard templates so that web pages have a consistent style, for example by developing cascading style sheets.

Typically the data which is published by the CMS is held in a relational database. The CMS has facilities for the management of access control at various levels, for workflow control so that content can be created by more than one person and for version control. Some CMSs have features for the management of FAQs (frequently asked questions). Some CMSs will have the ability to deal with non-Western character sets. Some authors have argued that wikis (see later in this chapter) and portals (see the beginning of this chapter) are content management systems.

On the output side, a CMS has the capabilities for publishing the material. Additional features include the ability to generate RSS feeds, a search facility and automatic site map creation.

CMSs can be used for the production of marketing material, operations manuals, newspapers, journals, newsletters and websites. In each of these applications CMS features such as version control and the ability for objects to be created by multiple authors can be important.

RECORDS MANAGEMENT SYSTEMS

In order to consider records management systems, it is necessary to make some brief comments about records management itself. Records management is a rapidly developing discipline which shares many characteristics with, but some differences from, information retrieval. Records management is concerned with the identification, capture, storage, retrieval and (where necessary) the destruction of the records which are necessary for a business to flourish. Examples of important records are medical records, tax records, applications data and financial records. In recent years the importance of records management has been emphasized by scandals such as those surrounding ENRON and the accountancy firm Andersens. The trend towards increasing electronic interaction between a government and its citizens and crimes such as identity theft have further emphasized the importance of records management in modern society.

A records manager is responsible for the creation, implementation and monitoring of an organization's records management policy. Such a policy should include a retention schedule which indicates where a key copy of a record is kept, for how long it is kept and when it should be destroyed.

An organization can keep records in either physical format or electronically. It is clearly the latter which are increasing in importance, though many organizations will now hold records in a mixture of physical and electronic formats. In this section of this chapter we consider briefly only electronic records management systems. A records management system is a software program which stores the records within an organization and keeps track of them so that they can be retrieved when needed and destroyed when appropriate. It is this need to be able to access electronic records which causes the similarities with information retrieval.

A particularly important issue as far as electronic records management is concerned is that of digital preservation. Much effort is going into research in this area as its importance is recognized not only in terms of records management but also in terms of the preservation of digital cultural heritage. As more and more information is available only in digital format, the importance of digital curation and preservation has increased. Current issues and developments are reported by Deegan and Tanner (2006).

IMAGE RETRIEVAL SYSTEMS

The advent of the Internet, and specifically the Web, has led to the availability of a huge range of images in digital form. Rather more attention has been paid to the creation of digital images than to the effective retrieval of those images. There are two approaches to image retrieval: concept-based image retrieval and content-based image retrieval (CBIR). Full explanations of both approaches are presented by Jorgensen (2003).

Concept-based image retrieval is logically the same as text-based retrieval; that is to say that the images are represented by some form of metadata, and retrieval is by matching query criteria against information object representations (the metadata). There are specific metadata schemas for images produced by the Visual Resources Association (known as VRA Core version 3.0) as well as versions of MARC for images. VRA Core 3.0 describes itself as a data schema for the description of works of visual culture and their images. Full details can be found on the VRA website but as an indication of the fact that the schema is designed specifically for visual culture, the element set includes materials, style period and culture (Visual Resources Association, 2002). There are also specific controlled vocabularies for the representation of image content. The best known of these are the classification scheme ICONCLASS and the Art and Architecture Thesaurus (AAT). ICONCLASS has been developed for the classification of art objects based upon the iconographic interpretation of those objects (<http://www.iconclass.nl/>). AAT has been developed to index objects in the fields of art, architecture and cultural history and is maintained by the Getty Museum (see <http://www.getty.edu/research/conducting_research/vocabularies/aat/>).

Content-based image retrieval (CBIR) has been developed from work in image processing. Given the huge volume of image material which is currently available on the Web, it is inconceivable that it can be indexed by conventional means; there is simply too much of it. In addition, digital objects in many areas (but especially art history) require interpretation; there is considerable difference between what is visible in an image and what the image is about (that is, what it represents). CBIR presents an alternative means of retrieving images. In CBIR systems, an image is represented by features derived from its pixel values. Typically the features used are one or more of colour, shape or texture. The features might be either global or local. Systems using local features divide the image into segments and thus provide a finer representation than do systems using global features. CBIR systems operate by matching the features of a query against the database of image representations using one of many available similarity measures. Whilst there are many experimental CBIR systems there are very few that have made it into operational systems. One readily available exception is IBM's QBIC (Query by Image Content) which has been implemented by the Hermitage Museum in St Petersburg (see <http://hermitagemuseum.org/>). The start of the QBIC search can be seen on the Museum's digital collections page which is presented in Figure 9.3. Whilst the use of a system which obviates the need for human indexing is attractive, CBIR systems face several serious problems which currently limit their widespread use. The two major problems are the so-called 'semantic gap' between what CBIR systems can do and what image information seekers require. Whilst there are well-defined areas such as engineering and architectural drawings where is it is easy to appreciate the potential of CBIR systems, there are other areas such as art history where the gap between achievement and need remains a chasm. The chasm is caused by the fact that in this subject the meaning of images is open to interpretation and is far more complex than can be achieved by matching the presence of colour or shape. The second major problem with CBIR systems is the difficulty of presenting the query to the CBIR database in a manner acceptable to users (Venters, Hartley and Hewitt, 2004).

WEB COMMUNITY TOOLS (WIKIS AND BLOGS)

One consequence of the very vastness of the Web has been the development of a range of tools which we term 'web community tools'; that is, software tools which have been developed to enable people to work in different ways, in particular to work collaboratively. One development from this movement of social computing to which we have already referred in Chapter 7 was social tagging and the emergence of a new type of semi-controlled vocabulary or 'folksonomy'. Two important software developments are wikis and blogs.

Wikis can be viewed from at least two perspectives. In one way they can be seen as simply sources of information on the Web, of which the original Wikipedia is by far the largest. On the other hand they can be viewed as simplified means of publishing information, usually in some collaborative way, on the Web. A wiki offers:

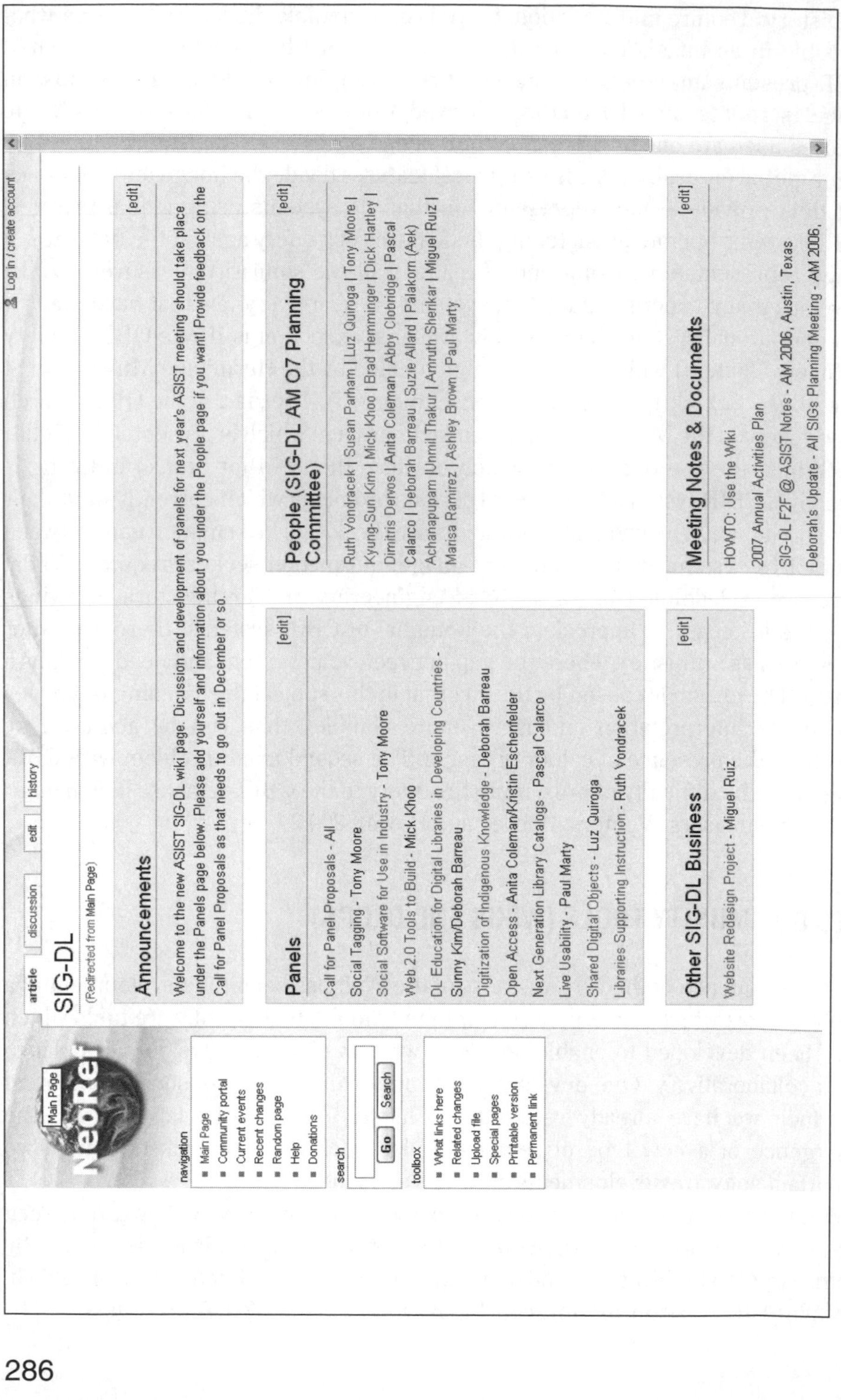

Figure 9.12 The ASIST Special interest Group on Digital Libraries' wiki being used to develop contributions to the ASIST Annual Meeting

- the ability to create text on the Web without the need for either installing local software or knowing HTML/XML
- the ability to edit documents without necessarily having special privileges
- a search function to retrieve information within the wiki.

Whilst completely open wikis can allow the editing of documents without special privileges, this can lead to problems of mis-information and even the publishing of malicious information, so many wikis have introduced some form of editorial control.

In addition to public access wikis such as Wikipedia and LISwiki (a wiki-based encyclopaedia of library and information science, see <http://liswiki.org/wiki/Main_Page>), wikis can be useful tools for operating within organizations, perhaps as laboratory notebooks for a research group or as a communication tool while a project is being developed, or indeed during any form of collaborative writing. However, by its very nature not a lot is known about this type of use and, as far as the use of wikis in the public sector is concerned, Guy (2006) has suggested that it is as well to treat claims of widespread uptake within the public sector with considerable caution, though she does offer some examples of their use.

A wiki has the potential for collaborative communication across international borders, for document development or for ideas sharing; Figure 9.12 demonstrates its use in the development of a panel session at a conference for the ASIST Special Interest Group for Digital Libraries (<http://bioivlab.ils.unc.edu/sandbox/SIG-DL/index.php/Main_Page>). However, it could be argued that this also shows the dangers of wikis, since it is evident that a certain amount of effort went into the creation of the wiki and its use is relatively limited.

Tonkin (2005) offers a comparative table of wiki software and speculates about the future development and application of the technology.

Blogs, or originally web logs, have developed from being relatively simple diaries to become something of a Web phenomenon: they are now so extensive that a search engine concentrating on blogs has been created. From those simple beginnings of being largely personal diaries and commentaries, the emergence of software with which to create blogs means that they have become powerful tools. Blog software now enables outsiders to comment on messages posted by the originator so that they have become a powerful form of communication. A major use of blogs is for commentary on current political events or for the dissemination of opinions which might not normally get into the conventional media. However, blogs are also being exploited by the conventional media and some BBC reporters maintain blogs on which they record views in their areas of expertise. In the library world, at least one library (the University of Bath) is making use of a blog to keep its academic users abreast with relevant developments in the library and a

Figure 9.13 The Talis Panlibus blog

blog has been used at MMU to keep colleagues aware of developments with the implementation of the virtual learning environment. Blogs written by leading thinkers within the library and information science community provide an increasingly useful means of keeping readers aware of developments and enabling the sharing of thoughts before they are appropriate for the more conventional sources such as journals. A good example is Lorcan Dempsey's blog (<http://orweblog.oclc.org/>), the home page of which is too complex to display. The library systems company Talis runs its own blog (Panlibus) which is shown in Figure 9.13.

SUMMARY

Previous chapters have concentrated upon the available approaches to knowledge organization which have evolved over many years through the efforts of librarians and information scientists. In this chapter we have explored the various systems in the digital environment which employed these various techniques. Thus we have seen their use in OPACs, digital libraries and concept-based image retrieval. In addition we have also seen how the techniques for providing access to knowledge have been extended by the application of ICT. For example, whilst the theory of citation indexes does not require the use of computers, in practice the production of large-scale citation databases, whether they are searched online or via the print product, could not be undertaken without computers. By definition all the material which is stored in digital libraries and the expanding number of institutional and subject-based repositories could not have been developed without the widespread application of ICT. The application of computers has provided completely new approaches to access to information. Retrieval of images on the basis of features such as colour, shape and texture is a completely new approach; whilst much work remains to be done to bridge the semantic gap between what is required and what can be achieved, CBIR offers a completely new approach to image retrieval. Finally, we have seen how the new tools of social networking are revolutionizing collaborative working, including approaches to the organization of knowledge.

REVIEW QUESTIONS

1. What do you understand by the term 'portal'?
2. In what ways are thesauri used in abstracting and indexing databases to aid retrieval?
3. What forms of knowledge organization are employed in an OPAC?
4. How is open access changing the organization of knowledge? How do institutional repositories contribute to the open access movement?
5. In what ways is it possible to retrieve images from knowledge organization systems?
6. Outline the unique method of retrieving information which is employed by the Web of Science.
7. Explain the ways in which digital libraries differ from conventional libraries in their approaches to the organization of knowledge.
8. What do you understand by the term 'personalization'?
9. Outline the strengths and weaknesses of search engines as a means of retrieving information.
10. How is social networking software impacting on the organization of knowledge?

REFERENCES AND FURTHER READING

Arms, W.Y. (2001) *Digital Libraries*. Cambridge MA: MIT Press.

Battelle, J. (2005) *The Search: How Google and its rivals rewrote the rules of business and transformed our culture*. London: Nicholas Brealey.

Bonnett, M. (2001) Personalization of web services: opportunities and challenges. *Ariadne*, 28 (<http://www.ariadne.ac.uk/issue28/personalization/>).

Borgman, C. (2000) *From Gutenberg to the Global Information Infrastructure: Access to information in the networked world*. Cambridge MA: MIT Press.

Brin, S. and Page, L. (2006) The anatomy of a hypertextual web search engine. Available at <http://infolab.stanford.edu/~backrub/google.html> [visited 22 December 2006].

Brophy, P. (2001) *The Library in the Twenty-First Century: New services for the information age*. London: Facet.

Butters, G. (2003) What features in a portal? *Ariadne*, 35 (<http://www.ariadne.ac.uk/issue35/butters/intro.html>) [visited 16 July 2006].

Deegan, M. and Tanner, S. (eds) (2006) *Digital Preservation*. London: Facet.

Guy, M. (2006) Wiki or won't he? A tale of public sector wikis. *Ariadne*, 49 (<http://www.ariadne.ac.uk/issue49/guy/>).

IBM (2003) Quoted by Liz Lyon in 'Enhancing access to e-resources', presented at RSC-SW meeting, Taunton, 2 July 2003. Available at <www.ukoln.ac.uk/ukoln/staff/e.j.lyon/rsc-sw-july2.ppt>.

Jorgensen, C. (2003) *Image Retrieval: Theory and research*. Lanham MD: Scarecrow.

Lesk, M. (2005) *Understanding Digital Libraries*, 2nd edn. London: Morgan Kaufman.

Lynch, Clifford A. (2001). Metadata harvesting and the open archives initiative. *ARL Bimonthly Report* 217 (<http://www.arl.org/newsltr/217/mhp.html>) [visited 21 December 2006).

The Open Archives Initiative – Protocol for Metadata Harvesting – v2.0 (<http://www.openarchives.org/OAI/openarchivesprotocol.html>) [accessed 21 December 2006].

Pearce, L. (2003) Apart from the weather, I think it's a good idea. *Ariadne*, 35 (<http://www.ariadne.ac.uk/issue35/pearce/intro.html>) File last modified 30 July 2004 [accessed 16 July 2006].

Rowley, J.E. (2000) Portal power. *Managing Information*, **7** (1), 62–4.

Tedd, L.A. and Large, J.A. (2005) *Digital Libraries: Principles and practice in a global environment*. Munich: K.G. Saur.

Tonkin, E. (2005) Making a case for a wiki. *Ariadne*, 42 (<http://www.ariadne.ac.uk/issue42/tonkin/>) [accessed 12 December 2006].

Venters, C.C., Hartley, R.J. and Hewitt, W.T. (2004) Mind the gap: CBIR and the user interface. In S. Deb, *Multimedia Systems and Content-Based Image Retrieval*, pp. 322–55. London: Idea Group.

Vise, D.A. (2005) *The Google Story*. London: Macmillan.

Visual Resources Association (2002) VRA Core 3.0 (<http://www.vraweb.org/vracore3.htm>) [accessed 22 December 2006].

10 The evaluation and design of information retrieval systems

INTRODUCTION

Evaluation is an activity which is carried on implicitly in everyday life almost whenever a decision is taken. For example, whenever a person decides whether to travel from A to B by train, car, coach or plane, he or she has, albeit subconsciously, evaluated the options available and based the decision on criteria relevant to the situation: price, travel time, convenience and so on. Similarly, users evaluate information retrieval (IR) systems implicitly when they decide to use a particular system, whether it is the decision to use an OPAC or a search engine. The precise mix of factors which determine a user's choice of IR system is complex and in itself has been the subject of research. However, the rapid emergence of Google to a position of pre-eminence has shown that speed of response and simplicity are key factors. Whilst Google's success is also clearly due to its ability to place relevant material at the top of its hit list, Hildreth has shown that, in the context of OPACs, interface simplicity is deemed more important than search effectiveness (Hildreth, 2001).

Whilst users' implicit evaluation is clearly important, the focus in this chapter is explicit evaluation, which has usually been undertaken by researchers or system operators, and the role it has played in the development of IR systems. Hernon and McClure define evaluation as:

> ... the process of identifying and collecting data about specific services or activities, establishing criteria by which their success can be assessed and the degree to which the service or activity accomplishes stated goals and objectives.
> (Hernon and McClure, 1990)

Whilst this is a helpful definition, it is worth adding that on occasion the purpose of evaluation is also to identify how system performance can be improved.

Much research in information retrieval over the last 40 years has been into evaluation and testing. Evaluation has made important contributions to the development of IR systems but has not been without its controversies. At the end of this chapter you will have learned about:

- criteria by which IR systems are evaluated and some of the more important measures used in evaluation
- methods by which IR systems can be evaluated and the arguments surrounding different approaches to evaluation
- the difference between formative and summative evaluation
- the major information retrieval experiments.

EVALUATION AND EVALUATION CRITERIA

IR systems can be evaluated by a number of criteria. By far the greatest effort and also controversy has surrounded effectiveness and its measurement. Although there is now reasonable agreement that effectiveness alone is not the sole criterion by which a system should be evaluated, there remains some disagreement about exactly which criteria are the most important and also the most appropriate means of measuring them. Some of the key criteria are:

- effectiveness
- usability
- satisfaction
- cost.

Each of these will be considered in turn below, but first it may be useful to reflect a little further on the nature of evaluation.

Evaluation is a process whose main purpose is to assess whether something works, or does what it is expected to do. This immediately raises three overarching issues:

1. Evaluation must start with the objectives of a system, decision, process or action. In the context of information retrieval systems the underlying assumed objective is that searchers can find the information that they want to complete a task, or in other words, as discussed above, its effectiveness. Increasingly, however, users apply other criteria because they expect the system to fulfil other objectives.
2. In order to assess whether a system meets its objectives it is essential to incorporate some measures which can be used to measure different levels of performance.
3. Different stakeholders, such as information professionals, systems designers

and users, may have different expectations of a system. This may lead to different stakeholders emphasizing different criteria. For example, an information professional may view it as essential that the system retrieves a significant proportion of the information available on a subject, whereas an end-user may be more concerned to retrieve two or three key articles in as short a time as possible.

The different evaluation criteria discussed below reflect the issues that have been discussed in the information retrieval literature.

EFFECTIVENESS

It is obvious that the primary concern of an IR system is to retrieve information objects which meet the needs of the user. However, it is less obvious what is meant by 'meeting the needs of the user'. For much of the development of IR evaluation, it has been assumed that the needs of the user are met by the retrieval of information objects which are relevant to the query presented to the IR system. By 'relevant' is meant an information object which contains information which in some way meets the information need which is behind the query. Therefore it has been assumed that effectiveness of an IR system is measured by its ability to retrieve items relevant to a given query and to not retrieve items which are not relevant. So, it is assumed that the perfect outcome would be for the system to present to the user every item which it contained relevant to the particular query and only items relevant to the query. The two most commonly used measures of system performance are the recall ratio and the precision ratio. These can be best understood by examination of Figure 10.1.

	Relevant	Not relevant
Retrieved	a	b
Not retrieved	c	d
Totals	a + c	b + d

Figure 10.1 The 2 x 2 table of retrieval effectiveness

This table suggests that in a search for documents or information objects there are four possible outcomes:

1. some relevant documents are successfully received – these we call *hits*
2. some items that are not relevant are retrieved – this is known as *noise*
3. the search fails to retrieve some relevant items – these are *misses*
4. some irrelevant items are not retrieved – these have been successfully *dodged.*

Recall is a measure of a system's ability to retrieve relevant information whilst *precision* is a measure of the system's ability to suppress irrelevant or unwanted material. Formally, they are defined as follows:

$$\text{Recall} = \frac{\text{Total relevant retrieved}}{\text{Total relevant in system}} \quad \frac{a}{a+c} \times 100$$

$$\text{Precision} = \frac{\text{Total relevant retrieved}}{\text{Total retrieved}} \quad \frac{a}{a+b} \times 100$$

By convention the ratios are multiplied by 100 and expressed as percentages.

Indexing systems and search software should be designed to maximize both recall and precision: that is, to minimize noise and misses. However, research has shown that there is a tendency for recall and precision to be inversely related; that is, as measures are taken to improve recall then precision is likely to decline, and vice versa. Whilst this will hold over a number of searches on a system, there may be some searches for which it does not hold.

It is thus unlikely to be possible to achieve a system that gives 100 per cent recall at the same time as 100 per cent precision. Thus, anyone designing a retrieval system must choose an appropriate blend of recall and precision for each individual application. Quite frequently a user will be satisfied with a few items on a topic as long as they are relevant and meet other criteria such as language, date and level. Here, high precision and low recall are satisfactory. On other occasions, as, for example, when planning a research project, a user may want every document or piece of information on a topic traced, and then high recall must be sought to the detriment of precision.

An indexing language has a number of devices that improve recall (see Figure 10.2), balanced by devices for improving precision (see Figure 10.3).

- *Entry vocabulary:* is there a good range of lead-in terms to guide the user from specific concepts to the terms used in the index to represent them?
- *Control of word form:* (number, grammatical form, word order, etc.) to prevent the loss of relevant documents through the scatter of different word forms.
- *Control of synonyms and quasi-synonyms:* to prevent their scattering under more than one heading.
- Hierarchical and associative relationships widen the search by suggesting closely related terms.
- *Structural display of relationships:* a classified or other systematic form of display gives the user a conspectus of closely related terms.
- *Exhaustivity of indexing* in computer-searchable databases is effectively a function of record length. The greater the number of terms used to index a document the greater the likelihood of a document being retrieved.
- *Truncation and wildcards:* these are features of most computer searching systems.
- *Relevance-ranking* of output, available in some computer searching systems.

Figure 10.2 Index language devices influencing recall

The first two (specificity and coordination) are by far the most important.

- *Specificity of the indexing language*: the greater the specificity the larger the number of terms and the more precise the subject specification.
- *Coordination of terms*: concepts required are described more accurately, and unwanted documents eliminated, by increasing the number of index terms in combination. This is done by the searcher in post-coordinate systems, and by the indexer in pre-coordinate systems.
- *Pre-coordination level*: multi-term concepts (e.g. COAL MINING) are introduced to ensure that subjects may be minutely identified. (A search on COAL AND MINING could lead to some false relationships.)
- *Relational indicators*: devices which label groups of associated controlled descriptors.
- *Weighting*: for differentiating between major and minor concepts within a record.
- *Exhaustivity of indexing* is a two-edged sword, influencing both recall and precision. The greater the number of terms available for searching, the greater the likelihood both of marginally relevant documents being retrieved and of false relationships (false drops).
- *Word proximity operators* reduce the number of false relationships.

Figure 10.3 Index language devices influencing precision

The measures of recall and precision were developed in the first major retrieval evaluation programme, the Cranfield tests (see section below headed 'Major retrieval evaluation projects'). A major finding of this research was that the recall ratio and the precision ratio are inversely proportional; that is to say, as one increases the other decreases. However, this inverse relationship is widely misunderstood and it is important to avoid the trap of that misunderstanding. The Cranfield researchers argued that in a given system and *over a number of searches*, there is a tendency for precision to increase as recall decreases, and vice versa. However, this does not mean that, for every single search on a system, as steps are taken to increase one of recall or precision then the other measure will decrease. This point is so important and so frequently misrepresented that it is worth quoting the late Cyril Cleverdon, who can rightly be viewed as the father of information retrieval evaluation, because of his pioneering efforts at Cranfield:

> Within a single system, assuming that a sequence of subsearches for a particular question is made in the logical order of expected decreasing precision, and the requirements are those stated in the question, there is an inverse relationship between recall and precision, if the results of a number of different searches are averaged.

> (Cleverdon, 1972)

It is apparent that this is a fairly cautious explanation of the inverse relationship which makes it clear that it does not apply to every single query.

Another measure, which has been quite widely used, is the fallout ratio. *Fallout* is a measure of the ability of a system to suppress, or not to retrieve, non-relevant material. Referring again to Figure 10.1, fallout can be presented as follows:

$$\text{Fallout} = \frac{\text{Total irrelevant retrieved}}{\text{Total relevant}} \quad \frac{b}{b+d} \times 100$$

This approach to the measurement of the performance of an IR system depends upon an acceptable means of determining the relevance of information objects to particular requests. This had been a continuing topic of argument and debate within the IR community for more than 35 years; Mizarro (1997) provides a review. The debate has been, and continues to be, both philosophical and practical. The practical matters which will be discussed further in the next section of the chapter relate to approaches to making relevance judgements and whether or not it is possible to make the binary judgement that a document is relevant or not to a given query. The philosophical argument, and if anything this is one that has gained weight in recent years, concerns whether or not relevance is an appropriate basis on which to measure system performance. However, the critics of relevance have been less successful at putting forward an alternative approach which has gained acceptance within the community. One interesting approach is Cooper's Utility Theory, which advocates document (information object) usefulness as the basis of measuring effectiveness (Cooper, 1973a; Cooper, 1973b). Whilst this is an interesting approach, it seems to suggest that a useful object is one that is new to the requestor and therefore it is a measure not just of system retrieval effectiveness but also of the existing knowledge of the requestor. Nevertheless an interesting development of the notion of utility was the use of documents read, encouraged by Cleverdon himself, but this unfortunately has not been developed further since it was initially proposed by Lantz (1981). Despite any shortcomings, currently there remains no serious alternative to relevance-based measures as the basis for measuring retrieval effectiveness.

Another concern is that it may be difficult to measure the total number of relevant documents in an information retrieval system. Strictly using this measure involves examining every document in the system for its potential relevance to a specific search query; obviously for Web search engines such as Google this is clearly impossible. Therefore, over the years there have been various approaches developed that seek to navigate this problem, including:

- *pooling* – asking a number of searchers to conduct a search, on the assumption that if a search is conducted on a sufficient number of occasions most of the relevant documents will be found
- *expert searching* – using the set of documents retrieved by one or more experts as a 'complete' set and measuring a novice searcher's performance against expert searchers

- *relative recall* – the ratio of retrieved relevant documents examined by the user and the number of relevant documents the user knows are in the system.

Whilst retrieval effectiveness remains a necessary criterion for IR system evaluation, it is widely recognized that alone it is no longer sufficient. This recognition is particularly important in the era of interactive systems intended for end-users rather than for professional intermediaries.

USABILITY

Usability, previously discussed in Chapter 4, has also become an increasingly important measure of information retrieval effectiveness. As a measure it draws a wider system boundary than traditionally associated with recall and precision, where the emphasis tends to be indexing, searching, the indexing language and search algorithms. Usability is a measure that embraces the interface through which the user interacts with the system, and also takes into account the user and their expectations, skills and experiences. The importance of usability is emphasized by some recent research concerning OPACs. Fast and Campbell have demonstrated that users prefer the familiarity of search engines over OPACs even though they are well aware of the superior quality control associated with resources located via OPACs rather than on the Web (Fast and Campbell, 2004). Similarly, Hartley and Booth (2006) have reported that users who cannot master a new system rapidly will soon revert to a familiar system.

SATISFACTION

It should be self-evident that user satisfaction is an important criterion by which to evaluate a retrieval system. Even if a system has been shown to perform well in terms of retrieval effectiveness and usability, it is of little value if its potential users are dissatisfied with the experience of using the system. If this is the case then they will simply 'vote with their feet' and not use the system. Unfortunately, apart from this statement of the obvious, the notion of user satisfaction is not at all clear. There is no agreed definition of user satisfaction within the information science and information systems communities.

The original proponents of user satisfaction as a criterion for IR system evaluation assumed that it was correlated with search success. However, there is considerable evidence that this is not the case; a fact which should become readily apparent from attempts at understanding the notion. In an early attempt to define satisfaction, Tessier, Crouch and Atherton stated that it is 'ultimately a state experienced inside the user's head' and so 'may be both intellectual and emotional' (Tessier et al., 1977, pp. 383 and 384). This line of argument makes it

297

clear that user satisfaction is not a measure of system performance alone – a line of argument which is further advanced by Applegate with her well-known and accepted concept of 'false positives' (Applegate, 1993). She indicates that 'false positives' occur when 'a consumer is satisfied with an inferior product'; in this case, poor search results. She outlines three different models of searcher satisfaction namely:

1. the material satisfaction model
2. the emotional satisfaction – simple path model
3. the emotional satisfaction – multiple path model.

Search results (presumably measured via some relevance-based measure) would be an appropriate measure of the material satisfaction model. However, both emotional satisfaction models are based upon subjective impressions and assessments which may be affected by factors such as search task, search setting and the searcher's state of mind at the time of the search. In a similar manner, Bruce has described satisfaction with information seeking as 'a state of mind which represents the composite of a user's material and emotional responses to the information-seeking context' (Bruce 1998).

Blair's extensive and careful evaluation of STAIRS is reported later in this chapter. At this point it is worth noting that an interesting finding of this research was the regularity with which his user group (lawyers) reported satisfaction with search outcome when in fact the researchers were able to demonstrate that their searchers has been sub-optimal. Applegate's research inspired Hildreth, working in the context of a university OPAC, to devise a carefully executed experiment to determine factors which influence searchers' satisfaction with a search (Hildreth, 2001). He concluded that 'Once again, the evidence indicates that actual search performance is not a predictor or determinant of a searcher's satisfaction with search results.' He goes on to point out that searcher perceptions of the system's ease of use and system usefulness during the search process do influence the searcher's satisfaction with search results. Little wonder then that practitioners have been known to refer to the problem of 'satisfied but inept user' (Plutchak, 1989).

Other perspectives on satisfaction are to be found in the service quality and website quality literatures. These literatures are concerned with the evaluation of the service experience in either physical environments, such as restaurants, retail outlets and libraries, or in digital environments such as the service delivered through websites. For example, in the service quality literature, quality is defined as the user's long-term judgement of the service experience, whilst satisfaction is seen as a transaction-specific measure. Both are defined in terms of the difference between the customers' perceptions (as they actually experience the serviced episode) and expectations (as they had expected to experience the service episode). In the context of information retrieval systems, the more recent development of the notions of service quality and satisfaction in digital environments are perhaps the most important.

Some of the studies of service quality have focused on website quality, whilst others take a wider service quality perspective. They all tend to try to develop a set of dimensions or factors that affect judgements of quality and satisfaction. Rowley (2006) offers an overview of this work and suggests the following core dimensions might contribute to quality and satisfaction judgements in digital environments: site features, security, communication, reliability, customer support, responsiveness, information, accessibility, delivery and personalization. Not all of these may be applicable in contexts where information retrieval and delivery is the prime concern, since many of the studies on which this list is based involve transactions, but there are certainly some lessons to be learnt as to the factors that might affect satisfaction in digital environments.

It should be apparent from this discussion that it is important to take account of user satisfaction and to measure it when appropriate as a part of an evaluation. However, it is also apparent that satisfaction is a complex, multi-dimensional concept which is not fully understood and is not a substitute for system performance as an evaluation criterion.

COST

The cost of creating an IR system is an obvious criterion by which it should be evaluated. Therefore, at first sight it is surprising that the literature on evaluation should be so devoid of reports on research into the cost of an IR system. However, a little reflection will reveal that meaningful accounting for the real costs of an IR system is remarkably difficult.

Let us take, as an example, the cost of providing an OPAC in a university. Certain costs will be fairly straightforward to ascertain. Examples are the salaries of the cataloguers and their various tools such as classification schemes, cataloguing rules and authority control tools. The annual cost of acquiring records externally will be known, however they are obtained. The cataloguing system is a part of an integrated library system. Without the catalogue database at its heart, the circulation system could not function. It is not at all obvious how to determine how to attribute the cost of the library system to the OPAC as opposed to the circulation system. Much less easy to determine will be a range of other costs. For example, externally acquired records will be delivered over a university network and a national network to which the university in some form or another makes a contribution. It is certainly not clear how to take into account such costs. Equally, access to an OPAC is increasingly remote from the library via a network using equipment which is not primarily bought for OPAC access. The real cost of providing an OPAC in a university is not readily calculated. Given the complexity of calculating costs, it is perhaps not surprising that little work has been undertaken to calculate either cost effectiveness or cost-benefit, which potentially might be other useful perspectives on evaluation.

Whilst there may be significant problems associated with the calculation of costs to the organization, the challenges associated with the calculation of costs to the searcher are yet more significant. Users may experience costs in terms of any payment that they need to make for system or document access, but perhaps their most significant cost is associated with the time that they expend in searching a system. Search algorithms, the options for the display of hits, the seamlessness of the stages in individual systems (for example, whether it is possible to click through to the full text of a document) and interoperability between systems (in the form, say, of searching across many databases) all affect the time that it takes the user to achieve what they regard as a satisfactory outcome.

METHODS AND APPROACHES TO EVALUATION

Attempts to measure the performance of a retrieval system began in an era when the systems were all manual, such as card catalogues and abstracts and indexes. In this context, usability was much less an issue and so it was no surprise that efforts were concentrated on retrieval effectiveness and little attention was paid to user satisfaction. At that time there was much argument about the relative merits of controlled vocabularies, such as classification schemes and thesauri, and the relatively new single-term systems (Uniterm). Working in an aeronautical engineering establishment, it is perhaps not surprising that Cleverdon decided that gathering evidence through testing in a laboratory environment was a means of throwing some light on the argument. It was in this context that retrieval testing was born. It is thus fair to say that laboratory-based testing was a logical development in the context of the issues being faced and the time and place at which the testing emerged. This work was important in establishing some of the fundamental concepts associated with the evaluation of information retrieval systems.

As systems have moved from manual retrieval to online interactive retrieval, it has become increasingly obvious that retrieval effectiveness alone is an inadequate criterion for evaluation. A combination of the continued (and sometimes valid) criticisms of the laboratory-based evaluation, the move towards interactive retrieval and increasing acceptance of the inadequacy of solely quantitative approaches to evaluation have led to an increasing use of qualitative approaches to evaluation and to evaluation in an operational context often using a combination of both obtrusive and unobtrusive data collection methods. This section briefly reviews the key approaches that have been used in the evaluation of information retrieval systems:

1. *Laboratory-based testing techniques.* The early information retrieval experiments were laboratory-based. Typically, laboratory-based testing requires, as a bare minimum, a set of documents, a set of queries and a set of relevance judgements for each document in respect of each of the queries. Laboratory experiments have the advantage that variability from different users with different levels of experience and system expectations and purposes can be controlled, so that the measures of systems effectiveness have a higher level of reliability and validity. On the other hand laboratory experiments have been criticized for their limited relevance to 'real-life' information retrieval.

2. *Transaction log analysis* has been used for approximately 25 years as a means of understanding searches. A transaction log is a record of the search statement received by an IR system and the system response. The precise nature of transaction logs varies from system to system but generally it will include a time stamp indicating when a search statement was received by the system, an indication of the origin of the search and, in some form, the system response to the search request. Generally, transaction logs are difficult to read but, because of their highly structured nature, they are amenable to the automated analysis of a large volume of data. A problem with transaction logs is the difficulty with which the start and end of a search can be determined. A more serious problem is that transaction logs only indicate what a searcher did. They do not shed any light on the searcher's intentions.

   An advance on transaction logs, where the data is captured on the searched system, is the use of screen logging software. In this case data capture is undertaken at the searcher's workstation, using software that can capture every keystroke of the searcher and the response from the system. An advantage of screen capture software is that it captures the entire transaction and not a cut-down version of it. Furthermore, it can be used in combination with other tools to better understand what the searcher is doing and why. An example is described by Griffiths et al. (2002).

3. *Measuring online activity.* Online activity can be measured, both at the level of web traffic and at the level of the behaviour of individual customers. In order to be able to collect data about specific individuals it is essential to be able to identify them, through registration. Particularly useful may be the collection of data relevant to:
   - access – an analysis of hits, servers and sessions, and the identification of sites that refer or attract the most traffic
   - activity – an analysis of what visitors are doing and what actions are taken;

this can give some general insights into searching behaviour, but may also contextualize searching behaviour in relation to other web navigation and transactions: activity is measured using the transaction logging methods outlined above.

4. *Thinking aloud.* Use has been made of 'thinking aloud' for nearly 30 years in IR research. The technique, as the name implies, requires searchers to describe what they are doing and, more importantly, to explain why they are doing it. The thoughts and comments of searchers are recorded and transcribed at a later time. Recent research has suggested that there are benefits to the thinking aloud taking place immediately after the searching rather than concurrently (Van den Haak et al., 2003). This process is facilitated by the existence of the screen capture software which is discussed above. This enables a researcher to play back a search to a searcher and ask what the searcher was attempting at any particular point in a search.

5. *Questionnaires and surveys.* These have been widely used to profile library use, and more recently e-mail surveys and questionnaires mounted in the space for virtual communities can be used to elicit information about users and their opinions, attitudes and behaviour. In the context of information retrieval systems, questionnaires and surveys may be used, for example, to:
   - elicit attitudes, opinions and behaviours associated with the implication of a new system
   - explore user behaviour, especially when used, for example, with the critical incident technique in which a user might be asked questions about their search behaviour in a recent information-seeking episode
   - to gather information about user satisfaction, perceptions of ease of use, and user requirements for system improvements.

6. *Interviews and focus groups.* These are useful for gathering facts, opinions and attitudes and should be used when more detailed data relates to why a user behaves in a certain way, or how the system supports or does not support the user towards a successful search outcome. Focus groups – groups of 8 to 10 people – create a more interactive environment in which members of the groups exchange attitudes, experiences and beliefs about the chosen topic. Online focus groups may take place through a bulletin board or discussion group.

In many evaluations more than one of these methods are used in parallel, either to achieve a response from a wider group, or to provide different perspectives and a detailed understanding of the system and its use. Questionnaires and interviews, for example, are often used in combination with transaction log analysis or screen capture and other observation methods.

Failure analysis is an important feature of IR system evaluation. As the name implies, it is the detailed analysis of retrieval failures, whether these are relevant items which have not been retrieved or irrelevant items which have been retrieved by a particular search of a particular system. As can be imagined, failure analysis is a lengthy business and therefore is rarely undertaken – a fact demonstrated by the paucity of items retrieved when searching library and information science abstracts for the subject. Lancaster (1979) notes that for each and every search failure it involves the evaluator in the examination of :

- the original document
- the index terms assigned to the document, including terms from a controlled vocabulary and/or classification scheme and any natural language terms
- the search request
- the search strategy.

It is only through such careful analysis of search failure that the reason(s) for the failure can be determined. In some cases it will not be possible to determine a single cause of retrieval failure; rather the failure may be attributed to several factors. In turn, identification of failures in a number of searches may enable system operators to make changes to the system which can lead to improved performance. Lancaster further reports that in his own detailed analysis of several hundred search failures, the major causes of precision failures were index language, searching user–system interaction and indexing. For recall failures the causes, in declining order, were indexing, searching user–system interaction and index language (Lancaster, 1979, pp. 137–9).

MAJOR RETRIEVAL EVALUATION PROJECTS

There have been thousands of evaluations undertaken since Cranfield, some major and some minor. Some have been undertaken rigorously and some less so. The more important ones are reviewed briefly in this section of the chapter.

Now more than 40 years old, the Cranfield tests remain of significance in information retrieval research and system evaluation. Whilst not as well-known as its successor, the first Cranfield test (Cranfield 1) was significant for two reasons. First of all, it demonstrated that it was possible to measure system performance in a systematic manner. Secondly, it was in the Cranfield 1 tests that the twin measures of recall and precision were developed. Cranfield 1 used a test collection of 18,000 documents and 1,200 queries to test the efficacy of four different index languages; namely, the UDC classification scheme, a faceted classification scheme, alphabetical subject headings and Uniterm. Cranfield 1 developed its queries through the use of source documents; that is to say that the queries were developed from the particular documents within the collection, and success was deemed to be the successful retrieval of that source document when a search was undertaken. The source document approach was subjected to considerable criticism and as a result a range of additional tests were undertaken which resulted in the development of recall and precision as measures of search effectiveness. The results of Cranfield 1 caused surprise since they suggested very little difference in performance between the different index languages. However, in retrospect the major achievement of Cranfield 1 was its demonstration, whatever the methodological criticisms, that retrieval testing was possible. The fact that developments of the Cranfield approach are still in operation today are testimony to its impact.

The better-known Cranfield 2 test used a collection of 1,400 documents and 279 queries to test the efficacy of 33 artificial index languages. The languages were artificially created combinations of different index language devices. Examples of the devices are term weighting, links and roles, word form variant confounding and synonym confounding. The intention in using artificial index languages was twofold. Firstly, it was hoped to avoid the controversy which surrounded Cranfield 1 by which proponents of different index languages had sought to challenge outcomes which did not accord with their preferences. Secondly, by combining index languages devices in different combinations, it was hoped to isolate the effects of particular index language devices and thereby demonstrate the relative merits of different devices. Once the Cranfield team had convinced itself that comparable results were achieved with smaller data sets, many of the tests were undertaken with the reduced set of 200 documents and 42 queries. The two major conclusions of the project team were:

> [1] Every set of figures supports the original hypothesis of an inverse relationship between recall and precision. It is immaterial which variable is changed to give a new system; it may be the coordination level …, the exhaustivity of indexing …, the recall devices …, the precision devices …; it has been impossible to find an exception to what can be claimed to be a basic rule.
>
> [2] Quite the most astonishing and seemingly inexplicable conclusion that arises from the project is that single term index languages are superior to any other type.

The Cranfield 2 tests set new standards of experimental rigour and reporting detail which marked the way ahead for retrieval testing for many years to come.

Whatever the criticisms of the Cranfield tests, even their detractors would agree that they have had a profound influence on the direction of information retrieval research. The original research reports are now difficult to acquire and so the best sources for further information are the paper by Cleverdon (1972) and the chapter by Spärck Jones in the book edited by her (Spärck Jones, 1981). One of the more thoughtful critics of the continued use of the Cranfield laboratory-based approach to evaluation has been Ellis. His review of the Cranfield tests also provides a useful exploration of Cranfield and its criticisms (Ellis, 1996, Chapter 1).

Much less well-known than the Cranfield tests is the under-reported work undertaken by Keen in Aberystwyth. The interest of this work lies in the fact that Keen, one of the researchers on the second Cranfield test and also for some time a worker with Salton on his widely reported SMART systems, extended the Cranfield methodology in an attempt to deal with some of the criticisms levelled at it (Keen, 1973; Keen, 1977). In particular, Keen demonstrated that it was quite possible to have a more complex approach to relevance judgement than the simple binary decision of relevant or not relevant. In his Information Science Index Language Tests (ISILT), he created definitions of relevant, partially relevant and two definitions of not relevant. Interestingly, these definitions were framed both in terms of the content of the document and their utility to the user. Given the criticisms of relevance-based measures, it is worth reproducing them in full and this is done in Figure 10.4. It should be noted that relevance is defined not solely in terms of the documents and their relationship to the query but also by a first recognition of the user in the definition or relevance (in column 2).

Degree of relevance	What the questioner wants	The documents
Relevant	The questioner would find this of medium or high volume	Documents that substantially or completely answer the question
Partially relevant	The questioner would want to see this as being possibly helpful or probably of some limited help	Documents that are a partial answer to the question, or answer part of the question only
Non-relevant type 1	The questioner would not want to see this document as it could not conceivably be said to be related to the question	Documents about which there is no doubt at all; that is, there is no need to examine more than the title
Non-relevant type 2	Although the questioner would not want to see this document, it does fall somewhere within the general subject area of the question	Documents about which there is some initial doubt; that is, there is a need to look twice at these, and read some or all of the abstract or text

Figure 10.4 Definitions of different levels of relevance
Source: Keen and Digger, 1972

These definitions have been used successfully in several subsequent investigations. Keen also demonstrated that it was then possible to calculate values for recall and precision at different levels of relevance. Keen sought not just to replicate the Cranfield method but to develop it both in terms of experimental rigour and also by measuring more than retrieval performance. Operating almost exclusively in the context of manual systems, he experimented with a range of measures for criteria beyond effectiveness, including page turns and search time taken.

Lancaster's MEDLARS evaluation was significant for three reasons. Firstly, it was the first research to demonstrate that it was possible to undertake controlled experiments with an operational system. Secondly it demonstrated that whilst the inverse relationship between recall and precision can be shown to hold over a number of searches, it does not hold for every individual query. Indeed, his scatter plots of recall against precision are an important demonstration of the dangers of this error. Finally, it was the first significant retrieval test to employ failure analysis as a part of the evaluation procedure.

The only other major evaluation of an operational system was the STAIRS evaluation undertaken and reported by Blair (Blair and Maron, 1985; Blair, 1986). This evaluation was important because it was the first major and thorough evaluation of a full-text retrieval system rather than one using only document surrogates. In addition, it was unusual in that the subject area of the system was law whilst many of the other evaluations have been undertaken in the areas of science, technology and medicine. Finally, whilst the work followed the Cranfield approach, the STAIRS evaluation was important because the researchers went to great lengths to overcome some of the methodological criticisms which have been made of Cranfield. Not only was the evaluated system one containing full text but it contained more than 350,000 documents and so the oft-voiced criticism about the unrealistically small size of the test collection was removed. Additionally, the researchers went to great lengths to identify possibly relevant documents by sampling subsets of the database likely to contain relevant documents.

Since 1992, the major retrieval test has been the annual Text REtrieval Conference (TREC) organized by the (American) National Institute of Standards and Technology (NIST). According to its website, the TREC workshop series has the following goals:

- to encourage research in information retrieval based on large test collections;
- to increase communication among industry, academia, and government by creating an open forum for the exchange of research ideas;
- to speed the transfer of technology from research labs into commercial products by demonstrating substantial improvements in retrieval methodologies on real-world problems; and
- to increase the availability of appropriate evaluation techniques for use by industry and academia, including development of new evaluation techniques more applicable to current systems.

(<http://trec.nist.gov/overview.html>)

Groups from both academia and industry can participate in TREC and they do so by using a standard test collection developed by NIST. TREC is organized into a series of tracks (or sub-problems within IR). Each track has its own test collection and series of queries. The range of tracks changes over time. Over time TREC has increased its interest in web-based retrieval and in multi-lingual retrieval. The full range of tracks in any one year can be seen on the TREC website (<http://trec.nist.gov>). Each track has its own set of documents and queries. The TREC series has addressed the concern that previous retrieval tests have used small document sets by using very large sets, measured in gigabytes. However, it still uses the relevance-based measures of recall and precision as its basic measures. Inevitably, with large test collections, it is not feasible to undertake relevance judgements on every document query combination and the 'pooling' method is used whereby the total number of unique relevant items located by each of the TREC participants is used as the substitute for the total number of relevant items in the collection.

There can be no doubt that TREC has made and will probably continue to make a valuable contribution to IR system evaluation. Its use of large test collections and the open nature of the discussion between groups ensures that this is the case. Of course it still does not address the argument that such laboratory-based tests are far removed from the reality of everyday retrieval.

Whilst there have been many more evaluation tests and experiments over the years, the ones reported here have made significant contributions either to the methodology of testing and evaluation or to our understanding of knowledge organization systems. In Figure 10.5, the major impacts of the selected retrieval tests and evaluations have been summarized and presented in chronological order.

CURRENT ISSUES IN EVALUATION

The evaluation of IR systems has been an area of active investigation for both researchers and service providers for nearly 50 years. Inevitably there has been considerable development in evaluation approaches and methods in that time. The results from evaluative research have had important impacts on information retrieval. Despite the marked developments, there remain numerous issues in the area of IR evaluation. Of these, the following remain current; they are the subject of debate and, hopefully, development within the IR community:

● evaluation on multiple dimensions
● evaluation from the perspective of a range of stakeholders and, specifically, end-users

Project	Importance/Impact
Cranfield 1	Demonstrated that retrieval testing could be undertaken and yield interesting results. Created the measures of recall and precision
Cranfield 2	Significant improvement in the testing methodology. Suggested the inverse relationship between recall and precision
MEDLARS	Demonstrated that testing could be undertaken with operational systems and not just in the laboratory. Illustrated the value of failure analysis
Aberystwyth	Attempted to tackle some of the criticisms of the Cranfield methodology by extending it. In particular, it produced very careful definitions of relevance and partial relevance, as indicated in Figure 10.4
STAIRS	Significant as the first detailed evaluation of a full-text retrieval system. Demonstrated significant gap between user satisfaction (high) and system performance (often low)
TREC	Has taken the laboratory-based approach to new levels of sophistication. Has produced a standard test-bed through which both commercial and academic researchers can test their systems. Has 'moved with the times' in the development of new evaluation tracks as the technology has advanced

Figure 10.5 Summary of the importance of major evaluation tests

- evaluation methods and methodological mix
- the shift from summative to formative evaluation and thus the link with system design.

Whilst these issues are clearly intertwined (for example, evaluation from the perspective of different stakeholders is related to the need to use multiple dimensions and therefore in turn to evaluation methods), an attempt will be made to discuss each in turn.

EVALUATION ON MULTIPLE DIMENSIONS

Evaluation following the Cranfield paradigm has concentrated on the measurement of retrieval performance, usually using the tried and tested measures of recall ratio and precision ratio, although (as has been noted) a whole range of other measures have either been proposed or used. However, there have been significant developments in retrieval systems since the days of Cranfield. In an era of interactive systems used largely by end-users, the measurement solely of retrieval effectiveness is no longer sufficient. Furthermore, in the case of huge dynamic IR systems epitomized by Internet search engines, the calculation of the recall ratio has become quite impossible. On that ground alone it has been necessary to determine other criteria and appropriate measures by which the performance of IR systems can be determined.

Whilst there is general recognition now that it is necessary to go beyond the measurement of effectiveness, through recall and precision, there has been less agreement on what further criteria should be evaluated. However, evidence from the literature indicates increasing evidence of concentration of users, their interaction with the system and their opinions of the system.

EVALUATION FROM THE PERSPECTIVE OF A RANGE OF STAKEHOLDERS AND SPECIFICALLY END-USERS

Closely related to the recognition of the need to move beyond the measurement of retrieval performance has been the increasing recognition that there is a need to evaluate IR systems from the perspective of a range of stakeholders. Principal amongst these are the system users.

Rather than seeking to determine for end-users the appropriate dimensions and criteria by which search engines should be evaluated, Johnson and his colleagues undertook a project which sought to allow those dimensions and criteria to be determined by a group of end-users, in this case students (Johnson, Griffiths and Hartley, 2003). This work has been further developed by Crudge and Johnson who have used the well-established repertory grid technique to elicit detailed constructs of users' evaluative criteria for search engines (Crudge and Johnson, 2004).

Another approach to evaluation which emphasizes the importance of stakeholders has been the adaptation of the service quality approach (SERVQUAL) to evaluate students' attitudes towards electronic resources (Griffiths, 2003).

In parallel with the developments in evaluation, there has been great interest in studying information-seeking behaviour and developing models of user behaviour. This huge body of work has been excellently reviewed by Case (2007); whilst Spink and Cole (2006) have edited a review of developments in information behaviour theories and models. Whilst this work has developed separately from IR system evaluation, there is a need for the two approaches to be brought closer together.

EVALUATION METHODS

For many years a major point of discussion has been the suitability of laboratory-based evaluation methods rather than testing in an operational environment. Whilst there is some logic to the argument that laboratory-based testing is so far removed from the real world in which people search retrieval systems, there is scant data to support the argument that laboratory findings are invalid. Whilst laboratory-based approaches have continued, there is now far greater use of evaluation in an operational environment. Rather than indulge in this debate it is better to accept that a far wider range of methods and approaches are now utilized; the most important factor is the use of research designs and methods which enable the required data to be collected and in a manner which, as far as possible, tests the phenomena under discussion. In short, both laboratory-based and real-world approaches have their place.

Alongside the debate about the use of laboratory or real-world evaluation, there has been a debate about the use of quantitative or qualitative approaches. Laboratory-based approaches, following the Cranfield model, concentrated on the quantitative approach. Essentially this approach has continued with the TREC experiments. Increasingly, as it has become apparent that there is a need to evaluate more than performance, there has been an increasing use of qualitative approaches. It is generally accepted that it can be appropriate to use one or other or even both approaches depending upon the objectives of the evaluation. Indeed, most evaluations these days will use a mix of data collection methods.

FORMATIVE AND SUMMATIVE EVALUATION

In the context of information retrieval, summative evaluation is the evaluation of an operational system or service. In contrast, formative evaluation is the evaluation of a system as it is being developed, with a view to helping the developers improve the system through the identification of weaknesses or shortcomings. There has been a clear trend towards an increased use of formative evaluation as well as summative evaluation. In the UK, this has been particularly apparent in the development work for the higher education community funded by the Joint Information Systems Committee (JISC). Indeed, in some cases the use of formative evaluation has been so extensive that there has been a blurring between the boundaries of design and evaluation: formative evaluation has frequently become a part of the design process.

SUMMARY

This chapter has outlined the major aims and methods of evaluation of information retrieval systems. It has explored the criteria by which retrieval systems are evaluated and the measures used to assess those criteria. So we have seen the initial importance attached to the measures of recall and precision but also the extension to other dimensions as a result of the recognition of both the limitations of recall and precision and the changing evaluation needs of evolving systems. The chapter has explored the development of different methods for evaluation and testing; it has noted the move from essentially laboratory-based testing to a broader range of test methods which now include methods for evaluating systems in a real-world environment, including transaction log analysis and social science methods such as questionnaires, interviews and focus group discussions. A selection of the major retrieval tests has been introduced and their impact on both evaluation methodology and the development of knowledge organization systems has been noted. Finally, current issues in the information retrieval system evaluation have been explored. The literature on the topic is vast and this chapter has only scratched the surface of a topic which has dominated IR research for years. An extensive review, which enables the reader to investigate the topic in greater depth than has been possible here, is that by Harter and Hert (1997).

REVIEW QUESTIONS

1. Define the major measures of retrieval effectiveness.
2. What are the strengths and weaknesses of the laboratory evaluation of an information retrieval system?
3. How do you distinguish between formative and summative evaluation?
4. What are the major devices which are available to promote (respectively) recall and precision?
5. What are the strengths and weaknesses of transaction log analysis?
6. What is the importance of satisfaction as a measure of information retrieval system search success?
7. What are the current issues in the evaluation of IR systems?
8. How did the Cranfield tests contribute to the development of information retrieval systems?
9. What role can failure analysis play in the evaluation of retrieval systems? Why is it so rarely employed?

REFERENCES AND FURTHER READING

Applegate, R. (1993) Models of user satisfaction: understanding false positives. *RQ*, **32** (4), 525–39.

Blair, D.C. (1986) Full text retrieval: evaluation and implications. *International Classification*, **13** (1), 18–23.

Blair, D.C. and Maron, M.E. (1985) An evaluation of retrieval effectiveness for a full-text document retrieval system. *Communications of the ACM*, **28**, 289–99.

Bruce, H. (1998) User satisfaction with information seeking on the Internet. *Journal of the American Society of Information Science and Technology*, **49** (6), 541–56.

Buttle, F. (1996) SERVQUAL: review, critique, research agenda. *European Journal of Marketing*, **30**, 8–32.

Case, D.O. (2007) Looking for information: a survey of research on information seeking, needs, and behavior. In D.O. Case, *Library and Information Science*, 2nd edn. London: Academic Press.

Cleverdon, C.W. (1972) On the inverse relationship of recall and precision. *Journal of Documentation*, **28**, 195–201.

Cooper, W.S. (1973a) On selecting a measure of retrieval effectiveness. Part 1, The 'subjective' philosophy of evaluation. *Journal of the American Society for Information Science and Technology*, **24**, 87–100.

Cooper, W.S. (1973b) On selecting a measure of retrieval effectiveness. Part 2, Implementation of philosophy. *Journal of the American Society for Information Science and Technology*, **24**, 413–424.

Crudge, S.E. and Johnson, F.C. (2004) Using the information seeker to elicit construct models for search engine evaluation. *Journal of the American Society for Information Science and Technology*, **55** (9), 794–806.

Ellis, D. (1996) *Progress and Problems in Information Retrieval*, especially Chapter 1. London: Facet.

Fast, K.V. and Campbell, D.G. (2004) 'I still like Google': university student perceptions of searching OPACs and the Web. In L. Schamber and C.L. Barry, *ASIS&T 2004, Proceedings of the 67th ASIS&T Annual Meeting*, **41** (1), 138–46.

Griffiths, J.R. (2003) Evaluation of the JISC information environment: student perceptions of services. *Information Research*, **8** (4). Available at <http://informationr.net/ir/8-4/paper160.html>.

Griffiths, J.R., Hartley, R.J. et al. (2002) An improved method of studying user-system interaction by combining transaction log analysis and protocol analysis. *Information Research*, **7** (4). Available at <http://www.informationr.net/ir/7-4/paper139.html>.

Harter, S.P. and Hert, C.A. (1997) Evaluation of information retrieval systems: approaches, issues and methods. *Annual Review of Information Science and Technology*, **32**, 3–94.

Hartley, R.J. and Booth, H. (2006) Users and union catalogues. *Journal of Librarianship and Information Science*, **38** (1), 7–20.

Hernon, P. and McClure, C.R. (1990) *Evaluation and Library Decision Making*. Norwood NJ: Ablex.

Hildreth, C. (2001) Accounting for users' inflated assessments of on-line catalogue search performance and usefulness: an experimental study. *Information Research*, **6** (2). Available at <http://InformationR.net/ir/6-2/paper101.html>.

Johnson, F.C., Griffiths, J.R. and Hartley, R.J. (2003) Task dimensions of user evaluation of information retrieval systems. *Information Research*, **8** (4). Available at <http://informationr.net/ir/8-4/paper157.html>.

Keen, E.M. (1973) The Aberystwyth index languages test. *Journal of Documentation*, **29** (1), 1–34.

Keen, E.M. (1977) On the processing of printed subject index entries during searching. *Journal of Documentation*, **33** (4), 266–76.

Keen, E.M. and Digger, J. (1972) *Report of an Information Science Index Languages Test*, Aberystwyth: College of Librarianship, Wales.

Lancaster, F.W. (1979) *Information Retrieval Systems Characteristics Testing Evaluation*. Chichester: Wiley.

Lantz, B.E. (1981) The relationship between documents read and relevant references retrieved as effectiveness measures for information retrieval systems. *Journal of Documentation*, **37**, 134–45.

Loiacono, E.T, Watson, R.T. and Hoodhue, D.L. (2002) WEBQUAL: measure of web site quality. *2002 Marketing Educators Conference: Marketing Theory and Applications*, **13**, 432–7.

Mizzaro, S. (1997) Relevance: the whole history. *Journal of the American Society for Information Science and Technology*, **48** (9), 810–832.

Oliver, R. (1981) Measurement and evaluation of satisfaction process in retail settings, *Journal of Retailing*, **57** (Fall), 25–48.

Parasuraman, A., Zeithaml, V. and Berry, L. (1985) A conceptual model of service quality and its implications for future research, *Journal of Marketing*, **49** (4), 41–50.

Plutchak, T.S. (1989) On the satisfied and inept user. *Medical Reference Service Quarterly*, **8** (1), 45–8.

Rowley, J. (2006) An analysis of the e-service literature: towards a research agenda. *Internet Research*, **16** (3), 339–59.

Spärck Jones, K. (1981) The Cranfield tests. In K. Spärck Jones (ed.), *Information Retrieval Experiment*. London: Butterworths.

Spink, A. and Cole, C. (eds) (2006) *New Directions in Human Information Behaviour*. Dordrecht: Springer.

Tessier, J., Crouch, W.W. and Atherton, P. (1977) New measures of user satisfaction with computer-based literature searches. *Special Libraries*, **68**, 383–9.

Van den Haak, M.J., De Jong, M.D.T. et al. (2003) Retrospective vs. concurrent think-aloud protocols: testing the usability of an online library catalogue. *Behaviour and Information Technology*, **22** (5), 339–51.

Zeithaml, V.A., Parasuraman, A. and Malhotra, A. (2002) Service quality delivery through web sites: a critical review of extant knowledge. *Journal of the Academy of Marketing Science*, **30** (4), 362–75.

11 Organizing knowledge without IT

INTRODUCTION

Knowledge and documents were organized before the advent of digital documents, search engines, metadata and the digital information environment. This chapter visits some key topics and approaches that are important where the user interacts with information in non-digital environments. In some ways this can feel like a journey down memory lane, but it is important to appreciate that such approaches still have significant relevance today. Printed indexes, such as the indexes to books, journals and other reference documents, and printed directories (such as telephone directories) are still created and used to fulfil information needs. In addition, significant proportions of the collections in archives, libraries and museums pre-date digitization, and despite major retrospective digitization projects, the only indexes or catalogues to some valuable collections remain in card or printed form. It is important, therefore, to review aspects of knowledge organization relevant in non-digital contexts. This review also encompasses some of the early uses of computers in information retrieval in the generation of printed indexes.

At the end of this chapter you will:

- understand the principles associated with document arrangement for effective browsing and document location
- understand the nature and components of printed and card catalogues and indexes
- be aware of the main approaches to the creation of printed indexes
- understand some techniques for the effective searching of printed indexes
- be acquainted with the key principles of book indexing
- appreciate the significance of filing sequences and some of the problems associated with establishing effective filing sequences.

315

DOCUMENT ARRANGEMENT

GENERAL PRINCIPLES

Documents in libraries or resource centres must be physically stored. With closed access collections, storage may be by factors that are not significant for retrieval, for example by size or by date added. Access is by means of indexes, and the information professional will act as an intermediary between the stock and the user. Open access environments are different: documents must be arranged or physically stored in an order which requires a minimum of explanation, and which matches as far as possible the search patterns of users.

The open access principle helps both management and users. Self-service was commonly available in libraries for many years before it was taken up by the retail trade. Managerially it is clearly cheaper to allow users to carry their own books off the shelves than to have to request them from a librarian and have them brought from a stack. The self-service principle also respects the privacy of the user. Users may not have clearly articulated their requirements in their own minds, and a library whose shelf arrangement and physical environment encourage browsing is one of the simple pleasures of civilization.

In some environments document arrangement may be the only retrieval device available to, or used by, users. Examples of such environments are bookshops, music shops, small public libraries and document filing systems. In larger document collections browsing the whole collection is not an option, but subsets of the collection may be examined by browsing. Various document characteristics that are rarely reflected in catalogues, such as the precise scope of the work and its level of difficulty, as well as its physical format, the quality of production and the design of the cover, can be identified. Hence, despite its relative lack of sophistication, document arrangement is an important and frequently used retrieval device.

APPROACHES TO DOCUMENT ARRANGEMENT

The arrangement in a collection is unlikely to follow one sequence for all types of material. As always, a balance must be struck between managerial priorities and user convenience. In this section, the various types of shelf arrangement that encourage browsing will be discussed, followed by the factors which may lead to sequences being modified or broken.

Detailed classified subject arrangement

Detailed, or 'close', classification is the commonest arrangement for the majority of open access stock in all but the smallest collections. Long sequences of books sharing the same class mark but having heterogeneous but related subjects are an irritation to purposeful browsing, and a detailed classified arrangement minimizes this. This arrangement is subject to the problems of classified order generally, whereby complex relationships have to be accommodated within a linear order, so only one relationship can be shown, and other related material is inevitably separated.

Broad classified subject arrangement

The principal drawback of detailed classification specifically is that shelf marks can become unmanageably long. Smaller libraries may opt for a less detailed version of a published classification – often DDC, which publishes an official abridged edition. Some public branch libraries have adopted 'reader interest' arrangement. This name is given to a whole group of single-facet classifications, mostly devised in-house. Reader interest arrangement is born out of exasperation – the exasperation of readers trying to find their way round DDC's unhelpful collocations and overlong notations, and of library staff trying to explain to them, for example, that DIY is classed at 643.7, except that carpentry is at 694, but not woodworking which is 684, unless it is marquetry and similar handicrafts, for which you will need 745.51. Reader interest arrangements are often intuitive and very broad, 30 to 40 classes sufficing for the whole collection, with simple, sometimes iconic, notations.

Verbal subject arrangement

This may be considered for a small collection with a restricted range of topics. However, verbal subject arrangement is quite indifferent to relationships, and gives an arbitrary sequence. The distinction between a verbal arrangement and a very broad classified arrangement is a fine one: some reader interest arrangements do not attempt to show relationships between subjects, and might be better considered as verbal subject arrangements. This is the kind of arrangement commonly found in bookshops. It also has its uses for the arrangement of small, specialist collections; for example, files of community information material or of photographs in a local collection.

Title arrangement

This method for direct retrieval is found mainly in the specialized context of periodicals, often within broad subject categories corresponding to the library's physical organization.

Author arrangement

This approach is traditionally found in the fiction section of public libraries, though even here it is increasingly common to find genre fiction grouped or labelled separately. Within a classified sequence, items are commonly sub-arranged by author, with the shelf mark indicating this.

Merchandising techniques and displays

There is an increasing awareness of the role of physical environments in service outlets in communicating with users and influencing their behaviour and satisfaction. In libraries a key aspect of the physical environment that facilitates a satisfactory outcome is the document arrangement. Whilst the first step is to ensure that documents are in a sequence that makes for straightforward location of books this is no longer sufficient; today libraries need to promote their services and resources. This has led to the development of more advanced display and promotion techniques similar to those used in merchandising in other retail outlets, such as:

- power spots – focused displays intended to draw the user's attention to specific items, such as selected new books
- end-caps – end-of-stack displays that attract attention by being out of the main shelving run
- theatre displays – displays that create a sense of theatre or performance, possibly including movement or lighting effects and inviting users to walk in and participate in some way.

Such techniques often integrate document display with the display of other items and services. For example, newspaper/coffee lounges might also have museum pieces and artwork on display, and even live entertainment.

PARALLEL SEQUENCES

Very few libraries arrange their classified stock in a single sequence. A variety of parallel sequences is almost universally found. Some situations that lead to sections of stock being shelved in a separate classified sequence are listed below.

Physical form

While improvements in packaging have made it possible to box up many videos, audio cassettes and other audiovisual materials in a way that makes them suitable for interfiling with books, many libraries prefer (for security or other reasons) to house such materials separately. This applies particularly if equipment – DVD players, video-cassette recorders (VCRs), PCs, fiche readers, slide viewers and the like – is needed to use such material within the library. Some items, such as graphic materials and portfolios, are simply too large or awkwardly shaped to be shelved with books. Books themselves often have one or more separate sequences for oversize items. Pamphlets, reports and similar items that are too slim to have a spine may be placed in separate sequences, possibly in filing cabinets.

Nature of use

Separate sequences may be established for items where special conditions are imposed on their use, for example short-loan collections in academic libraries. Lending and reference stock are commonly segregated, and there is often a separate quick reference sequence for yearbooks, directories and other materials that are designed for rapid consultation.

Readership level

Separate undergraduate collections may be found in academic libraries. School and public libraries often split the stock into categories reflecting the child's level of reading and emotional development.

GUIDING

Library guiding is essentially the system–user interface as described in Chapter 4, but writ large, and static rather than interactive. The range of sequences that are likely to be found even in quite small libraries underlines the need for users to be given clear information about the whereabouts of every item of stock. Such guidance may take forms that are specific to individual environments, but may include:

- group or individual instruction in the layout and use of the collection: within the catalogue, shelf marks must clearly indicate the sequence within which an item is housed
- users of the catalogue should have easy access to information guiding them to each sequence
- clear and explicit guidance that is visible within the library
- guidance as necessary on book stacks and shelves.

LIMITATIONS OF DOCUMENT ARRANGEMENT

Document arrangement is a crude retrieval device that normally needs to be supported by other approaches. Specifically, its limitations are that:

- Documents can be arranged in only one order, and grouped according to one characteristic.
- Any given document can only be located in one place in any given sequence.
- The document arrangement adopted is often broken; parallel sequences are common, and additional complexity may be introduced by the need to accommodate large collections on several different floors of a library building.
- Only part of the library collection will normally be visible on shelves or in filing cabinets. Documents that may be available through a library, but which will not be evident through browsing, include: digital documents such as e-journals, e-books and e-maps, documents on loan, documents which might be obtained by interlibrary loan, and any collections that are maintained on closed access.

While document arrangement has some significant limitations for the retrieval of both documents and the information contained within those documents, it is important to remember that document arrangement is used widely in libraries, archive collections and paper-based filing systems, and, overall, has an important impact on information retrieval.

PRINTED AND CARD CATALOGUES AND INDEXES

Computer-based information retrieval has become the norm, and print, card and other forms of non-computerized catalogues have faded in their significance. Nevertheless there remain a range of contexts in which they are still compiled and used. In addition they have had a significant influence in defining cataloguing, indexing and metadata standards used in digital environments, because today's systems evolved from these earlier systems. Indeed, the first applications of computers to information retrieval were in the generation of printed indexes, printed bibliographies, and card and microfiche catalogues.

PRINTED CATALOGUES

Any catalogue comprises a number of entries, each entry representing or acting as a surrogate for a document (see Chapters 2 and 3). There may be several entries per document, or just one. Each entry comprises three sections: the heading, the description and the location.

Headings determine the order of a catalogue sequence. The entries in an author catalogue will have authors' names as headings, and the catalogue will be organized alphabetically according to the author's name.

The common types of catalogue are:

- *Author catalogues*, which contain entries with authors' names as access points. Authors may be persons or corporate bodies; the term 'author' is normally extended to include illustrators, performers, producers and others with intellectual or artistic responsibility for a work. A variant sometimes found is the *name catalogue*, which includes in addition personal names as subjects and, sometimes, corporate bodies.
- *Title catalogues*, which contain entries with titles as access points.
- *Author/title catalogues* contain a mixture of author entries and titles entries; since both are alphabetical these can be interfiled into one sequence.
- *Subject catalogues* use subject terms as access points.
  - *alphabetical subject catalogues* use verbal subject headings as headings
  - *classified subject catalogues* use notation from a classification scheme as a heading: as this order is not self-evident, classified catalogues require a subject index, an alphabetical list of subjects and their class marks.

Normally a combination of these catalogue sequences will be used. There are two different approaches:

- *classified catalogue*, which has the following sequences: an author/title catalogue or index (or separate author and title catalogues), a classified subject catalogue and a subject index to the classified subject catalogue
- *dictionary catalogue*, which has only one sequence (like a dictionary) with author, title and alphabetical subject entries interfiled.

PRINTED INDEXES

Two basic types of indexes are common: author indexes and subject indexes. A subject index has alphabetical terms or words as headings. Entries are arranged in alphabetical order according to the letters of the heading. An author index may be created; here entries are arranged alphabetically by authors' names. The descriptive part of an entry in an index depends upon the information or document being indexed. Three important contexts in which printed indexes are encountered are:

1. *Book indexes.* A book index is an alphabetically arranged list of words or terms leading the reader to the numbers of pages on which specific topics are considered, or on which specific names appear. Many non-fiction books and directories include an index; this is often a subject index. The section below explores some of the principles of the creation of book indexes in greater detail.
2. *Periodical indexes.* A periodical index is an index to a specific periodical title (for example, *Proceedings of the London Mathematical Society* or *Managing*

Information). Usually indexes are generated at intervals to cover several issues; annual indexes are common. Periodicals may have subject, author and/or title indexes.

3. *Indexing journals* and the indexes to printed abstracting journals are alphabetical indexes to the literature of a subject area. Usually many of the entries relate to the periodical literature, but monographs, conference proceedings and reports may also be covered. The indexing journal normally comprises an alphabetical subject index, possibly also supported with an author index. The 'description' is the bibliographical citation that gives details of the document that is being indexed. Different approaches to generating these indexes in printed form are discussed below in the section headed 'Creating printed indexes'.

ENTRIES AND REFERENCES

In catalogues or indexes there are two possible approaches to the provision of multiple entries for one work. One of these is to use *main* and *added entries* (see also Chapter 8 under the heading 'Catalogues and their functions'). The main entry includes the complete catalogue record of the document. In a classified catalogue the main entry will be the subject entry in the classified sequence. In a dictionary catalogue the main entry will be as determined by AACR2 or whichever catalogue rules are in use – normally the principal author. Added entries will be made for additional access points or headings. For example, in an author catalogue added entries might be expected for collaborating authors, writers, editors, compilers and illustrators (see Chapter 8). Typically, added entries do not include all of the components of the description that are used in the main entry, but only the minimum needed for identification. The second approach is the use of *unit entries*; in a unit entry catalogue all entries are equivalent and contain the same descriptive detail. This approach is commonly found in card catalogues. Printed catalogues and indexes tend to prefer the main and added entry format, which uses less space.

Entries are usually supplemented by references. A reference provides no direct information about a document but, rather, refers the user to another location or entry. References take less space than added entries in a printed index, and require less detail to be printed on a card. There are two types of reference: *see* and *see also*. These operate in a similar way whether they are used to link authors' names or subject headings.

A *see* reference directs the user from a name, title, subject or other term which has not been used as an entry heading to an alternative term at which words occur as a heading or descriptor. *See* references may link two subjects with similar meanings (for example, Currency *see* Money) or variant author names (for example, Council for the Education and Training of Health Visitors *see* United Kingdom. *Council for the Education and Training of Health Visitors*). Some bibliographies use references in situations where AACR2 would require an added entry, as with second authors. For example, the added entry:

Frink / Edward Lucie-Smith and Elisabeth Frink. – Bloomsbury, 1994. – 138p. – ISBN 0-7475-1572-7

from Figure 3.9 would be replaced with the reference

Frink, Elisabeth *see* Lucie-Smith, Edward *and* Frink, Elisabeth

A *see also* reference connects subject headings or index terms which have a hierarchical or associative relationship (Chapter 5). For example, the following *see also* reference links two headings under which entries may be found:

Monasteries *see also* Abbeys

The searcher is recommended to examine entries under both index terms if it is likely that documents might prove to be relevant. *See also* references between personal names, corporate bodies and uniform titles are prescribed also by AACR2 in a very limited number of circumstances; for example, where the same person's works are listed under different pseudonyms or where a corporate body has changed its name.

Explanatory references may be either *see* or *see also* references that give a little more detail than merely the direction to look elsewhere. An example might be:

Devon, Sarah
For works of this author published under other names see
Murray, Jill; Treves, Kathleen

Association of Assistant Librarians
See also the later name:
Library Association. *Career Development Group*

PROS AND CONS OF PRINTED AND CARD CATALOGUES AND INDEXES

Printed and card indexes and catalogues will continue to be used for those collections where no digital index or catalogue has been developed, and in contexts in which the printed format is more convenient. This section discusses further some of the advantages and disadvantages of such indexes and catalogues.

Availability and accessibility

The biggest advantage of printed indexes, in particular, is their availability. This operates on two levels:

- Printed indexes are available to all of the users of a library. Access to digital resources is often restricted to certain classes of users under the terms of licensing arrangements; for example, in university libraries, external users often have limited access to digital resources.
- Where printed indexes accompany or are an integral part of printed documents, such as journals, or books, a printed index is the most appropriate navigation tool.
- In some countries and locations, digital networked environments and even stable electricity supplies are unavailable, or only available to the privileged few; printed documents are the only option.
- As has been noted earlier, there are collections that can only be accessed through printed indexes or catalogues.

Currency

The currency of manual indexes of all types is usually inferior to that of electronic information retrieval systems, as time is taken up for physical production and for the distribution of published indexes. In 'the good old days', card indexes often had a backlog of entries for filing, as the work involved is slow and tedious and at the same time requires great accuracy and a knowledge of complex filing procedures.

Static lists

A static list is any index that has a physical substrate – printed page, card, microform or the physical arrangement of library materials. The list is permanent, or nearly so, and is not altered by use. These lists are costly to compile and (where applicable) to distribute, and they take up physical space. Access is by consulting relevant sections of the list. A search is only able to retrieve what is on the list, so queries have to be tailored to what the list can offer. In contrast, with computer-based systems the physical ordering of records is hidden from the user. Interrogation of the system produces dynamic lists. These are the records that have been retrieved from the system in response to a specific query. Each list is tailored to its query. Depending on the sophistication of system and user, it may be possible to fine-tune a list in respect of record format and file arrangement.

Access points

Because of the cost in space and time of producing and maintaining static lists, information organizations make them as simple as they can, by limiting both the amount of data in the individual record and the number of access points available. Access points in non-computerized systems typically consist of: the first word of the title, the author and one or more subject access points, which together rarely exceed four or five. This contrasts with online systems where the number of access points depends on the size of the record, the number of indexed fields and on whether a keyword search facility is available.

Searching

Non-computerized systems are often pre-coordinate systems, where a single access point may carry two or more elements of information. The searcher has to scan through static lists, and modifying a search is laborious. However, because the exhaustivity of indexing is limited, false coordinations are uncommon, and the precision of a search can be high. Scanning and browsing can be affected by layout and typography.

Search output

Output from a search of a printed or card index has to be memorized or copied, using manual copying, photocopying or digital scanning. All options are time-consuming. On the other hand, output from computer systems can be relatively easily printed or downloaded, provided that there are no licensing or access constraints controlling such processes.

CREATING PRINTED INDEXES

One of the first applications of computers in information retrieval was in the production of printed indexes. Computers were used for in-house indexes to reports lists, local abstracting and indexing bulletins, patents lists, etc., and for the production of published indexes to many of the major abstracting journals.

Particularly for the large abstracting and indexing organizations, computerization of indexes and indexing yielded considerable savings in the production and cumulating of indexes. Originally index production was an isolated operation. Now, many indexes are merely one of a range of database products. Although much searching is now conducted online, there are still contexts in which printed indexes are created and used. Several different access points may be used in printed indexes. The most important of these are subject and author; but chemical formulae, trade names, company names and patent numbers are all possible access points.

All indexes consist of a series of lead terms, arranged usually in alphabetical order. Each lead term may be qualified and must have a link that leads the user to other lists or documents. Computer-generated indexes may rely on automatically assigned index terms or intellectually assigned terms. Each of these possibilities will now be considered.

Keyword indexes

A keyword-in-context (KWIC) index is the most basic of natural language indexes. KWIC indexes were popular because they are straightforward to create. In the most basic of KWIC indexes, words in a title are compared with a stop list, in order to suppress the generation of useless index entries. The stop list or stopword list contains words under which entries are *not* required, such as 'them', 'his', 'her', 'and'. Each word in the title is compared with those in the stop list and if a match occurs it is rejected; but if no match is found, the term is designated a keyword. These keywords are used as entry words, with one entry relating to the document for each word. The word is printed in context with the remainder of the title (including stop words). Entry words are arranged alphabetically and aligned in the centre or left column. A single line entry, including title and source reference, is produced for each significant word in the title. The source reference frequently amounts to no more than a document or abstract number, but may extend to an abbreviated journal citation. Alternatively, a full bibliographic description, with or without abstract, can be located in a separate listing. Entries under one word are arranged alphabetically by title. Figure 11.1 presents an example of a KWIC index layout from the Biological Abstracts database. This index is more user-friendly than some, making good use of white space. Even so, many titles are drastically truncated on any given index line. The index uses title enrichment: subject terms are added to the title to enhance or clarify it. The slash (/) appears at the end of the title and separates it from the added subject terms.

Subject context	Keyword	Subject context	Ref No.
CONTROL WEED CONTROL/	**ALTITUDINAL**	DISTRIBUTION OF THE LANT	205
LIMIT TEMPERATURE/ECOLO		OWNSTREAM REPLACEMENT	3128
ZONATION SYNONYMY/A SU		RA-SPLENDENS VEGETATION	1458
. . .			
ED CONTROL/ ALTITUDINAL	**DISTRIBUTION**	OF THE LANTANA LACE BUG	205
IVORY COAST CAMEROON/		OF THE MATING TYPE ALLE	9684
URE BRAIN DEVELOPMENT/		OF THE NOVEL DEVELOPME	7907
. . .			
ANCE BIOLOGICAL CONTROL	**WEED**	CONTROL/ ALTITUDINAL DIST	205
ING AND FREQUENCY SEED		CONTROL/COTTON GOSSYPI	172
HUS-RETROFLEXUS GROWTH		CONTROL/PETROLEUM OIL A \	9759

Figure 11.1 KWIC index

The merits of title indexes derive mainly from the low human intervention. Since a simple KWIC index is entirely computer-generated, a large number of titles can be processed quickly and cheaply. The elimination of personal interpretation enhances consistency and predictability. Indexing based on words in titles reflects current terminology, automatically evolving with the use of the terminology. Also, the creation of cumulative indexes (to, say, cover five annual volumes) is easier and does not demand any added intellectual effort, only an extra computer run.

However, for all their convenience, title indexes are open to criticism on several counts:

- Some titles do not accurately mirror the content of a document. Titles can always be found which are misleading or eye-catching rather than informative; for example, 'On the care and construction of white elephants' – an article on the value of catalogues.
- Basic KWIC indexes are unattractive and uncomfortable to read, due to their physical arrangement and typeface, and the limited information that they contain.
- There is no vocabulary control, leading to irrelevant and redundant entries, and scatter under different terms.

There are a variety of potential enhancements on the basic KWIC index concept, such as KWOC (keyword-out-of-context), KWAC (keyword-and-context) and Double-KWIC (based on pairs of words, that mitigate some of these limitations.

Indexes based on string manipulation

The alternative to the use of title words is to use terms from controlled indexing languages for the entries in a printed index. In this context, computers are used in the formatting and sequencing of entries in indexes and in generating files for cumulative indexes. In the process of sequencing printed indexes, string manipulation is important. The human indexer selects a string of index terms from which the computer, under appropriate instructions, prints a series of entries for the document to which the string of index terms relate. Figure 11.2 shows an example.

One important articulated subject indexing system that used a controlled vocabulary was PRECIS, which was developed and used to index the *British National Bibliography* for many years. The syntax for PRECIS was based on a system of over 30 role operators and other manipulation codes. These have three functions. They indicate the role of each term within the subject statement or string. They determine the citation order. Finally, they pass instructions to the computer for the precise pattern of rotation of the index entries under each lead term, as well as their typography, punctuation and capitalization. Figure 11.3 shows an example of this process.

Topic: Testing of bored concrete piles by ultrasonics

The indexer inserts manipulation codes into this string, thus:
    <Testing> of <Bored <Concrete <Piles>>> by <Ultrasonics>
which the computer turns into a set of index entries:

Testing of Bored Concrete Piles by Ultrasonics
Bored Concrete Piles. Testing by Ultrasonics
Concrete Piles. Bored. Testing by Ultrasonics
Piles. Bored. Concrete. Testing by Ultrasonics
Ultrasonics. Testing of Bored Concrete Piles

This example is based on Craven's NEPHIS (NEsted PHrase Indexing System).

Figure 11.2   Articulated subject index

Title: Education and the Third Age in the South-West

Subject in natural language: Education of the elderly in Devon to 1990

PRECIS concept string: (0) Devon _
                                    (1) old persons_
                                    (2) educationv $d to 1990_

where (0), (1) and (2) are role operators denoting Environment, Key system, and Action / Event respectively, and $d is a manipulation code introducing date. _ against a term indicates that a lead (entry) is required under that term. The indexer rewrites these instructions as a machine-readable *manipulation string*:

$z01030$dDevon$z11030$aold persons$z21030$aeducation$dto 1990

Index entries are generated from these coded instructions:

Devon.
    Old persons. Education, *to 1990*

Old persons. Devon
    Education, *to 1990*

Education. Old persons. Devon
    to 1990

References are recalled automatically from a machine-held thesaurus:

Aged persons *see* **Old persons**

Elderly persons *see* **Old persons**

England
    see also Names of individual counties

Great Britain
    see also Names of individual countries, regions and districts

Figure 11.3   PRECIS worked example

Access from subordinate terms in subject headings

Many subject headings consist of a single concept only, but many more contain two or more concepts, or facets. In machine-searched systems any facet is equally retrievable, but manually searched indexes need to provide some mechanism for gaining access from terms that are not in the lead (filing) position. Most indexes employ some form of *rotation*: a subject heading consisting of the facets A, B, C and D, and filed at A, can also be retrieved by means of references or additional citations at B, C and D.

There are a number of different ways of rotating subject headings. All of the following are commonly found in indexes:

- *Cycling*. Successive index entries move the final term across to the lead position:

  Football. Clubs. Management. Scotland.   *[citation or address]*
  Management. Scotland. Football. Clubs.   *[citation or address]*
  Clubs. Management. Scotland. Football.   *[citation or address]*
  Scotland. Football. Clubs. Management.   *[citation or address]*

- *Keyword out of context (KWOC)*. With this technique (which has many variations) the lead term is followed by either the whole of the string, or (as in the example) the remainder of the string:

  Football. Clubs. Management. Scotland.   *[address]*
  Clubs. Football. Management. Scotland.   *[address]*
  Management. Football. Clubs. Scotland.   *[address]*
  Scotland. Football. Clubs. Management.   *[address]*

- *Rotation, or keyword in context (KWIC)*. The whole string is slid forward in successive index entries, so that each term in turn appears in the lead position:

  Football. Clubs. Management. Scotland. *[address]*
  Football. **Clubs**. Management. Scotland. *[address]*
  Football. Clubs. **Management**. Scotland. *[address]*
  Football. Clubs. Management. **Scotland**. *[address]*

- *Shunting*. This method is used by PRECIS, and has a two-line format:

  Scotland.
     Football. Clubs. Management.   *[citation or address]*
  Football. Scotland.
     Clubs. Management.   *[citation or address]*
  Clubs. Football. Scotland.

Management.   *[citation or address]*
Management. Clubs. Football. Scotland.   *[citation or address]*

SEARCHING PRINTED INDEXES

Many of us today are so accustomed to conducting all our searches online that the techniques specific to printed indexes are apt to be forgotten. This brief checklist of practical factors to be aware of supplements the discussion of the characteristics of print and card indexes and catalogues above.

- *Coverage.* Check – either by examining any prefatory material or by direct inspection – how the subject (or other) field has been defined, and what range of material is included. If the coverage appears marginal to the information need, then *either* bear this in mind when searching *or* check literature guides and other secondary sources for more appropriate indexes. Is retrospective coverage adequate? Be aware that a long retrospective search through annual cumulations will be slow, repetitive and often heavy work.
- *Depth of treatment.* Are there indexes only, or are there abstracts also? How exhaustive is the indexing? If there are abstracts, are they informative or merely indicative? In many cases, where there are print and electronic formats of the same database, the printed index will offer far fewer search keys, even within the same field; for example, by not making minor descriptors available for searching.
- *Up-to-dateness.* Some indexes have a time-lag of several months or even a year or two. Verify by spot-checking. If unacceptably dilatory, then see if more up-to-date hard-copy alternatives are available, or check electronic databases as they are usually more up to date.
- *Arrangement.* Indexes are basically either one-stage or two-stage:
  - A one-stage, or dictionary, index has all approaches interfiled in a single A–Z sequence. A variant has a single A–Z subject sequence with a separate author index.
  - A two-stage index has, firstly, a bibliography (citations with or without abstracts), often in a broadly classified subject grouping to permit browsing. For specific searching the bibliography is accessible via, secondly, author and subject indexes, occasionally other indexes also. Author indexes may give a full citation, more usually just a reference. Depending on the nature of the subject, other specialist indexes may be found. For example, Biological Abstracts has the following: a biosystematic index composed of taxonomic categories; a generic index (giving entries according to genus or genus-species names); and a subject index, a computer-produced index in which keywords in the titles and abstracts are arranged in alphabetical sequence.

- *Subject approaches*. Check the subject indexing approach that is adopted and beware of its limitations. Possible approaches include those discussed above, such as KWIC, indexes based on string manipulation, and indexes using subject headings lists. Specifically consider the level of vocabulary control and pre-coordination and therefore the extent of the need to search under alternative terms or headings.

Some other points to check are:

- Use library catalogues and guides, literature guides, etc., to ascertain what is available in the subject area. Check both hard copy and electronic sources.
- Instructions for using indexes are often found at the front of the index. Sometimes there are separate guides, from the publisher or produced by the library, or even video tutorials for the more complex indexes.
- Layout and arrangement of bound volumes and unbound issues. How do the issues cumulate? Are the indexes in separate volumes? Current (uncumulated) issues of many abstracting journals may lack some or all indexes.
- Be aware of the filing rules in use.
- For subject searches, start with the most recent issue and work systematically back.
- If there is an accompanying thesaurus, use it to suggest alternative approaches.
- Do not expect too much of printed indexes. Many are less exhaustively indexed than their electronic versions and, increasingly, printed indexes may not be designed for easy use.
- Know when to stop. The Law of Diminishing Returns applies. At what point do citations become so old as to cease to be useful?

BOOK INDEXING

Book indexes are one type of printed index. They are important in assisting the user to locate concepts within the text of a book. Since book indexes can be compiled by authors or by professional indexers, the quality of such indexes varies considerably. A small extract from an index in a book (a book on indexing) was given in Figure 5.2. Entries may be the names of persons, corporate bodes or places, or alphabetical index terms to represent subjects, followed by number of those pages on which the information is to be located. The purposes of an index are, according to the relevant British Standard (BS 3700: 1988), to:

- identify and locate relevant information within the material being indexed

- discriminate between information on a subject and passing mention of a subject
- exclude passing mention of subjects that offer nothing significant to the potential user
- analyse concepts treated in the document so as to produce a series of headings based on its terminology
- indicate relationships between concepts
- group together information on subjects that is scattered by the arrangement of the document
- synthesize headings and subheadings into entries
- direct the user seeking information under terms not chosen for the index entries to the headings that have been chosen, by means of cross-references
- arrange entries into a systematic and helpful order.

The same principles can be used to guide the creation of entries in book indexes, as are outlined elsewhere in this book. The indexer creates an informal controlled vocabulary, one that is based on the language used by the author. Headings for persons, places and corporate bodies can follow the model offered by AACR2 in matters such as the identification of best-known names and the use of abbreviations of names. For subject entries, the problems associated with the variability of language and the indication of relationships between subjects still need to be addressed. Figure 5.2 shows clearly how the index groups together subjects that the document scatters. In this particular index the grouping would be assisted by the frequent use of *see also* references (not shown in Figure 5.2), for example:

alphabetization *see also* filing order; sorting

See references are also found, as:

audience *see* readers

Where subentries have been used, the indexer should provide appropriate access points. For example, the index used in Figure 5.2 also has such entries as:

alphabetization
    of abbreviations, 130

and

double-posting
    of abbreviations, 130

Indexes should subdivide entries rather than offer long lists of page numbers. Any main heading with more than five or six reference locators should be considered for subentries, as long undifferentiated lists of page or section numbers are a

332

hindrance to the user. Many word-processing packages support an indexing function, but they are relatively unsophisticated. Dedicated indexing software is available and is appropriate for all but the simplest indexes. The features found in dedicated software include:

- editing and display features: copying a previous entry; transposing (flipping) main heading and subheading; searching and find-and-replace entries; creating a subset of the index for the indexer to work on; verifying cross-references; onscreen editing
- sorting features: word-by-word or letter-by-letter alphabetizing, immediate sorting of entries, page number sort, merging of index files
- formatting and printing features: removal of duplicate entries or page references; automatic formatting and printing of the index in a range of styles, including user-selected formats; creation of user-defined style sheets.

The indexer is required to judge which items of information are relevant and which are to be passed over. The depth of indexing required will be affected by the nature and length of the book. An average ratio of index pages to text pages is 3 per cent, but for reference books this may be much higher. A well-structured book may be easier to index than a less well-structured one. Specificity of index headings can also be guided by the content of the book.

FILING ORDER AND SEQUENCES

Earlier sections have considered in some detail the headings and search keys to be used in catalogues and indexes. In any situation where a number of such headings or terms are to be displayed one after another in a static list, some well-recognized filing order must be adopted. Thus, in printed and card catalogues and indexes, the filing order is important in assisting the user in the location of a specific heading or term. In computer-based systems, lists of index terms or search keys or references are sometimes encountered, and here it is also useful to work with a defined filing order. If no filing order is adopted, the only way in which appropriate headings and their associated records can be retrieved is by scanning the entire file.

Since most headings in catalogues and indexes comprise primarily Arabic numbers and letters of the roman and other alphabets, it is these characters that must be organized and for which a filing order must be defined. While the letters of the alphabet do have a canonical order, letters, unlike numbers, are not primarily handled for their ordinal values. The larger the file, the slower and more complex the consultation process, and some users will have difficulty finding their way through large, complex files. As much help and assistance should be given, both within and outside the catalogue or index, as is reasonably possible.

Maintaining a coherent sequence requires, first, a set of filing rules. It also requires that these rules be followed accurately and consistently. In the production of printed indexes filing is done automatically, which ensures absolute consistency. Modern filing rules take into account the requirements of both manual and computer-based filing. Typically such rules address the problems and principles discussed below.

PROBLEMS AND PRINCIPLES IN ALPHABETICAL FILING SEQUENCES

Filing value of spaces and punctuation symbols

If spaces between words are given a filing value, word-by-word filing results; if not, the order is letter-by-letter. These give:

Word-by-word	*Letter-by-letter*
Leg at each corner	Legal writing
Leg ulcers	Leg at each corner
Legal writing	Legends of King Arthur
Legends of King Arthur	Leg ulcers

Word-by-word order is the more common, at least in the English language, but letter-by-letter filing is by no means dead. Hyphenated words are a related problem: where would *Leg-irons* file within either of the above sequences? And dashes also, which are not the same as hyphens: how would *Leg – bibliographies* file?

Acronyms fall within this category, as their filing value may be affected by whether they incorporate full stops and possibly spaces. Does *A.L.A.* file near the head of the sequence of As or somewhere between *Al Capone* and *Alabama*? What if it is written *A. L. A.*? Or *A L A*? Or *ALA*?

Subject headings beginning with the same word may be interfiled in different ways according to the filing value given to inverted headings, phrase headings and subdivided headings. Frequently the filing value accorded to a subdivided heading (where the punctuation is a dash) may be different from that for inverted headings (which use commas), which may lead to deviations from the strict and most obvious alphabetical sequence. Where certain symbols have a filing value, they introduce a classified element into an alphabetical file (see Figure 11.4).

'As if' and 'File as is' filing

Some kinds of character string may file otherwise than as given. Filing rules designed with automated filing in mind tend to minimize the amount of 'as if' filing, and to file as given in most cases. Examples include:

- abbreviations, particularly of terms of address; for example, *Dr* and *St* filing as *Doctor* and *Saint*

- ampersands (&) may file as they stand – an ampersand generally files before numbers and letters. 'As if' filing would have to translate & as *and*, *et*, *und*, etc., according to the language of the document
- diacriticals: should *Müller* file as *Muller* or *Mueller*? Also ligatures: does *Æthelred* file under E or A? 'As if' filing uses the first, 'As is' the second, in each case.
- numbers: should Arabic numbers file as numbers, in a sequence preceding letters? In an ordinal sequence, or as characters? Should roman numbers file as numbers or as letters? And if as letters, how will this affect the filing of headings like Pius VIII, *pope* and Pius IX, *pope*? How should more complicated numbers, or strings containing numbers and other characters (such as $50, 1/10, 3rd, πr^2, 0.5), file?
- Scottish and Irish names beginning with Mac and variants: filing rules of British origin often interfile Scottish and Irish names beginning with Mac, Mc and M'.

Many of the problems touched on here are illustrated in Figures 11.4, 11.5 and 11.6, which have been adapted from the National Library of Australia's ABN Cataloguing Manual, September 1990 (URL: <widow.nla.gov.au/2/abn/catman.html>).

COOKERY	*Word(s) alone*
COOKERY, AFRICAN	*Word(s) followed by a comma and qualifying word*
COOKERY, CHINESE	
COOKERY (APPLES)	*Word(s) followed by parenthetical qualifier*
COOKERY (MEAT)	
COOKERY FOR ALLERGICS	*Word phrases*

In any subject heading, subdivisions (subordinate elements following a double or em dash) are grouped in the following order:

ART—19th CENTURY	*Period subdivision*
ART—20th CENTURY	
ART—BIBLIOGRAPHY	*Form and topical subdivision*
ART—PHILOSOPHY	
ART—AFRICA, WEST	*Geographical subdivision*
ART—NEW YORK (CITY)	

The following example provides a comprehensive illustration of filing:

COOKERY	*Word(s) alone*
COOKERY—1965	*Word(s) alone, period subdivision*
COOKERY—BIBLIOGRAPHY	*Word(s) alone, form/topical subdivision*
COOKERY—HISTORY	

COOKERY, AMERICAN—BIBLIOGRAPHY	*Word(s), comma, word and word with form/topical subdivision*
COOKERY, AMERICAN—MARYLAND	*Word(s), comma, word and geographical subdivision*
COOKERY, INTERNATIONAL	*Word(s) followed by a comma and word*
COOKERY (BABY FOODS)	*Word(s) followed by parenthetical qualifier*
COOKERY (MEAT)	
COOKERY FOR ALLERGICS	*Phrase beginning with word in above subject heading*

Figure 11.4 Filing values of subject headings

Czolowski, Ted
D., H.   *(D is a word)*
Da Costa, Beverly   *(Da is a word)*
Da Ponte, Lorenzo, 1749–1838
Dabbs, James McBridge, 1896–1970
De George, Richard T.
De Young Memorial Museum
De, Kay L.
DeArmond, Frederick Francis, 1893–
Maass, John, 1918–
MacArthur, Robert H.
Madden, David, 1933–
Mazzeo, Henry
McAllester, Susan
McWilliams, Margaret
Mead, Cary Hoge, 1897–
Segal, Lore Groszmann
Segal (Martin E.) *(Firm) see* Martin E. Segal and Company, Inc.
Segal, Sydney
Washington, Jim
Washington
Washington (*State*). *Attorney General's Office*
Washington (*Territory*). *Governor*
Washington/Alaska Regional Medical Program
Washington and Lee University
Washington Association of Soil and Water Conservation Districts
Washington Metcalfe, Thomas
Washington Sea Grant Program
Washington State Association of Counties

Figure 11.5 Comprehensive punctuation and filing in the author index

Non-filing elements

Many headings include an additional non-filing element. Most commonly, definite and indefinite articles (*The, A, An*) at the beginning of titles are ignored. Some computer filing algorithms incorporate in their sort procedures a routine for

1, one dancing drum	('1' is a word and files before all titles beginning with the letter A)
2rabbit, 7wind	
1100 words you need to know	
The 1971 deer population	
8,000 stones	
The AAAS science book list for children	('AAAS' is a word)
The abacus	
ABCs of tape recording	
Able seaman, deckhand, cowman	
The advertising man	('The' at the beginning of a title is disregarded for filing purposes)
AEIHover policy studies	('AEI' is a word)
The Aeneid of Virgil	
Cyrano de Bergerac	
D. B. Kabalevsky's Joey the clown	('D. B.' files as 'D B', as if 'D' and 'B' were separate words)
D. W. Griffith: his life and work	
Daddyji	
Do you remember England?	
Doctor Spock	
Doctoral students in schools of social work	
Down's syndrome	('Down's' files as 'Downs')
Dr. Sam: an American tragedy	('Dr.' files as 'Dr')
Dracula	
Encyclopedia directory of ethnic newspapers and periodicals in the United States	
An end and a beginning	('An' at the beginning of a title is disregarded for filing purposes)
The end of nowhere	
Enemies	
Epidemiology as medical ecology	
EQMM annual	('EQMM' is a word)
Equal justice	
I, Pig	
I. Q. in the meritocracy	('I. Q.' files as 'I Q', as if 'I' and 'Q' were separate words)
I remember it well	
II VI semiconducting	('II' files as alphabet letters)
The IU cult ('IU' is a word)	
Ira sleeps over	
Once upon a Christmas	
One acre and security	('One' files alphabetically)
The two worlds of Jim Yoshida	
The U.N. Convention on the elimination . . .	('U.N.' files as 'U N', as if 'U' and 'N' were separate words)
U.S.A. and the Soviet Myth	
U.S. Foreign economic policy and the domestic economy	
The UFO experience	('UFO' is a word)
The underwater war	
UNESCO collection of representative works	
The unforgotten	
United Nations peacekeeping operations	
The United States, 1492–1877	

Figure 11.6   Comprehensive punctuation and filing in the title index

automatically ignoring initial articles – or more precisely, title strings beginning with A An or The. This is satisfactory provided all the titles are in the same language, though even here there could be the occasional misfit of the type *A Apple pie*. Another non-filing element commonly met is *Sir* and similar terms. in British titles of honour of the type: Reynolds, *Sir* Joshua.

Different types of headings beginning with the same word

Headings may arise as author, title and subject, and all types of headings may commence with the same word. 'Black', 'Rose', 'London' are all words that could be part of author, title or subject headings. The problem is whether to adopt a strict alphabetical sequence or whether the user would find it helpful to have entries of the same type grouped together.

Arrangement of entries under the same heading

A prolific author may be responsible for a number of books, or a subject heading may be assigned to several books that discuss the same subject. The preferred sequence for multiple entries under the same heading or term needs to be established. First, it is normal to distinguish between references and added entries, and then to group references at the beginning of the sequence associated with a given term or heading. Next, it is necessary to order the works for which entries are made under a specific subject or author heading. Often the title is used for this purpose but sometimes chronological order may be preferred.

SUMMARY

The rapid growth of the World Wide Web has introduced an expectation of one-stop shopping in relation to information retrieval, and has led to a growing attitude that any information that cannot be located electronically is not worth searching for at all. This is an unsound attitude, for a number of reasons. First, there are many parts of the world where the infrastructure to support machine-based systems is inadequate or lacking. Even in developed areas there may be power failures or system downtime. Secondly, many information resources are still only available in hard copy. Many of these are very specialized, either because they appeal to a small clientele or because they extend a long way back in time (which amounts to much the same thing). In other contexts such as book indexes, or indexes to other printed documents, printed indexes are likely to persist for as long as the documents themselves are created and used in print form. Accordingly, this chapter has visited some of the important themes associated with document arrangement, and the nature and development of printed and card catalogues and printed indexes. Book indexes (e-books excepted) remain in printed form, and deserve specific attention. Finally, the chapter explored the issue of filing orders. Superficially straightforward, filing sequences are in fact extremely complex, and whilst in digital environments both information professionals and users are less exposed to the headache of esoteric filing sequences, filing sequences remain important in a number of contexts.

REVIEW QUESTIONS

1. Outline some of the alternative approaches to document arrangement. Why is document arrangement important?
2. Describe the different types of printed catalogues.
3. What is the difference between a *see* and a *see also* reference in a printed index or catalogue? How do references differ from entries?
4. Explain why in a 'digital age' there remains a place for printed indexes.
5. Compare and contrast keyword indexes with indexes based on string manipulation.
6. Make a checklist of the key points that a searcher needs to remember when using a printed index.
7. What are the purposes of a book index? Indicate some of the key decisions that a book indexer needs to make.
8. Explain, with examples, the difference between word-by-word and letter-by-letter filing.
9. Discuss the issues associated with establishing filing sequences for subject headings, and names of persons and corporate bodies.
10. Summarize why it is necessary to consider filing sequences in a digital age.

REFERENCES AND FURTHER READING

American Library Association, RTSD Filing Committee (1980) *ALA Filing Rules*. Chicago: ALA.

British Standard Institution (1985) *British Standard Recommendation for Alphabetical Arrangement and the Filing Order of Numbers and Symbols*. BS 1749: 1985. London: British Standard Institution.

British Standard Institution (1988) *British Standard Recommendation for Preparing Indexes to Books, Periodicals and Other Documents*. BS 3700: 1988. London: British Standard Institution.

Cleveland, D.B. and Cleveland, A. (1990) *Introduction to Indexing and Abstracting*, 2nd edn. Littleton CO: Libraries Unlimited.

Foskett, A.C. (1996) *The Subject Approach to Information*. London: Library Association.

Knight, G.N. (1979) *Indexing, the Art of*. London: Allen & Unwin.

Lancaster, F.W. (2003) *Indexing and Abstracting in Theory and Practice*. London: Facet.

Mulvany, N.C. (2005) *Indexing Books*, 2nd edn. Chicago IL: University of Chicago Press.

Stauber, D.M. (2004) *Facing the Text: Content and structure in book indexing*. Eugene OR: Cedar Row.

University of Chicago Press Staff (2003) *Indexes: A chapter from 'The Chicago Manual of Style'*. Chicago IL: University of Chicago Press.

Wellisch, H. (1991) *Indexing from A to Z*. New York: H.W. Wilson.

12 Management of knowledge systems

INTRODUCTION

The earlier chapters in this book, with the exception of Chapter 9, have tended to focus on the micro-level of the organization of knowledge, concerning themselves with databases, records and, in particular, the wide range of different types of metadata that are used in the organization of knowledge. Access to digital resources is dependent not only on how those resources are organized, or even on the usability of the user interface, but also on the information systems that store and provide access to the databases that contain knowledge. This chapter, then, draws together a number of systems management themes that are relevant in a wide variety of the different types of systems (as outlined in Chapter 9) that facilitate the organization of and access to knowledge. At the end of this chapter you will:

- understand the need to update controlled indexing languages and maintain authority control records
- be aware of systems management issues, including maintenance, security and user support
- have considered the evolving nature of information systems, including the processes associated with systems analysis and design and managing people in change
- be aware of knowledge networks, and the relationships between organizations in the information and knowledge industry.

Some of these themes are considered in greater detail in texts on business information systems. The most important message embedded in this chapter is that systems for the organization of knowledge are dynamic. Users, information professionals and others involved with the design and maintenance of such systems are at the frontiers of the significant changes associated with the development of knowledge societies and economies. They have no choice but to proactively engage with and manage the change in knowledge and information systems.

MAINTAINING AUTHORITY CONTROL AND UPDATING CONTROLLED INDEXING LANGUAGES

All databases or other knowledge repositories need to be kept up to date; in other words, new information needs to be added. There are three different kinds of amendments that can be made to a database:

1. addition of new records
2. amendment of existing records
3. deletion of existing records.

Bibliographic databases are updated primarily by adding new records to the established collection of records. Catalogue databases may be updated by adding new records to correspond to additions to stock but, also, amendments may be made to existing records to accommodate, for example, the relocation of a document or the removal of documents from the collection. Other databases, such as directory databases, are primarily updated with corrections to existing records, such as changes of address, or amendments to an entry to reflect the latest social or technological developments.

AUTHORITY CONTROL

A key issue in updating bibliographic records is authority control – the concern for maintenance and application of standard access points or index terms. Authority control consists of the creation of authority records for established headings, the linking of authority and bibliographic records, and the maintenance and evaluation of an authority system. Such control can be exercised locally or within a regional or international network.

Three kinds of authority control can be maintained: for names (of persons, corporate bodies and places), for subjects and for classification.

Name authority control

This has three purposes:

- to ensure that works by an author are entered under a uniform heading
- to ensure that each heading is unique; that is, to prevent works by more than one author from being entered under the same heading (in other words, to manage the collocative function of the catalogue)
- to save having to establish the heading every time a work is catalogued.

342

Name authority covers more than names of authors (personal or corporate); it also includes geographical names and lists of artist names (see <http://www. getty.edu/research/conducting_research/vocabularies/> for an example of each).

When a personal or corporate name or place name is used for the first time, a *name authority record* is made, using AACR guidance in determination of the appropriate heading. Normally the name authority file is linked to the bibliographic file so that names associated with new documents are checked as they are entered. If a heading is not on file close matches are displayed and on this basis the cataloguer can proceed to create a new heading, and enter that heading in the name authority file. Authority control may also be exercised on other fields of the record, such as names of publishers. As with terms in thesauri discussed in Chapter 5, authority lists may be made available to support searching on personal, corporate and place names.

Subject authority control

This exists to ensure that subject headings, and their references, are applied uniformly and consistently. A *subject authority record* is made whenever a new subject heading is established. The type of subject authority control depends on the context and the subject access system in place. There is a fine dividing line between:

- updating a dynamic controlled indexing language such as a thesaurus or an ontology, as discussed below, and
- updating the record of the terms that have been used for indexing in a specific database.

In relation to LCSH, for example, headings that are in use may be synthesized by the use of subdivisions that do not specifically appear in the list, or that may be personal, corporate or geographic names which are excluded from the list. These headings are published by the Library of Congress and are available in a variety of formats. On the other hand, in dynamic ontologies the use of the term may automatically provoke the updating of the 'authority list' of the language.

UPDATING CONTROLLED INDEXING LANGUAGES

Thesauri, classification schemes and lists of subject headings need to be kept up to date. New subjects emerge and need to be represented within the scheme. The key issues in the maintenance of such lists are:

- the identification of new subjects, as they arise in the literature to be indexed
- a process for agreeing on the notation or terms that are to be used to represent those new subjects

- the identification of relationships between new subjects and existing subjects
- processes for recording both new subjects and their relationships with other terms
- processes for notifying all indexers using the scheme of the modification
- processes for ensuring that searchers have access to an up-to-date version of the controlled indexing language.

When a controlled indexing language is used only to index one database or document, it is relatively straightforward, especially with the aid of special software for thesaurus maintenance, to maintain a current version of a thesaurus, to which all indexers may have access. On the other hand, for the large classification schemes, such as the Dewey Decimal Classification, or subject headings lists such as the Library of Congress Subject Headings list, agreement on new terms may require elaborate and extensive consultation. Indexers all around the world may need to be notified of changes, and changes could have a potential impact on many libraries, search intermediaries and end-users. In the context of subject terms and classification codes two issues cause complexities:

1. As well as the addition of a term, it is necessary to ensure that all relationships between that term and earlier and related terms have been adequately indicated. Significant new areas of knowledge may require new sections in classification schemes, or a collection of new related terms in a subject headings list or thesaurus.
2. Many subject terms and classification codes are drawn from published lists or schemes, and revision requires agreement on the introduction of such terms. This agreement may inject a delay in the updating of the lists or schemes. The issue of revision for classification schemes has been explored further in Chapter 6.

Reclassification may involve a once-and-for-all migration to a different classification scheme, or the routine updating of the existing scheme. Changes affecting the physical distribution of stock in a library may involve significant effort and disruption to the library's normal operation. The components of this exercise are as follows:

- retrieve documents
- retrieve records
- amend class mark on document and record
- re-file documents
- re-file records.

Measures which may be taken to reduce the disruption include the following:

- rolling reclassification – separate classes are reclassified one by one over a period of time

- reclassification by osmosis – new accessions only are classified by the new system: existing stock is gradually weeded out, leaving only a small nucleus of old stock to be reclassified.

MANAGING SYSTEMS FOR KNOWLEDGE ORGANIZATION

The hardware and software platforms that support access to knowledge need to be managed and users need to be supported in their access to such systems. Typically, this involves attention to day-to-day maintenance issues and system integrity, security and user support.

SYSTEM MAINTENANCE

System maintenance is concerned with keeping the hardware and software working. This involves:

- Monitoring the quality and integrity of databases, from a more technical perspective than outlined above. In other words, it is important that all of the most recent version of the database is available to those users who are authorized for access.
- Dealing with any hardware or software malfunctions, such as faulty workstations or software bugs.
- Making sure adequate backups of databases are taken.
- Troubleshooting any situations where the system does not work as it might and, in general, having and being able to implement contingency plans in a crisis.
- Implementing upgrades of software and hardware to existing systems. This might include the installation of new workstations or further developments to an existing network. Upgrades to software may offer new features and facilities; users need to be informed of any changes that affect their interaction with the system.
- Liaison with hardware and software suppliers, in relation to both new and future developments.

SECURITY

The other side of access to information is security. Proper attention to information security ensures:

- *availability* – all users have access to the databases and functions for which they are authorized

345

- *confidentiality* – no users have access to databases and functions for which they are not authorized
- *authenticity and integrity* – the accuracy of information is maintained.

Loss of security occurs from both accidental and deliberate threats. Accidental threats arise from poor system features such as overloaded networks or software malfunction. Deliberate threats arise from human intent, and include theft, computer fraud, vandalism and other attempts to break the system. Typically such threats may lead to:

- the interruption of data preparation and data input
- the destruction or corruption of stored data
- the destruction or corruption of software
- the disclosure of personal or proprietary information
- injury to personnel
- removal of equipment or information.

Design of security for a system involves risk analysis. Organizations need to be aware of the information assets that they are seeking to protect, and their value. A threat assessment identifies the threats to information security, and an impact assessment establishes the implications for the organization of information assets being compromised (such as breach of confidentiality or licence breach). On the basis of these assessments, the organization can develop an appropriate level of security controls, counter-measures to minimize any risk, and a disaster recovery plan that prioritizes information assets and processes in the event of something going wrong.

Conventional notions of security assume organizational ownership of systems and databases, and control over the roles exercised by specific individuals. The Internet has been described as the 'Wild West', in which rules and controls that can be effectively exercised in other systems contexts do not apply, and even where there is an identified owner of a database considerable efforts need to be exercised in order to ensure its integrity. Security and control of collaborative 'open' information resources such as wikis raise a range of ethical, policy and practical complexities around security, threats, risks and disaster recovery. Essentially, the more open the access, the more complex the security issues become.

Acceptable use policies that specify rules for using information systems and networks from a user perspective are particularly useful in many information organizations. These may cover users' responsibilities in relation to accounts and passwords, identify allowable and unacceptable use of the system, and reiterate any legal obligations.

Security is a particular challenge in systems where the users are not members of the staff of a specific organization. Libraries, online search services and publishers will want to implement security that is linked to the licensing arrangements that have been contracted with organizations or individual users. Security issues in this context cover everything from the security of items in the library's collections, to privacy concerning user information. As a quick checklist, some of the issues are:

- authentication of the user, so that users can only access their own accounts
- security of hardware, to avoid theft or vandalism
- prevention of hacking into networks, leading to access to other databases that should not be publicly accessible
- data privacy, concerning user information
- item identifiers, and ensuring that these are unique
- building design, to increase hardware and user security
- education to ensure that staff and users are security-conscious
- the design and use of processes to avoid security breaches.

Systems often facilitate user access to the databases of publishers or aggregators, as well as library resources in a number of libraries and document collections. The systems must tackle issues concerning liability, control of copyright, licensing and collecting of appropriate payments. Such systems may also need to accommodate the assessment and evaluation of resources by those involved in a decision-making process about their purchase.

Systems need to be able to manage who is allowed access to what, when, for how long or to what maximum charge, payment strategy and associated rights. They need to manage copyright issues as an integral function, and will need to be linked to the systems of publishers, editors, indexers, picture libraries and authors.

Security is increasingly being linked to charging, and needs even more attention as we move into the realm of transactions and payment. Providing access to the wealth of Internet resources is expensive; smartcards that record customers' transactions may be used to support charging, and can also act as the security device for access to a range of organizational and external information resources.

USER SUPPORT

This is concerned with ensuring that all potential users of a system can make effective use of that system. Support will be offered through one or more of the following:

- *Interface design* – a well-designed web page embeds implicit support. Appropriate labels in menus and good icon design, coupled with different

347

interfaces for quick search and advanced search, can do much to make the search process intuitive.

- *Printed documentation* – lists of key operations, commands and menu options are particularly helpful in print format. In addition the extensive manuals associated with some online systems are more easily perused on paper.
- *Help systems* – online help systems using, for instance, frequently asked questions (FAQs) and contextual help are common. Often, different levels of detail and approaches to help text style and contexts are available to support basic and advanced search options.
- *Training* – through courses, seminars and one-to-one hands-on sessions. Users of library systems fall into two categories: staff and library users. User training for staff can proceed as with many other systems, although, due to the exigencies of other duties, much training may need to be conducted on a one-to-one basis. Training for library users is much more difficult to achieve in many libraries. The position is better in academic and organizational libraries than in public libraries, but there is always some fluidity of clientele and, generally, a lack of interest in systematic training.
- *Help desks* and other in-person support – available either remotely or at the location where the user is likely to perform the search. These are particularly valuable for problem solving, troubleshooting and supporting the new user.

EVOLVING AND MIGRATING SYSTEMS

Over the past 20 years technological developments have led to many changes in system platforms. Changing the platform on which a database is mounted, or which provides user access to information or knowledge, is a significant project which will affect both operations as conducted by information professional staff and the services available to, and accessed by, users. It is therefore important that the transition from one system to another be managed effectively and efficiently. There are two perspectives on such a transition; those offered by:

1. information systems development
2. strategies for the management of change.

INFORMATION SYSTEMS DEVELOPMENT

Information systems are almost always under development, although major changes which may involve new technology, and/or significant changes to functionality working practices or user service, are often managed as specific projects. Such systems development projects are undertaken through the process of systems analysis and design, which is often guided by an information systems methodology. Such a methodology provides a clear structure to a systems analysis and design project, providing recommendations about:

- phases, sub-phases and tasks
- when to use which and their sequence
- what sort of people should perform each task
- what documents, products, and reports should result from each phase
- the management, control, evaluation and planning of developments.

Such methodologies use:

- computer-aided software engineering (CASE) tools to support the necessary drawing of diagrams, and the logical design of the system
- diagrams, such as hierarchy charts, data-flow diagrams, data dictionaries, entity life histories and entity relationship diagrams, to assist in the design of the software and information architectures for the system.

Information system methodologies have been developed by systems developers and designers as tools to aid in modelling information systems and designing computer-based systems that meet the requirements of the user of the information. The adoption of a systematic approach to information systems development offers a number of advantages; namely:

- control over planning, since progress can be charted, and financial allocations can be predicted
- standardized documentation which assists in communication throughout the system's planning and life
- continuity, provided as a contingency against key members of staff leaving the systems staff.

Many of the early information systems methodologies were based on the waterfall model of systems development which has the following stages:

- initiation
- analysis
- design
- development
- implementation
- maintenance.

More details of each of these stages are shown in Figure 12.1. The waterfall model assumes a linear project path from the definition of objectives, through design and programming to implementation and maintenance. This model will not fit all situations, and the emphasis of different stages may vary even where they are all relevant, but the model offers a useful checklist of the actions that are involved in a systems development project.

There are also a number of other approaches to information systems development which may be used alone or embedded in a larger project based on the waterfall model. These include:

- *Prototyping* – in which a demonstration system is built from users' initial requirements specification; this is used to gather further user feedback; and an iterative process of prototype building and user feedback continues until an acceptable system emerges. Rapid applications development (RAD) is a type of prototyping in which interactive tools for developing the user interface speed up the development process.
- *Application software packages* – where commercially available software, such as word-processing software, a library management system or a search engine technology, is acquired and integrated into the organization's systems.
- *End-user development* – in which end-users are provided with the tools and technical support to develop their own systems; the advantage of this approach is that the end-users have clear ideas of what they want the system to do.
- *Object-orientated development* – where the key issues are the identification and classification of objects and the relationships between classes of objects. Object orientation is based on re-usable components, and it is therefore easier to manage systems under continual evolution. The Unified Modelling Language (UML) was developed to provide a common approach for modelling object-oriented systems. UML describes systems in terms of a range of object-oriented diagrams. Two examples of such diagrams are use case diagrams and class responsibility collaborator (CRC) cards.

STRATEGIES FOR THE MANAGEMENT OF CHANGE – PROJECT MANAGEMENT

Far too few systems projects are delivered on time and to budget. Accordingly, there has been an increasing emphasis on the use of project methodologies in systems development, alongside the information systems methodology. Project management is concerned with the planning, scheduling and controlling of those activities that must be performed to achieve project objectives. Project management involves:

- putting in place an effective temporary organization to implement, manage, control and direct the project
- planning activities so that outputs are produced to the required quality, on schedule and within budget
- managing risk to ensure that opportunities and benefits are fully evaluated

- managing benefits to make sure that the investment makes an optimum contribution to improved performance
- controlling the project to make sure that the right resources are committed at the right place and right time
- bringing together the main interest groups and encouraging their participation.

The project management process involves:

- *estimation* – identifying the work and activities needed

Development stage	Purpose	Inputs	Process	Output
Initiation Why and how is the system to be developed?	Start-up phase	Business case for the system	Assess feasibility Project planning	Feasibility analysis Project plan Decision to proceed
Analysis What should the system do?	Define requirements of the organization and system users	Business case and requirements from users	Determine requirements from users and documentation	Requirements document Test plan Decision to proceed
Design How will the system deliver requirements?	Specify how the system will be delivered	Requirements document	Evaluation of design options for creating and integration of systems components	Design document for information architecture, software process and system architecture Decision to proceed
Development Programming and configuring the system	Implement the design	Design document	Bespoke solutions: programming system. Off-the-shelf or tailored systems: configuration of input to and outputs from the system or integration of different systems components	The different physical components of the system Deployment plan Decision to proceed

Implementation Installing and testing the system Changeover from old to new system	System deployed into the organization	Systems component Test plan	Migrating data, testing the system and managing the changeover to the live system	Live system signed off by business as satisfactory, meeting the user's and business requirements Project close-down report Decision to proceed
Maintenance Monitoring and revising the system	To keep the system running smoothly and to enhance it	Signed-off system	Monitoring the system and enhancing it as problems and opportunities arise	Upgrades or patches to the system

Figure 12.1 Summary of stages in systems analysis and design

- *resource allocation* – identifying who has the skills to do the work and complete it
- *scheduling* – planning which tasks are to be completed when
- *budgeting* – managing and controlling project costs and expenditure
- *monitoring and control* – ensuring that the project is progressing and that each stage is completed to schedule.

MANAGING PEOPLE IN CHANGE

The discussion in the previous sections, whilst making the occasional reference to the participation and consultation of system users, is rather focused on changing the systems. All changes in technology mean changes for users, whether they be in 'customer', 'client' or 'employee' roles. Changing technology is not the only factor that leads to changes in systems development. Changes in organizational structures, marketplace, product and service ranges, legal requirements and user expectations and behaviour are just a few of the factors that may lead to the need for changes in information systems. The literature on the management of change recognizes that change will only be successful if people as well as systems change. Information systems are often at the forefront of change within organizations as we move towards a knowledge-based society. For many systems, user change occurs by gradual evolution punctuated by occasional incremental change.

Employees, and other users, must feel able to adjust to systems change if they are to continue to create and use the databases upon which the organization of knowledge depends.

Users may find change inconvenient and it may not suit their interests. Systems change means learning a new system, and may also affect job security, job role and work relationships. This means that in the change management literature there is much discussion about 'resistance to change'. Individuals resist change if they perceive change to be damaging or threatening to themselves. These perceptions may arise from:

- parochial self-interest – in which an individual is 'protecting their corner'
- misunderstanding of the nature of change and lack of trust as to the consequences for another individual
- individuals' varying assessments of the impact of change for them, relative to the assessment that a system professional is making
- low tolerance for change.

There are six well-known techniques for managing resistance to change:

- *Education and commitment* – if those affected by change understand the benefits for them, and feel confident that they can use the new system without difficulty, this can reduce resistance.
- *Participation and involvement* – involvement in planning and implementation change, say through engagement in a prototyping exercise, not only enhances system fit, but also encourages commitment.
- *Facilitation and support* – sometimes users with new systems need support and coaching in the use of the new system, to carry them through any initial resistance.
- *Negotiation and agreement* – particularly with users who are employees, negotiation and agreement may lead to a system that may not be technically superior, but which accommodates the perspectives of strong interest groups and is therefore accepted.
- *Manipulation* – in which proposals are offered that deliberately appeal to certain interest groups in order to get the system accepted.
- *Implicit and explicit coercion* – this approach to the management of resistance may be the only option. Within an organization this might involve management being directive and countering any resistance by taking actions that benefit those who do not resist.

In general there is an acknowledgement that participative change management is effective in ensuring buy-in, as well as being able to capitalize on the expertise of users. On the other hand, this can sometimes be very time-consuming, delaying a systems development project. Where it is difficult to reach an agreement another approach may be adopted. Many information retrieval systems have two levels of users – information professionals and end-users. The change management approach for these two groups may be very different. Much more consultation is likely to take place with the expert users, the information professionals, and rather less with end-users. It is therefore important that the interests of end-users are not overlooked.

In relation to end-users, the notion of adoption has been popular. Users or consumers have the choice as to whether they use, say, the Internet to learn, gather information or engage in transactions. So, typically, the acceptance of any new system can be profiled by an adoption curve which shows the percentage of the potential user population that has adopted the new system at any point in time. This gradual adoption process is further modelled by the technology acceptance adoption model (TAM).

KNOWLEDGE NETWORKS

The organization of knowledge is achieved through the activities of various information professionals, such as cataloguers, indexers, knowledge workers and others. These individuals are usually employed by organizations such as libraries, library consortia, abstracting and indexing services, publishers and Internet search engine providers. Libraries in particular have a long history of collaboration in their efforts to organize knowledge in order to preserve and develop the cultural heritage of our society. In general, the Internet offers an infrastructure which supports a wide range of different types of document and information exchange. While these exchanges could be performed on an ad hoc basis, they are usually facilitated by the development of a range of relationships, otherwise described as a network. Such networks may comprise users, libraries, national libraries, publishers and a range of other agencies in the information industry. These relationships may be the basis for exchange of, or provision of, access to a range of databases and document types. Figure 12.2 summarizes the key relationship types.

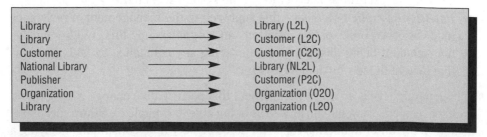

Figure 12.2   Relationship types in knowledge networks

The ultimate aim of most networking is to make documents, information or knowledge accessible to the end-user. However, there may be a number of other relationships in the supply chain which supports this end-user delivery, including (in particular) those roles concerned with document creation. Figure 12.3, for example, is a summary of the roles in document creation and delivery, and identifies some of the organizations and individuals that might adopt these roles in the digital information marketplace. It is perhaps particularly significant that some organizations and professional groups may be involved in a number of these stages or, to put it another way, may control several stages in the supply chain. In addition, the shift from print documents to electronic journals and e-books, alongside competing 'free' information available on the Web, is challenging the business viability of many of the actors who currently fulfil many of these roles. For example, journal publishers' earlier business models were based on revenue from subscriptions, most of which were with libraries. Libraries are now purchasing many of their journals under licence agreements, and competition amongst publishers is intense. Newspaper publishers face a similar challenge, with circulations falling due to news being available through a range of other channels; it is difficult for newspaper publishers to compete with news delivered over the Web to people's desks. The future security and role of specific actors in the knowledge marketplace may change, causing shifts in network relationships, but the essential roles identified in Figure 12.3 will persist.

Librarians have long engaged in cooperative ventures, or networks and consortia. The early objectives of these networks were associated with exchange

Role	Examples
Producer of intellectual content	Authors, illustrators, multimedia creation teams
Controller of intellectual content, with reference to quality standards and suitability	Editors, referees, reviewers
Publisher – establishes a corporate brand image and acts as an interface between producer of intellectual content and distributor	Publishers, printers, database producers, ISPs
Distributor – ensures that the document/ information reaches the potential customers and engages in appropriate promotion	Subscription and supply agents, booksellers, search engines, portals and subject gateways, online search services, aggregators, publishers
Archiver – maintains archival copy for later retrieval	Libraries, private collectors
Re-distributor – makes documents or information available to others, copying for students	Libraries, educational institutions, information consultants
User	Corporate and individual users

Figure 12.3   Stakeholder roles in the digital information marketplace

of catalogue records and print-based document delivery or interlibrary loan. These functions still remain important, but they are now facilitated by electronic exchange and keeping of records. Often, print document delivery has been supplemented by electronic document delivery.

Groups of libraries have maintained union catalogues for many years. The earliest union catalogues were large card catalogues whose creation was a labour of love and which were very difficult to keep up to date. Similarly, interlibrary loan arrangements existed between libraries long before computer-based systems and data networks. However, under these arrangements, interlibrary loan was often a slow process. Cooperation is generally seen as a means of sharing resources or containing cataloguing costs. In recent years, networks have increasingly made use of telecommunication networks and computer systems. The first computer-based cooperative ventures, while ambitious for their time, would seem very basic now. Batch systems, with too much paper, little connectivity between processors and limited online access, pre-dated the much more streamlined systems that we find easy to take for granted today. Systems have undergone major development since the late 1960s and early 1970s. Nevertheless, the central objectives of networking remain constant. These are to:

- reveal the contents of a large number of libraries or a large number of publications, especially through accessibility of catalogue databases, using OPAC interfaces
- make the resources shown in these catalogue databases available to individual libraries and users when and where they need them
- share the expense and work involved in creating catalogue databases through the exchange of records and associated activities.

Ancillary functions that might also be fulfilled by networks include:

- distribution and publication of electronic journals and other electronic documents
- end-user access to other databases, such as those available via the online search services
- value-added services such as electronic mail, directory services and file transfer
- exchange of bibliographic and authority records, usually in MARC format.

In the beginning, networks were established with limited and well-defined objectives. As the use of networking has become more pervasive and as the infrastructure has become available which makes data transfer more common, consortia and their participants are likely to be linked to each other. The end-user can choose more than one route through the maze of networks in order to locate a given document. Barriers are already less defined by the physical limitations of networks than by licensing and access arrangements. Technology imposes fewer constraints, but politics and economics remain powerful influences on network membership.

Two important categories of hubs in the networks of knowledge organizations are:

1. Large national libraries or centralized cataloguing services which create large bibliographic databases and, in some instances, provide leadership in document delivery; for example, the Library of Congress, the British Library and the National Library of Australia.

2. Cooperatives set up by groups of libraries who feel that they and their users can profit by resource sharing, such as might be associated with interlibrary loans and document delivery, and sharing in the creation of a union catalogue database; for example, the Research Libraries Group (RLG), the Consortium of University Research Libraries (CURL), London and South-East Region Libraries (LASER) and UTLAS International (University of Toronto Library Automated Systems). Many of these organizations are now independent businesses with a range of business relationships with other knowledge organizations. Figure 12.4 summarizes the service offered by OCLC, and thereby illustrates the diverse roles of some of these organizations.

SUMMARY

This chapter has explored a number of issues associated with the management of systems for the organization of knowledge and information retrieval. Authority control over the form of names and subject terms helps to instil consistency into

- *Cataloging and metadata* – Cataloguing service including: full service online cataloguing, simple copy cataloguing, MARC record collections, offline cataloguing, customized OCLC cataloging, automated copy cataloging. The administration of the Dewey Decimal Classification.
- *Collection management*, including collection development services, targeted collection analysis tools, and shelf-ready collections of non-English materials.
- *Digitization and preservation*, including digitization, microfilm and archival services, support for managing special collections, access to skilled preservation centre staff.
- *E-content*, including e-books from NetLibrary, e-audiobooks from NetLibrary and recorded books, full-text e-journals, a variety of online reference databases.
- *Reference*, including FirstSearch, which offers online access to full-text documents, abstract and indices, and WorldCat, a powerful bibliographic database, and a virtual reference service (in partnership with the Library of Congress).
- *Resource sharing*, including the creation, sending and tracking of interlibrary loan requests with WorldCat Resource Sharing, ILLiad and ILL management system.

Figure 12.4   A list of OCLC services
Source: based on <www.oclc.org/services> [accessed 4 October 2006]

the database, and thereby assists with database quality. Controlled indexing languages need to evolve and be updated. Other issues in the management of systems include maintenance, security and user support. Systems are dynamic; the evolution of systems needs to be managed. Information systems methodologies and other approaches to the management of change can assist in this context. There are many organizations that are involved in the organization of knowledge. Significant among these are the national libraries and the library consortia or networks, which make a significant contribution to the sharing of resources. They also share the work associated with the compilation of databases that are an essential prerequisite for full access to the resources which can be accessed through a number of different libraries and other information providers.

REVIEW QUESTIONS

1. What is authority control and why is it important?
2. Why is it necessary to update controlled indexing languages? What are the key issues in the maintenance of such tools?
3. What are the key issues in the maintenance of information systems?
4. Discuss the challenges associated with maintaining the availability, confidentiality, authenticity and integrity of digital information resources.
5. What are the different options open to information organizations for the provision of support to information users?
6. Discuss the notions of an information systems methodology. In what way is project management relevant to information systems development?
7. Why, when systems change, is it necessary to manage people through change? What are some of the approaches that can be adopted in this process?
8. Explain the different roles that different parties play in the digital information marketplace.
9. What role do knowledge networks and library networks play?

REFERENCES AND FURTHER READING

Angelis, G., Gritzalis, S. and Lambrinoudakis, C. (2004) Mechanisms for controlling access in the global grid environment. *Internet Research*, **14** (5), 347–52.

Buchanan, D. and Huczynski, A. (2004) *Organizational Behaviour*, 5th edn. Harlow: Prentice Hall.

Chaffey, D. and Wood, S. (2005) *Business Information Management: Improving performance using information systems*. Harlow: FT Prentice Hall.

Curtis, G. and Cobham, D. (2005) *Business Information Systems: Analysis, design and practice*. Harlow: FT Prentice Hall.

Evans, G.E. (2002) Management issues of consortia. Part 2. *Library Management*, **23** (6/7), 275–86.

Hudomalj, E. and Jauk, A. (2006) Authentication and authorization infrastructure of the mobility of users of academic libraries: an overview of developments. *Program*, **40** (1), 63–73.

Hughes, M. (2006) *Change Management: A critical perspective*. London: CIPD.

Malhan, I.V. (2006) Developing corporate culture in the Indian university libraries: problems and challenges of change management. *Library Management*, **27** (6/7), 486–93.

Mitchell, V. (2003) Implementing the first library management system at Merthyr Tydfil Public Libraries: an overview and impact on staff. *Program*, **37** (2), 103–8.

Nfila, R.B. and Darko-Ampem, K. (2002) Developments in academic library consortia from the 1960s through to 2000: a review of the literature. *Library Management*, **23** (4/5), 203–12.

Pearlson, K.E. and Saunders, C.S. (2006) *Managing and Using Information Systems: A strategic approach*, 3rd edn. New York: Wiley.

Sayers, R. (2004) A smart place in the sun: futureproofing the Queensland Government Libraries Consortium. *Library Management*, **25** (6/7), 283–92.

Spacey, R. and Goulding, A. (2004) Learner support in UK public libraries. *Aslib Proceedings*, **56** (6), 344–55.

Tidd, J., Bessant, J. and Pavitt, K. (2005) *Managing Innovation: Integrating technological, market and organizational change*. Chichester: Wiley.

Index